WHITE PINE AND BLUE WATER

Also by Henry Beston

THE OUTERMOST HOUSE

NORTHERN FARM

THE ST. LAWRENCE RIVER

AMERICAN MEMORY

WHITE PINE
AND BLUE WATER

A STATE OF MAINE READER

Edited by Henry Beston

———————

DOWN EAST MAGAZINE

CAMDEN / MAINE

To Maurice and Beatrice Day of
Damariscotta, Maine, with
grateful affection old and ever new

PREFACE

The editor wishes to acknowledge his debt to the following authors, publishers and other holders of copyrights whose good will made possible the reprinting of selections from copyright material in the Maine Reader.

Appleton-Century-Crofts, Inc. for *The Pioneer Arrives Downeast* from *Barton's Mills* by A. Hyatt Verrill.

The Atlantic Monthly Company for *The Old Woman* by Isabel Hopestill Carter.

Coward-McCann, Inc. for *Pillars of Smoke* from *Here I Stay* by Elizabeth Coatsworth; for *Maine Sunshine* from *The Little Locksmith* by Katharine Butler Hathaway; and for *A Duplicious Incident* from *Where Flows the Kennebec* by Arthur R. MacDougall, Jr.

Thomas Y. Crowell Company for *Pursuit at Sea* from *High Tide at Noon* by Elisabeth Ogilvie.

Marion E. Dodd and The Hampshire Bookshop for *Oxen* from *Cloudman Hill Heritage* by Charles Dunn, Jr.

Duell, Sloan and Pearce, Inc. for *The Corduroy Pants* from *Jackpot* by Erskine Caldwell.

The Falmouth Publishing House of Portland, Maine, for *The First Aroostook Potatoes* and *The Founding of "New Sweden"* from *Land Under Heaven* by Pearl Ashby Tibbetts.

Jessie Wheeler Freeman together with The Stephen Daye Press for *No More Sea* from *Town Down East* by Jessie Wheeler Freeman.

Leland Hall for *The Snowstorm* from *They Seldom Speak* by Leland Hall, published by Harcourt, Brace and Company.

Charlotte W. Hardy for *The Rescue* from *The Penobscot Man* by Fannie Hardy Eckstorm.

Harper and Brothers and E. B. White for *Coon Hunt* from *One Man's Meat* by E. B. White.

Henry Holt and Company, Inc. for *Coast Children of the Eighteen Nineties* from *A Goodly Heritage* by Mary Ellen Chase.

Houghton Mifflin Company and Ben Ames Williams for *Spring Flood on Bangor River* from *The Strange Woman* by Ben Ames Williams.

Alfred A. Knopf, Inc. for "A Farmer Remembers Lincoln" from *Grenstone Poems* by Wytter Bynner.

J. B. Lippincott Company for *Lumber Camp: Modern Mood* and *The Maine Guide* from *We Took to the Woods* by Louise Dickinson Rich.

The MacMillan Company for *The Fields in Spring* from *As the Earth Turns* by Gladys Hasty Carroll; for "This Green Field" from *Country Poems* by Elizabeth Coatsworth; for "Making the Spring" from *One Horse Farm* by Robert P. Tristram Coffin; for "Frost Is on the Bunchberry" from *The Bright North* by Abbie Huston Evans; for *The Launching of "The Rainbow"* from *Time Out of Mind* by Rachel Field; for *Graveyard in the Woods* from *Maine Charm String* by Elinor Graham; for *The Flowering of a Maine Lumber Town* from *Holy Old Mackinaw* by Stewart H. Holbrook.

Gardiner J. Maxcy and The Old Squire Bookstore for *The Outlaw Dogs* from *When Life Was Young* by C. A. Stephens.

William Morrow and Company, Inc. for *Baked Beans* from *The House that Jacob Built* by John Gould; and *The Catch of the Halibut* from *Spoonhandle* by Ruth Moore.

W. W. Norton and Company, Inc. for *The Old West India Trade* from *The Maritime History of Maine* by William Hutchinson Rowe.

John Richards for "The Northern Lights" from *Songs of a Schoolmaster* by John Richards, published by the Rumford Press, 1928.

Rosalind Richards for *A Northern Countryside* from *A Northern Countryside* by Rosalind Richards, published by Henry Holt and Company, Inc.

Rinehart and Company, Inc. for *The Sound of the Pond Ice* and *The Waters of Early Spring* from *Northern Farm* by Henry Beston; and for *The Ice Trade on the Kennebec* from *Kennebec: Cradle of Americans* by Robert P. Tristram Coffin.

Charles Scribner's Sons for "Pasa Thalassa Thalassa" by Edwin Arlington Robinson from *The Collected Works of Edwin Arlington Robinson.*

The Viking Press for *The Difference* from *An Afternoon* by Elizabeth Parsons Warner.

Harold Vinal of Vinalhaven, Maine, together with the Falmouth Publishing House of Portland, Maine, for "The Rowers" from *Selected Poems of Harold Vinal,* Portland, 1948.

Mildred Coes Wasson for *The Rote* from *Home from the Sea* by George S. Wasson.

The editor also wishes to express his gratitude for the help so generously given him by a number of friends. He is much beholden to Mrs. Marion Cobb Fuller, late of the State Library of Maine, and to the staff of that institution; he is likewise much indebted to Miss Marian B. Rowe, Librarian of the Maine Historical Society. His grateful thanks are due Walter Muir Whitehill, Esq., Librarian of the Boston Athenaeum, for calling his attention again to the work of George Wasson; to Richard Matthews Hallet, Esq., of Portland, for help with aspects of the history of the state; and to Captain William M. Berry of the *Sunbeam* for his information concerning the eighteenth-century course from Boston to Monhegan. He wishes to thank Mrs. John Linsky, Jr. for the careful typing of a rather complicated manuscript. In particular he wishes to thank his wife, Elizabeth Coatsworth Beston, for a world of editorial good counsel and for every help with the preparation of the Reader.

HENRY BESTON

Chimney Farm,
Nobleboro, Maine

Contents

13 MAINE WINTER

14 THE FOREST AND THE LOGGERS

15 THE RESCUE

16 THE MAINE OF LIVING MEMORY

17 THE ROTE

18 ENTER THE SUMMER VISITOR

19 FARMING COUNTRY

20   MIRRORS HELD UP TO MAINE

21   A "DUPLICIOUS" INCIDENT

22   THE CORDUROY PANTS

INTRODUCTION

THE state of Maine, unlike the New England lying to the south and west, has its roots in the eighteenth century rather than in the seventeenth. Though the region was known and settlements had been made since the early days of the North Atlantic fisheries, it was not till after the fall of Quebec and the surrender of French Canada that the province could be regarded as safely ready for plantation. Those interested in the quality of Maine will find it important to note that being of the eighteenth century, the state had no background of seventeenth-century Massachusetts Calvinism, which the passing years had modified to something less fanatical and grim. Maine was never Puritan, in the historical and theological sense of that unyielding term. The earliest settlements had been Anglican, an influence still vigorous in the life of the state; the present mood is evangelical.

Not till the second great struggle of the age, the American Revolution, had been won did pioneers arrive in numbers, following with their oxen a primitive coast road already blazed or disembarking from some small vessel which had made the run "downeast" from the ports of Massachusetts. (The term "downeast" is a sailors' phrase for the country to which the course from Massachusetts lay "down" the prevailing southwest wind of summer; the "east" has reference to the fact that the Maine coast lay about due northeast magnetic from Boston in the later eighteenth century. As there is an annual variation, the magnetic course has since altered.) What lay ahead was New England's contemporary frontier, and on they came, the adventurous and the hardy, the seafarers and the people of the barn and plow, following that north star which was later, and with such wise insight, made to figure on the state shield. A wilderness paradise both awaited and confronted them. The "province of Maine" had remained as Nature had made it, clothed in the green of the ancient forest, and in its being, unsullied and remote. The woods teemed with game, the rivers, ponds, and coastal waters were aswarm with fish, and the great pines stood massed and untroubled in the wilderness.

On they came, and defending itself against the arrival of Man, the earth put on its armor of snow and sometimes arctic cold. To use a favorite word of the Maine vocabulary, its prizes were to be for the "ruggéd"; from the first it would have no headlong frontier scramble, disorderly and squalid; it demanded courage, character, and endurance. To this day, the state grants its people the inestimable boon—inestimable in twentieth-century America—of not having things both passive and too easy. It makes demands.

Those who would understand the particular quality of Maine must first, perhaps, take thought of this element of the frontier. For the frontier is still a part of our lives, the state being today the one state in the east possessed of a frontier with the wilderness; indeed, Maine is probably the only state in the Union in which an eighteenth-century heritage confronts the immensities of timeless North America. Beyond the coast and the farming country opening inland along the rivers lies the great north woodland, thousands of square miles of it, flowing earthwise across the mountains to the political frontier of Canada—with the noble fortress of Katahdin at its heart. Though it is not country for the plow, being much of it upland and elemental, it is not a region off-the-human in quality as is the lunar landscape of the desert west; it is on the contrary profoundly human in its nature, a forest world of blue mountains, hidden ponds, and the pleasant sound of running streams. Always a great part of the consciousness of the state, it is used, and visited and cherished; some neighbor having always gone "to Katahdin" or into "the woods."

What does the possession of such a frontier mean to the way of life? It means the presence of the genuine North America and the earth influences rising from its green and archaic mystery. It means that the State of Mainer still has room to breathe physically and metaphorically. A moose may take it into its head to cross Route 1, but there is no pressure of the tragic, crowded, and inescapable mass to confuse and smother one about; one does not have to elbow or gasp to remain an individual and a human being. Modern mass pressures, too, of their very selves, mean a compulsion towards a nonhuman specialization, and this the State of Mainer has happily avoided; in the old American tradition, he can still do many things and do them well. An element which is perhaps a social inheritance of the kind of pioneering which did occur is the good will and the neighborliness of a Maine community. To make one last point, the people remain in relation to Nature, for there is no "conquest of Nature" here— evil phrase!—and never will be. The people hold on to the sense of reality which springs from a relation to Nature, and to that other wisdom called common sense.

The other pillar of the State is certainly the presence of the sea. The North Atlantic brings to the coast, and, indeed, to the entire region, another aspect of physical and spiritual freedom and enlargement. Let it be remembered that no coastal people is ever provincial.

I cannot close without remarking that Maine enjoys being Maine. Something of the eighteenth-century gusto of living continues here, and there is a positive enjoyment of adventure, character, and circumstance. Bulwarked by the tradition of an ancestral New England, by the discipline of the wilderness and the ordinances of the sea, the way of life has faced the age of the machine and preserved its communal good will and the human values. Here one still thinks of life as life and not as existence. The great northeasters bear down upon us laden with the deep February snows, and are for us an adventure when the ice goes out of the ponds and the blue estuaries open in the bright

WHITE PINE AND BLUE WATER

1. The Rivals for the Coast

IN PRAISE OF HIS PROVINCE TO THE NORTH

[1622]

by

SIR FERDINANDO GORGES

For better satisfaction of the reader in his behalf, we have thought it fit, by the way, to acquaint him first with the nature of the place where we have settled ourselves, whereby he may see reason for what we have done, remembering him likewise, that in settling of plantations, there is principally to be considered; the air, for the health of the inhabitants; the soil, for fertility fit for corn, and feeding of cattle wherewith to sustain them; the sea, for commodity of trade and commerce, the better to enrich their publick and private state, as it shall grow to perfection; and to raise employments, to furnish the course of those affairs.

Now for the quality of the air, there is none of judgment but knows it proceedeth either from the general disposition of the sphere, or from the particular constitution of the place.

Touching the disposition of the sphere, it is not only seated in the temperate zone, but as it were in the centre, or middle part thereof, for that the middle part of that country stands in the

From *Gorges and the Grant of the Province of Maine,* edited by Henry S. Burrage and published by authority of the State of Maine (Portland, 1923). The original source is Gorges' *Brief Relation of the Discovery and Plantation of New England 1622.*

forty-fourth and forty-fifth degrees of the northern latitude, that is, twenty degrees from the fiery tropick, and as much from the freezing artick circle; under the same climate and course of the sun that Constantinople, and Rome, the ladies of the world; Italy, and France, the gardens of Europe, have their situation, within the limits of the fifth and sixth climate, after the latter computation; having their longest day fifteen hours and some odd minutes.

Touching the constitution of the place (which is about fifty degrees by sea from our continent westerly) the maritime parts thereof are somewhat colder, than the nature of the clime otherwise affordeth; for that the beams of the sun are weakened, partly by the unstable reflection of the same upon the sea, and partly by being laden with abundance of moisture it exhales out of the vast ocean, whereby the nature thereof is not so violently there expressed, as in the like parallel further into the main is accustomed. Nor is that sea coast so subject to droughts or want of rain in seasonable times, as other parts are of like latitudes, and by that reason the sea coasts are at all times more cold than is the inland. And the eastern coast which receiveth the rising of the sun, is likewise colder than are the western parts, towards the declining of the same, as our morning airs (for example) even in the heat of summer are cold and quick, when the day and evening are very sweltering. And this makes those parts more suitable to the nature of our people, who neither find content in the colder climates, nor health in the hotter; but (as herbs and plants) affect their native temperature, and prosper kindly no where else.

And indeed, the hot countries yield sharper wits, but weaker bodies, and fewer children; the colder, more slow of conceit, but stronger of body, and more abounding in procreation. So that, though the invention of arts hath risen from the southern nations, yet they have still been subject to the inundation, and invasions of the more northerly people, by reason of their multitudes, together with the strength of their body, and hardness of their constitutions.

But this country, what by the general and particular situation, is so temperate, as it seemeth to hold the golden mean, and indeed is most agreeable to the nature of our own, which is made manifest by experience, the most infallible proof of all assertions; in so much as our people that are settled there, enjoy their life and health much more happily, than in other places; which can be imputed to no other cause, than the temperature of the climate.

Now, as the clime is found to be so temperate, so delicate, and healthful, both by reason and experience; such is the soil also, some parts thereof yielding wonderful increase, both of the corn the natives have most use of; as also of our own, of all sorts: with infinite variety of nourishing roots, and other herbs, and fruits, common among them, but rare with us.

Besides, the coast doth abound with most convenient havens, and harbours, full of singular islands, fit for plantations; replenished with plants and wood of all sorts; as oak, cedars, spruce, fir, pine, walnut, chestnut, elm, sassafras, plum trees, and calamus aromaticus, &c.

The people are tractable (if they be not abused) to commerce and trade with all, and as yet have good respect for us. The seas are stored with all kinds of excellent fish, and in many places upon the coast, fit to make salt in. The country aboundeth with diversity of wild fowl, as turkeys, partridges, swans, cranes, wild geese of two sorts, wild ducks of three sorts, many doves, especially when strawberries are ripe.

There are several sorts of deer in those parts, and some that bring forth two, three, and four young at once, which is a manifest proof of the fertility of the soil, or temper of the clime, or both together.

There is also a certain beast, that the natives call a moose, he is as big bodied as an ox, headed like a fallow deer, with a broad palm, which he mues* every year, as doth the deer, and neck like

---

* To change. Johnson's Dictionary.

a red deer, with a short mane, running along the reins of his back, his hair long like an elk, but esteemed to be better than that for saddlers' use, he hath likewise a great bunch hanging down under his throat, and is of the colour of our blacker sort of fallow deer, his legs are long, and his feet are big as the feet of our oxen, his tail is longer than the single of a deer, and reacheth almost down to his huxens, his skin maketh very good buff, and his flesh is excellent good food, which the natives use to jerkin and keep all the year to serve their turn and so proves very serviceable for their use. There have been many of them seen in a great island upon the coast, called by our people Mount Mansell, whither the savages go at certain seasons to hunt them; the manner whereof is, by making of several fires; and setting the country with people, to force them into the sea, to which they are naturally addicted, and then there are others that attend them in their boats with bows and weapons of several kinds, wherewith they slay and take their pleasure. And there is hope that this kind of beasts may be made serviceable for ordinary labour with art and industry.

The known commodities of that country, are fish of several sorts, rich furs, as beavers, otters, martins, black fox, sables, &c. There are likewise plenty of vines, of three kinds, and those pleasant to the taste, yet some better than other. There is hemp, flax, silkgrass, several veins of ironstone, commodities to make pitch, rosin, tar; deal boards of all sorts, spars, masts, for ships of all burdens; in a word, there comes no commodity out of France, Germany, or the Sound, but may be had there, with reasonable labour and industry.

Further we have settled at this present, several plantations along the coast, and have granted patents to many more that are in preparation to be gone with all conveniency. Those of our people that are there, have both health and plenty, so as they acknowledge there is no want of any thing, but of industrious people, to reap the commodities that are there to be had, and they are indeed so much affected to the place, as they are loath to be drawn from thence, although they were directed to return to give satisfaction to those that sent them, but chose rather to perform that office by letters, together with their excuse, for breach of their duty in that behalf. And thus you see there is no labour well employed, but hath his reward at one time or other.

These encouragements have emboldened us to proceed, to the engaging of ourselves, for the building of some ships of good burden, and extraordinary mould, to lie upon the coast for the defence of merchants and fishermen, that are employed there, as also to waft the fleets, as they go to and from their markets: and we purpose from henceforth to build our shipping there, where we find all commodities fit for that service, together with the most opportune places, that can be desired.

Lastly, finding that we have so far forth prevailed, as to wind ourselves into familiarity with the natives, (which are in no great number) along the coast for two hundred leagues together, we have now despatched some of our people of purpose, to dive into the bowels of the continent, there to search and find out what port, or place, is most convenient to settle our main plantation in, where we mean to make the residence of our state and government, as also to be assured, what other commodities may be raised for the publick, and private benefit of those that are dealers in that business, and willing to be interested in any the lands there: whither is gone this year already, for trade and fishing only, thirty sail of the better sort of ships, belonging to the western parts, besides those who are gone for transportation of the planters, or supply of such as are already planted, whose return (as is supposed) will amount (at the least) to thirty thousand pound, the greater part whereof comes home in bullion.

And therefore as touching the third happiness of these parts, which is the sea, there needeth no other or greater commendation than this benefit of fishing assured unto us by common experience; although it affords many other hopes both in regard of the facility of the navigation, the boldness of the coast, the conveniency of roads, havens and harbours, for performance of all manner of employments; yet is there also found shows of pearl, ambergris, great numbers of whales, and other merchantable means to raise profit to the industrious inhabitants or diligent traders.

Here you may see to what profit our industry and charge hath been employed; what benefit our country is like to receive by it, and whether it be reason we should be so traduced, as we have been, we seeking nothing more than the glory of God, the enlarging of his highness' dominions, and general good of all his majesty's loyal subjects, and striving for the better accomplishment thereof to keep order, and settle government in those affairs, to preserve from ruin and confusion so fair a foundation, whereon is likely to be built the goodliest frame that hath ever been undertaken to be raised by our nation.

A FRENCH JESUIT MISSION ARRIVES
AT MT. DESERT

[1613]

by

FATHER PIERRE BIARD, S.J.

They fitted up a ship in France to take the Jesuits away from Port Royal,* and to found a new French settlement in a more suitable place.

The chief of this expedition was Captain la Saussaye, who was to winter in the country with thirty persons, counting in the two Jesuits and their servant, whom he was to take up at Port Royal. He had with him, besides, two other Jesuits, Father Quantin and Gilbert du Thet, whom he was to take there, but they were to return to France in case two at Port Royal were

From: *The Jesuit Relations: the extract given as translated in Forerunners and Competitiors of the Pilgrims and Puritans,* edited by Charles Herbert Levermore (Brooklyn, N. Y.: The New England Society of Brooklyn, 1912).
* Now Annapolis Royal, N. S.

not dead, of which there was some doubt. The entire company, counting the Sailors, numbered 48 persons. The master of the ship was Charles Flory of Habbe-ville, a discreet, hardy and peaceable man. The Queen in her goodness had contributed four of the King's tents or pavilions, and some munitions of war. Sieur Simon le Maistre had devoted himself earnestly to the freighting and provisioning, and Gilbert du Thet, the Jesuit lay brother, a very industrious man, had not spared himself; so they were amply provided with everything for more than a year, besides the horses and goats which were being taken over for domestic purposes. The ship was of a hundred tons burthen.

This expedition, thus fitted out, departed from Honfleur on the 12th of March, 1613, and landed first at Cap de la Hève on the coast of Acadie, on the 16th of May, having consumed two entire months in the passage. At Cap de la Hève Mass was said and a Cross erected, upon which was placed the coat of arms of Madame la Marquise de Guercheville, as a sign of having taken possession of it in her name. Thence putting to sea again, they came to Port Royal.

At Port Royal they only found five persons; namely, the two Jesuits, their servants, the Apothecary Hebert, and another. Sieur de Biencourt and the rest of his people were all quite far away, some here, some there. Now because Hebert was taking the place of the sieur, they presented to him the Queen's letters, which contained the royal command to release the Jesuits and to let them go wherever they pleased; so the Jesuits took away their property in great peace. And on that day as well as on the following, they made it as pleasant for Hebert and his company as they could so that this arrival would not be a cause of sadness to them. At their departure, (although they were not in need of anything) they left them a barrel of bread and some bottles of wine, that the Farewell might be received with equally good grace.

Unfavorable winds kept us about five days at Port Royal, and then a propitious Northeaster arising, we departed, intending to go to the river Pentegoet, to the place called Kadesquit,[1] the site destined for the new colony, and having many great advan-tages for such a purpose. But God ordained otherwise. For when we were to the Southeast of the Island of Menano,[2] the weather changed, and there came upon the sea such a dense fog that we could see no more by day than by night. We had serious misgivings in this time of danger, because in this place there are breakers and rocks, against which we were afraid of striking in the darkness; the wind not permitting us to draw away and stand out to sea. We continued thus two days and two nights, veering now to one side, now to the other, as God inspired us. We were moved by our affliction to offer prayers and vows to God, that he might be pleased to deliver us from the danger, and direct us to some place for his glory. In his goodness he hearkened to us, for when evening came on we began to see the stars, and by morning the fogs had all disappeared. We recog-nized that we were opposite Mount Desert, an Island, which the Savages called Pemetig.[3] The pilot turned to the Eastern shore of the Island, and there located us in a large and beautiful port, where we made our thanksgiving to God, raising a Cross and singing to God his praises with the sacrifice of the holy Mass. We called this place and port Saint Sauveur.

Now here in this Port of St. Sauveur a great contention arose between the Sailors and our company, or us other passengers, because the charter party and contract, drawn up in France, stipulated that the Sailors should be held at anchor in a Port of Acadie, which we should name to them, and should remain there for the space of three months; the sailors maintained that they had arrived at a Port of Acadie, and that therefore the said term of three months should begin to run from the time of this arrival.

---

[1] The river Kenduskeag, which empties into the Penobscot near the site of the present city of Bangor.
[2] I.e., Menano—Grand Manan Island.
[3] Or, Pemetic. They came to Frenchman's Bay.

It was explained to them that the Port was not the one that had been designated to them by the name of Kadesquit, and therefore the time would not begin to be counted until they were there. The pilot obstinately opposed this, maintaining that a ship had never gone as far as Kadesquit, and that he had no intention of becoming a discoverer of new routes; there was also some mistake about the name Acadie meaning Norambegue, which strengthened the dispute; reasons here, reasons there; nothing but argument, a bad augury for the future.

During these quarrels, the Savages signaled to us with smoke. This means that we can go and find them if we need them, which we did. The Pilot incidentally remarked to these Savages that the Port Royal Fathers were in his ship. They answered that they would like very much to see the one with whom they had become acquainted two years before at Pentegoet.* This was Father Biard, who went immediately to see them, and in asking about the route to Kadesquit, said he wished to go there to live. "But," said they, "if thou wishest to stay in these regions, why dost thou not rather remain here with us, who have truly as good and beautiful a place as Kadesquit?" And they began to sing the praises of their home, assuring him that it was so healthy, and so agreeable, that when the Savages are sick in other parts, they have themselves brought to this place and here recover. These blessings did not affect Father Biard much, for he knew that the Savages did not lack that with which almost everyone is abundantly provided, namely, the ability to praise their own wares. But they knew well how to use their machinations against him to carry him off. "For," said they, "it is necessary that thou comest since Asticou, our Sagamore, is sick unto death; and if thou dost not come he will die without baptism, and will not go to heaven. Thou wilt be the cause of it, for he himself wishes very much to be baptized." This argument, so naively deduced, astonished Father Biard, and fully persuaded him to go there, especially as it was only three leagues away, and in all there

* Now Castine, Maine.

would result no greater loss of time than one afternoon; so he got into one of their canoes with sieur de la Motte, Lieutenant, and Simon the interpreter, and went off.

When we arrived at Asticou's cabins, we found him truly sick, but not unto death, for it was only a cold that troubled him; so having assured ourselves of his good condition, we had plenty of leisure to go and visit this place, so greatly boasted about and so much better for a French settlement than Kadesquit. And in truth we found that the Savages were not wrong in praising it so highly, for we ourselves were wonderfully astonished; and having carried the news to the chiefs of our company, and they having come to view the place, all unanimously agreed that we ought to stay there and not look for anything better, especially as it seemed as if God told us to do so through the fortunate events which had happened to us, and through an evident miracle, which he performed in the restoration of a child of which we shall speak elsewhere.

This place is a beautiful hill,* rising gently from the sea, its sides bathed by two springs; the land is cleared for twenty or twenty-five acres, and in some places is covered with grass almost as high as a man. It faces the South and East, and is near the mouth of the Pentegoet, where several broad and pleasant rivers, which abound in fish, discharge their waters; its soil is dark, rich and fertile; the Port and Harbor are as fine as can be seen, and are in a position favorable to command the entire coast; the Harbor especially is as safe as a pond. For, besides being strengthened by the great Island of Mount Desert, it is still more protected by certain small Islands which break the currents and the winds, and fortify the entrance. There is not a fleet which it is not capable of sheltering, nor a ship so deep that could not approach within a cable's length of the shore to unload. It is situated in latitude forty-four and one-third degrees, a position still less northerly than that of Bourdeaux.

---

* Still visible as the fine slope of open land rising from the waters of Somes Sound on the west side of the entrance. Now known as "Jesuits Field." H. B.

Now having landed at this place and planted here the Cross we began to work; and with the beginning of work also began the quarrels, a second sign and augury of our ill luck. The cause of these dissensions was principally that la Saussaye, our Captain, amused himself too much in cultivating the land, while all the chiefs of the enterprise were urging him not to employ the laborers for that purpose, but to get to work without delay upon the houses and fortifications, which he did not wish to do. From these disputes sprang others, until the English brought us all to an understanding with each other, as you will hear immediately.*

ENGLISH AND INDIANS HAVE IT
OUT AT PEMAQUID

[1689]

by

JOHN GYLES

On the second day of August, 1689, in the morning, my honored father, THOMAS GYLES, Esq., went with some laborers, my two elder brothers and myself, to one of his farms, which laid upon the river about three miles above fort Charles,† adjoining Pemmaquid falls, there to gather in his English harvest, and we labored securely till noon. After we had dined, our people went

---

From *Memoirs of Odd Adventures, Strange Deliverances etc. in the Captivity of John Gyles* (Boston, 1736).

* In September 1613, Captain Samuel Argall, acting under the orders of British authorities in Virginia, destroyed this southern outpost of the French settlements.

† Fort Charles stood on the spot where fort Frederick was, not long since, founded by Colonel Dunbar. The township adjoining thereto was called Jamestown, in honor to the duke of York. In this town, within a quarter of a mile of the fort, was my father's dwelling-house, from which he went out that unhappy morning.

to their labor, some in one field to their English hay, the others to another field of English corn. My father, the youngest of my two brothers, and myself, tarried near the farm-house in which we had dined till about one of the clock, at which time we heard the report of several great guns at the fort. Upon which my father said he hoped it was a signal of good news, and that the great council had sent back the soldiers to cover the inhabitants; (for on report of the revolution they had deserted.) But to our great surprise, about thirty or forty Indians,* at that moment, discharged a volley of shot at us, from behind a rising ground near our barn. The yelling of the Indians, the whistling of their shot, and the voice of my father, whom I heard cry out, "What now! what now!" so terrified me (though he seemed to be handling a gun), that I endeavored to make my escape. My brother ran one way and I another, and looking over my shoulder, I saw a stout fellow, painted, pursuing me, with a gun, and a cutlass glittering in his hand which I expected every moment in my brains. I soon fell down, and the Indian seized me by the left hand. He offered me no abuse, but tied my arms, then lifted me up and pointed to the place where the people were at work about the hay and led me that way. As we went, we crossed where my father was, who looked very pale and bloody, and walked very slowly. Then when we came to the place, I saw two men shot down on the flats, and one or two more knocked on their heads with hatchets, crying out "O Lord," &c. There the Indians brought two captives, one a man, and my brother James, who, with me, had endeavored to escape by running from the house when we were first attacked. This brother was about fourteen years of age. My oldest brother, whose name was Thomas, wonderfully escaped by land to the Barbican, a point of land on the west side of the river, opposite the fort, where several fishing vessels lay. He got on board one of them and sailed that night.

---

* The whole company of Indians, according to Charlevoix, was one hundred. —S. G. Drake. The attack had the backing of the French in Canada, H. B.

After doing what mischief they could, they sat down and made us sit with them. After some time we arose, and the Indians pointed for us to go eastward. We marched about a quarter of a mile, and then made a halt. Here they brought my father to us. They made proposals to him, by old Moxus, who told him that those were Strange Indians who shot him, and that he was sorry for it. My father replied that he was a dying man, and wanted no favor of them, but to pray with his children. This being granted him, he recommended us to the protection and blessing of God Almighty; then gave us the best advice, and took his leave for this life, hoping in God that we should meet in a better. He parted with a cheerful voice, but looked very pale, by reason of his great loss of blood, which now gushed out of his shoes. The Indians led him aside!—I heard the blows of the hatchet, but neither shriek nor groan! I afterwards heard that he had five or seven shot-holes through his waistcoat or jacket, and that he was covered with some boughs.

The Indians led us, their captives, on the east side of the river, towards the fort, and when we came within a mile and a half of the fort and town, and could see the fort, we saw fire and smoke on all sides. Here we made a short stop, and then moved within or near the distance of three-quarters of a mile from the fort, into a thick swamp. There I saw my mother and my two little sisters, and many other captives who were taken from the town. My mother asked me about my father. I told her he was killed, but could say no more for grief. She burst into tears, and the Indians moved me a little farther off, and seized me with cords to a tree.

The Indians came to New Harbor, and sent spies several days to observe how and where the people were employed, &c., who found the men were generally at work at noon and left about their houses only women and children. Therefore the Indians divided themselves into several parties, some ambushing the way between the fort and the houses, as likewise between them and the distant fields; and then alarming the farthest off first, they killed and took the people, as they moved toward the town and fort, at their pleasure, and very few escaped to it. Mr. Patishall was taken and killed, as he lay with his sloop near the Barbican.

On the first stir about the fort, my youngest brother was at play near it, and running in, was, by God's goodness, thus preserved. Captain Weems, with great courage and resolution, defended the weak old fort two days; when, being much wounded, and the best of his men killed, beat for a parley, which eventuated in these conditions:

1. That they, the Indians, should give him Mr. Patishall's sloop.

2. That they should not molest him in carrying off the few people that had got into the fort, and three captives that they had taken.

3. That the English should carry off in their hands what they could from the fort.

On these conditions the fort was surrendered, and Captain Weems went off; and soon after, the Indians set on fire the fort and the houses, which made a terrible blast, and was a melancholy sight to us poor captives, who were sad spectators.

After the Indians had thus laid waste Pemmaquid, they moved us to New Harbor, about two miles east of Pemmaquid, a cove much frequented by fishermen. At this place there were, before the war, about twelve houses. These the inhabitants deserted as soon the rumor of war reached the place. When we turned our backs on the town, my heart was ready to break! I saw my mother. She spoke to me, but I could not answer her. That night we tarried at New Harbor, and the next day went in their canoes for Penobscot. About noon, the canoe in which my mother was, and that in which I was, came side by side; whether accidentally or by my mother's desire, I can not say. She asked me how I did. I think I said "pretty well," but my heart was so full of grief I scarcely knew whether audible to her. Then she said, "Oh! my child! how joyful and pleasant it would be if we were going to old England, to see your uncle Chalker and other friends there! Poor babe, we are going into the wilderness, the Lord knows where!" Then bursting into tears, the canoes parted. That night following, the Indians with their captives, lodged on an island.

A few days after, we arrived at Penobscot fort, where I again saw my mother, my brother and sisters, and many other captives. I think we tarried here eight days. In that time, the Jesuit of the place had a great mind to buy me. My Indian master made a visit to the Jesuit, and carried me with him. And here I will note that the Indian who takes a captive is accounted his master, and has a perfect right to him, until he gives or sells him to another. I saw the Jesuit show my master pieces of gold, and understood afterward that he was tendering them for my ransom. He gave me a biscuit, which I put into my pocket, and not daring to eat it, buried it under a log, fearing he had put something in it to make me love him. Being very young, and having heard much of the Papists torturing the Protestants, caused me to act thus; and I hated the sight of a Jesuit.* When my mother heard the talk of my being sold to a Jesuit, she said to me, "Oh! my dear child, if it were God's will, I had rather follow you to your grave, or never see you more in this world, than you should be sold to a Jesuit; for a Jesuit will ruin you, body and soul!" † It pleased

---

* "It is not to be wondered at that antipathy should be so plainly exhibited at this time, considering what had been going on in England up to the latest dates; but that children should have been taught that Catholics had the power of winning over heretics by any mysterious powders, or other arts furnished them by his satanic majesty, is a matter, to say the least, of no little admiration."—S. G. Drake.

† It may not be improper to hear how the Jesuits themselves viewed these matters. The settlement here was, according to the French account, in their dominions, and the English settlers "incommoded extremely from thence all the Indians in the adjacent country, who were the avowed friends of the French, and caused the government of Acadia no less inquietude, who feared, with reason, the effect of their intrigues in detaching the Indians from their alliance. The Indians, who undertook to break up the post at Pemmaquid were Penobscots, among whom a Jesuit, named M. Thury, a good laborer in the faith, had a numerous mission. The first attention before setting out of these brave Christians was to secure aid of the God of battles, by confessions and the sacrament; and they took care that their wives and children performed the same rites, and raised their pure hands to heaven, while their fathers and mothers went out to do battle against the heretics." See Charlevoix.—S. G. Drake.

God to grant her request, for she never saw me more! Yet she and my two little sisters were, after several years' captivity, redeemed, but she died ere I returned. My brother, who was taken with me, was, after several years' captivity, most barbarously tortured to death by the Indians.

My Indian master carried me up Penobscot river to a village called Madawamkee, which stands on a point of land between the main river and a branch which heads to the east of it. At home I had ever seen strangers treated with the utmost civility, and being a stranger, I expected some kind treatment here; but I soon found myself deceived, for I presently saw a number of squaws, who had got together in a circle, dancing and yelling. An old grim-looking one took me by the hand, and leading me into the ring, some seized me by the hair, and others by my hands and feet, like so many furies; but my master presently laying down a pledge, they released me.

ISLAND WATERS: "THE ROWERS"

by

HAROLD VINAL

Always we were aware of the islands, the interminable sea
Against our ears, drawn by the tides seaward;
Yet we remained in those estuaries, those island waters,
While the seasons drifted. Leeward.

Vast tides climbed savagely between crags;
Leeward, gulls flew in perpetual, unending arcs of white.
It was a landscape where birds moved in joy,
Their movements praise for undying light.

From *Selected Poems,* by Harold Vinal (Falmouth Publishing House: Portland, Maine, 1948).

And we, rowers between crags, the gigantic cliffs,
Moved to a tide change, the endless rhythm
Of the mighty waters, held in the hand of God,
Transfixed in a vast and an eternal prism.

Always we were aware of the islands, glad of time
Whose sandals were slow, glad of day without motion.
We have left upon the sand the signature of our love;
You will find it there by the soft and blue-tongued ocean.

2. Of Battles Long Ago

FROM THE INFORMAL ILIAD OF THE ARNOLD EXPEDITION TO QUEBEC

by

CAPTAIN JOHN TOPHAM

(1775)

(Oct.) 6 Carry'd our boats and provisions across and proceeded
On our way about 7 miles—here is seven islands
Fairly encompassed by the water; the most of them
Lies on the east side of the river—now we began
To see the mountains that lay ahead, these appeared
Dismal in our sight, thinking we had them to
Pass—here I shall observe that we had no pilot.

7 This day we proceeded on our way to the great
Carrying place—the land here is low and very fine
Grass, but on the edge of the river it appears to
Be overflowed in the spring—now it begins to be
Mountainous and appears to be less fertile here.—
I travelled by land till I came to the above
Carrying place, traveling through several small
Rivers; at length I came to the carrying place
And much fatigued—

From *The Journal of Captain John Topham* (*The Magazine of History,* No. 50: Tarrytown, N. Y., 1916).

8 This day Lt. Church came back and gave Accounts
Of the first carrying place being three miles ¼,
Then a pond. I shall give an account of
Then as I pass by them—encamp'd and
Were employed in clearing the road for
Carrying our boats—it rain'd all day and
Occasioned our work not going on as it
Would have done if fair; we have been favored
Hitherto with extraordinary good weather for
The season of the year. At 3 O'Clock all our boats
And most of our men came up—here we
Remained, here was all the rifle Men helping to
Clear the roads—they'd killed a moose, I saw the
Skin and it appeared to be as big as that of an
Ox that would weight 600^{wt}—they're very
Plenty and we can scarcely go 50 yards
Without meeting with their tracks.

9 Detach'd 2 Subbarltons and 36 men to clear the
Roads to the first pond, which was perfected at 12
O'Clock and the rest of our men were employ'd
In getting our pork on sticks and carrying our
Baggage and boats across to the first pond.
This carrying place is four miles—here is very
Fine trout of which we caught a great number.

(10) This day we were employed in getting our
men across the pond—this carrying place is
Half a mile, then proceed'd to the second pond.

(11) Crossed the 3rd carrying place, which is about
4 miles & came to the rivulet that leads
Into Dead river so call'd.

(12) Had a very fine prospect of a high mountain* which
bears S. W. being 15 miles; round this pond
It is boggy and wet—here is a bogg

---

* Mt. Bigelow.

About 1 mile across which we was oblig'd
To carry our boats across, and at every step we .
Sunk half leg high into mud and water;
Which made it very difficult, and to make it
Much worse there was ice on the top which
Broke through.

13 Proceed'd on our march about 3 miles and
Encamp'd—

14 Proceeded on our way, not going above 10
Miles because of the current runs so swift
And the shore so Bold that our setting poles
Will not reach the bottom in many places, so
That we are oblig'd to hall our boats along
By the bushes that hang over the river.

15 We despached two Indians and one white man
To quebec with a letter to a gentleman in that
City,·and they are expected to meet us in
10 or 12 days. Here we waited some time
For a company that was in our rear to come
Up—employ'd in cleaning our guns.

16 Being very short of provisions and brought
To one half pint of flower for each man now,
Waiting untill 9 O'Clock for the Rifle
Companies in order to get some supplys &
They not coming up, we proceeded on our
Way—came to an Indian hut where one
Satanniss lived, as big a rogue as ever liv'd—
Still proceed'd on our march about 4 miles
And encamp'd, and Col Arnold came up in
The evening at 8 O'Clock and hearing of our wants
Of bread, order'd 4 Battoes with 32 men
Of each companies to return to the rear for a
Supply of provision in the morning—here
We had not more than 5 or 6 lb of flower
Pr. man.

24 Received accounts of its being 25 miles to the
   Height of land, and we almost distitute
   Of provision being brought to 1 half pint
   Of flower p^r. man and having no more
   To deliver out it being the last we have; it snow'd
   This evening & continued part of the night.

25 We stayed for Col green, who is gone foreward
   To hear what we must do for provisions—we are in
   An absolute danger of starving: however I hope for
   The best but if we do not receive no supply from
   The french we shall be poorly off. This day there
   Was a sub^n. & 48 men of the sick and unfit for duty
   Went back with 3 boats of each of 3 companies.
   The river is narrow and exceeding swift, the
   Going by land is very difficult, which much
   Disheartn'd our men and are desirous to return.
   However if their bellies were full I believe
   They'd rather go forward—we are out and must
   Go on.

THREE FIGURES FROM THE HISTORY
OF THE CAMPAIGN

I AND II   THE TWO WOMEN WHO CROSSED THE WILDERNESS WITH
THE TROOPS, MRS. SERGEANT GRIER AND MRS. JEMIMA WARNER.
III   THE PURBLIND DRUMMER

by

JOHN JOSEPH HENRY

I   Mrs. Sergeant Grier

This morning, the first of November, breakfasting on our
bleary,* we took up the line of march through a flat and boggy
ground. About ten o'clock A.M. we arrived, by a narrow neck of
land at a marsh which was appalling. It was three fourths of a
mile over, and covered by a coat of ice, half an inch thick. Here
Simpson concluded to halt a short time for the stragglers or
maimed of Hendrick's and Smith's companies to come up. There
were two women attached to those companies, who arrived before we commenced the march. One was the wife of Sergeant
Grier, a large, virtuous and respectable woman. The other was
the wife of a private of our company, a man who lagged upon
every occasion. These women being arrived, it was presumed that
all our party were up. We were on the point of entering the
marsh, when some one cried out "Warner is not here." Another
said he had "sat down sick under a tree, a few miles back." His
wife begging us to wait a short time, with tears of affection in
her eyes, ran back to her husband. We tarried an hour. They

From *An Accurate and interesting account of the Hardships and Sufferings of
that Band of Heroes who traversed the Wilderness in the Campaign against
Quebec in 1775* by John Joseph Henry, Esq. (Lancaster, Pa., 1812).

* A gruel made of flour and water.

came not. Entering the pond, (Simpson foremost,) and breaking
the ice here and there with the buts of our guns and feet, as occasion required, we were soon waist deep in the mud and water.
As is generally the case with youths, it came to my mind, that a
better path might be found than that of the more elderly guide.
Attempting this, in a trice the water cooling my armpits, made
me gladly return into the file. Now Mrs. Grier had got before
me. My mind was humbled, yet astonished, at the exertions of
this good woman. Her clothes more than waist high, she waded
before me to the firm ground. No one so long as she was known
to us, dared intimate a disrespectful idea of her. Her husband,
who was an excellent soldier, was on duty in Hendricks' boat,
which had proceeded to the discharge of the lake with lieutenant
M'Cleland. Arriving at firm ground, and waiting again for our
companions, we then set off, and in a march of several miles,
over a scrubby and flat plain, arrived at a river flowing from the
east into the Chaudiere lake.

II   Mrs. Jemima Warner

The fate of James Warner, among others, was really lamenta-
ble. He was young, handsome in appearance, not more than
twenty-five years of age; he was athletic and seemed to surpass
in bodily strength. Yet withal, he was a dolt. His wife was beautiful, though coarse in manners. The husband on the other hand,
was a poor devil, constantly out of view, or in the back-ground
of the picture.

We heard nothing of them after entering the marsh, and until
a month had elapsed at Quebec. In December, the wife or widow
of poor James Warner, came to our quarters on the Low-grounds,
bearing her husband's rifle, his powder-horn and pouch. She appeared fresh and rosy as ever. This arose from the religious and
gratuitous spirit of the Canadians.

The story Mrs. Jemima Warner told, was extremely affecting,
and may be worth remembering, as it is something like a sample
of the whole of our distresses and intolerable disasters.

The husband was a great eater. His stores of provisions, after the partition, at the head of the Chaudiere, were in a little time consumed. The consummate wife ran back from the marsh, and found her beloved husband sitting at the foot of a tree, where he said he was determined to die.

The tender-hearted woman, attended her ill-fated husband several days, urging his march forward; he again sat down. Finding all her solicitations could not induce him to rise, she left him, having placed all the bread in her possession, between his legs with a canteen of water. She bore his arms and ammunition to Quebec, where she recounted the story. The nephews of Natanis, afterwards at Quebec, confirmed the relation of this good woman. For when going up, and returning down the river with our inestimable friend M'Cleland, she urged them, suffused in tears to take her husband on board. They were necessarily deaf to her entreaties. Thus perished this unfortunate man, at a period of his age, when the bodily powers, are generally in their full perfection. He and many others, who died in the wilderness, lost their lives by an inconsiderate gluttony. They ate as much at a meal, as ought to have been in our circumstances the provision of four days, and a march of one hundred miles. Young men, without knowledge or a previous experience, are very difficult to govern by sage-advice, when the rage of hunger assails.

III   The Purblind* Drummer

On the 30th of October, we set forward. The men were told by the officers that orders would "not be required in the march," each one must "put the best foot foremost." The first day's march was closed by a charming sleep on fir-branches. The gentlemen of our mess lay together, covering themselves, with the blankets of each one. My memory does not serve, to say, that any stir was made by any one, during the night. Happening to be the first who awaked, in the morning, the blanket was suddenly thrown from my head, but what was my surprise to find, that we had

---

* "almost blind"

lain under a cover of at least four inches of snow. We scarcely had risen and had our kettle on the fire, when our drummer, (we had no bugles,) John Shaeffer, came slipshod to our fire, complaining, that all his cakes had been stolen from him. A more wretched figure was scarcely ever beheld. He was purblind. This circumstance, though he was my townsman, and acquainted with me from my earliest infancy, was yet unknown to me until this last march, ascending the "Dead-river," commenced. My station in the line of march, which was in the single file, (or Indian, as it was then called,) was next to the captain; the drummer followed. Here it was his defect of sight was most effectually shewn. Smith was lithsome and quick afoot, as we all were, (except poor Shaeffer.) In the course of this toilsome march, without a path, many deep ravines presented, over these lay many logs, fallen perhaps many years before. The captain took the log, preferring it to a descent of 20 or 30 feet into the gulph below, which at times was quite abrupt. Following me, Shaeffer would frequently, drum and all, tumble headlong into the abyss. His misfortunes in this way, for he was a laughing stock, excited contempt in the soldiers, but in me compassion. Often, he required my aid. On this latter occasion, our kettle, boiling a bleary, which was no other than flour and water, and that without salt, my solicitations prevailing, the mess gave him a tin cup full of it. He received from me my third cake. This man, blind, starving, and almost naked, bore his drum (which was unharmed by all its jostlings) safely to Quebec, when many other hale men died in the wilderness.

PARSON BAILEY, LOYALIST AND CHURCHMAN, SAILS TO HALIFAX FROM COLONIAL POWNALBORO*

by

JACOB BAILEY

June 7th, 1779. We arose this morning before the sun and began to prepare for our expulsion, our hearts replete with apprehension, anxiety and distress.

As the rising sun tinged the various objects around us, I beheld the once delightful scenes with bitter emotions of grief. This, in a word, was the silent language of our faces, as we looked upon each other, and it was agreeable to the inward impulse. Must we, after all the trouble, harrassment and cruel persecution we have endured for the cause of truth and virtue, must we leave these pleasing scenes of nature, these friendly shades, these rising plants, these opening flowers, these trees swelling with fruit, and yonder rising river, which appears through the umbrageous avenue, to revive and elevate the mind? We must no longer behold the splendid orb of day peeping over the eastern hills to dissipate the fog, and to brighten the field and the forest. We must hear no more the sweet music of the tuneful tribe, amidst the trembling grove, to gladden, charm and animate the desponding heart.

But we quickly perceived other objects approaching to take a mournful farewell, which made a still deeper and more lasting impression on the wounded spirits, I mean a number of our honest, kind and generous parishioners, who came to offer us their last assistance, and to let fall a parting tear!

From *The Frontier Missionary*, edited by William S. Bartlet (Boston, 1853).
* Parson Bailey's house was near the present village of Dresden Mills.

In the forenoon we carried our beds, and the shattered remains of our fortune, the whole not worth forty dollars, on board our schooner, a little vessel, not more than fifteen tons, with such slender conveniences that we were obliged to make provision for lodging in the hold.

June 9th. About nine we got under way with a gentle breeze from the south-west, and fell down between Parker's Island and Jeremisquam into Sheepscot River. The country hereabouts made a romantic appearance, fine groves of tall trees, shrubby evergreens, craggy rocks, cultivated fields and human habitations, alternately presented themselves to view, and yielded a profusion of pleasure to the imagination.

When we entered the Sheepscot River the rolling ocean presented itself in open prospect, and we perceived a number of vessels sailing at a distance. About two o'clock we got into the sea, and began to steer towards the east, but the wind failing we made but slow progress.

We attempted to avoid a fishing vessel in our neighborhood, lest some accident should interrupt our voyage, but we were unable to carry our intention, for she came alongside, and we found the schooner belonged to Dennis Gatchell, of Bodingham, a late convert from rebellion and independence. He gave us a little salt, and pronounced his benediction.

As night approached it grew perfectly calm, and we were obliged to anchor in Cape Newaggen harbour, a little to the west of Booth Bay. This is an excellent station for small shipping. The land rises with an easy slope from the water's edge on the north and partly on the east, while the remainder is surrounded with islands on which were erected fishermen's huts. Between these islands you pass into the harbour through very small inlets.

Soon after our arrival, Mr. Gatchell came in and dropped an anchor near us. As I am always impatient to go on shore whenever it is possible, I persuaded our men to get the boat in readiness, and Mr. Palmer and Mrs. Bailey, her niece and little son, accompanied me; we landed upon the northern shore.

The land, from the water to some considerable distance, was destitute of trees and covered with grass exceedingly green and flourishing, notwithstanding the dryness of the season; the soil, though rocky, is rich, and we observed that the plants and flowers, which grew in abundance, were large and thriving. We followed some of the winding paths towards the east, till the prospect opened into Townsend harbour, which stretches a long way from the sea up to the northward. After we had diverted ourselves awhile with walking among these romantic scenes, we returned near the landing, and reposed upon the grass till evening advanced to spread abroad her cooling and refreshing shades. While we continued here, I observed at some distance, the ruins of an human habitation, with the vestiges of a garden, constructed among the rocks. This, Mr. Palmer informed me, was formerly the abode of an hermit, who, meeting with a cruel disappointment in a love matter, retired from all society, and spent the remainder of his days, to extreme old age, in this forsaken retreat. After supper, the persons belonging to my family took possession of the hold, and spread our beds upon the hard stones which were collected for ballast, a most humble and gloomy situation. We had not long been composed to sleep, before we were aroused by thunder, and saw lightning flashing through the crevices with tremendous glare, while the rain, pouring through the leaky deck, fell upon us in streams.

June 10th. This morning, after a succession of fine showers, which greatly refreshed the face of nature, the wind began to breeze from the north-west. This favourable incident determined us to weigh anchor and to display our sails. We soon ran down to Pemaquid, and saw at a distance, up a large opening to the northward, a number of fine settlements around the ancient port, while to the S. W., we had a pleasing prospect of Damariscove Island, mostly cleared land, with one or two habitations; to the

S. E., the Isle of Monhegan rose like a mountain out of the ocean. We discovered a topsail schooner standing to the south, which was afterwards taken, as we understood, by the Blonde frigate. We now approached Pemaquid point, an extensive, narrow headland, running out into the sea for many miles. The shores, I observed, were very high, rocky and rude, covered with a fine appearance of trees, but destitute of any improvements or human habitations. We were obliged to beat all the way, for eighteen miles, up to Broad Cove, in order to discharge Mr. Palmer. In our passage, we passed by a beautiful island in possession of the famous Will Loud, containing several hundred acres of rich land. Opposite to this estate, on the western shore, was situated Round Pond, encircled with a number of elegant settlements.

We came to an anchor a little above Loud's Island, and took our leave, with regret of our zealous friend, Mr. Palmer. After he was gone, in order to divert our melancholy, while the people were filling their casks with water, we went on shore to a neighboring house, where we met with a friendly reception. About four in the afternoon we set sail, and proceeded almost to St. George's Island, under the assistance of a propitious breeze, but, on a sudden, the wind shifted to the south-east, and blew with some degree of violence, which compelled us to alter our course, and to stand up the river towards the settlements in Broad Cove.* Nothing could be more romantic and pleasing than the prospects around us.

As we sailed up the harbour a number of islands of various shapes and sizes, partly cultivated, and partly in their primeval wildness, presented themselves to view in alternate succession, till we had a distant appearance of the Dutch plantations at Broad Bay, lying contiguous on both sides of the river. At length the fine settlements on the Bristol shore suddenly opened upon us, the fields arrayed in virgin green, gently sloping down to the water, exhibited an idea of cheerfulness and joy. The reflection,

* A bay on the west side of the Medomak River near Waldoboro.

however, that we were doomed to abandon these pleasant scenes, checked the rising emotions of the heart, and filled our minds with the glooms of melancholy and sorrow.

When we came to anchor, the two brothers conducted us on shore, and we walked through a range of fields and pastures to the habitation of Mr. Rhodes, who received us with sincere expressions of hospitality. The sun was now descending towards the margin of the western horizon, and every object was brightened by his beams and softened with the cooling breezes of evening. We were soon provided with a dish of tea, which, after our fatigue and sickness upon the water, afforded us a seasonable refreshment. After this grateful repast, we walked among the rural scenes, and surveyed them with a pleasing regret, and having spent the remainder of the evening in conversation, supper and devotion, we went to repose, and slept quietly till the morning.

June 16th. This morning, when we awoke, a little before sunrise, we had the agreeable information that the weather was fine and clear, and the wind beginning to breeze from the west. This intelligence revived our spirits, but we were obliged to wait for the tide till after breakfast, for it being spring tides, the water had ebbed out so low that we were aground. It was with great impatience that we waited till the element returned to assist our escape; at length, about nine, we came to sail, and passed through a narrow channel, and stood towards Owl's Head, under favour of a propitious gale, with a view to discover, if possible, some of the British fleet. We stood away to the northward till we had a fair prospect into Owl's Head Harbour, but no vessels appearing, we had some dispute whether we should proceed up Penobscot Bay, or direct our course for Nova Scotia. I was inclined to favour the former proposal, but the rest of our company being anxious to visit Halifax, and Mrs. Bailey expressing her fears that instead of finding British ships, we should fall among rebel cruisers, I gave directions to cross the Bay of Fundy. Nothing could be more flattering than the prospect before us; the sky was serene, with a gentle gale from the west northwest, and a number of small clouds over the land, promised a propitious season. We were, besides, charmed with the various appearances around us,—the ocean, interspersed with a multitude of fine islands, of different shapes and dimensions; to the north, Penobscot Bay opened into the land, with its numerous islands, covered with lofty trees, except here and there an infant plantation, while beyond, the Camden Mountains arose in majestic grandeur, throwing their rugged summits above the clouds; these, as we approached the Fox Islands without, began gradually to diminish till their dusky azure resembled the seat of a thunder-tempest, advancing to discharge its vengeance on some distant shore. But while we were viewing these romantic scenes with a mixture of delight and veneration, and taking leave of our native regions with melancholy regret, the wind suddenly shifted into the S. S. W., and a thick fog covered the surface of the ocean in such a manner as to exclude every object. This incident afforded us abundance of perplexity, as we had to pass through a multitude of islands and rocks, none of which could be discovered at the distance of ten rods. We however ventured to continue our voyage in this uncertain situation. The wind continued to blow a moderate gale, though it remained so scanty that we were obliged to go close-hauled. In the afternoon the weather for several hours was obscure and gloomy, and gave us uneasy apprehensions of an approaching storm, a circumstance no ways agreeable to persons confined to such a little shallop, in so threatening a tract of the ocean as the Bay of Fundy. These apprehensions continued to disturb our repose till about an hour before night, when the sun brake forth in all the brightness of his departing glory, and tinged the summits of the rolling waves with his level beams. At the same time we had a distant view of Mount Desert, at an immense distance, settling like a hillock on the water. All our company by this time were extremely sick, except the Captain, who was obliged to continue at the helm till the returning light began to disperse the shades of darkness. The wind continued somewhat favourable till after midnight, when it died away for more than two hours, then sprang up S. E., almost ahead; about sunrise came to the east, then N. N. E., where it freshened up into a severe gale. It was now tide of flood, and the current proceeding in direct opposition to the wind, a sharp and dangerous sea commenced. After reefing we attempted to scud, but the seas rolling over the vessel obliged us to bring to. The tempest still increased; the wind roared like thunder in the shrouds; the ocean around us was all ragged and deformed, and we were filled with great agitation and dread, expecting every moment to be swallowed up in the immense abyss. We were unable to take any refreshment, and continued till the storm abated confined to our miserable apartments.

June 21st (Halifax). We were now plainly sensible that our uncouth habits and uncommon appearance had, by this time, attracted the notice of multitudes, who flocked towards the water to indulge their curiosity. These inquisitive strangers threw us into some confusion, and to prevent a multitude of impertinent interrogations, which might naturally be expected by persons in our circumstances, I made the following public declaration, standing on the quarter-deck: "Gentlemen, we are a company of fugitives from Kennebeck, in New England, driven by famine and persecution to take refuge among you, and therefore I must entreat your candour and compassion to excuse the meanness and singularity of our dress."

I that moment discovered among the gathering crowd Mr. Kitson, one of our Kennebeck neighbors, running down the street to our assistance. He came instantly on board, and after mutual salutations, helped us on shore. Thus, just a fortnight after we left our own beloved habitation, we found ourselves landed in a strange country, destitute of money, clothing, dwelling or furniture, and wholly uncertain what countenance or protection we might obtain from the governing powers. Mr. Kitson kindly offered to conduct us either to Mr. Brown's or Capt. Callahan's; and just as we had quitted our vessel, Mr.

Moody, formerly clerk to the King's Chapel, appeared to welcome our arrival. But as it may afford some diversion to the courteous reader, I will suspend my narration a few moments to describe the singularity of our apparel, and the order of our procession through the streets, which were surprisingly contrasted by the elegant dresses of the gentlemen and ladies we happened to meet in our lengthy ambulation. And here I am confoundedly at a loss where to begin, whether with Capt. Smith or myself, but as he was a faithful pilot to this haven of repose, I conclude it is no more than gratitude and complaisance to give him the preference. He was clothed in a long swingling threadbare coat, and the rest of his habit displayed the venerable signatures of antiquity, both in form and materials. His hat carried a long peak before, exactly perpendicular to the longitude of his aquiline nose. On the right hand of this sleek commander shuffled along your very humble servant, having his feet adorned with a pair of shoes, which sustained the marks of rebellion and independence. My legs were covered with a thick pair of blue woolen stockings, which had been so often mended and darned by the fingers of frugality that scarce an atom of the original remained. My breeches, which just concealed the shame of my nakedness, had formerly been black, but the color being worn out by age, nothing remained but a rusty grey, bespattered with lint and bedaubed with pitch. Over a coarse tow and linen shirt, manufactured in the looms of sedition, I sustained a coat and waistcoat of the same dandy grey russet; and, to secrete from public inspection the innumerable rents, holes, and deformities, which time and misfortunes had wrought in these ragged and weather-beaten garments, I was furnished with a blue surtout, fretted at the elbows, worn at the buttonholes, and stained with a variety of tints, so that it might truly be styled a coat of many colours, and to render this external department of my habit still more conspicuous and worthy of observation, the waist descended below my knees, and the skirts hung dangling about my heels; and to complete the whole a jaundice-coloured

3. The Pioneer Arrives Downeast

by

A. HYATT VERRILL

THE ox cart creaked, swayed and jolted down the rock-strewn slope towards the river. With rolling eyes, foam-slathered muzzles and with splayed feet slipping and sliding on pebbles and gravel, the steers strained against their yoke.

"Hay, Star! Ho, Buck! Gee! Haw!" Encouraged, urged, admonished by the shouts of their driver, the oxen made the grade, and, halting at the brink of the stream, buried their noses in the cool water. Their driver, a lean young giant in rough homespun and high cowhide boots, leaned on his goad and regarded the beasts with a tolerant smile.

"Reckon the critters be plumb tuckered out," he observed, turning to the woman perched on the rough plank seat of the vehicle. "Been a derned long pull an' hotter'n Tophet. Sakes alive! Malviny, ye must be shook most to pieces, and wearied to death, most. Shucks! I'd oughta pulled up an' spelled ye a bit. Well, ye'll have a chance to rest up, just as soon's we ford the crick. Plumb purty spot for a camp, this intervale. Plenty of grass, good water, wood handy, an' trout an' deer for the askin'."

The woman, small, frail-looking, almost girlish, smiled as she removed her poke bonnet and shifted the weight of the infant in her arms.

"No, Dan'l, I be'n't a mite wearied," she denied bravely. "An' Eunice has been sleepin' fine. The joltin's been like a rockin' cradle to her. But I guess Bud here'll be mighty glad to quit ridin'. Land's sake, Dan'l, ye must be footsore, what with trompin' 'longside them critters ever since sunup."

The freckle-faced youngster beside her scrambled from his seat and held out his arms. "Hey, Pop, lif' me down," he shrilled.

"Not yet, son," replied his father. "Soon's ever we're acrost the crick ye can romp an' run all ye mind to. Now holt tight, Bud, we're a-goin' along over."

Wading ahead of his oxen, Daniel, sounding the depth of water with his goad, led the way across the shallows to the farther bank. Refreshed with the water, and with acres of lush meadow before them, the steers bent to the yoke and dragged the cumbersome vehicle up the bank and into the shelter of a clump of willows.

"Here we be," exclaimed Daniel as he unyoked the tired oxen and lifted the boy and helped his wife to the ground. "Now set down an' rest in the shade whilst I git the truck out," he added as he stooped and kissed her, and with a callused finger chucked the infant Eunice under the chin.

Tethered to the rear of the cart was a milch cow mooing complainingly as she watched the steers browsing on the rich grass. Turning her free to graze, Daniel proceeded to rummage in the cart body which was filled to overflowing with a most amazing assortment of goods and chattels—all the earthly possessions of the Bartons.

There was a coop containing several hens and a cockerel; there was a wobbly-legged calf; a willow withe crate imprisoned a couple of young pigs and another held two plaintively bleating lambs. A huge iron kettle was packed full of kitchen utensils and cutlery; there were pewter dishes, bedding, a side of tanned leather; shovels, hoes, pitchforks and a scythe; axes and a maul; a chest of carpenters' tools; sacks of grain, potatoes and seeds; some odd pieces of simple furniture and even an anvil with blacksmith's tools and iron bars. A cannister of powder, a bag of shot, a bullet mold and a pig of lead were stowed in one corner of the cart, and, hanging to the bows above, were a fowling piece and a long rifle, both carefully cleaned and oiled and both loaded. Having secured a skillet, pewter plates, a few pieces of cutlery and other necessities, Daniel slipped the straps of shot pouch and powderhorn over his shoulders and primed his fowling piece.

"No use wastin' time huntin' a deer naow," he observed. " 'Pears to me some pa'tridge'll be moughty tasty for our supper, eh, Malviny? An' mebbe I kin hook up a few trouts. Calc'late we kin spare a mite o' po'k for to fry 'em in. Now jest set an' rest for a spell an' I'll be back in less'n no time 'tall."

The woman glanced somewhat timorously about the meadow and the fringe of woodland beyond.

"Ain't no Injuns about, be they?" she asked.

The man shook his head. "Nary sign on 'em," he assured her. "An' if they be they ain't hostyle. Nawthin' but Abenakis in these parts, the folks to Po'tlan' said." Then, after a slight pause— "Calc'late ye mought as well have the rifle handy, though—no knowin' but a b'ar or wolf or some such varmint mought come rummagin' round arter the heifer or other critters."

Securing the rifle he primed it, and placing it within easy reach of his wife he strode off towards the forest. Crooning the baby to sleep the woman stretched her weary body on the soft grass and idly watched the boy as he played near, chasing the butterflies that flitted about the buttercups and gentians and chortling with glee when he stumbled upon a wandering box tortoise. Presently the dull report of a gun came from the forest, and rousing herself with a sigh the woman commenced gathering twigs and dry wood for a fire. Frail-looking as she was, she wielded the ax with strength and skill that would have been the envy of many a man, until she had accumulated enough fuel to last through the night. Meanwhile, she had heard a second gunshot, and, knowing for a certainty that her husband would soon be back with game, she struck flint and steel, blew the tinder to a glow and lit the campfire.

Suddenly she started, seized the rifle and wheeled about all in one swift motion, as a shout came from the direction of the river. For an instant she stared, incredulously. Then, lowering her weapon, she stood gazing towards the ford. Rattling and bumping down the rocky bank was a lumbering cart drawn by a span of horses driven by a stout, red-bearded man, with a woman on the seat beside him.

Malviny could scarcely believe her eyes. White folks! Company! Another woman here in the wilderness! As the horses splashed and floundered through the stream she seized Bud—who was having a glorious time with his tortoise and a captive toad—hastily brushed the dirt and litter from his clothes and person, smoothed her own garments, donned her discarded bonnet and tucked the wisps of her rebellious hair from sight.

"Howdy, miss!" greeted the new arrival as he drew his panting horses to a halt a few yards from the ox cart. "Ain't no objection to our stoppin' here for to camp, have ye?" Then, glancing about —"Men folks out huntin', ain't they? Thought I heerd a gunshot a spell back. Ain't ye skeered all by herself here?"

Malviny shook her head. "Not a mite," she declared. "Dan'l says they ain't Injuns about, an' I kin shoot's well as any man. Land! I forgot my manners. Howdy! Ye're right welcome. Seems like ages sence I've seen white folks. We come all the way from Kit'ry, an' ox carts are lots slower'n hosses an' wagons. Step right down an' make yerself to home, Mrs. ——"

"Wildredge," supplied the man as he lifted the woman to the ground. "I'm Ephraim Wildredge from Northfield an' she's Mary. Now——"

A childish voice from the interior of the wagon interrupted

him and a girl of three appeared clambering over the seat. "I wanta get out an' play," she shrilled.

"All right, sis," laughed Ephraim as he swung the child to the ground. "There ye be, an' a nice little lad to play with. Got a turkle an' hop-toad, too."

Like old friends the two women were chatting and laughing, and Ephraim, filling and lighting a homemade birchwood pipe, proceeded to unharness his team. As he turned the horses loose to graze, Daniel appeared with a string of trout and several grouse.

"Howdy!" he greeted the newcomers. Then, after welcoming them and the mutual introductions, "Where ye boun' for?" he asked.

Wildredge scratched his head and cast a glance about the intervale. "Wasn't boun' no place in pertickler," he replied. "Any place where they's likely land an' far enough from the cities. Kinder calc'late I'll settle right here—purty place, good grass, good water, timber handy an' no pesky clearin' to be done. That is," he added, "if so be you ben't minded to stop here."

Daniel shook his head. "No," he said. "We're a-travelin' on. I'm aimin' for to git farther away. 'Twon't be no time at all afore folks'll be a comin' in here'bouts thicker'n flies about a 'lasses jug. I'm aimin' to find some likely place in the timber. I ain't no medder man."

"An' I ain't no woodsman," grinned the red-bearded giant. "Every man to his taste, ye know. Wall, guess I'd better be gettin' me a mess of trout."

The stream, which had never been fished, fairly teemed with trout that literally fought to be caught, and while the two women busied themselves with culinary duties Daniel helped Wildredge unload his wagon. Like the Bartons, the Wildredges had brought practically everything they owned. There was the usual collection of live stock—poultry, two pigs, three lambs and a cow. There were tools, implements and household furnishings; grain and seeds, firearms and necessary supplies such as leather, flax, wool and other raw materials, with a meager supply of salt pork, bacon, corn meal and other provisions.

But these were reserved for emergencies, for the pioneers relied upon their guns and fishing tackle to supply them with food until such time as they garnered their first crops. And as the streams and ponds were filled with fish, and the forests held an abundance of game, and as berries covered the bushes and could be gathered by the peck, food was the least of their problems.

By settling upon the open, grassy meadow land beside the river, Ephraim eliminated many of the difficulties that Daniel would have to face. But even then he was embarking on an undertaking that would have appalled many a man. Unaided, save by his wife, he would be forced to build a house, plow the land, till the soil, plant and cultivate his crops and meanwhile provide for his family. And all must be done in the few short months before the hard New England winter set in. And there was the ever present menace of Indians.

It was largely of this that the two men conversed as, with appetites satisfied, with the children sleeping soundly in the carts, and with the women engaged in discussing feminine affairs, Daniel and Ephraim stretched themselves on the grass with pipes aglow.

"Don't 'pear like they's Injuns here'bouts," remarked Ephraim. "An' I ain't seen ary one since we left Lovell."

"Come that way, did ye," muttered Daniel. "We seen quite a passel our way, down around Sebago. Met up with one village an' stopped the night with 'em—purty good folks, they was. An' run acrost a party salmon fishin' on the Androscoggin. All of 'em Abenakis an' friendly. Wore clothes, they did, an' most of 'em talkin' some English."

"Injuns is Injuns," observed Ephraim with conviction. "I don't trust none of 'em. Long's they let me be I let 'em be, but I don't hanker for 'em."

"No more alike than white folks be," declared Daniel. "When I was a younker I played with Injuns much as I did with white lads. L'arned a powerful lot 'bout the woods an' critters from 'em, too. My idee is that ef ye treat a Injun right he'll treat ye right. 'Course they's some bad uns. Them Mikmaks fer instance. Derned lucky they ain't none o' that breed here'bouts. They'll sculp ye soon's tarnation. Wall, it's gittin' mighty late. Calc'late I'll be gittin' myself some sleep. We got to git goin' right early tomorrer."

4. The Old West India Trade

by

WILLIAM HUTCHINSON ROWE

SHE proved to be the Schr. *Venis* of St. Kitts from St. Kitts bound to Quebec laden with Rum, Sugar and Molasses.— *The Log of the Privateer Schooner Teazer, August 17, 1812*

> Old horse! Old horse! how came you here?
>   From Sacarap to Portland Pier
> I've toted boards for many a year.
>   Until worn out by sore abuse
> They salted me down for sailors' use.
>   The sailors they do me despise,
> They turn me over and damn my eyes,
>   Cut off my meat and pick my bones
> And throw me over to Davy Jones.

Regardless of what was to be a Maine boy's occupation or profession, an indispensable part of his upbringing was a voyage or two in the West India trade. In the days when the privateers of France and England, not to mention the piratical craft swarming in the Caribbean, might be sighted at any time and in almost any latitude, this opened up endless vistas of adventure before the young sailor. In *The Hardscrabble,* Elijah Kellogg spins a

Reprinted from *The Maritime History of Maine* by William Hutchinson Rowe by permission of W. W. Norton & Co., Inc. Copyright 1948 by the Publishers.

44

yarn of the building of a sloop by four boys. They manned her, filled her with ventures, and took her out to Martinique, where, according to Kellogg, "Pluck and principle won the day" and each came home with "What in those days was considered a handsome property."

The facts do not belie the fiction. For example, in 1791 Captains Asa Clapp and William McLellan were witnesses to the frightful massacre of the white population of Haiti during the revolution precipitated by Toussaint L'Ouverture. And thereby hangs a tale of the shrewd guile by which a Maine skipper snatched in the face of disaster, a cargo and a profit.

The insurrection was hardly over when a down-east captain sailed into the port of San Domingo with a cargo of lumber worth $7,000. As soon as he dropped anchor a squad of Toussaint's black soldiers came aboard and took possession. The captain put up no resistance and learned from the sergeant that Toussaint was in camp near by and would be glad to meet any one from the United States, for which country he had a high regard. Now at this time every vessel in foreign trade carried a sea letter calling on all kings, rulers, and potentates to render aid to vessels or crews in distress. They were issued by the governments, and the one carried by the captain was signed by President Washington. The captain told the sergeant that he had a letter from General Washington which he wished to read to his commander.

They went ashore and found the "Black Napoleon" lying in a hammock dressed in full uniform. The announcement that Washington had written him a letter brought him to his feet with a bound, and he ordered the letter read. Thereupon the captain read and the sergeant translated. Immensely pleased by the craftily inserted praise of himself, Toussaint asked what cargo the captain had brought and what he wished to take back. Thereupon he directed that the lumber be discharged and the vessel be loaded cargo for cargo with sugar and coffee. No brig ever had its capacity more fully tested. Every nook and corner was used, and the sailors complained that they had no place to sleep. The profits of this voyage were over $80,000.

The Bay Colony quite early developed a thriving trade with "the Islands." In 1676 Edward Randolph, the "Surveyor, collector and searcher for New England," reported that Boston should be "esteemed the mart town of the West Indies." On the Maine coast, while there is record of early voyages to the Caribbean, this trade came to its maturity much later. By the middle of the seventeenth century Thomas Cutts was in the Barbados acting as agent for his brothers, receiving their cargoes of Piscataqua fish and lumber and shipping West India goods in return. Later he came to Kittery and carried on an extensive business in this line. Somewhat later The William Pepperells built up and maintained a vigorous trade with the islands.

Even before their settlement was safe from Indian attack the people of York joined together in partnership to build and fit out a vessel to send to the West Indies. By 1745 they had some twenty craft engaged in that trade. At the time that Wells included the present town of Kennebunk, it also had its fleet and varied its trips to the southward with voyages to Halifax and Montreal, where there was a ready market for cattle. This was a profitable but precarious cargo. There is a case on record where one skipper had his entire deckload of thirty-nine head washed overboard the first night out. Colonel Thomas Cutts, a former clerk of the Pepperells in Kittery, came to Saco in 1758, where he soon developed a large business with warehouses and a wharf at Saco Ferry. He is said to have netted a profit of $100,000 on a cargo of molasses which was taken in exchange for one of lumber and which arrived in time to be sold on a high market.

When the people on the neck at Falmouth were engaged in the masting trade, there had sprung up a West India trade of considerable extent. It was carried on principally by Ezekiel Cushing and William Simonton, who had a large valuable wharf in the cove in South Portland which now bears Simonton's name.

Farther on down East the records are of a later date. For example, the first voyage to that part of the world out of Blue Hill was made in 1768. Ellsworth's first vessel, the *Susan and Abigail,* cleared in 1773 on a voyage, which thereafter became an annual affair, to Demerara with a cargo of oak staves and shingles turned out by Captain Isaac Smith's neighbors.

The products of the Islands furnished many of the staples of pioneer life. In 1759, after the call of Canada, new settlements were established well back from the coast. This increased the demand. Thus merchants in the coast towns not only supplied local needs but became wholesalers for the many little general stores up country, whose signs "W–I Goods" proclaimed them as the depots for rum and treacle. Barter was then the order of the day. The fisherman and the farmer found the merchant an indispensable middleman, whose warehouses and wharves became the center of an ever-growing import and export trade.

Before the Revolution, what with free access to the British islands, plenty of smuggling with the Spanish ports, and trade with the French, American shipowners had been carrying on a most profitable business and were by way of making large fortunes. By the Treaty of Paris, which recognized our independence, the doors of the British West India ports were "slammed in our faces." Parliament told the planters of the islands that they would find their supplies in the Canadian provinces. But the English merchants and the inhabitants of these islands wanted American produce. Yankee captains could supply them more promptly, with better quality, and at lower prices than could their own people in Nova Scotia.

Moreover, the Yankee captain would take in trade West India goods, particularly molasses, which had no ready sale in Europe, or, if need be, he could pay cash. The governors of the islands appointed the collectors and the judges. Backed by them, these officials found many excuses for winking the official eye, and most vessels entering their ports loaded to the scuppers with Maine products went out light. Provided the most important part of the transaction was not omitted and that a five-joe piece crossed an English palm, stress of weather, relief for-a starving population, the need for rebuilding after a hurricane, a British charter acquired in Nova Scotia, a Spanish one in Trinidad, or an ancient register dating from before the Revolution, was quite enough. So it was that when Horatio, later Lord, Nelson was sent out in 1786 to enforce the Navigation Acts, he wrote home saying:

When I arrived in Barbadoes, the Bay was so full of American vessels, lading and unlading without molestation from the customs house officers that there were more American flags than English and had I been set down from the air I should most assuredly have been convinced that I was in an American instead of a British port.

At this time, by virtue of treaties, American vessels had access to the French islands as well as to the Dutch—St. Eustatius, St. Martin, and Curaçao—and the Swedish—St. Bartholomew. The commerce of the island of Cuba was in theory a complete monopoly, but its inhabitants, as well as those of the other Spanish colonies, encouraged smuggling. Thus there was built up an enormous contraband trade which all the fleets of Spain were unable to prevent. It was with this island that the largest amount of the trade from the Maine coast was carried on. Havana in particular offered a ready market for ship timber and spars for the large number of Spanish men-of-war that were being built there.

The vessels engaged in the West India trade seem surprisingly small today. They comprised large sloops, two-masted schooners, and brigs. For two decades after the Revolution, the average size of a vessel out of the Kennebec was but 129 tons. As this figure includes ships, the majority were much smaller. Being of moderate draft, they were able to take the more direct route to Cuba across the Great Bahama Bank. Over this route traveled a goodly part of the output of the Maine forests in the shape of masts, spars, boxes, shingles, and staves.

In the early days they were built in forgotten yards all along the shore and on the small rivers from the Kennebec westward to the Piscataqua. Near Smelt Hill and the first falls of the Presumpscot River, which enters into Casco Bay, was a popular location. Here the Merrills, Lunts, Moodys, Batchelders, Knights, Hamiltons, and Smelledges put afloat the full-rigged, hermaphrodite, and jackass brigs which were so popular in the West India trade. At one time nearly a hundred of them hailed from Portland.

These vessels cost no more than fifteen or twenty dollars a ton, since the lumber for them could be cut within a few rods of the building ways. Their floors were of red oak or beech and their tops of pitch pine, Norway pine, spruce, hemlock, or anything that came to hand. Spruce limbs saturated with pitch furnished good treenails. However rough in appearance they might be, they were staunch and lasted well. For example, in 1810 Captain Ezekiel Dyer built himself the brig *Cordelia* at Ferry Village opposite Portland. Thirty-nine years later an item in the Portland *Transcript* announced that she was soon to sail for the West Indies on her ninetieth voyage.

The cargoes they carried were varied. Almost every necessity of life was welcome in islands whose only products were luxuries. There was lumber—sawed lumber and masts, spars, and hewn timbers for the shipyards of Havana. On top of a deckload of lumber and on the decks of other vessels there would often be carried the small-flat-bottomed craft known as "moses boats," which were in great demand in the sugar islands. The planters used them in lightering molasses out of the narrow streams bordering their plantations to the brigs awaiting their cargoes in deep water.

The products of the cooper's trade formed a considerable item. There were shooks with the staves jointed and crozed, hoops shaved, the headings fitted to put in place. These are terms in the cooper's trade. Shooks are bundles of staves, hoops, and heads, each bundle containing the number sufficient to make up a single hogshead, tierce, cask, or barrel. Boxes knocked down and shipped in bundles are also called shooks. The saving in cargo space is obvious. This aspect of the West India trade has survived into our own time.

Then also there were house frames all ready to put up, oxen and horses for the plow, the sugar and the treadmill, farm produce such as parsnips, potatoes, onions and grain, beef, mutton, pork, pickled fish, soap, candles, and dried codfish in "drums" of from five to eight hundred pounds each. Indeed, the manifests of these vessels read like the inventory of a country store. And what profits they paid! Lumber from the banks of Maine rivers which cost there $8.00 a thousand sold in Havana for $60.00. Beets and parsnips brought $16.00 a barrel in the French islands. Flour sold for $21.00 a barrel, beef for $24.00, and pork for $27.00. How completely this trade absorbed the maritime activity of these early years is shown by the fact that in 1787 seventy-three out of the eighty-nine clearances from Portland were for some port in the West Indies.

With prosperity came the desire for better facilities to take care of this rapidly increasing business. Old wharves and breastworks disappeared. In Portland, Union, Long, and Commercial Wharves pushed far out into the harbor. On these were constructed substantial stores, warehouses, and distilleries. At Kennebunk prodigious efforts were made to improve the harbor with the ill-fated Mousam Canal and thereafter with the more successful piers at the mouth of the Kennebunk River. King's Wharf was built at Bath, and others were constructed at Wiscasset. Up to this time the District had been dependent on Boston for its banking facilities. In 1799 the Portland Bank was chartered, to be followed in 1802 by the Maine Bank. That year also saw the start of the Lincoln and Kennebec Bank at Wiscasset.

Under the name of the Portland Monument Association a

company of merchants, headed by Captain Lemuel Moody, in 1807 subscribed for the construction of an observation tower then and since known as "The Observatory." Standing atop of Munjoy Hill and rising two hundred and twenty-seven feet above sea level, it commanded all the approaches by sea. They furnished it with a powerful French telescope. The octagonal brown tower was supported by eight large white-pine posts which rose from a deep foundation of stone eighty-two feet to a sheltered observation deck.

Here Captain Lemuel Moody stood watch from sunrise to sunset. With the glass he could identify a vessel twenty miles off shore. On three flagstaffs—one for ships and barks, another for brigs, and a third for schooners and later for steamers—he set well-known signals which told the town what shipping was in the offing. A foreign vessel was announced by its national flag, and if it was a war vessel, a black ball was set just below. Various pennants told of a ship in distress or a vessel ashore and various other tales. Most valuable was the display of the private house flags of the merchants in town. The setting of these warned them of the arrival of their vessels several hours before they reached harbor.

Here on September 5, 1813, Captain Moody watched the *Enterprise* whip the *Boxer* and recounted the progress of the battle, in the manner of a modern radio commentator, to an expectant crowd at the base of the tower. From this vantage a fleet of two hundred little barks and brigs could be seen sailing out of the harbor on the twenty-ninth day of April in 1844. With their white sails glistening in the sun they made, in the words of a contemporary editor, "a fine sight in the offing."

Many of the finest houses in Maine were built in the last decade of the eighteenth and the first of the nineteenth century. There are the beautiful mansions of Wiscasset which reached "the apogee of the Georgian style and the culmination of the colonial and early national architecture." The Nickels, Hodge, Smith, Tucker, Cook, Lee, Wood, and Carlton houses of this town belong to this period. So also does the Hamilton house at South Berwick, the Sewall at York, the Lyman and Robert Lord at Kennebunk, the Thomas Cutts mansion at Saco, the Cobb, Ingraham, Wingate, and Ebenezer Storer houses at Portland, the Cotterill at Damariscotta and the Kavanagh at New Castle. Many attempts have been made to give the credit for the beauty of form and line of these houses to foreign architectural plans. In most instances they were the work in both design and execution of local carpenters and joiners—the very same men who set the frames of their vessels "by the eye." Indeed, no better education in beauty of line could be obtained than by the designing of ships. Ship carpenters framed and erected, ship joiners finished the interiors, and ship carvers, turning from figureheads, trailboards, and stern ornaments, carved with equal facility mantels, stairways, and wainscoting.

The news of the Treaty of Ghent, which concluded the three years of "Mr. Madison's War," reached the coast of Maine in midwinter. Many vessels were stripped of their gear and all but their lower masts. Indeed, some were frozen in the ice of the creeks and rivers where they had been hidden away. By April 1816 many little brigs were bearing away on their old courses to the southward. Their masters hoped to find good markets awaiting them, but in this they were disappointed. Very few made saving voyages. Although commerce slowly revived, it did not flourish as it had at the beginning of the century. It was not until some time after the European wars that it became more stable and developed a character all its own. This period from the close of the second war with England until 1840 came to be known to oldtimers as the "old West India trade."

The ships and the rigs which were peculiarly adapted to the West India trade have completely disappeared from the seas. They were small craft, on the average around 200 tons, although after 1830 vessels of 300 and over were launched. Drawing but little water, they were able to look into almost any creek or river that emptied into a cove or bay in search of a likely cargo. Being very full-bodied, they could load to advantage. The pros and cons of the various types—not to mention the quarrel-provoking question of their proper designation—have formed a favorite topic of maritime debate wherever those of a sea turn of mind may foregather.

This period is pre-eminently that of the brig—now obsolete for three-quarters of a century. In the building of these Maine had a near monopoly. The full-rigged brig had both masts, main and fore, in three spars and was wholly square-rigged save that on the mainmast was a standing gaff to which was bent a small fore-and-aft sail called the spanker. The snow was much akin to the brig, the difference being that the snow set her spanker on a trysail mast stepped on deck a foot or so abaft the mainmast and secured aloft to the trestletrees of the mast.

These gave way to the hermaphrodite brig. This was a cross between a brig and a schooner, being square-rigged on the foremast and fore-and-aft-rigged on the mainmast. Fewer men were required to handle her, and her economy made her exceedingly popular. A modification of this was that familiarly known as the "jackass brig." This carried one or more square sails on the mainmast. Out of Maine waters the hermaphrodite and particularly the jackass brig was often called a brigantine. But on the coast of Maine the brigantine carried the sails of a brig on her foremast and her mainmast was made in two spars having the rig of a topsail schooner with at least one square main topsail and sometimes a main topgallant sail. This was thought to be a more weatherly rig than the others, for the big fore-and-aft sail was a powerful pusher when close-hauled on the wind.

Then there was the familiar "tops'l schooner," which was widely used though never quite as popular in the District as the brig rigs. Here the masts and sails were those of a fore-and-after, save that on the foremast she carried a topsail and sometimes a topgallant sail, the latter two being square sails. Finally there was the completely forgotten but quite popular "tops'l sloop."

One is described by Elijah Kellogg in *The Hardscrabble*. In addition to her mainsail, she carried a full suit of square sails—course, topsail, topgallant sail, and royal. Says the author:

Her lower mast was rather short in proportion to the top, topgallant and royal masts. The mainmast was set well aft, and raked a good deal. The bowsprit and jib-boom were long. She had a sprit-sail yard and double martingale. The forebraces led to the end of the bowsprit, the others to the end of the jib-boom. In bad weather they had preventive-braces that led aft to the rail. She carried fore-topmast staysail, jib and flying-jib.

The number of smart little vessels of all these types and rigs which were owned in the various ports is amazing. Two trips a year was a rule. A vessel would leave the Maine coast in the latter half of December, and arrive at the islands at the end of the three-week Christmas holidays. She would unload, take on a return cargo, and reach home around the last of February. Immediately she would reload and go out on her second voyage, reaching port again sometime in the latter part of April. Then they would lay her up over the summer months, during the yellow fever and hurricane season in the islands and the planting and haying season at home. In October the most industrious would go on a coasting voyage.

As time went on the larger merchants established business connections with merchants in the West Indies. This gave assurance of a market and a return cargo and permitted the brigs to sail almost with the regularity of a packet. Others, who comprised the majority, cleared merely to the West Indies with no particular port in view, seeking a market where the best opportunity offered. These voyages did not always bring the warmth, sunshine and delight of the tropics together with enormous profits. A typical experience is that of Captain Theodore Wells in the schooner *Friendship*, bound from Wells to St. Vincents with a cargo of hewed lumber. This his owners had ordered him not to dispose of unless he could get one hundred gallons of molasses for a thousand feet of lumber. He had a short and pleasant voyage down to St. Vincents but found no market there. The captain tells his own tale:

From St. Vincents I sailed for Grenada where not finding a market from thence I left for Trinidad where I was still unable to effect a sale. Proceeding northward I touched at Port Royal in the island of Martinico. Here I failed to find a satisfactory sale. From this port I proceeded to Bastarre in the Island of Guadaloupe where the same disappointment awaited me. I next touched at Nevis but could not dispose of my freight without trusting it in hands of doubtful solvency. From here I sailed for St. Thomas. At this point there was no demand for a cargo like mine. I attempted to reach Porto Rico which was the last island where molasses was to be found excepting Cuba but in this failed because of a fresh blow and thick stormy weather which drove me by it when I ran for Aquin in the Island of St. Domingo and here as elsewhere I found a dull market and no sale.

To cut short this catalogue of frustration, he ran from San Domingo to Aux Cayes, to Jeremie, to Mariguana, and to Port-au-Prince, where he found a large number of vessels that were making losing sales in an overstocked market. Leaving there, he sailed to St. Marks. At last he returned to Jeremie, from whence, after spending twenty-eight days in making a sale, and forty more in waiting for his cargo of coffee, he sailed for home, only to lose both his vessel and his cargo when but a few days out.

Neither dull markets nor the reefs of the Bahama cays were the worst hazards of a West India voyage. There was piracy. During the long years of the American and Napoleonic wars the islands and cays had become infested with pirates of the lowest type. Encouraged by the authorities, they preyed openly on American commerce. In November 1821 eleven pirate vessels were cruising from Maisi on the southeast coast of Cuba. Five worked together as a squadron off Cape San Antonio on the southwest coast and five more east of Matanzas on the north. Between Matanzas and Havana a flotilla of small boats kept constant watch for vessels becalmed in the offing, attacking them as soon as darkness fell. Still another nest of small boats operated at Cape Cruz, the crews living in caves on the shore. The ship news of the period is full of accounts of the atrocious attacks by these gangs of cutthroats who were guided by the maxim, "Dead cats don't mew."

The brig *Dolphin* of Nobleboro was attacked in August 1821 off Cape Antonio, the mate stabbed and the men hoisted up by the neck to compel them to tell where money was concealed. The *Alliance* of Kennebunk fell into the hands of the same gang the next January. The members of the crew were robbed of everything, even their shirts, and were beaten, put into the long-boat and set adrift. The *Mary Jane,* the *Evergreen,* the *Milo,* the *Dispatch,* and the *Cobbseconte* were given like treatment, the last when only four miles out from Morro Castle, Havana. The Portland brig *Mechanic* was burned and the crew murdered. The murder of Captain Clement Perkins of the Kennebunk brig *Belisarius* was particularly horrible. In March 1823, when off Campeche, she was boarded by the crew of a piratical schooner of some forty tons. They were vicious brutes. The captain told them where they could find what money there was aboard. Disappointed in not finding as much as they hoped, they cut off first his right arm, then his left, and finally his leg above the knee. Not satisfied with this, they filled his mouth with oakum, saturated it with oil, and, setting it on fire, ended his sufferings.

The murder of all but one of the crew of a Maine brig, the story told by this survivor, and the nationwide publicity given to it are said to have brought about a campaign of extermination that all but cleared the Caribbean of these pests. On the twenty-eighth of November, 1824, the brig *Betsey* sailed from Wiscasset with a cargo of lumber for Matanzas. She was under the command of Elias Hilton with two mates, three seamen, and a cook. On a December night, the brig struck a rock off the Double Head

Shot Keys. The crew took to the boats, eventually landing on one of the Cuba keys. This they found to be inhabited by five fishermen, the leader of whom the captain recognized as one with whom he had previously traded at Matanzas. Feeling that he could trust him, the captain made arrangements with him to take the party to the island in the morning. This opinion was not shared by the mate. His suspicions were aroused by the secret departure of the fishermen during the night and all but confirmed by his finding evidence of violence in a hidden cove of the key.

As they were leaving the following morning, their vessel was attacked by ten Spaniards in an open boat. Aided by the fishermen, the Spaniards bound them all and carried them to the cove which the mate had discovered the evening before. When they arrived at the head of the cove, they assured their victims that "Americans were very good beef for their knives." Then they began their work of death by decapitating Captain Hilton and murdering all but one of the others in a manner too barbarous to describe. The executioner to whom the second mate, Daniel Collins, had been assigned slipped up. His glancing blow cut the cord with which Collins was bound. Despite his severe wound he was able to escape to the mangrove bushes. Here, creeping in water up to his chin, he reached the edge of the island. Sleeping in the mangroves at night and swimming from key to key by day, tormented by hunger and thirst, the heat, and mosquitoes, he at last reached the island of Cuba.

The eighteen-thirties and the roaring forties were days of great activity for the ports of Maine. The railroads had not been built, and the shortest route to the seaboard from northern New Hampshire beyond the White Mountains and from all northern Vermont to Derby Line was through Crawford Notch. There was little money in the new country. Trade was almost entirely by barter. The farmer brought his produce to the seaboard merchant and took "store pay" in return. All this country produce had to be transported to market and exchanged for the flour, salt fish, coffee, rum, and "long sweetening," as molasses was called, which were necessities of life in the pioneer settlements. So in winter the "Vermonters" came down the present Roosevelt trail in long strings of red pungs. On a projecting board stood the driver, clad invariably in a long blue frock, guiding his team over the frozen road. In the pung were his round hogs, his butter, and his lard, together with the large round box which held his provisions—generally huge chunks of cheese and molasses doughnuts.

The whole country was awakening to the economic value of the back country. In 1825 the Erie Canal was completed, and in Maine various attempts were made to open up the expanding frontier. Lakes and ponds were joined by canals to facilitate the bringing of lumber and other products to a shipping point. From 1820 to 1840 the Maine legislature granted charters for twenty-five such enterprises. The most important was the Cumberland and Oxford Canal. Completed in 1830, it opened up the whole Sebago Lake region with its wide branching system of lakes and ponds. Moving slowly down the twenty miles from White's Bridge in Windham to Portland Harbor, the flat-bottomed boats, *Whirlwind, Major Downing, Honest Quaker, Reindeer,* and others added their cargoes to the holds of the waiting West India brigs.

When a cargo of coffee or molasses came alongside a wharf or when lumber was being loaded aboard, the waterfront resounded with the song of the Negro stevedores. They hoisted the hogsheads from the holds by a tackle (pronounced "taykel") and fall, all the time singing:

> "Everybody he lub something,
> Hoojun—John—a hoojun,
> Song he set the heart a-beating,
> Hoojun—John—a hoojun."

There were no winches in those days. It is said that after they were introduced Negroes disappeared from the northern seaports, for they refused to work with a winch, as with that sort of labor their songs had no place. Adding to the confusion were the busy lumber surveyors who ran from one ox load to another with a shingle for their record in one hand and a rule staff for their scaling in the other. On the wharf, as the cargo came out, stood the gauger checking the hogsheads and boxes against the manifest. Since this document sometimes failed to list all the cargo, there sometimes arose the question as to how this surplus could be landed without detection by the customs officer. It was often solved by the owner taking the inspector home with him to dinner and lingering rather long over the wine. Then a few more hogsheads of molasses or boxes of sugar would be hoisted out and stored in the warehouses without appearing on the tally.

On the inventories of the West India Stores as in the manifests of the West India brigs, rum, coffee, and molasses lead all the rest. After the Revolution rum from Jamaica and the other English islands or from St. Croix and the Dutch ports lost its place in the imports. Before that time old Falmouth had its distillery wharf. With the cost of molasses at thirteen pence per gallon and the cost of distilling it five and a half, Maine merchants were quick to perceive the large profits to be had in manufacturing rum at home. There were seven distilleries at one time in Portland, one in Bath, another in Wiscasset, and Vaughan's great establishment at Hallowell. The amount consumed was surprising. During one winter a country store in Pittston disposed of ninety hogsheads. A boatman on the Cumberland and Oxford Canal reported that during the season he alone delivered three hundred barrels to the towns along his route.

Coffee was the most desired cargo. This was because of its small bulk as against its value. Haiti, which before the insurrection of the blacks had been the richest of the islands, produced much of the fragrant bean. Cuba also was a high producer before the great hurricane of 1844 destroyed her coffee groves. But the islands of the Spanish Main were growing a steadily increasing amount. Brazil, too, was fast attaining the pre-eminence that has made the name of her principal port, Rio, synonymous with coffee. As the years passed, coffee figured less and less in the manifests of the Maine brigs. More and more the cargoes consisted entirely of molasses. In the marine news the romantic names of the Saints of the Leeward and Windward Island occur with less frequency. They are replaced by a monotonous iteration of Havana, Cardenas or Matanzas in Cuba, and San Juan Guayama in Porto Rico. The brigs built for this trade at Pipe Stave Landing on the Piscataqua by Sarah Orne Jewett's grandfather were known as the Berwick "molasses brigs."

Havana had long been a favorite port for Maine captains. As early as 1826 over one-tenth of the 117,796 tons of shipping which entered this beautiful harbor in that year hailed from Maine. Cuba not only took a great deal of lumber from the state, the best was also demanded. "Large, handsome lumber suitable for the Havana market," so read the orders. In the six years from 1856 to 1861, there went 1,207 cargoes of this staple to this island. As the sugar and molasses trade grew in the later forties and fifties, Cuba turned to the Maine woods for her sugar boxes, molasses hogsheads, and tierces. In 1856 eight vessels sailed from Bath to Havana carrying 12,368 such boxes and 3,102 hogsheads. Portland monopolized the shook trade and became a collecting center for them. During the six years which have been noted above, only 17 of the 1,040 lumber cargoes from here went to any other than Cuban ports. Sugar boxes are claimed to have been first manufactured at Saccarappa. This is the present city of Westbrook on the Presumpscot River. As with the "molasses brigs," the vessels carrying these shooks came to be known as "Saccarappas."

Many small sawmills were busy sawing and fitting the box boards to proper lengths all ready to be set up and nailed on the sugar plantations. The cooper's trade in the manufacture of hogshead and tierce shooks was one of the best paid in the towns near the coast. In 1867 there were 263 such shops in the state. As has been explained, the shook was a package of red-oak staves and heading, numbered and ready to be set up as a hogshead, a tierce, or a cask when needed. This was done by the coopers on the plantations or by State of Maine coopers who went out to the islands for that purpose. They ranged in price from 50 cents to $1.50. Since the going rate was from 30 to 35 cents for the rough stock, a man who could complete four or five sets in a day made a good day's wage for the times.

Molasses was cheap, fetching some fifty cents a gallon at retail. Hence it was consumed in enormous quantities in the country, and particularly in the logging camps. As one writer has put it:

Foresters float down timber that seamen may build ships and go to the saccharine islands of the south for molasses; for without molasses no lumberman could be happy in the unsweetened wilderness. Pork lubricates the joints, molasses gives tenacity to his muscles.

A variation in sweetening was the raw brown sugar. This was known to the trade as "muscovado" and was procurred by draining the molasses through holes in the bottom of the hogshead after the crystallization of the cane syrup had begun. Another variety was the "clayed" form. This name derived from the fact that the containers were sealed with moist clay. This latter type was shipped mostly from Havana in long wooden boxes, while the muscovado came from Matanzas in hogsheads weighing around a half a ton. White sugar was looked upon as a luxury. Refined of its impurities, it was marketed in a cone or loaf at a price much higher than that of raw sugar.

There were profits to be had in the process of refining. This was perceived by the West India merchants of Portland, one of the first of whom was John Bundy Brown. In partnership with others in 1845 he erected what is said to have been the third sugar house in the United States. By perseverance and constant experimentation he developed a process that produced an excellent quality of granulated sugar. His famous Portland Sugar House was incorporated in 1855. An immense establishment with warehouses and wharves was erected, and the main refinery was eight stories high. With a capital of $400,000 there were employed two hundred persons. It turned out some 250 barrels of sugar a day and processed 30,000 hogsheads of molasses in a year.

In the sixties the demand of the Brown establishment, coupled with that of two other sugar houses of good capacity operating in the city and the market in the vast territory opened to the west and the east by the Grand Trunk and Maine Central Railroads, made Portland a molasses port that was a close rival of New York. In 1860 the national total was 31,000,000 gallons. New York was in the lead with 8,500,000, and Portland was second with 5,700,000. In 1868, Portland's peak year of importation, there came into the harbor cargoes totaling 59,510 hogsheads and in addition 10,055 hogsheads and 16,800 boxes of sugar.

This was the trade and those were the days for the rugged individualist. In the year 1865 Captain Benjamin Webster contracted for the building of the brig *Emma*. She was built in ninety days. When the men were in the woods in January cutting her frame, Captain Webster contracted for her cargo with a Portland West India merchant. On the third of April she cleared fully loaded and sailed out of Portland Harbor with a fine northwest wind, reaching Cuba in time to secure a return cargo.

5. A Fair Wind on the Coast

THE LAUNCHING OF THE "RAINBOW"

by

RACHEL FIELD

ROADSIDES were bright with asters and goldenrod all the way, and mountain ash trees loaded with fiery fruit. Bo picked a branch as we passed and Nat had a bunch for his button-hole and I one to wear in my brown straw hat. Once we got on the turnpike all sorts of rigs were headed in the same direction,— old buggies and farm-wagons and prosperous carriages from Little Prospect and neighboring harbors. It might have been election or County Fair day from the cluttered roads and deserted houses, and from the white triangles of sail all headed for Fortune's Ship Yard.

It seemed as if everyone would be there before us and we three worked ourselves into a fever of impatience before the five mile ride was ended. But at last we were there and the place as gay with bunting as the fall trees had been along our way. I had thought to keep with Nat and Rissa but once we were set down from the carriage Henry Willis bore the two away to join their Philadelphia cousins and I was left with mother and the Jordan family. Jake Bullard was there in his best Sunday suit and though he had scowled at sight of my two companions, he joined me after awhile and we prowled about together. He and some of his cronies had been there for hours and it pleased him to show off the sights and answer my foolish questions.

"I'll show you the best place to see from," he volunteered. "We got plenty of time before we eat supper."

I followed him up a ladder into an old sail loft where the view was uninterrupted by tall bodies, or hurrying workmen. I had only been in the brick office once, so I had had no notion what a bustling ship-yard could be on the eve of a launching. No vessel in harbor had ever looked so vast as this one,—set high and dry, with stern to sea and great wooden timbers holding it like giants' arms.

"That's the cradle she sets in," Jake told me. "It has to cant just that much and no more. If 'twas half an inch out there'd be trouble when they started the blocking."

I didn't understand till after it was over what he had been talking about, but I listened as if I did. All the time he pointed this or that out to me I was thinking how the figures of the men working on the hull below us looked no bigger than dark bees clustering on an enormous hive. The hammers and men's voices mingled into a sort of gigantic buzzing.

Even without her masts, which Jake explained would not be set up till she lay at the wharf, the "Rainbow" loomed like a monster. High and dry she rose above the water that was steadily rising to receive her. A rich smell I had never known before hung low over the whole yard. There has been none like it since, for it was made up of lesser smells,—the steam of hot iron from the blacksmith's forge; boiling tar; hemp rope; freshly sawed lumber, and the tallow greasing the ways under that untried keel. My nose quivers yet at remembrance of it.

"There's Cousin Sam," I pointed out. "I didn't know he'd be working on it."

"Why, he's a master hand at the blocking," Jake told me scornfully. "I guess there couldn't be a launching without him. He'll knock the last block out, most likely."

"Is that hard to do?" I ventured, there being no one else about to hear my ignorance.

"Holy Moses, yes! You just wait and see. He'll have to be quick as lightning. Sometimes there ain't even time for him to get out 'fore she starts. He'll deal that last block a regular knock and then maybe he'll have to throw himself down quick and let it go right over him down the ways."

"Oh, my, Jake, won't he be all squashed?"

"No, Sir, he won't. He says there's plenty of room if he lays flat. It's loose timbers and blocks flying round he has to watch out for. I wish they'd let me do it."

I couldn't help staring at Jake with new admiration, for he looked as if he really could do it with those big-knuckled fists of his. My expression must have pleased him for when we went down the ladder again he did not leave me to join the Little Prospect boys. We found mother and the Jordan tribe and though I missed Nat and Rissa, still I was glad of Jake and his wide grin and pushing elbows in all the crowd.

We ate our supper, picnic fashion on a point not far from the yards. Besides Jake there were other schoolmates about me,— Abbie Stanley and her brother Joe; Dan Gilley and Mollie and his older sister Sadie, as well as Cousin Martha Jordan's Ruth and Hilda. I felt shy at first after being with Nat and Rissa all summer long. But little by little it got to seem like recess in the school yard again, and we ate apples and crullers, and eggs and pie as lively as could be. Only I couldn't forget those other two, not even when we skipped stones and played tag on the strip of shingle, getting as near the tide line as we dared without wetting our best shoes. I was careful not to talk with them the way I did with Nat and Rissa, for I knew they wouldn't like it, and would say I was getting stuck up and full of corn-starch airs. I'd heard them talk among themselves about the Fortune pair before now. As it was, Abbie and Ruth and even tall Sadie got discussing Rissa's clothes till I was ready to fly out at them.

"Did you see her?" Sadie laughed to the others. "Why she

looks all rigged up like a Maypole. Mother says it's a shame and she's only going on thirteen!"

"And him in a jacket like the one the monkey wore in the circus!" Jake jeered.

"A regular Miss Nancy that's what he is!" Joe Stanley was scornful.

It would have ended in a squabble most likely and I wouldn't have been able to hold my own against so many dissenting voices, only just then the others called us to help carry the baskets back to the wagons. Already the sun had set and the red afterglow was dwindling behind the spruces on the western point. A fall chill was in the September air and I felt glad of mother's old paisley shawl though it was so long I had to hold up its fringes with both my hands. We found good places near enough to see the busy men on the dark hull. The noise of hammering and shouting had grown louder. The very air was charged with a kind of current from all the human beings gathered together in that place. But at the time I could not guess that. I only knew that under my layers of shawl and dress my heart began to beat in time to the hammers. Flaring torches had been lit and in the yellow flickering light the ship-yard looked vast and strange. All the familiar faces about me wore an unnaturally sharp, bright look. The tide was well up now and still rising. I could not see how far the timbers Jake had called the cradle stretched into the dimness, but I know that nothing again will ever seem so tremendous to me as the "Rainbow" before she took to water. There still lacked some minutes before the September moon would be up.

"Kate," I suddenly heard Nat's voice at my side and felt his hand. "I thought I'd never find you in all these people. Come on with me."

"But, Nat," I began, "there isn't room, is there?"

"Hurry," he urged me, "Father won't notice, and he won't care anyhow, he's too busy. You can squeeze in by me on the platform."

Mother nodded and we began picking our way back between all the close pressed legs and skirts. It wasn't till we were safely up on the rough piece of scaffolding above all the heads and almost overhanging the great bows, that I knew how disappointed I had been not to see it all with those two. I could not get close to Rissa, but we smiled at each other, and I knew they were both glad I was there. She wore a long red cloth cape over her finery. It made her look taller and more grown up than she had in the afternoon. She stood beside her father and her Aunt and the two Philadelphia cousins, the bottle with all its ribbons pressed close to her chest and her lovely face a little pale and anxious.

"Rissa's a whole lot prettier'n your cousins," I whispered to Nat.

"Yes," he nodded, "and I think her clothes are nicer too, but she doesn't now she's seen their's have got fur trimming."

"Moon's up—over there!" someone cried above the poundings as an orange rim began to show above the wooded ridge of Ragged Island.

"There's a sight for you, Esther," I heard Major Fortune say to his sister with a wave of his arm, as if he had somehow contrived to make it rise.

Up and up it crept till the shining ball had cleared the black trees. The red drained out as it climbed, and at last it hung, round and golden, above its own broad silver track. The farther islands swam in that brightness like bristling-backed monsters, and though I was already used to moonlight over sea and islands, yet somehow this was different from all other moons. I turned to Nat who stood quiet beside me.

"Nat," I said because I felt somehow frightened by it. But before I could speak or he could answer me, the hammer blows were beginning to fall with curious heavy thuds on the wooden blocks. "It's begun," I cried to him above the sudden commotion. He nodded and from that moment his eyes got big and dark and far removed from me.

There will never be any sound like that for me till the day I

die. The air was alive with a great throbbing pulse of hammer beats, hundreds of them all going it together. At last those quickening blows and my own heart beats became one in some strange and indescribable way. I lost all count of time and nothing was real to me but that sound and the dark shapes of men's bodies and arms rising and falling in the smoky glare below me. They made me think of the little men going through their motions on the clock in the east parlor. I tried to tell Nat, but he hardly seemed to hear me. His cheeks had grown red, the way they never were except when he played the piano and he kept time to the hammers, beating with his clenched fist on the wooden railing as if he were part of it all.

The blocks of wood were falling away under the blows so fast it made me giddy to watch. And then there was a pause, and a whisper went round that it was time for the christening.

"Friends," Major Fortune's voice went out to the farthest corners as he stepped to the edge of the make-shift platform and leaned out over the "Rainbow's" forepart, "there's no call for me to make a speech. I'm not much given to words as most of you know. Timber and canvas and cargoes are my line and I'll back my last dollar on them every time. I don't need to tell you that my father and my father's father sent Fortune ships round the globe and that the best went into their making then and now." Someone broke in there with a cheer and other voices took it up in a mighty cheer that silenced the Major for more than a minute. I could see his eyes were pleased under their beetling brows, though there was a sort of heaviness in his voice as he went on. "Times may not be what they were and shipping may not be so prosperous as it once was, but I'm not one to break with the past for any new notion afloat. Fortunes have always built the finest wooden ships that sailed, and this vessel here on the ways is sound in every beam, that's all I've got to say."

He stepped back to more cheers as the Reverend Chase took his place to pronounce a blessing. Peering under my hat brim as he prayed I stole a look at Rissa. She had slipped out of the red cape and I could see her hands shaking about the bottle.

"Oh, Lord," I prayed in a more personal petition than the Reverend Chase, "please let it break good and hard when she throws it."

Only those of us who stood close could hear Rissa say:—"I christen thee 'Rainbow,'" but a rewarding splinter of glass followed, and a sharp fragrance rose from the bows. A moment later the poundings began with renewed vigor. Now they were coming faster and faster, with a kind of ringing wildness that was like a storm of sound. Then the last blows fell. Braces cracked and solid blocks spurted as if they were no more than chips flying before an axe. Suddenly there was a rending and splintering the like I have never heard before or since, and the whole great mass began to move, as if it were breaking up there in front of my eyes. Those sweat-glazed men leaped aside as the great hull settled down into her cradle. It slid with her while she moved steadily on and out over the greased ways. Above the noise of ripping wood and rushing water, a cry went up:—

"She's floated! Hip-hip-hooray, Rainbow!"

Nat's cold fingers were gripping mine. My heart seemed to swell inside me, and my whole body to be swallowed up in its beating. I knew that I was shouting along with the rest, and the usually demure Rissa was hopping up and down and waving her handkerchief. Only the Major stood quiet, with head craned forward, to watch the welcoming surge of water.

"Took it neat as a dolphin," he cried out to Henry Willis, relieved and jubilant.

SOCIAL LIFE AT OLD HALLOWELL

by

REV. JOHN H. INGRAHAM

In that day people were more hospitable and social than in our modern times. If then a gentleman came down from Boston to visit for a few days some family, a party was at once got on foot to do him honor. Invitations would be sent to all genteel families within thirty miles of Hallowell, from Old General Chandler's in Monmouth, round by the Howards and Conys to Augusta, to the Lithgows, and others at Dresden and Wiscasset, and so over to the Kings at Bath, and to the Stanwoods at Brunswick. Everybody came that was invited. No weather kept them back, and in those days the rivers were unbridged, and sometimes the lively guests would drive a dozen miles around to get to a ferry. If it were winter, so much the better; for if the river were frozen they could make a good sleighing frolic of the ride home and back. Snow five feet deep was no obstruction to these joyous party-goers. Then, when they reached the mansion where the party was to be given, they would find the house brightly lighted up, every room glowing, fifty sleighs standing around it, the horses all covered with bear skins and blankets, for buffaloes were then very rare. At the door one or two well dressed servants, (often in livery, too, dear reader) would take their smoking horses by the head, and the master of the house, forewarned by the jingling sleigh-bells, would step out to receive his guests bareheaded, fearless of the frosty air, his hair powdered, his knee and shoe buckles glittering, and his face covered with smiles. With old-fashioned politeness, he would assist the lady from her sleigh,

From *Old Hallowell on the Kennebec* by Emma Huntington Nason (Augusta, Maine, 1909).

hand her in to the wardrobe woman who would hurry her past the glittering drawing rooms to a warm back apartment, there to disrobe; while her husband after a hearty shake of the hand would be conducted to another for the same purpose by the gentleman, who, before the newcomer had time to throw aside his overcoat, would lead him to a sideboard and make him take half a tumbler of hot brandy toddy which was kept constantly hot and mixed by a white-headed old Negro in attendance. Then a nice glass of toddy was sent in to the lady in the disrobing room, and usually came back emptied! Those days of 'old times' were not exactly temperance times.

Then when they entered the rooms they found everybody dancing, on the very tiptoe of hilarious enjoyment. There was no waltzing; dances of that character were then unknown, but minuets and contra dances (called then country dances) were in vogue. By and by there was a movement into one of the rear or perhaps an upper room where a long table was set out, laden with every sort of a delicacy from a roast pig and a roast turkey to a barberry tart. Wines and strong waters sparkled red and amber in the rich decanters, and for the old folks there were pitchers of nice cider. Everybody was suited and everybody enjoyed themselves. The minister was always there. They used to have but one minister in those primitive days! And his venerable head is still among us to bless us! He always asked a blessing, (or rather made a prayer as was the custom) before they began to demolish the fair show upon the board.

After the feast they returned to dancing, which, when they were tired of it, was changed for games, such as "Button, Button, Who's Got the Button," "Hunt the Slipper," and "Blind-man's-Buff." They usually wound up with "Oats, Peas, Beans, and Barley O": but not before the day began to dawn! Then such a general bundling up and bundling into sleighs; such leave-takings screamed out and shouted from male and female voices; such jingling of bells was never heard except on like occasions when the next parties came off. Those who lived on the same road usually stopped to start together and so they went off in various parties and always in high glee.

Sometimes a heavy snow storm would come on in the night and before the morning the roads would be so blocked up as to become impassable. Such an event was always a source of great satisfaction to the hospitable host of that day; as he foresaw a continuance, at least, of the party for two or three days longer. One party that had assembled at General C——'s (Chandler's), at Monmouth, was thus detained three days; and the spirit of joyous misrule reigned for three days within the walls of that hospitable mansion. Day and night King Frolic had full ascendancy. The Negro fiddler fairly broke down, and the gentlemen who were amateurs, resolving not to give it up so, took the fiddles and kept up the merriment.

Those were days of the Olden Time! And since then times have changed! In all this frolicking there was no lack of courteous bearing. The gentlemen of that day were, in manners, models that we might imitate; for courtly manners have sadly fallen away. The ladies, too, were stately and beautiful, and although they went in hand and foot for frolic, they knew when to be dignified. Do we not now bear witness to this when we speak of one and say he is a "gentleman of the old school," or of a lady, "she is one of the old school dames"?

"YELLOW JACK" IN THE WEST INDIES

by

CAPTAIN THEODORE WELLS

Through the following summer I was employed at farming and brickmaking. It was believed that the Embargo would be

From *The Life and Adventures of Captain Theodore Wells* (Biddeford, Maine, 1874).

raised in the early part of the winter, at the first session of Congress. Acting under this impression, vessels were loaded and run into deep harbors for the purpose of an early start when the embargo should be removed. In the month of October, I entered on board the ship, General Green, Captain Jefferds, and proceeded to Portsmouth, N. H., where we lay about two months, but finding the embargo was not to be removed at that time, we were discharged. The following March, the embargo having been removed, I became attached to the brig, Herald, Captain Darby, bound to Havana.

We sailed from Kennebunk the twenty-fourth of April. Soon after, a storm of wind and rain came on from the eastward. We had a good crew of six able seamen, but four of them were very seasick. We had been exposed to a cold rainstorm through the day, and shortened sail before night and set the watches. At ten o'clock in the evening all hands were called to take in sail. The wind blew heavily, and the rain fell in torrents. We were drenched with water, and having all of us been from sea for more than a year, we were as seasick as green hands. It was one of the most suffering nights I ever spent on the ocean. We succeeded in getting under short sail, and the next day the gale abated and the weather became favorable and we proceeded on our passage rapidly. The sixth day after sailing we discovered a phenomena which I have never seen before or since. It was a hazy morning when there appeared in the southern horizon a brown colored circle in the form of a rainbow, but higher than rainbows form, being about sixty degrees in the centre from the plane of the visible horizon and touching the plane at each end, and in this circle were seven bright sun-dogs.

We had a sharp blow for about one hour in the middle of the day, followed by clear, pleasant weather, and on the fifteenth day out made the hole in the wall, on the island of Abico, one of the Bahama islands. On the great Bahama banks there is from two to two and a half fathoms of water, the bottom cream color and plainly visible. Sailing about sixty miles on this bank we entered deep water, and soon after sighted the Moro Castle, which is a strong fortification on the easterly side. At the entrance of the harbor of Havana there is also a fort on the west side called St. Mary's. The city is walled, and abounds with magnificent structures of various models of architecture, towering churches, fine-toned bells, priests and friars in abundance. The harbor is spacious and safe, and the landscapes in the interior of the city are delightful. Here the cargo was disposed of, and while landing it an accident occurred which I will record. The lumber is taken away by teams as fast as it is landed. These teams consist of a cart, one pair of oxen with an awkward apology for a yoke, and reins thrust through the nose, between the nostrils, with a long goad in the hand of the driver, who rides on his cart, light or loaded, carrying forty boards to a load, great or small.

In consequence of all this, two men were sufficient to land the lumber as fast as it was taken away. Having arrived at the mole in the morning with a raft of lumber, and having forgotten to take water with us, I was directed by the Captain to return to the brig and bring some. I proceeded to obey this order, and returning to the raft found several passage boats laying near the raft. These passage boats are very neat, having an awning over the stern, and are rowed by one man. Their vocation is to carry persons to the vessels and different parts of the harbor. Endeavoring to make my way between these boats I accidently touched one of them, for which I received a blow with the blade of an oar, which very nearly brought me down. My castigator was near me, and I could easily have retaliated, but I thought best to pocket the outrage, fearing if I did otherwise that a knife would be substituted for an oar. It was now the last of May or first of June, and sickness had begun to prevail among the fleet of shipping and was very mortal, several vessels having lost their entire crews.

We escaped till about the tenth of June. Early in the afternoon I was sent aloft by the mate with another young man to set up the fore-topmast shrouds. While engaged in this service I observed the man who was with me stooping with his hands on his knees.

I inquired what was the matter, when he informed me that he had a severe pain in his head and back. I advised him to go down and send up another man, which he did. Having finished my work I came down and found him in his berth in great distress. I made report to the mate and the doctor was called, but on account of other engagements, he did not come on board till near night, when it was too late. He did what he could but gave no relief, and in forty-five hours from the time he was taken he was dead. It was on Thursday, at two o'clock, this man was taken, and the following night another of our men became violently sick, and on Friday another, and on Friday night another. It was difficult to get the attention of a doctor in season; but he attended our men and afforded them some relief. On Saturday morning I was ordered by the Captain to go with four hired Negroes to unmoor a launch and take to the mole to load with sugar boxes. I had felt unwell in the morning but I succeeded in loading the launch and bringing it along-side of the brig, and was employed through the forenoon in the launch, slinging sugar boxes while the men on deck hoisted them in, till the launch was nearly unloaded, when I became so distressed in my head and back that I was obliged to go on board, and another man took my place. I had to moor the launch as no one else knew where to find the buoy by which it was moored.

I came on board in extreme pain, and made my way to my berth in the forecastle. The doctor was sent for and soon came on board. He first attempted to take blood, but failing in this (for some cause blood refused to run) he gave me a very large portion of medicine, I know not of what kind, and about sunset another powerful dose was given me by the mate, and in the early part of the night the mate came forward and said he wanted me to take some gin. I did not believe him, but obeyed, and took down half a pint of castor oil, and before morning was some relieved. The day previous the captain had provided a place for us at the West Meglus, a small town at the southern extremity of the bay, three miles distant, and Sunday morning

we were taken in the boat with our bedding and with the assistance of men from other vessels, for we had only two well men
on board, were taken, four in number, to a private hospital
which was superintended by a woman, known by the name of
French Mary. There were six of us in a small room entirely destitute of furniture. Our bedsteads were made by four pieces of
joist secured together with strips of board nailed on crosswise,
and were very narrow. Our bedding consisted of our sea bedsacks
and blankets, and some of us had a pillow. The flies were exceedingly numerous and troublesome, and those filthy birds, the
turkey buzzards, would light on the sills of the windows.

Here we were nursed and attended by the doctor. Our diet
consisted of a small cup full of thin soup three times each day.
We had liberty to suck the juice of a sweet orange and a small
draught of port wine in the morning, and occasionally at other
times. I believe this woman understood the duties of a nurse, but
she failed in attention to it. We were attended to mainly by two
female servants, a Negress and mulatto. They would come into
the room and switch the flies off, and before they were gone out
we would be nearly covered with them. I had reason to believe,
from the first, my case to be dangerous, and readily took the
medicine which the doctor prescribed, and carefully followed his
directions. While we were here, Captain Bourne of Kennebunk,
who died here soon after, came to our lodging and inquired how
Captain Darby's men were. The doctor replied that he thought
they would recover. Captain Bourne further inquired, "How is
young Wells? Captain Darby told me yesterday he feared he
should lose him." The doctor, who was a rough, profane man,
replied, "There is no danger of him. He would eat an apothecary's shop."

When we had been here five or six days, we entreated the Captain to take us on board. He was a very kind man and soon
after yielded to our request and took three of us on board the
brig. The other, who was the cook, was left there, being too sick
to be removed, and the next day died of black vomit, as did also

the other two men who were in the room with us, belonging to another vessel. Our captain had employed an Irishman who was familiar with cooking and nursing to cook for the vessel and take care of us, and who came home with us. We lived in the day time on the quarter deck under the awning, and ate fowl soup and sago, and soon began to recruit. After being on board a few days, the captain inquired of me if I was able to go in the long boat and take care of it, with four Negroes who were employed boating off sugar, bidding me not to do any work. I went and after bringing off two or three boat loads, I became vexed with the lazy Negroes, and sent them all on the mole and stowed the boat myself. The next morning I was prostrate. Captain Darby reproved me for disobeying his orders, and it was several days before I recovered from this act of imprudence.

THE ENTERPRISE AND THE BOXER

[1813]

by

CAPTAIN GEORGE PRINCE

There has always been more or less dispute as to the exact locality in which the famous naval battle between the American ship Enterprise and the British ship Boxer took place.

This brilliant naval battle was witnessed from the towns of St. George, Pemaquid, St. George's islands, Monhegan, Damariscove, and from the mountains of Rockland. Hundreds of people from those points were witnesses; a few may be still living. The writer has gathered the following incidents from many of them, and also from two of the sailors who served on board of the Enterprise, Capt. William Barnes of Woolwich and Capt. James

From *The Rockland Courier Gazette* (Rockland, Maine).

Springer of Bath, also from one sailor who served on board of the British brig Boxer, and who was wounded in the action, Mr. Nelson of Bath.

The brig Enterprise had seen service in the wars with France and Algiers. She had been rebuilt in 1811. At the opening of the war, like other small gun-rigs of our navy, she was over-loaded and over-manned. By crowding guns into her bridle ports she mounted fourteen 18-pound carronades and two long 9's, with 102 men. Lieut. Burrows who had served during the Tripolitan war under Commodore Edward Preble was given the command of the Enterprise, which was fitted out to hunt along the Maine coast for the Boxer, that had been committing depredations on the sea-coast villages. The Enterprise labored under many disadvantages when she sailed from Portland on the afternoon of Saturday, September 4, 1812, with a fresh, untried crew, many of whom were mere boys.

The Boxer, commanded by the gallant Capt. Samuel Blythe, mounted twelve 18-pound carronades and two sixes, with a crew of seventy-eight men. She was a new and strong vessel, fitted out at St. John, N. B., with every care bestowed upon her equipment, and a selected crew, who had had about a week's drill before meeting the Enterprise. The first day after leaving St. John, she entered the harbor of Eastport, hauled aback her head sails— opened her ports, run out her guns and thus lay for a while threatening the town with a broadside. After indulging in this threatening act, she again stood out of the harbor and headed for the westward. The writer is indebted to the Hon. William Singer of Thomaston for this incident. He was one of the soldiers of Fort Sullivan, Eastport, at the time.

After despoiling many fishermen and some seacoast villages the Boxer came to anchor under St. John's island, Pemaquid harbor, Saturday, Sept. 4. The inhabitants, fearing an attack, quickly withdrew into the woods. During the evening they could hear the music on board.

Sunday morning, Sept. 5 opened clear, balmy and bright; not

a breath of wind stirred the listless ocean. The Enterprise found herself almost becalmed as she drifted by Fisherman's island, and opened out the Pemaquid shore, where she saw far up in the harbor the Boxer lying at anchor. The Boxer, having sighted the Enterprise immediately got under way and giving a parting shot over St. John's island into the village, started out to meet the Yankee brig. Both vessels headed off the land for more sea room. The Enterprise changed one of her forward guns aft, running it out of the cabin window to be ready for an attack in the rear.

It was nearly calm until about noon when a light breeze sprang up from the south southwest. The Enterprise, shortening sail edged away toward the enemy. By 3 o'clock they had gained a sufficient offing, and each stripped to fighting canvas. The vessels were both on the starboard tack heading nearly due east, the Enterprise to the windward. They had gradually shortened their distance, running nearly abreast until they had approached within pistol shot of each other, some four or five miles from the shore.

Hundreds of eyes gazed anxiously and hearts beat rapidly as their owners waited breathless for the coming death grapple. At about quarter past three the Boxer fired a gun and gave a loud cheer. The Enterprise answered by firing a musket and giving three hearty cheers. At this moment the Boxer poured in her first broadside which was immediately returned by the Enterprise, and the desperate battle now began in earnest, the belching cannon pouring out destruction and death amidst the defiant cheers which rose above the roar of battle; the Boxer fighting with her starboard guns, the Enterprise with her port batteries. Both commanders were shot early in the engagement. A portion of the Boxer's crew stationed forward finding the place too hot for them, abandoned their guns and rushed aft. Capt. Blythe declared that the guns should be served, rallied the men of the retreating division and led them forward again to the abandoned guns. Here he was met by a perfect torrent of balls, and while exclaiming, "Great God, what shots!" he was struck by an 18-pound ball, which, nearly cutting him in twain, killed him instantly. Very nearly at the same time on board the Enterprise, the commander finding that the crew of one of his quarter deck guns was reduced in numbers and unable to manage it, seized hold of the tackle to help run it out. While in the act he was struck and mortally wounded by a musket ball. He refused to be carried below but laid himself down on deck leaning against a shot rack, continued to encourage the men until the close of the action, which lasted only thirty minutes. The command was assumed by Lieut. Edward McCall.

For the first fifteen minutes they fought broadside with but little advantage to either side. At 3:30 the Enterprise drew ahead, and finding this advantage quickly sheered across the Boxer's forefoot firing the gun that had been run out of the cabin window which did great execution. The enemy was now allowed to come upon the American's starboard quarter, and received a broadside which raked her fearfully, carrying away her maintopmast. The Enterprise then shot ahead and the after gun again did fearful execution. She was thus enabled to maneuver at will across the Boxer's bow and rake her lengthwise with terrible effect. In a venturous attempt to board, the Boxer's flying jibboom came in over the stern of the Enterprise, holding her for a moment there, which was improved by the American's after gun with renewed effect. At 3:45 the Boxer ceased firing and made signals of surrender. When ordered to haul down their flag they replied that it was "nailed aloft!" This foolish bravado undoubtedly caused the sacrifice of many lives. The number killed aboard the Boxer is unknown, as they were thrown over-board as fast as they fell—there were 14 wounded. The Enterprise had one killed outright, and 13 wounded. The gallant Burrows lived till noon the next day. Midshipman Waters and one man died in Portland of their wounds.

The ensign of the Boxer is among the trophies of the Naval Academy at Annapolis, and the tattered folds of the Enterprise are arrayed with those of the Bonhomme Richard at Fort

McHenry (now in the National Museum, Washington, D. C.).

When the first lieutenant of the Boxer came on board to deliver up the sword of Capt. Blythe, the dying Burrows laid his hand on it and said, with a deep sympathizing sigh, "Keep it, sir, yourself, you are richly worthy of it."

The two vessels were taken into Portland on the 7th where the bodies of both gallant commanders were brought on shore draped with the flags they had so well defended. They each received the same honors, and were interred side by side in the cemetery at the foot of Mt. Joy hill (now called Munjoy Hill). Capt. Blythe had been one of the gallant Lawrence's pall bearers.

As some contrary statements have been made in regard to the exact locality of this naval engagement, we will give the statement made by Capt. William Barnes of the Enterprise, who has been over the locality many times since his fearful experience there. He says that the surrender was at a point some four or five miles east from Pemaquid point, four miles southwest of East Egg Rock at the mouth of the Georges river and about seven miles west north west of Monhegan.

THE PORTLAND OF LONGFELLOW'S BOYHOOD: "MY LOST YOUTH"

by

HENRY WADSWORTH LONGFELLOW

> Often I think of the beautiful town
>   That is seated by the sea;
> Often in thought go up and down
> The pleasant streets of that dear old town,
>   And my youth comes back to me.
>   And a verse of a Lapland song

From *The Poetical Works of Henry Wadsworth Longfellow.*

Is haunting my memory still:
"A boy's will is the wind's will,
And the thoughts of youth are long, long thoughts."

I can see the shadowy lines of its trees,
   And catch, in sudden gleams,
The sheen of the far-surrounding seas,
And islands that were the Hesperides
   Of all my boyish dreams.
     And the burden of that old song,
     It murmurs and whispers still:
   "A boy's will is the wind's will,
And the thoughts of youth are long, long thoughts."

I remember the black wharves and the slips,
   And the sea-tides tossing free;
And Spanish sailors with bearded lips,
And the beauty and mystery of the ships,
   And the magic of the sea.
     And the voice of that wayward song
     Is singing and saying still:
   "A boy's will is the wind's will,
And the thoughts of youth are long, long thoughts."

I remember the bulwarks by the shore,
   And the fort upon the hill;
The sunrise gun, with its hollow roar
The drum-beat repeated o'er and o'er,
   And the bugle wild and shrill.
     And the music of that old song
     Throbs in my memory still:
   "A boy's will is the wind's will,
And the thoughts of youth are long, long thoughts."

I remember the sea-fight far away,
  How it thundered o'er the tide!
And the dead captains, as they lay
In their graves, o'erlooking the tranquil bay,
  Where they in battle died.
    And the sound of that mournful song
    Goes through me with a thrill:
  "A boy's will is the wind's will,
And the thoughts of youth are long, long thoughts."

I can see the breezy dome of groves,
  The shadows of Deering's Woods;
And the friendships old and the early loves
Come back with a sabbath sound, as of doves
  In quiet neighborhoods.
    And the verse of that sweet old song,
    It flutters and murmurs still:
  "A boy's will is the wind's will,
And the thoughts of youth are long, long thoughts."

I remember the gleams and glooms that dart
  Across the school-boy's brain;
The song and the silence in the heart,
That in part are prophecies, and in part
  Are longings wild and vain.
    And the voice of that fitful song
    Sings on, and is never still:
  "A boy's will is the wind's will,
And the thoughts of youth are long, long thoughts."

There are things of which I may not speak;
  There are dreams that cannot die;
There are thoughts that make the strong heart weak,
And bring a pallor into the cheek,

And a mist before the eye.
  And the words of that fatal song
  Come over me like a chill:
 "A boy's will is the wind's will,
And the thoughts of youth are long, long thoughts."

Strange to me now are the forms I meet
  When I visit the dear old town;
But the native air is pure and sweet,
And the trees that o'ershadow each well-known street,
  As they balance up and down,
    Are singing the beautiful song,
    Are sighing and whispering still:
   "A boy's will is the wind's will,
And the thoughts of youth are long, long thoughts."

And Deering's Woods are fresh and fair,
  And with joy that is almost pain
My heart goes back to wander there,
And among the dreams of the days that were,
  I find my lost youth again.
    And the strange and beautiful song,
    The groves are repeating it still:
   "A boy's will is the wind's will,
And the thoughts of youth are long, long thoughts."

6. Later Years at Sea

THE OLD WOMAN

by

ISABEL HOPESTILL CARTER

YOUNG Caroline trod majestically into the sunny parlor, balancing on her head a round brown box. This was a scheme to attract the attention of old Caroline and lead up naturally to the matter of suggesting the charming box as a token of esteem from the old to the young. However, old Caroline was both unseeing and, in the main, unseen, for two veiny hands held outspread before her the Bath DAILY TIMES; her feet, bony and jointy in those thin leather shoes that old women manage to buy somewhere, rested flatly on a red wooden footstool that served her comfort when she sat at the window in the high-backed rocker; her lean old legs were draped in a cotton gown printed with red forget-me-nots. The light, striking through a single thickness of paper, revealed the fact that she studied the inside of the back page, devoted to news of Boothbay, Popham, Winnegance, Woolwich, Wiscasset, and Dresden. The breeze from the Kennebec rustled the curtain against the paper; there was no other sound.

Baffled, young Caroline flung herself on the old sofa, resting her neck on the back and stretching long legs out into the middle of the hideous carpet. Idly she polished the flat box on her thigh and contemplated the familiar Bailey gods. The carpet; on the

By permission of *The Atlantic Monthly* (Boston, July, 1926).

opposite wall the oil painting, not so bad as some, of the ship Mary Spaulding, and a print, in a chipped green frame, on the bark Arethusa; a cut-velvet picture and a little mirror in a mahogany frame with an intricately cut outline; a round framed photograph of Winchester Cathedral and another of an Indian temple. On the white mantel there were two beautiful Chinese vases and, in sociable juxtaposition, a large and sinfully ugly red-pottery pig which held a mass of goldenglow; an old fat Buddha sat there, too, beside a sandglass. Above young Caroline's dark head hung a gilt-framed mirror with a colored farm scene at its top, a mirror known to be capable of performing wonders in the way of distorting even the most symmetrical features. The chairs were old and severe, and thoroughly disapproved of a black-and-silver lacquered table that gleamed wanton from a corner.

Somewhere a clock in a great hurry banged six times in bursts of two. Old Caroline began a struggle to get the paper to collapse into its creases; the accursed single sheet in the middle seized the opportunity to slide out and skid across the floor, only to be captured and returned to the fold by young Caroline. Old Caroline vented small irritated sounds while she strove with the frenzied TIMES, but, at last subduing it with some well-placed blows, she laid it on the arm of the sofa and folded her hands on her beflowered stomach. She became aware of young Caroline alert in the offing.

"Oh!" she said. "Where's Joel?"

"He's out on the porch. Look, Aunt Caroline, may I have this box? I found it in that bureau in my room. It hasn't anything in it but some old hat-trimming." She crushed it to her breast, wrenching off the tight cover. "Those were pretty little birds. Look, auntie." Old Caroline, stretching a shaky hand, took the box into her lap. There were three dried skins of birds, with heads iridescent and gorgeous; one imagined them rushing brilliantly from flower to flower in a tropic forest. She smoothed their

shining crowns, the two that were splendidly green and the one
that was brown with a golden cap.

"Did you have them on one of those absurd hats people used
to wear?" inquired young Caroline. "They look like real birds,
don't they? I don't see how anyone could put them on a hat."

"Hat!" Old Caroline's voice was faintly surprised. Her eyes
grew dreamy. "No, I never had them on a hat—" A long silence
fell. She sat very still in the tall black rocker with the little long-
dead birds in her old hand and the round brown box in her lap.
She was old and serene; her thin gray hair was neatly disposed to
cover, as far as possible, the pink scalp; her absent eyes were a
faded blue, beset by a million wrinkles. Her life, one felt, had
been placidly happy.

Old Caroline was young Caroline in that far time, and she had
been married a year and three days. Hot and miserable and uncomfortable she lay on her back in the wide built-in bed with
the thick posts reaching to the ceiling of the cabin; the light in
the outer room dimly illumined the stateroom, and it gleamed
on the brass rim of the compass bolted to the ceiling over the
bed; the compass card bobbed and bobbed with the weary plunge
of the ship. She could not read the compass and the light was
faint, but it seemed to her that the card flopped back and forth
and back and forth across the vertical black line that was the
ship—back and forth, back and forth. With every aimless lunge
in the swell she heard the lifeless flap of canvas and the jerk of
heavy yards. On the poop deck just above her head the wheel
creaked unceasingly, and the mate's soft footfalls padded across
the deck and back, across and back, across and back; from time
to time he stopped and she knew he leaned his elbows on the
house and stared at the stars and the dangling telltale and the
lazy sails; then he began again his endless pacing. For an eternity
she had heard these same noises.

The mate jogged down the starboard side. The man at the
wheel began to sing softly—it must be Mads. Only yesterday

morning when she went on deck she had found Mads at the wheel and had said to him, "Just a few days more, Mads!" He had looked quickly at her, and cast his vigilant blue eyes down at the compass, murmuring, "Yasss, ma'am." Rise and fall, creak and groan, flap, flap. Even if they were a week later than Joel had estimated at the beginning as the very limit of a long passage, there would still be time for her. At dinner Mr. Adams and Joel no longer bothered to exchange their figures on the day's run, which was encouraging. But dinner itself was tiresome with the flour almost gone, the butter and sugar all gone, and beans their staple diet; Joel fumed like an old woman over the food. Well, it probably wasn't so good for the baby, but they would be arriving soon.

She rolled hotly over on her side and stared at Joel sitting under the hanging lamp. Every night he read like that. After they had finished reading aloud from the sea-worn green Shakespeare and she had gone to bed, he still sat out there and read. Now he leaned back, gazing across the cabin with knitted brows. As she watched he half-closed the book to feel in a pocket for a pipe, and she recognized the tan leather cover of the book. Old Bowditch! Why, he must know old Bowditch by heart!

"Oh, Joel!" she called softly. He started. "What are you doing?"

"Reading."

"What are you reading?"

"Oh—A Midsummer-Night's Dream," he responded. She was on the point of remarking in her surprise that the Shakespeare was green, but it hardly seemed worth while. It was doubtless some joke of Joel's.

"Will you get me a drink, Joel? I'm so hot." He rose instantly, laying the book on the wide arm of the chair, unconscious of her observation. Why, that wasn't old Bowditch, either; old Bowditch had a broken back sewed up with string. What was that book? She rolled back into her own corner as Joel stepped back from the forward cabin with the water. She had seen it somewhere, a thick tan book with a wide red name-piece on the back binding. She drank the warmish water gratefully. Joel was a good boy to her, but if she had known that a bridal trip around the world would end in discomfort like this—

That was the medicine book! That was what he read every night with such grimness.

It explained everything. Over on the chart table the chart, which used to be held open all the time with the parallel rulers and the dividers and the corner of the chronometer, lay curled up tight in the provoking way of charts, discouraging to investigation. So Joel thought it was going to happen at sea. She was frightened. . . .

Old Caroline rubbed the box. "The comprador gave it to me in Shanghai," she said. "On my wedding trip. It had a beautiful silk embroidered handkerchief in it. A big silk handkerchief, a yard square, I guess, embroidered in flowers, soft and lovely. I kept Joel's father's watch in it, which Joel prized. He never used it at sea, of course. It wasn't much good, anyway."

It turned out to be a rather good baby, not very big, but very slippery. Caroline found herself constantly snatching him just in the nick of time by a fat leg or an arm; but he was perfectly good-natured about that and about almost everything except his meals. Joel became a very clever nurse in a short time, and exhibited his son to the mate and the second mate. The steward begged permission to take him out to show to the men, and as he claimed to be an adept in the dandling of babies,—one pictured him as juggling three or four babies at once, keeping them constantly in motion in the air without the slightest slip,—the favor was granted and he withdrew, carrying the little red pig in a comfortingly professional manner. He returned in triumph, bearing gifts and compliments and promises of more gifts. Ben had almost completed a particularly neat Turk's head. Old Bill had presented an Alaskan salmon-spear, five feet long. The carpenter had begun forthwith on a labyrinthine rattle; Tom was doing some wood-carving, and very mysterious he was about it, too—the steward thought, sniffing, that it was going to be a doll. The bo's'n, ready for any occasion, presented a very useful walrus tusk. A pair of ivory dice, loaded, had been rejected by the steward, in his official capacity, as an unsuitable gift for a moral infant.

Joel set the baby down in the logbook with the utmost exactness as to latitude and longitude. He marked a red star in the margin opposite the entry.

In a few days Joel calmed down after his ordeal and Caroline began to recover somewhat from hers. Then, for no apparent reason, everyone got into a state of nerves. Caroline, not greatly interested, suspected that some old wretch of a seaman in a bad temper had said babies on a ship brought mean weather, and so all the silly sailors were wrought up over that. Certainly the sails still slatted and pounded, the ship lumbered about, and, though they were far beyond the equator, it grew hotter day by day. Caroline could not sleep much for the heat and the requirements of her offspring, and Joel seemed not to sleep at all. Repeatedly at night he went on deck "to get a breath of air."

One day Caroline took a short walk. It had been excessively hot in the cabin, but nevertheless she felt rather well, as she had not suffered any nervous shocks that day from having her little greased pig try to elude her and dash his ten-day-old brains on the deck. So she wobbled along through the forward cabin to the high doorsill that kept the bad-weather seas from rolling across the main deck and making themselves unwelcome in the cabin. This obstacle she awkwardly surmounted, stepping across the grating outside on to the deck. It was like a griddle; the black stuff between the planks oozed up soft and gummy and stuck to her shoes. The broiling sun menaced her, and her legs unhappily turned to macaroni. Her dazzled eyes were caught by a group of men on the fo'c'sle doing some extraordinary thing with the big boat—painting it, perhaps. As she turned to flee from the glare to the dimness of the cabin she saw in the mizzen rigging a long string of limp gay flags—there was probably a ship in sight. Possibly they were going to borrow some potatoes or something. She reached the haven of the big chair just as Joel's deliberate steps sounded on the companionway stairs.

"I went on deck, Joel," she volunteered, much elated. "But it was so hot I didn't stay." He filled a pipe, sitting down on the ugly red divan. His glance at her as he sucked the flame of the match down to the bowl of the pipe was very gentle.

"Is there a ship near?" she pursued. Joel might sit there for a year and not think to tell her! "I saw the flags. Are you speaking her?"

"No," he answered slowly. "It's only a signal. The ship is on fire, Caroline."

It came like a blow; for a moment it seemed impossible that those quiet words had actually been uttered. Her eyes grew to be huge blue spots on the pallor of her face—staring blue spots. "Don't be frightened, dear," he murmured. (Her pride, indignant, administered a sharp prod to her courage. "Anybody who can have babies at sea can be shipwrecked creditably," it admonished. She must say some bold words.)

"Shall—shall we have to leave the ship?" she quavered. ("Now, could there be a more idiotic question?" remonstrated pride. "Everyone will think you are a fool and a coward besides.")

"The hatches are battened down," he replied. She did not know what that meant. "But I think we'll have to abandon the ship tonight or tomorrow. You'd better get a few things together. This isn't what I would have chosen for a wedding trip for you, Caroline!" The cry broke unexpectedly through his teeth, and he dropped his head in his big brown hands. His pipe fell and scattered embers about. "I am so sorry," he muttered, struggling to regain his admirable calm.

"There, there, Joel," she comforted. "I don't mind." ("Now that sounds better," remarked her pride to her courage; "shipwrecks are nothing to babies.")

So she gathered a few things. She arrayed herself in her best black silk, made for her wedding outfit, according to the tradi-

tional New England custom. She took the round wooden box
containing Joel's father's watch carefully folded in the rich
silk handkerchief. She collected a few meagre supplies for the
baby, some vaseline and what not. Then a brown cashmere
shawl, and she was ready—tremendously composed, she flattered
herself, with her hands and knees trembling and her heart
pounding her to bits. Joel was making some leisurely preparations, too; he put together in a neat pile his sextant, some instruments, a chart, a few bottles from the medicine chest, the green
Shakespeare and old Bowditch, a big new oilskin coat from the
slop chest, the ship's papers, the logbook.

"What do you take the Shakespeare for?" babbled Caroline.

"Why, I take it everywhere!" responded faithful old Joel.

All the afternoon Caroline listened to strange sounds of preparations, holding her fat pig in her arms for fear she might abandon ship and forget him, not having had him so long as Joel had
had that old green book. The steward came and went in the
pantry, and Joel conversed briefly with him in low tones about
condensed milk and hardtack. There were unusual creakings
and thumpings outside the forward cabin windows, which Caroline, very erect and ready, opined to be related to the boat
davits. She wondered how they'd get the big boat down off
the fo'c'sle. She would like to know how near the land they
were, but she hesitated to ask lest Joel think her frightened;
she was just as calm as anybody, she was sure. Calmer.

In the morning they took the final steps. Caroline sat for
the last time on the poop in the barrel chair, with her baby
and her bundle, like an immigrant woman, and watched everything. Three boats there were—Joel said that any one of them
was as big, almost, as Christopher Columbus's ship, but Caroline knew better than to believe that. The second mate was the
first to go; he came up, with the ship's cat under his arm, to
say good-bye and to shake hands with Caroline. Joel gave him
some sailing directions for the mainland.

"You can't miss it," he said. "Of course, it's farther than

Juan Fernandez, but you can't navigate. You've got the younger men in your boat—you may have to push them some unless you get picked up. Mr. Adams and I will make for Juan Fernandez." They shook hands, and presently the boat floated off from the side of the ship. Wisps and ribbons of smoke were coming through the deck near the main hatch. How far from land could they be, thought Caroline.

Men were dropping into the second boat. Mr. Adams shook hands with Caroline and the baby and with Joel. He had Joel's own chronometer in his hand, and he uttered a parting protest.

"The ship's is all right," responded Joel. "You will have to push your crew a little with your provisions. You may get picked up. If not, we'll see you later. Good luck!" The mate's old brown felt hat vanished. They must be a long, long way from land.

Two or three sailors got into the third boat. Joel took Caroline's bundle and the baby, and shortly she saw the bundle disappear over the rail. Joel gave the baby to Mads, and Caroline in a sudden frenzy of anxiety hastened to the side; but Mads managed the baby as if climbing up and down the tall sides of burning ships with slippery babies were the regular work of an able seaman. The sailors ran up and down like monkeys. Then it was Caroline's turn; she hated those up-and-down wiggly ladders.

She crouched on the rail, clinging to Joel's hand on one side and to a tarred black rope on the other, and peered outward and downward at a diminutive boat bouncing below and at the white specks that were the faces of seamen gazing up. At Joel's command one of these began to mount the ladder.

"Turn around, Caroline." That was the pinch—to let go of the things you had hold of and turn around quickly enough to snatch at them again with the other hand, and to go down that ladder backward with your face to the black ship, like a woodpecker—terrifying. "Turn around, Caroline." She turned. She was successful; she clutched Joel with her right hand now, and stretched her foot down, down. Where was it going? Why didn't it light on something? Oh, there! "Take hold of the ropes. There —step down." This was an endless ladder. She tried to look down between the ladder and her body to find the next step, but her skirt caught up on every step and she had to keep taking one hand off to brush it down decently. Why, she had put her black silk dress on over her gray one—how could she have done that? "Keep hold of the rope!"

The places for her feet were farther apart every time. Joel said something, but not to her. She lifted her face and saw him miles above her. "Go on, Caroline. Step down." She put her blind foot down, down—oh! A hand caught the feeling foot, pulled gently, and placed it on a step. A big red hand covered with shiny hair appeared below her own on the rope, and a gentle surrounding pressure told her that she did not have to finish her acrobatic feats alone—a red hand always beside her and an unseen hand that found a place for her nervous feet. If she ever went to sea again she would practise on ladders first. Another step, another, and her foot touched something hard that yet sank sickeningly under her—that was the boat. She turned enormous blue eyes over her shoulder, and many hands reached to steady her, and many grins greeted her from seamen who in their remarkable way seemed to be holding the boat to the ship's side by the palms of their hands.

Now she sat down in the stern of the boat, exhausted in mind and body. The baby, wrapped in the brown shawl, lay screaming energetically on the deck boards. There were five sailors. Why didn't Joel come? Where was he? An uncle of Caroline's had gone down with his ship. Joel couldn't mean to stay on board. He had said once— But it was all right, after all. There were still some men on board. Everywhere she looked now she saw little whiffs of smoke, just like a firecracker about to explode. Someone dropped an umbrella like a harpoon into the boat, and the sailors laughed gruffly. Four more sailors came down, monkey-like, and then they waited, waited. Then two more. After an interminable time Joel descended the dangling ladder, as casually as he might a staircase, with some papers in one hand and a bundle under his arm.

"Shove off," he said.

The ship very soon was leaking gray mist all over like a smoky stove, and anon it leaped into flame, fire running up the tarred rigging, chasing the colored flags that were not needed any longer to tell that the ship Mary Spaulding was in peril by fire. Wood and rope and canvas, pitch and tar and oil—they make a gallant conflagration! Thick black smoke and orange flame! Suddenly Caroline wept. The poor ship! It was so small and forlorn, sitting there on the flat sea and burning up; and, even though it had behaved in a most untrustworthy way, a boat, just a plain boat with no cover, was in comparison utterly contemptible.

This boat had a mast and a small sail, but for a day or two there was no wind, only sun, and Joel made the men take turns laboring with four heavy oars. They were far from skillful at first, but after a little practice they managed very well, though not, to be sure, like a racing crew. They grunted a good deal, and during the day they became simply impossibly red in the face; but so did Caroline. Mads was a sort of officer and took turns with Joel sitting in the stern and steering. The boat barely moved. It rested on the light-blue hot water like a double boiler, and she and Joel and Mads and the fat pig and all the sailors were being steamed in it like rice; and swelling, too, like rice. The sky was the bright blue cover of the boiler, and the sun made one red-hot spot on the cover. When the wind at last came, it dried up everybody's face and hands, and the sun and wind together burned and cracked the skin like a paper put over a cake in the oven.

The first two or three days nothing happened. And after that nothing happened but the wind; however, Caroline had only fragmentary recollections of the later days. For a long time, for hours, she sat on the hard seat till she ached in every bone. Then she stood up; but it was difficult to keep her balance and it made her feel like Washington Crossing the Delaware, and tired her, too, and she sat down, laughing foolishly. No one else ever laughed. The sailors who were not rowing lolled about red and sweating; those who rowed waved back and forth and back and forth and gave out more gusts of heat to the already hot air. Caroline sat beneath her umbrella and peeped out at them surreptitiously and occasionally intercepted a returning stare. There was nothing to do. Time could scarcely be said to pass at all. It was hard to sit still so long on the wooden seat. Everyone edged about imperceptibly. Caroline shifted now to this position and now to another, and always a board or seam or edge began to dig into some soft piece of flesh until she simply had to move again. She tried sitting in the bottom of the boat, and all the hard places came most heavenly in different spots, so that she dozed against the edge of the seat until that hurt her back; and then she tried the seat once more. Oh, oh! Joel was the only one who had any change—except Mads and the baby and the sailors who rowed the boat. Joel stood up and took the sun in the glare of noonday; he sat down and figured and looked at the chronometer and the chart, and he penciled a point on the chart and measured with the long-legged brass dividers and the parallel rulers; he scowled over the bright white paper. Mads steered and watched Joel, who hunched above the chart and pondered or else napped a little—the heat made one drowsy and the boards kept one awake. He talked in low tones to Mads, whose answers were all alike monotonous. "Yass, sir, a little." "Yass, sir, iss far." "Yass, sir, I tink sso, ssir." Only a thousand times he said "yassssir," and the s's hissed like a wet finger on a flatiron. It made her sleepy.

After she had been nodding and waking and changing her position, dozing and waking, for hours, the sun was still high in the sky. Under the protection of the umbrella she fed the baby, giggling hysterically with that shelter toward the supposedly baffled company. It felt Mother Goose-ish; but, try as she would, the exact verses dealing with the woman who lived under an umbrella eluded her, though she recollected other surprising situations which had been ably recorded. She appealed to Joel. Joel, however, murmured that once when he was a wild young man, the second mate of the Orion, he had been in a Black Sea port, and he and another wild young second mate from another ship had gone on a jaunt to a neighboring beach to discover the truth of the rumor that men and women went in bathing together stark naked. Yes, they did. It was true. Very sensible and matter-of-course. For forty years Caroline remembered Joel sitting before her, brown and serious, with his old hat pulled low, staring at her and the fat pig and telling them that tale.

The tedium of heat and aches was broken at last by sunset and a repast of hard-tack with a meagre dose of water. Joel bullied her to drink some condensed milk; just a little bit, he urged, because it was good for her and the baby. Why was it good for her to drink something she loathed? He wasn't a doctor. She would not; and then she did. The awful bluish sweetness that made her so thirsty—gulp, gul-lup—two choking spoonfuls. Ugh! She gnawed on the hard-tack like a dog on a bone; she kept a bit in her lap and crunched it from time to time. In the middle of the night she chewed on it and tried to sleep. She could not get comfortable lying down on the boards, for they were not the right shape, and she was not comfortable either when she sat up and leaned against the seat; she could not be comfortable anywhere because her bones and her figure were always in the way. It was terribly public, too, and what good was an umbrella that bounded out of one's hand if one dozed off when one sat and was quite inadequate when one lay? Joel slept and Mads sat at the tiller and crooned to the baby, who was trying to cry. Mads went away and Joel sat at the tiller. A hundred times in the night the wild animal that she had borne screamed for food,—he wasn't just a pig, but a ravening wolf,—and she hid herself with him in the brown cashmere shawl and was thankful for the darkness.

A hot dawn and no wind. All day raged the struggle about the condensed milk. She threw a can overboard, which angered Joel, who called her a savage and a pig; so, contrite, she consumed three large nauseating spoonfuls, even to lapping the spoon, and fell to on her hard-tack to take away the vile taste.

She dozed and waked and held the baby, glistening with vaseline, on her lap under the umbrella in the fierce sunshine. The baby clamored to eat every living instant, so finally Joel held him, or Mads. Peering out from time to time from the shade of the shawl under which she sat on the bottom of the boat, she viewed an unnautical tableau: either Mads or Joel seated under an umbrella at the tiller ropes, cleverly balancing on his knees a disagreeable red infant that Joel strove to soothe with "Camp Town Races" and to which Mads crooned, in the ribs and trucks of a once melodious voice, his repertoire of sad Scandinavian tunes. Whenever, after napping for an age, she wakened because the boards were so merciless and her legs had gone to sleep, she found the sun still standing overhead. Sometimes Joel whispered commands to the men, and behind her she heard their hoarse answering whispers. It was fantastic. Usually when Joel wanted something done he spoke firmly to the mate or to the second mate, and they at once sped roaring up and down the deck and the men ran and shouted, "Aye, aye, sir," and "A-all fast!" and there was no secrecy or whispering whatever, and one realized with a thrill how powerful Joel was. Maybe it might be silly for Joel to bellow like a bull to the men in such a small boat, but at the same time it would make the boat seem bigger, particularly if one did not look over one's shoulder. However, it might wake the baby. He lay for the moment on the brown shawl beside her while Joel scratched in the log; he was like a chicken ready to roast, with his poor fat legs cramped up. In a burst of pity for his discomfort Caroline bent over and straightened his legs, but as soon as she removed her hand they doubled up again; moreover, the touch of her hand seemed to remind him of something and he began to whimper.

The days were hard to tell apart.

Again and again she roused from a heavy dream in a panic of fear that she had somehow lost Joel; frantic, she popped her head from the enshrouding shawl, opening her eyes suddenly in the light. But always he was there, an awful spectacle indeed, cheering her with a grimace of a grin. He looked the master, silent, sure; he was burned and haggard, his lips were parched, a scraggly beard flourished exceedingly upon his countenance, but his red narrowed eyes restlessly searched the horizon, watched the sail, squinted over the dazzling chart. All was yet well. Then, blinded either by the sun or by Joel's shining presence, she slipped back into the shadows.

Nothing was continuous. She wakened—a picture flashed on the screen and was gone. Rarely she spoke.

Once she saw Joel leaning toward Mads, who held the baby on his lap and a condensed-milk can in one hand, and tried to dribble a little milky substance into the pink, yelling mouth of that wild animal, who flourished tiny hands and kicked his red legs in a temper monumental for his size. Two, or perhaps more, sailors hovered just behind her, watching.

"He ain't like it," commented Mads hoarsely. His conclusion seemed completely accurate. Joel grunted.

"I don't like it either," whispered Caroline in an effort to justify her son's peculiarities. "I hate it, too." Several pairs of eyes turned to her, red-rimmed eyes in hairy faces.

"It's all there is, Caroline," she heard Joel reply as the picture faded away.

Another time she saw almost the same scene save that the baby was sucking voraciously on a wisp of grayish rag dabbled frequently into the glittering can.

"I don't believe it's good for him," muttered Joel.

"He ain't got the teeth for hard-tack, sir," submitted a remote voice which resembled that of the donor of the Alaskan salmon-spear.

Again, in the passage of days, Caroline came to herself, an

anxious parent, and whispered an inquiry of Joel as to whether someone had attended to her child's diapers.

"We got 'em trailing on the end of a line," reported that reliable sea dog and, straining, she glimpsed indeed a patch of white leaping in the wavering path of the boat.

"Salt water," she protested. "I think it will hurt his poor legs." But Joel patted her hand and she drifted off again to where her mother was making gingerbread in the breezy kitchen in Wiscasset.

Days and days and days. . . .

She dreamed that she was sitting on the splintery yellow kitchen floor in the bright warm oblong beside the screen door, and a big bad fly was on the outside, buzzing and buzzing, and pushing to get in—no, a hand was pressing on her shoulder and a familiar croak called to her.

"Caroline! Caroline! An island!" She was still in the boat. She opened her heavy eyes and blinked, but there was no island to be seen. No island. None at all. She put her head down once more, but the inexorable voice went on and on—a voice with a hint of authority.

"Caroline! Wake up! It's an island—for you and the baby and everybody." For the baby. Oh, yes, for the baby. She had almost forgotten him. He had cried all day and all night and had been as bad as beans, but he was good now; he had heard about the island. "Where?" she moved her stiff lips soundlessly.

"Starboard bow," said Joel's voice, quite close. Was starboard right or left? And if one looked toward the back of the boat, where was it then? She raised her head and peered at the dazzling tin-can sea with a strip of paper unrolling along it. There was no island. Joel was crazy. But he was so persistent.

"It's Juan Fernandez!" His husky whisper slid away from her, but his hand was inescapably tight on her bony shoulder. "Robinson Crusoe's island. Listen, dear, we can get to Valparaiso and take a steamer home to Bath." Robinson Crusoe was in a bright blue book with gilt letters, on the top shelf; he was the man who was cast away on a desert island with savages and goats. He tamed the goats and milked the savages—on Friday. No, he milked the savages and tamed the goats on Friday. He made a coat of an old nanny-goat, and what do you s'pose made him do so? The baby might like goat's milk better than condensed milk in a shiny can with a blue cow on the label—he was so unreasonable—but if there were milk only on Friday and he wanted milk every minute—

Joel mumbled on and on and pinched her shoulder.

"Look forward!" He turned her reluctant chin. There it was! It was a vision of mountain tops and green trees rising from a shining sea, cool trees and bushes. Shade and a desert island— a better place for women to live in than the seclusion of an umbrella in an open boat with many men. She remembered the piece of hard-tack in her hot hand and lifted it to her lips, grinding it feebly with her teeth; it hurt her face to open her mouth even a little. For a while she stared at a delightful dark spot in a bright universe; it was at her right, a short distance off. Presently she made it out to be the umbrella, under which sat a fearful reddish giant covered with golden hair, with her own amiable little pig on his knee. A maternal jealousy stirred her.

"I want to hold him," she whispered. Joel's hand bit into her shoulder, and he did not answer.

"He iss assleep now, ma'am," Mads hissed at her. "If I moof him, he cries, maybe."

"He doesn't like me!" she lamented. "He's a bad boy."

"Sssh, sssh!" reproved Joel. "He's been a good boy, and we are taking him to Robinson Crusoe's island. A feller should be older when he goes to sea." He achieved a ragged, gasping laugh.

"When he grows up—" began Caroline; but she was tired of talking and forgot what she had had in mind to say.

Juan Fernandez was a pleasant place to rest. She had a canvas hammock made from the lifeboat's sail stretched under the trees that smelled like sandalwood. She lay in the shade and was contented. The wind blew on her steadily, and the sun shone only in little patches through the leaves. The pretty sunshine. There were millions and millions of goats and quantities of strong milk and coarse meat and fish and fruit; there were a few curious people who seemed eager to get her what she wanted, though really all she wanted was to lie in the shade and watch the flowers and the birds. There were innumerable humming birds, as swift and bright as fireflies; some were bright brown with gold heads, and others, more beautiful still, were royally green, and their heads shone with a greenish-golden crown. They were prettier than any of the birds in Bath. She lay in her hammock or sat in the heavenly shade and reached out unsuccessfully to pat the swift things when they flew near.

When she came away, an old woman of the islands, expecting to please, gave her the dried skins of three of those little birds. The poor dead pretties. . . .

"You haven't told me a thing!" complained young Caroline. "Not one thing! You said there was a handkerchief in the box! Where did the birds come from? And where's the handkerchief and Uncle Joel's father's watch?"

"He was only a little baby, you know," murmured old Caroline, faded eyes fixed on the past; "and Joel wrapped him in the handerchief—to bury him."

In the old parlor the curtains blew in and out, and the pattern of the many-paned windows lay bright on the heathenish carpet. Old Caroline dreamed of her wedding trip, and young Caroline beat her restless feet on a stupid rug and was fiercely discontented with the present.

"How old were you then?" she burst out, hoping against hope.

"Why, I was twenty-four, I guess. No, maybe I was twenty-five," old Caroline replied, frowning and calculating. Young Caroline snorted bitterly.

"I'm thirty-two! I've never been anywhere except to New York and Boston and Philadelphia! There aren't any sea captains for

me to marry and I'll never have enough money to go anywhere
—anywhere!"

"It isn't anything much to go places," said old Caroline re-
motely.

PASA THALASSA THALASSA
(The Sea is everywhere the Sea)

by

EDWIN ARLINGTON ROBINSON

I

Gone—faded out of the story, the sea-faring friend I remember?
Gone for a decade, they say: never a word or a sign.
Gone with his hard red face that only his laughter could wrinkle,
Down where men go to be still, by the old way of the sea.

Never again will he come, with rings in his ears like a pirate,
Back to be living and seen, here with his roses and vines;
Here where the tenants are shadows and echoes of years un-
            eventful,
Memory meets the event, told from afar by the sea.

Smoke that floated and rolled in the twilight away from the
            chimney
Floats and rolls no more. Wheeling and falling, instead,
Down with a twittering flash go the smooth and inscrutable
            swallows,
Down to the place made theirs by the cold work of the sea.

Roses have had their day, and the dusk is on yarrow and worm-
      wood—
Dusk that is over the grass, drenched with memorial dew;
Trellises lie like bones in a ruin that once was a garden,
Swallows have lingered and ceased, shadows and echoes are all.

II

Where is he lying tonight, as I turn away down to the valley,
Down where the lamps of men tell me the streets are alive?
Where shall I ask, and of whom, in the town or on land or on
      water,
News of a time and a place buried alike with him?

Few now remain who may care, nor may they be wiser for
      caring,
Where or what manner the doom, whether by day or by night;
Whether in Indian deeps or on flood-laden fields of Atlantis,
Or by the roaring Horn, shrouded in silence he lies.

Few now remain who return by the weed-weary path to his
      cottage,
Drawn by the scene as it was—met by the chill and the change;
Few are alive who report, and few are alive who remember,
More of him now than a name carved somewhere on the sea.

"Where is he lying?" I ask, and the lights in the valley are
      nearer;
Down to the streets I go, down to the murmur of men.
Down to the roar of the sea in a ship may be well for another—
Down where he lies to-night, silent, and under the storms.

7. Housekeeping at Brunswick

by

HARRIET BEECHER STOWE

MY DEAR Sister,—Is it really true that snow is on the ground and Christmas coming, and I have not written unto thee, most dear sister? No, I don't believe it! I haven't been so naughty—it's all a mistake—yes, written I must have—and written I have, too—in the night-watches as I lay on my bed—such beautiful letters—I wish you had only received them; but by day it has been hurry, hurry, hurry, and drive, drive, drive! or else the calm of a sick-room, ever since last spring.

I put off writing when your first letter came, because I meant to write you a long letter,—a full and complete one; and so days slid by,—and became weeks,—and my little Charley came . . . etc. and etc.!!! Sarah, when I look back, I wonder at myself, not that I forget any one thing that I should remember, but that I have remembered anything. From the time that I left Cincinnati with my children to come forth to a country that I knew not of almost to the present time, it has seemed as if I could scarcely breathe, I was so pressed with care. My head dizzy with the whirl of railroads and steamboats; then ten days' sojourn in Boston, and a constant toil and hurry in buying my furniture and equipments; and then landing in Brunswick in the midst of a drizzly, inexorable northeast storm, and beginning the work

From *Life and Letters of Harriet Beecher Stowe* by Mrs. Annie Fields (Boston, 1907).

of getting in order a deserted, dreary, damp old house. All day long running from one thing to another, as, for example, thus:—

"Mrs. Stowe, how shall I make this lounge, and what shall I cover the back with first?"

MRS. STOWE. "With the coarse cotton in the closet."

WOMAN. "Mrs. Stowe, there isn't any more soap to clean the windows."

MRS. STOWE. "Where shall I get soap?"

"Here, H., run up to the store and get two bars."

"There is a man below wants to see Mrs. Stowe about the cistern. Before you go down, Mrs. Stowe, just show me how to cover this round end of the lounge."

"There's a man up from the depot, and he says that a box has come for Mrs. Stowe, and it's coming up to the house; will you come down and see about it?"

"Mrs. Stowe, don't go till you have shown the man how to nail that carpet in the corner. He's nailed it all crooked; what shall he do? The black thread is all used up, and what shall I do about putting gimp on the back of that sofa? Mrs. Stowe, there is a man come with a lot of pails and tinware from Furbish; will you settle the bill now?"

"Mrs. Stowe, here is a letter just come from Boston inclosing that bill of lading; the man wants to know what he shall do with the goods. If you will tell me what to say, I will answer the letter for you."

"Mrs. Stowe, the meat-man is at the door. Hadn't we better get a little beefsteak, or something, for dinner?"

"Shall Hatty go to Boardman's for some more black thread?"

"Mrs. Stowe, this cushion is an inch too wide for the frame. What shall we do now?"

"Mrs. Stowe, where are the screws of the black walnut bedstead?"

"Here's a man has brought in these bills for freight. Will you settle them now?"

"Mrs. Stowe, I don't understand using this great needle. I can't make it go through the cushion; it sticks in the cotton."

Then comes a letter from my husband, saying he is sick abed, and all but dead; don't ever expect to see his family again; wants to know how I shall manage, in case I am left a widow; knows we shall get in debt and never get out; wonders at my courage; thinks I am very sanguine; warns me to be prudent, as there won't be much to live on in case of his death, etc., etc., etc. I read the letter and poke it into the stove, and proceed. . . .

Some of my adventurers were quite funny; as for example: I had in my kitchen-elect no sink, cistern, or any other water privileges, so I bought at the cotton factory two of the great hogsheads they bring oil in, which here in Brunswick are often used for cisterns, and had them brought up in triumph to my yard, and was congratulating myself on my energy, when lo and behold! it was discovered that there was no cellar door except one in the kitchen, which was truly a strait and narrow way, down a long pair of stairs. Hereupon, as saith John Bunyan, I fell into a muse,—how to get my cisterns into my cellar. In days of chivalry I might have got a knight to make me a breach through the foundation walls, but that was not to be thought of now, and my oil hogsheads, standing disconsolately in the yard, seemed to reflect no great credit on my foresight. In this strait I fell upon a real honest Yankee cooper, whom I besought, for the reputation of his craft and mine, to take my hogsheads to pieces, carry them down in staves, and set them up again, which the worthy man actually accomplished one fair summer forenoon, to the great astonishment of "us Yankees." When my man came to put up the pump, he stared very hard to see my hogsheads thus translated and standing as innocent and quiet as could be in the cellar, and then I told him, in a very mild, quiet way, that I got 'em taken to pieces and put together,—just as if I had been always in the habit of doing such things. Professor Smith came down and looked very hard at them and then said, "Well, nothing can beat a willful woman." Then followed divers negotiations with a very clever, but (with reverence) somewhat lazy gentleman of jobs, who occupieth a carpenter's shop opposite to mine. This same

John Titcomb, my very good friend, is a character peculiar to Yankeedom. He is part owner and landlord of the house I rent, and connected by birth with all the best families in town; a man of real intelligence, and good education, a great reader, and quite a thinker. Being of an ingenious turn, he does painting, gilding, staining, upholstery jobs, varnishing, all in addition to his primary trade of carpentry. But he is a man studious of ease, and fully possessed with the idea that man wants but little here below; so he boards himself in his workshop on crackers and herring, washed down with cold water, and spends his time working, musing, reading new publications, and taking his comfort. In his shop you shall see a joiner's bench, hammers, planes, saws, gimlets, varnish, paint, picture frames, fence posts, rare old china, one or two fine portraits of his ancestry, a bookcase full of books, the tooth of a whale, an old spinning-wheel and spindle, a lady's parasol frame, a church lamp to be mended, in short, Henry says Mr. Titcomb's shop is like the ocean; there is no end to the curiosities in it.

In all my moving and fussing Mr. Titcomb has been my right-hand man. Whenever a screw was loose, a nail to be driven, a lock mended, a pane of glass set,—and these cases were manifold, —he was always on hand. But my sink was no fancy job, and I believe nothing but a very particular friendship would have moved him to undertake it. So this same sink lingered in a precarious state for some weeks, and when I had nothing else to do, I used to call and do what I could in the way of enlisting the good man's sympathies in its behalf.

How many times I have been in and seated myself in one of the old rocking-chairs, and talked first of the news of the day, the railroad, the last proceedings in Congress, the probabilities about the millennium, and thus brought the conversation by little and little round to my sink! . . . because, till the sink was done, the pump could not be put up, and we couldn't have any rain-water. Sometimes my courage would quite fail me to introduce the subject, and I would talk of everything else, turn and get out of the shop, and then turn back as if a thought had just struck my mind, and say:—

"Oh, Mr. Titcomb! about that sink?"

"Yes, ma'am, I was thinking about going down street this afternoon to look out stuff for it."

"Yes, sir, if you would be good enough to get it done as soon as possible; we are in great need of it."

"I think there's no hurry. I believe we are going to have a dry time now, so that you could not catch any water, and you won't need a pump at present."

These negotiations extended from the first of June to the first of July, and at last my sink was completed, and so also was a new house spout, concerning which I had had divers communings with Deacon Dunning of the Baptist church. Also during this time good Mrs. Mitchell and myself made two sofas, or lounges, a barrel chair, divers bedspreads, pillow cases, pillows, bolsters, mattresses; we painted rooms; we revarnished furniture; we— what didn't we do?

Then came on Mr. Stowe; and then came the eighth of July and my little Charley. I was really glad for an excuse to lie in bed, for I was full tired, I can assure you. Well, I was what folks call very comfortable for two weeks, when my nurse had to leave me. . . .

During this time I have employed my leisure hours in making up my engagements with newspaper editors. I have written more than anybody, or I myself, would have thought. I have taught an hour a day in our school, and I have read two hours every evening to the children. The children study English history in school, and I am reading Scott's historic novels in their order. To-night I finish the "Abbot"; shall begin "Kenilworth" next week; yet I am constantly pursued and haunted by the idea that I don't do anything. Since I began this note I have been called off at least a dozen times; once for the fish-man, to buy a codfish; once to see a man who had brought me some barrels of apples; once to see a book-man; then to Mrs. Upham, to see about a drawing I promised to make for her; then to nurse the baby; then into the kitchen to make a chowder for dinner; and now I am at it again, for nothing but deadly determination enables me ever to write; it is rowing against wind and tide.

I suppose you think now I have begun, I am never going to stop, and, in truth, it looks like it; but the spirit moves now and I must obey.

Christmas is coming, and our little household is all alive with preparations; every one collecting their little gifts with wonderful mystery and secrecy. . . .

To tell the truth, dear, I am getting tired; my neck and back ache, and I must come to a close.

Your ready kindness to me in the spring I felt very much; and why I did not have the sense to have sent you one line just by way of acknowledgment, I'm sure I don't know; I felt just as if I had, till I awoke, and behold! I had not. But, my dear, if my wits are somewhat wool-gathering and unsettled, my heart is as true as a star. I love you, and have thought of you often.

This fall I have felt often sad, lonesome, both very unusual feelings with me in these busy days; but the breaking away from my old home, and leaving father and mother, and coming to a strange place affected me naturally. In those sad hours my thoughts have often turned to George; I have thought with encouragement of his blessed state, and hoped that I should soon be there, too. I have many warm and kind friends here, and have been treated with great attention and kindness. Brunswick is a delightful residence, and if you come East next summer, you must come to my new home. George[1] would delight to go a-fishing with the children, and see the ships, and sail in the sailboats, and all that.

Give Aunt Harriet's love to him, and tell him when he gets to be a painter to send me a picture.

Affectionately yours,

H. Stowe.

---

[1] Her brother George's only child.

8. The Moosehead Country in 1853

by

JAMES RUSSELL LOWELL

FRIDAY the 12th.—The coach leaves Waterville at five o'clock in the morning, and one must breakfast in the dark at a quarter past four, because a train starts at twenty minutes before five— the passengers by both conveyances being pastured gregariously. So one must be up at half past three. The primary geological formations contain no trace of man, and it seems to me that these eocene periods of the day are not fitted for sustaining the human forms of life. One of the Fathers held that the sun was created to be worshipped at his rising by the Gentiles. The more reason that Christians (except, perhaps, early Christians) should abstain from these heathenish ceremonials. As one arriving by an early train is welcomed by a drowsy maid with the sleep scarce brushed out of her hair and finds empty grates and polished mahogany, on whose arid plains the pioneers of breakfast have not yet encamped, so a person waked thus unseasonably is sent into the world before his faculties are up and dressed to serve him. It might have been for this reason that my stomach resented for several hours a piece of fried beefsteak which I forced upon it, or, more properly speaking, a piece of that leathern conveniency

From *Literary Essays* by James Russell Lowell (Houghton Mifflin and Company: Boston, 1890).

which in these regions assumes the name. You will find it as hard to believe, my dear Storg, as that quarrel of the Sorbonists, whether one should say ego amat or no, that the use of the grid-iron is unknown hereabout, and so near a river named after St. Lawrence, too!

To-day has been the hottest day of the season, yet our drive has not been unpleasant. For a considerable distance we followed the course of the Sebasticook River, a pretty stream with alternations of dark brown pools and wine-colored rapids. On each side of the road the land had been cleared, and little one-story farm-houses were scattered at intervals. But the stumps still held out in most of the fields, and the tangled wilderness closed in behind, striped here and there with the slim white trunks of the elm. As yet only the edges of the great forest have been nibbled away. Sometimes a root-fence stretched up its bleaching antlers, like the trophies of a giant hunter. Now and then the houses thickened into an unsocial-looking village, and we drove up to the grocery to leave and take a mail-bag, stopping again presently to water the horses at some pallid little tavern, whose one red-curtained eye (the bar-room) had been put out by the inexorable thrust of Maine Law. Had Shenstone travelled this road, he would never have written that famous stanza of his; had Johnson, he would never have quoted it. They are to real inns as the skull of Yorick to his face. Where these villages occurred at a distance from the river, it was difficult to account for them. On the river-bank, a saw-mill or a tannery served as a logical premise, and saved them from total inconsequentiality. As we trailed along, at the rate of about four miles an hour, it was discovered that one of our mail-bags was missing. "Guess somebody'll pick it up," said the driver coolly: "'t any rate, likely there's nothin' in it." Who knows how long it took some Elam D. or Zebulon K. to compose the missive intrusted to that vagrant bag, and how much longer to persuade Pamela Grace or Sophronia Melissa that it had really and truly been written? The discovery of our loss was made by a tall man who sat next to me on the top of the coach, every one of whose senses seemed to be prosecuting its several investigation as we went along. Presently, sniffing gently, he remarked: " 'Pears to me's though I smelt sunthin'. Ain't the aix het, think?" The driver pulled up, and, sure enough, the off fore-wheel was found to be smoking. In three minutes he had snatched a rail from the fence, made a lever, raised the coach, and taken off the wheel, bathing the hot axle and box with water from the river. It was a pretty spot, and I was not sorry to lie under a beech-tree (Tityrus-like, meditating over my pipe) and watch the operations of the fire-annihilator. I could not help contrasting the ready helpfulness of our driver, all of whose wits were about him, current, and redeemable in the specie of action on emergency, with an incident of travel in Italy, where, under a somewhat similar stress of circumstances, our vetturino had nothing for it but to dash his hat on the ground and call on Sant' Antonio, the Italian Hercules.

There being four passengers for the Lake, a vehicle called a mud-wagon was detailed at Newport for our accommodation. In this we jolted and rattled along at a livelier pace than in the coach. As we got farther north, the country (especially the hills) gave evidence of longer cultivation. About the thriving town of Dexter we saw fine farms and crops. The houses, too, became prettier; hop-vines were trained about the doors, and hung their clustering thyrsi over the open windows. A kind of wild rose (called by the country folk the primrose) and asters were planted about the door-yards, and orchards, commonly of natural fruit, added to the pleasant home-look. But everywhere we could see that the war between the white man and the forest was still fierce, and that it would be a long while yet before the axe was buried. The haying being over, fires blazed or smouldered against the stumps in the fields, and the blue smoke widened slowly upward through the quiet August atmosphere. It seemed to me that I could hear a sigh now and then from the immemorial pines, as they stood watching these camp-fires of the inexorable invader. Evening set in, and, as we crunched and crawled up the long

gravelly hills, I sometimes began to fancy that Nature had forgotten to make the corresponding descent on the other side. But
erelong we were rushing down at full speed; and, inspired by
the dactylic beat of the horses' hoofs, I essayed to repeat the opening lines of Evangeline. At the moment I was beginning, we
plunged into a hollow, where the soft clay had been overcome
by a road of unhewn logs. I got through one line to this corduroy
accompaniment, somewhat as a country choir stretches a short
metre on the Procrustean rack of a long-drawn tune. The result
was like this:—

"Thihis ihis thehe fohorest prihihimeheval; thehe mur-
    hurmuring pihines hahand thehe hehemlohocks!"

At a quarter past eleven, P. M., we reached Greenville, (a little
village which looks as if it had dripped down from the hills,
and settled in the hollow at the foot of the lake,) having accomplished seventy-two miles in eighteen hours. The tavern was
totally extinguished. The driver rapped upon the bar-room window, and after a while we saw heat-lightnings of unsuccessful
matches followed by a low grumble of vocal thunder, which I
am afraid took the form of imprecation. Presently there was a
great success, and the steady blur of lighted tallow succeeded the
fugitive brilliance of the pine. A hostler fumbled the door open,
and stood staring at but not seeing us, with the sleep sticking
out all over him. We at last contrived to launch him, more like
an insensible missile than an intelligent or intelligible being, at
the slumbering landlord, who came out wide-awake, and welcomed us as so many half-dollars,—twenty-five cents each for
bed, ditto breakfast. O Shenstone, Shenstone! The only roost
was in the garret, which had been made into a single room, and
contained eleven double-beds, ranged along the walls. It was like
sleeping in a hospital. However, nice customs curtsy to eighteen-
hour rides, and we slept.

Saturday, 13th.—This morning I performed my toilet in the
bar-room, where there was an abundant supply of water, and

a halo of interested spectators. After a sufficient breakfast, we embarked on the little steamer Moosehead, and were soon throbbing up the lake. The boat, it appeared, had been chartered by a party, this not being one of her regular trips. Accordingly we were mulcted in twice the usual fee, the philosophy of which I could not understand. However, it always comes easier to us to comprehend why we receive than why we pay. I dare say it was quite clear to the captain. There were three or four clearings on the western shore; but after passing these, the lake became wholly primeval, and looked to us as it did to the first adventurous Frenchman who paddled across it. Sometimes a cleared point would be pink with the blossoming willow-herb, "a cheap and excellent substitute" for heather, and, like all such, not quite so good as the real thing. On all sides rose deep-blue mountains, of remarkably graceful outline, and more fortunate than common in their names. There were the Big and Little Squaw, the Spencer and Lily-bay Mountains. It was debated whether we saw Katahdin or not, (perhaps more useful as an intellectual exercise than the assured vision would have been), and presently Mount Kineo rose abruptly before us, in shape not unlike the island of Capri. Mountains are called great natural features, and why they should not retain their names long enough for these also to become naturalized, it is hard to say. Why should every new surveyor rechristen them with the gubernatorial patronymics of the current year? They are geological noses, and as they are aquiline or pug, indicate terrestrial idiosyncrasies. A cosmical physiognomist, after a glance at them, will draw no vague inference as to the character of the country. The word nose is no better than any other word; but since the organ has got that name, it is convenient to keep it. Suppose we had to label our facial prominences every season with the name of our provincial governor, how should we like it? If the old names have no other meaning, they have that of age; and, after all, meaning is a plant of slow growth, as every reader of Shakespeare knows. It is well enough to call mountains after their discoverers, for Nature

was a bear, and a bear at least eighteen hands high. There is something pokerish about a deserted dwelling, even in broad daylight; but here in the obscure wood, and the moon filtering unwillingly through the trees! Well, I made the door at last, and found the place packed fuller with darkness than it ever had been with hay. Gradually I was able to make things out a little, and began to hack frozenly at a log which I groped out. I was relieved presently by one of the guides. He cut at once into one of the uprights of the building till he got some dry splinters, and we soon had a fire like the burning of a whole wood-wharf in our part of the country. My companion went back to the birch, and left me to keep house. First I knocked a hole in the roof (which the fire began to lick in a relishing way) for a chimney, and then cleared away a damp growth of "pison-elder," to make a sleeping place. When the unsuccessful hunters returned, I had everything quite comfortable, and was steaming at the rate of about ten horse-power a minute. Young Telemachus[1] was sorry to give up the moose so soon, and, with the teeth chattering almost out of his head, he declared that he would like to stick it out all night. However, he reconciled himself to the fire, and, making our beds of some "splits" which we poked from the roof, we lay down at half past two. I, who have inherited a habit of looking into every closet before I go to bed, for fear of fire, had become in two days such a stoic of the woods, that I went to sleep tranquilly, certain that my bedroom would be in a blaze before morning. And so, indeed, it was; and the withes that bound it together being burned off, one of the sides fell in without waking me.

Tuesday, 16th.—After a sleep of two hours and a half, so sound that it was as good as eight, we started at half past four for the hay-makers' camp again. We found them just getting breakfast. We sat down upon the deacon-seat before the fire blazing between the bedroom and the salle à manger, which were

---

[1] This was my nephew, Charles Russell Lowell, who fell at the head of his brigade in the battle of Cedar Creek.

simply two roofs of spruce-bark, sloping to the ground on one side, the other three being left open. We found that we had, at least, been luckier than the other party, for M. had brought back his convoy without even seeing a moose. As there was not room at the table for all of us to breakfast together, these hospitable woodmen forced us to sit down first, although we resisted stoutly. Our breakfast consisted of fresh bread, fried salt pork, stewed whortleberries, and tea. Our kind hosts refused to take money for it, nor would M. accept anything for his trouble. This seemed even more open-handed when I remembered that they had brought all their stores over the Carry upon their shoulders, paying an ache extra for every pound. If their hospitality lacked anything of hard external polish, it had all the deeper grace which springs only from sincere manliness. I have rarely sat at a table d'hote which might not have taken a lesson from them in essential courtesy. I have never seen a finer race of men. They have all the virtues of the sailor, without that unsteady roll in the gait with which the ocean proclaims itself quite as much in the moral as in the physical habit of a man. They appeared to me to have hewn out a short northwest passage through wintry woods to those spice-lands of character which we dwellers in cities must reach, if at all, by weary voyages in the monotonous track of the trades.

By the way, as we were embirching last evening for our moose-chase, I asked what I was to do with my baggage. "Leave it here," said our guide, and he laid the bags upon a platform of alders, which he bent down to keep them beyond reach of the rising water.

"Will they be safe here?"

"As safe as they would be locked up in your house at home."

And so I found them at my return; only the hay-makers had carried them to their camp for greater security against the changes of the weather.

We got back to Kineo in time for dinner, and in the afternoon, the weather being fine, went up the mountain. As we landed at the foot, our guide pointed to the remains of a red shirt and a pair of blanket trousers. "That," said he, "is the reason there's such a trade in ready-made clo'es. A suit gits pooty well wore out by the time a camp breaks up in the spring, and the lumberers want to look about right when they come back into the settlements, so they buy somethin' ready-made, and heave ole bust-up into the bush." True enough, thought I, this is the Ready-made Age. It is quicker being covered than fitted. So we all go to the slop-shop and come out uniformed, every mother's son with habits of thinking and doing cut on one pattern, with no special reference to his peculiar build.

Kineo rises 1750 feet above the sea, and 750 above the lake. The climb is very easy, with fine outlooks at every turn over lake and forest. Near the top is a spring of water, which even Uncle Zeb might have allowed to be wholesome. The little tin dipper was scratched all over with names, showing that vanity, at least, is not put out of breath by the ascent. O Ozymandias, king of kings! We are all scrawling on something of the kind. "My name is engraved on the institutions of my country," thinks the statesman. But, alas! institutions are as changeable as tin-dippers; men are content to drink the same old water, if the shape of the cup only be new, and our friend gets two lines in the Biographical Dictionaries. After all, these inscriptions, which make us smile up here, are about as valuable as the Assyrian ones which Hincks and Rawlinson read at cross-purposes. Have we not Smiths and Browns enough, that we must ransack the ruins of Nimroud for more? Near the spring we met a Bloomer! It was the first chronic one I had ever seen. It struck me as a sensible costume for the occasion, and it will be the only wear in the Greek Kalends, when women believe that sense is an equivalent for grace.

The forest primeval is best seen from the top of a mountain. It then impresses one by its extent, like an Oriental epic. To be in it is nothing, for then an acre is as good as a thousand square miles. You cannot see five rods in any direction, and the ferns, mosses, and tree-trunks just around you are the best of it. As for solitude, night will make a better one with ten feet square of pitch dark; and mere size is hardly an element of grandeur, except in works of man,—as the Colosseum. It is through one or the other pole of vanity that men feel the sublime in mountains. It is either, How small great I am beside it! or, Big as you are, little I's soul will hold a dozen of you. The true idea of a forest is not a selva selvaggia, but something humanized a little, as we imagine the forest of Arden, with trees standing at royal intervals,—a commonwealth, and not a communism. To some moods, it is congenial to look over endless leagues of unbroken savagery without a hint of man.

9. The State of Maine and the War for the Union

JULY 2nd 1863, LITTLE ROUND TOP AND THE TWENTIETH MAINE

by

COLONEL JOSHUA L. CHAMBERLAIN

IN COMPLIANCE with the request of the colonel commanding the brigade, I have the honor to submit a somewhat detailed report of the operations of the Twentieth Regiment Maine Volunteers in the battle of Gettysburg, on the 2nd and 3rd instant.

Having acted as the advance guard, made necessary by the proximity of the enemy's cavalry, on the march of the day before, my command on reaching Hanover, Pa., just before sunset on that day, were much worn, and lost no time in getting ready for an expected bivouac. Rations were scarcely issued, and the men about preparing supper, when rumors that the enemy had been encountered that day near Gettysburg absorbed every other interest, and very soon orders came to march forthwith to Gettysburg.

My men moved out with a promptitude and spirit extraordinary, the cheers and welcome they received on the road adding

From *Strong Vincent and His Brigade at Gettysburg* by Oliver W. Norton (Chicago, 1909).

to their enthusiasm. After an hour or two of sleep by the road-side just before daybreak, we reached the heights southeasterly of Gettysburg at about 7 a. m. July 2.

Massed at first with the rest of the division on the right of the road, we were moved several times farther toward the left. Although expecting every moment to be put into action and held strictly in line of battle, yet the men were able to take some rest and make the most of their rations.

Somewhere near 4 p. m. a sharp cannonade, at some distance to our left and front, was the signal for a sudden and rapid movement of our whole division in the direction of this firing, which grew warmer as we approached. Passing an open field in the hollow ground in which some of our batteries were going into position, our brigade reached the skirt of a piece of woods, in the farther edge of which there was a heavy musketry fire, and when about to go forward into line we received from Colonel Vincent, commanding the brigade, orders to move to the left at the double-quick, when we took a farm road crossing Plum Run in order to gain a rugged mountain spur called Granite Spur, or Little Round Top.

The enemy's artillery got range of our column as we were climbing the spur, and the crashing of the shells among the rocks and the tree tops made us move lively along the crest. One or two shells burst in our ranks. Passing to the southern slope of Little Round Top, Colonel Vincent indicated to me the ground my regiment was to occupy, informing me that this was the ex-treme left of our general line, and that a desperate attack was expected in order to turn that position, concluding by telling me I was to "hold that ground at all hazards." This was the last word I heard from him.

In order to commence by making my right firm, I formed my regiment on the right into line, giving such direction to the line as should best secure the advantage of the rough, rocky, and stragglingly wooded ground.

The line faced generally toward a more conspicuous eminence

southwest of ours, which is known as Sugar Loaf, or Round Top. Between this and my position intervened a smooth and thinly wooded hollow. My line formed, I immediately detached Company B, Captain Morrill commanding, to extend from my left flank across this hollow as a line of skirmishes, with directions to act as occasion might dictate, to prevent a surprise on my exposed flank and rear.

The artillery fire on our position had meanwhile been constant and heavy, but my formation was scarcely complete when the artillery was replaced by a vigorous infantry assault upon the center of our brigade to my right, but it very soon involved the right of my regiment and gradually extended along my entire front. The action was quite sharp and at close quarters.

In the midst of this an officer from my center informed me that some important movement of the enemy was going on in his front, beyond that of the line with which we were engaged. Mounting a large rock, I was able to see a considerable body of the enemy moving by the flank in rear of their line engaged, and passing from the direction of the foot of Great Round Top through the valley toward the front of my left. The close engagement not allowing any change of front, I immediately stretched my regiment to the left, by taking intervals by the left flank, and at the same time "refusing" my left wing, so that it was nearly at right angles with my right, thus occupying about twice the extent of our ordinary front, some of the companies being brought into single rank when the nature of the ground gave sufficient strength or shelter. My officers and men understood my wishes so well that this movement was executed under fire, the right wing keeping up fire, without giving the enemy any occasion to seize or even to suspect their advantage. But we were not a moment too soon; the enemy's flanking column having gained their desired direction, burst upon my left, where they evidently had expected an unguarded flank, with great demonstration.

We opened a brisk fire at close range, which was so sudden and effective that they soon fell back among the rocks and low trees in the valley, only to burst forth again with a shout, and rapidly advanced, firing as they came. They pushed up to within a dozen yards of us before the terrible effectiveness of our fire compelled them to break and take shelter.

They renewed the assault on our whole front, and for an hour the fighting was severe. Squads of the enemy broke through our line in several places, and the fight was literally hand to hand. The edge of the fight rolled backward and forward like a wave. The dead and wounded were now in our front and then in our rear. Forced from our position, we desperately recovered it, and pushed the enemy down to the foot of the slope. The intervals of the struggle were seized to remove our wounded (and those of the enemy also), to gather ammunition from the cartridge-boxes of disabled friend or foe on the field, and even to secure better muskets than the Enfields, which we found did not stand service well. Rude shelters were thrown up of the loose rocks that covered the ground.

Captain Woodward, commanding the Eighty-third Pennsylvania Volunteers, on my right, gallantry maintaining his fight, judiciously and with hearty co-operation made his movements conform to my necessities, so that my right was at no time exposed to a flank attack.

The enemy seemed to have gathered all their energies for their final assault. We had gotten our thin line into as good a shape as possible, when a strong force emerged from the scrub wood in the valley, as well as I could judge, in two lines in echelon by the right, and, opening a heavy fire, the first line came on as if they meant to sweep everything before them. We opened on them as well as we could with our scanty ammunition snatched from the field.

It did not seem possible to withstand another shock like this now coming on. Our loss had been severe. One-half of my left wing had fallen and a third of my regiment lay just behind us, dead or badly wounded. At this moment my anxiety was increased by a great roar of musketry in my rear, on the farther or northerly slope of Little Round Top, apparently on the flank of the regular brigade, which was in support of Hazlett's battery on the crest behind us. The bullets from this attack struck into my left rear, and I feared that the enemy might have nearly surrounded the Little Round Top, and only a desperate chance was left for us. My ammunition was soon exhausted. My men were firing their last shot and getting ready to "club" their muskets.

It was imperative to strike before we were struck by this overwhelming force in a hand-to-hand fight, which we could not probably have withstood or survived. At that crisis, I ordered the bayonet. The word was enough. It ran like fire along the line, from man to man, and rose into a shout, with which they sprang forward upon the enemy, now not 30 yards away. The effect was surprising; many of the enemy's first line threw down their arms and surrendered. An officer fired his pistol at my head with one hand, while he handed me his sword with the other. Holding fast by our right, and swinging forward our left, we made an extended "right wheel," before which the enemy's second line broke, and fell back, fighting from tree to tree, many being captured, until we had swept the valley and cleared the front of nearly our entire brigade.

Meantime, Captain Morrill with his skirmishers (sent out from my left flank), with some dozen or fifteen of the U. S. Sharpshooters who had put themselves under his direction, fell upon the enemy as they were breaking, and by his demonstrations, as well as his well-directed fire, added much to the effect of the charge.

Having thus cleared the valley and driven the enemy up the western slope of the Great Round Top, not wishing to press so far out as to hazard the ground I was to hold by leaving it exposed to a sudden rush of the enemy, I succeeded (although with some effort to stop my men, who declared they were "on the road to Richmond") in getting the regiment into good order and resuming our original position.

Four hundred prisoners, including two field and several line officers, were sent to the rear. These were mainly from the Fifteenth and Forty-seventh Alabama Regiments, with some of the Fourth and Fifth Texas. One hundred and fifty of the enemy were found killed and wounded in our front.

At dusk, Colonel Rice informed me of the fall of Colonel Vincent, which had devolved the command of the brigade on him, and that Colonel Fisher had come up with a brigade to our support. These troops were massed in our rear. It was the understanding, as Colonel Rice informed me, that Colonel Fisher's brigade was to advance and seize the western slope of Great Round Top, where the enemy had shortly before been driven. But, after considerable delay, this intention for some reason was not carried into execution.

We were apprehensive that if the enemy were allowed to strengthen himself in that position, he would have a great advantage in renewing the attack on us at daylight or before. Colonel Rice then directed me to make the movement to seize that crest.

It was now 9 p. m. Without waiting to get ammunition, but trusting in part to the very circumstance of not exposing our movement or our small front by firing, and with bayonets fixed, the little handful of 200 men pressed up the mountain side in very extended order, as the steep and jagged surface of the ground compelled. We heard squads of the enemy falling back before us, and, when near the crest, we met a scattering and uncertain fire, which caused us the great loss of the gallant Lieutenant Linscott, who fell, mortally wounded. In the silent advance in the darkness we laid hold of 25 prisoners, among them a staff officer of General (E. M.) Law, commanding the brigade immediately opposed to us during the fight. Reaching the crest, and reconnoitering the ground, I placed the men in a strong position among the rocks, and informed Colonel Rice, requesting also ammunition and some support to our right, which was very near the enemy, their movements and words even being now distinctly heard by us.

Some confusion soon after resulted from the attempt of some regiment of Colonel Fisher's brigade to come to our support. They had found a wood road up the mountain, which brought them on my right flank, and also in proximity to the enemy, massed a little below. Hearing their approach, and thinking a movement from that quarter could only be from the enemy, I made disposition to receive them as such. In the confusion which attended the attempt to form them in support of my right, the enemy opened a brisk fire, which disconcerted my efforts to form them and disheartened the supports themselves, so that I saw no more of them that night.

Feeling somewhat insecure in this isolated position, I sent in for the Eighty-third Pennsylvania, which came speedily, followed by the Forty-fourth New York, and, having seen these well posted, I sent a strong picket to the front, with instructions to report to me every half hour during the night, and allowed the rest of my men to sleep on their arms.

At some time about midnight, two regiments of Colonel Fisher's brigade came up the mountain beyond my left, and took position near the summit; but as the enemy did not threaten from that direction, I made no effort to connect with them.

We went into the fight with 386, all told—358 guns. Every pioneer and musician who could carry a musket went into the ranks. Even the sick and footsore, who could not keep up in the march, came up as soon as they could find their regiments, and took their places in line of battle, while it was battle, indeed. Some prisoners I had under guard, under sentence of court-martial, I was obliged to put into the fight, and they bore their part well, for which I shall recommend a commutation of their sentence.

The loss, so far as I can ascertain it, is 136—30 of whom were killed, and among the wounded are many mortally.

Captain Billings, Lieutenant Kendall, and Lieutenant Linscott are officers whose loss we deeply mourn, efficient soldiers and pure and high-minded men.

In such an engagement there were many incidents of heroism and noble character which should have place even in an official report; but, under present circumstances, I am unable to do justice to them. I will say of that regiment that the resolution, courage, and heroic fortitude which enabled us to withstand so formidable an attack have happily led to so conspicuous a result, that they may safely trust to history to record their merits.

About noon on the 3d of July, we were withdrawn, and formed on the right of the brigade, in the front edge of a piece of woods near the left center of our main line of battle, where we were held in readiness to support our troops, then receiving the severe attack of the afternoon of that day.

On the 4th, we made a reconnaissance to the front, to ascertain the movements of the enemy, but finding that they had retired, at least beyond Willoughby's Run, we returned to Little Round Top, where we buried our dead in the place where we had laid them during the fight, marking each grave by a headboard made of ammunition boxes, with each soldier's name cut upon it. We also buried 50 of the enemy's dead, in front of our position of July 2. We then looked after our wounded, whom I had taken the responsibility of putting into the houses of citizens in the vicinity of Little Round Top, and, on the morning of the 5th, took up our march on the Emmitsburg Road.

A FARMER REMEMBERS LINCOLN

by

WITTER BYNNER

'Lincoln?—
Well, I was in the old Second Maine,
The first regiment in Washington from the Pine Tree State.
Of course I didn't get the butt of the clip;
We was there for guardin' Washington—
We was all green.

'I ain't never ben to the theayter in my life—
I didn't know how to behave.
I ain't never ben since.
I can see as plain as my hat the box where he sat in
When he was shot.
I can tell you, sir, there was a panic
When we found our President was in the shape he was in!
Never saw a soldier in the world but what liked him.

'Yes, sir. His looks was kind o' hard to forget.
He was a spare man,
An old farmer.
Everything was all right, you know,
But he wasn't a smooth-appearin' man at all—
Not in no ways;
Thin-faced, long-necked,
And a swellin' kind of a thick lip like.

Reprinted from *Grenstone Poems* by Witter Bynner by permission of
Alfred A. Knopf, Inc. Copyright 1917, 1926 by Alfred A. Knopf, Inc.

'And he was a jolly old fellow—always cheerful;
He wasn't so high but the boys could talk to him their own
    ways.
While I was servin' at the Hospital
He'd come in and say, 'You look nice in here,'
Praise us up, you know.
And he'd bend over and talk to the boys—
And he'd talk so good to 'em—so close—
That's why I call him a farmer.
I don't mean that everything about him wasn't all right, you
    understand,
It's just—well, I was a farmer—
And he was my neighbor, anybody's neighbor.
I guess even you young folks would 'a' liked him.'

10. A Northern Countryside

by

ROSALIND RICHARDS

OUR county lies in a northern State, in the midst of one of those districts known geographically as "regions of innumerable lakes." It is in good part wooded—hilly, irregular country, not mountainous, but often bold and marked in outline. Save for its lakes, strangers might pass through it without especial notice; but its broken hills have a peculiar intimacy and loveableness, and to us it is so beautiful that new wonder falls on us year after year as we dwell in it.

There is a marked trend of the land. I suppose the first landmark a bird would distinguish in its flight would be our long, round-shouldered ridges, running north and south. Driving across country, either eastward or westward, you go up and up in leisurely rises, with plenty of fairly level resting places between, up long calm shoulder after shoulder, to the Height of Land. And there you take breath of wonder, for lo, before you and below you, behold a whole new countryside framed by new hills.

Sometimes the lower country thus revealed is in its turn broken into lesser hills, or moulded into noble rounding valleys. Sometimes there are stretches of intervale or old lake bottom, of

From *A Northern Countryside* by Rosalind Richards (Henry Holt and Company: New York, 1916).

real flat-land, a rare beauty with us, on which the eyes rest with delight. More often than not there is shining water, lake or pond or stream. Sometimes this lower valley country extends for miles before the next range rises, so that your glance travels restfully out over the wide spaces. Sometimes it is little, like a cup.

As you get up towards the Height of Land you come to what makes the returning New Englander draw breath quickly, the pleasure is so poignant: upland pastures dotted with juniper and boulders, and broken by clumps of balsam fir and spruce. Most fragrant, most beloved places. Dicksonia fern grows thick about the boulders. The pasturage is thin June-grass, the color of beach sand, as it ripens, and in August this is transformed to a queen's garden by the blossoming of blue asters and the little nemoralis golden-rod, which grew unnoticed all the earlier summer. Often whole stretches of the slope are carpeted with mayflowers and checkerberries, and as you climb higher, and meet the wind from the other side of the ridge, your foot crunches on gray reindeer-moss.

Last week, before climbing a small bare-peaked mountain, I turned aside to explore a path which led through a field of scattered balsam firs, with lady-fern growing thick about their feet. A little further on, the firs were assembled in groups and clumps, and then group was joined to group. The valley grew deeper and darker, and still the same small path led on, till I found myself in the tallest and most solemn wood of firs that I have ever seen. They were sixty feet high, needle-pointed, black, and they filled the long hollow between the hills, like a dark river.

The woods alternate with fields to clothe the hills and intervales and valleys, and make a constant and lovely variety over the landscape. Sometimes they seem a shore instead of a river. They jut out into the meadow-land, in capes and promontories, and stand in little islands, clustered around an outcropping ledge

or a boulder too big to be removed. You are confronted everywhere with this meeting of the natural and indented shore of the
woods, close, feathery, impenetrable, with the bays and inlets
of field and pasture and meadow. The jutting portions are apt
to be made more sharp and marked by the most striking part
of our growth, the evergreens. There they grow, white pine and
red pine, black spruce, hemlock, and balsam fir, in lovely sister-
hood. Their needles shine in the sun. They taper perfectly,
finished at every point, clean, dry, and resinous; and the fragrance distilled from them by our crystal air is as surely the
very breath of New England as that of the Spice Islands is the
breath of the East.

Our soil is often spoken of as barren, but this is only where
it has been neglected. Hay and apples give us abundant crops;
indeed our apples have made a name at home and abroad.
Potatoes also give us a very fine yield, and a great part of
the State is rich in lumber. When it is left to itself, the land
reverts to wave after wave of luxuriant pine forest. Forty miles
east of us they are cutting out masts again where the Constitution's masts were cut.

The apple orchards are scattered over the slopes. In the more
upland places, sheep are kept, and the sheep-pastures are often
hillside orchards of tall sugar maples. We have neat fields of oats
and barley, more or less scattered, and once in a while a buckwheat patch, while every farm has a good cornfield, beans, pump-
kins, and potatoes, besides "the woman's" little patch of "garden
truck." A good many bees are kept, in colonies of gray hives
under the apple trees.

The people who live on the farms are, I suppose, much like
farm people everywhere. "Folks are folks"; yet, after being much
with them, certain qualities impress themselves upon one's
notice as characteristic; they have a dry sense of humor, and
quaint and whimsical ways of expressing it, and with this, a
refinement of thought and speech that is almost fastidious; a

fine reticence about the physical aspects of life such as is only found, I believe, in a strong race, a people drawing their vigor from deep and untainted springs. I often wonder whether there is another place in the world where women are sheltered from any possible coarseness of expression with such considerate delicacy as they find among the rough men on a New England farm.

The life is so hard, the hours so necessarily long, in our harsh climate, that small-natured persons too often become little more than machines. They get through their work, and they save every penny they can; and that is all. The Granges, however, are increasing a pleasant and wholesome social element which is beyond price, and all winter you meet sleighs full of rosy-cheeked families, driving to the Hall for Grange Meeting, or Sunday Meeting, or for the weekly dance.

Many of the farm people are large-minded enough to do their work well, and still keep above and on top of it; and some of these stand up in a sort of splendor. Their fibres have been seasoned in a life that calls for all a man's powers. Their grave kind faces show that, living all their lives in one place, they have taken the longest of all journeys, and traveled deep into the un-map-able country of Life. I do not know how to write fittingly of some of these older farm people; wise enough to be simple, and deep-rooted as the trees that grow round them; so strong and attuned to their work that the burdens of others grow light in their presence, and life takes on its right and happier proportions when one is with them.

If the first impression of our country is its uniformity, the second and amazing one is its surprises, its secret places. The long ridges accentuate themselves suddenly into sharp slopes and steep cup-shaped valleys, covered with sweet-fern and juniper. The wooded hills are often full of hidden cliffs (rich gardens in themselves, they are so deep in ferns and moss), and quick brooks run through them, so that you are never long without the talk of one to keep you company. There are rocky glens, where you meet cold, sweet air, the ceaseless comforting of a waterfall, and moss on moss, to velvet depths of green.

The ridges rise and slope and rise again with general likeness, but two of them open amazingly to disclose the wide blue surface of our great River. We are rich in rivers, and never have to journey far to reach one, but I never can get quite used to the surprise of coming among the hills on this broad strong full-running stream, with gulls circling over it.

One thing sets us apart from other regions: our wonderful lakes. They lie all around us, so that from every hill-top you see their shining and gleaming. It is as if the worn mirror of the glacier had been splintered into a thousand shining fragments, and the common saying is that our State is more than half water. They are so many that we call them ponds, not lakes, whether they are two miles long, or ten, or twenty.* I have counted over nine hundred on the State map, and then given up counting. No one person could ever know them all; there still would be new "Lost Ponds" and "New Found Lakes."

The greater part of them lie in the unbroken woods, but countless numbers are in open farming country. They run from great sunlit sheets with many islands to the most perfect tiny hidden forest jewels, places utterly lonely and apart, mirroring only the depths of the green woods.

Each "pond," large or little, is a world in itself. You can almost believe that the moon looks down on each with different radiance, that the south wind has a special fragrance as it blows across each; and each one has some peculiar, intimate beauty; deep bays, lovely and secluded channels between wooded islands, or small curved beaches which shine between dark headlands, lit up now and then by a camp fire.

Hill after hill, round-shouldered ridge after ridge; low nearer

---

* The legal distinction in our State is not between ponds and lakes, but between ponds and "Great Ponds." All land-locked waters over ten acres in area are Great Ponds; in which the public have rights of fishing, ice-cutting, etc. R.R.

the salt water, increasing very gradually in height till they form the wild amphitheatre of blue peaks in the northern part of the State; partly farming country, and greater part wooded; this is our countryside, and across it and in and out of the forests its countless lovely lakes shine and its great rivers thread their tranquil way to the sea.

11. The Red Man

THE PILLARS OF SMOKE

by

ELIZABETH COATSWORTH

A FEW mornings later, something happened for which Margaret had not dared to hope. When the possibility occurred to her, she dismissed it quickly, not wishing to allow her mind the comfort of delusion; last year it had not taken place, and she had no reason to expect it this year.

Nevertheless, when on this particular morning she stepped out into the early dawn with her milking pail in her hand and glanced as always toward Horn Pond, she saw two thin pillars of smoke rising quietly into the sky, and drifting away into the blue. The water lay very still, and mirrored the pillars with a faint sparkle of silver. It was so long since she had seen here any smoke but her own! She stood leaning against the door frame, gazing out quietly at the rising smoke, letting its message slowly fill her heart.

She was sure that she knew who had lighted the cooking fires and who sat about them now, there across the pond near the water's edge. It was just where her father and she had seen them two summers ago, on such a morning as this. He had gone down to welcome the strangers and had found a family of wandering

Reprinted from *Here I Stay* by Elizabeth Coatsworth by permission of Coward-McCann Inc., Copyright 1938, by Elizabeth Coatsworth Beston.

Indians, headed by an old bow-legged and rum-smelling man dressed in cast-off English clothes and a red flannel waistcoat, who said that he was called Captain Bob Bandylegs and that the rest were his sons and daughters and their husbands and wives. They had at first been rather sullen with the white man, pretending to speak little English, staring at him with the black expressionless eyes which some people likened to a snake's. But Mr. Winslow had been patient with them. After a little, he found that they were accustomed to come here on certain summers when the mood struck them to plant their corn in the clearing where his cabin now stood. Where were they to plant now? What right had the white man to seize their clearing and to drive them away from the places which had always been their hunting and fishing grounds?

For once, they found a settler who agreed with them. True, he had bought the land, but from white men who had no real right to sell an Indian clearing, and very willingly he bought it again from Captain Bob Bandylegs, paying for it with blankets and an iron kettle and an old musket. As to the hunting and fishing rights, he freely left them to their original owners. Surely the land was large enough for them all.

But the friendship had been cemented by a far more human incident. One day Mr. Winslow and Margaret saw the old man coming up the slope, holding something in his arms. This something proved to be a favorite grandson, little more than a baby, and when the white man saw the small hand, swollen and dark-looking, and the child's hot face, he looked grave indeed.

"Fishhook," said Captain Bob. "Try larch-cones, try spruce gum—no good. You try now."

"I'll do what I can, Captain Bob," Mr. Winslow said, "but mind you, I can't promise. Margaret, bring me clean lint, thyme water, and mallow ointment."

She could see him now, deft and careful, hurting no more than he could help; she could see the child still in his grandfather's arms, trusting the white man, and stoical in spite of his littleness.

Margaret made up a bed for him in a corner by the hearth, and there he lay for three days with Captain Bob sitting beside him and her father re-dressing the wound at all hours of the day and night. She could see the men's heads bent together over the small tortured hand, or Captain Bob gravely feeding the child with broth.

In three days the worst danger was over, but for a fortnight Captain Bob brought the child with him every day to have his wound re-dressed.

Now, as Margaret stood leaning against the door frame remembering these things, she saw once more the two figures climbing the slope. They might be climbing out of the past, except that now the little boy was thinner and taller than he had been, no longer half a baby. Quickly she shut Ajax into the cabin, since he was a stranger to these people, and with Rambler bounding ahead, hurried down to meet the newcomers.

Captain Bob eyed her black dress.

"You are alone?" he asked directly.

"My father is dead," she answered, sure of his sympathy. He made a gesture with his hands.

"The leaves fall," he replied. There was a beautiful calm look on his face that seemed to have nothing to do with his body in its ill-fitting, ill-matched, and dirty clothes.

He said very little, but walked with Margaret about the farm.

"The hay is ready," he remarked at last.

"Yes," she answered. She did not tell him how she had already taken the scythe and spent long back-breaking afternoons in the upper field, with so little accomplished that she felt sick with discouragement.

He praised her corn, for she had planted only the Indian crops of corn and beans and squash, together with a few potatoes, since these were the crops that would bring the largest yield at the least cost of strength.

When they came back to the cottage, she invited Captain Bob and the child in, laid a new cloth, and brought them fresh milk and corn bread spread with wild strawberry preserve. She saw the old Indian glance once about the room.

"All is the same," he said.

She nodded.

"Only he is gone," she thought to herself.

Gravely, the man and the little child ate and ate. At last they pushed back their chairs—chairs that her father had made, with deerskin seats—but when Margaret asked, "Are you through, Captain Bob?" the Indian shook his head.

"I'm resting," he said, and in a few moments fell to again and ate as much more. Every time she saw it, the girl was surprised at the quantities that Indians could eat when there was food to be eaten. The other side of the coin, she knew, was how little they could live on for weeks and months even, when food was scarce, and with what patience they starved and waited for the gift of food to come once more from the hand of the Good Spirit.

When her guests were gone, Margaret went about her work as usual and saw no more of the Indians for that day.

But next morning, when the first light was graying the room, she was awakened by the sound of voices outside the cabin—a lovely sound, indeed, to her ears!—and hurrying to the door, with her hand on Ajax' collar, found on the great field-stone doorstep two perch, gleaming in the morning light, and beyond in the middle of the dew-drenched field saw a group of three or four squaws, Captain Bob's daughters and daughters-in-law, each armed with a sharp knife, and busy cutting hay. It was still too early in the morning for the grass to fall easily, wet as it was, but already they had made a wide swale, and seeing her at the door, they called out to her, smiling, and then went back to their work, close-bunched together, talking as busily as a flock of blackbirds in a field of stubble.

Margaret, excited and happy, cooked and ate the fish quickly, did the necessary chores in the barn, and then joined the women with her scythe. All day the great clouds crossed the blue sky; all day their shadows crossed the hayfield where the winds were

making pulsing cat's paws down the slope. All day the Indian
women worked with Margaret among them, cutting valiantly.
And although the girl perhaps never learned the whole art of
the scythe, she did, working with renewed hope, learn to take
more time for whetting her blade, and slowly came to feel the
proper swing and jerk of the handle in her hands, which had
escaped her when she was working alone and made desperate by
the magnitude of the task.

So, deserted by her own kind, Margaret was befriended by
the shadowy people of the forest, and by their help the hay was
made and finally carried into the barn. She sometimes felt as
though she were living in a dream. For the first few days the
women had been shy with her, and hid their faces, giggling,
when she spoke to them.

But one day during the haying, as she sat resting a little
apart from the others, an older woman came up to her, and shaking her head, felt her shoes, whose thick soles were almost worn
through.

"No good. Molly Molasses make moccasins," she grunted, and
in a moment the brown girls were clustered about Margaret,
touching, feeling her clothes, laughing, exclaiming over the
smallness of her feet, their reserve suddenly broken through.

Molly Molasses made Margaret take off her shoes and stockings while she marked a pattern on the deerskin which one of
the young women brought from the camp, and then the whiteness of her feet, untanned by sun and wind, brought forth another volley of exclamation.

They begged her to pull up her sleeves and unfasten her
collar.

"All over birch bark!" they cried, and giggled again.

From then on there was no formality between them. They
watched her milk Laura and Daisy and drank the warm milk.
They shook their heads over the time she spent in keeping her
sheets white and fresh, when to their minds a bed of balsam
boughs and a bear-skin would do as well and make much less

work. They peered into her delicate mirror and laughed to see
their own broad faces there. They handled her cups and dishes,
sneezed at the smell of her dried herbs, wondered at the cats,
looked at everything and exclaimed over everything, but did no
harm to anything.

For well over a week the winds held from the southwest, hot
and dry, fine weather for haying, but wearying for flesh and
blood. Still the women worked on uncomplaining, and at dusk
they would beg Margaret to sing to her harp, which was a never-
failing wonder to them. It seemed strange and beautiful to the
girl to sit in the falling dusk, with the light of the fire moving
faintly on the walls, and sing the old ballads of another world
while the Indian women sat motionless on the floor watching
from dark pensive faces.

> "There were twa sisters in a bower,
>   Binnorie, O, Binnorie;
> There cam' a knight to be their wooer,
>   By the bonny milldams o' Binnorie.
>
> He courted the eldest wi' glove and ring,
>   Binnorie, O, Binnorie;
> But he lo'ed the youngest, a-boon a' thing—
>   By the bonny milldams o' Binnorie."

What went on in those shadowy minds? Margaret wondered,
as she sang. What did they understand of love as the Scotch had
sung it? But whether they were moved by the very strangeness,
or by the haunting sadness of the tune, or by Margaret's hands
plucking the strings, they called for the ballad again and again.
They would have listened until late in the night if at last
Molly Molasses had not risen from her seat on a drawer pulled
out from the chest—she always refused a chair—and wakened
the others from their dream, saying that Margaret must rest,
and in a moment more they would fade into the dusk and
Margaret would be left once more to her solitary housekeeping,

watched now only by the attentive eyes of the hounds and Chloe and the green-eyed kitten.

It was a curious and happy time for Margaret, a period of truce with the forest, when she went as silently as the Indian women in her new moccasins decorated with strawberries of dyed porcupine quills. Molly had refused all payment for them except a single penny which she added to a store, kept in a doeskin pouch worn about her neck, apparently as a charm.

"I take out penny," she exclaimed. "I see who gave it. See him big. What him doing. Him well, him sick. I see everything."

The Indian men never appeared until after the last armful of hay had been carried into the loft of the barn, but then Captain Bob and two or three of the younger men suddenly took form, carrying a haunch of venison, which the women roasted over an outdoor fire, while Margaret, weary, but at ease now for the stock during the coming winter, made johnnycake and opened her preserves with a reckless hand.

When the little feast was over, the girl, standing apart with Captain Bob, tried to give him her purse with the cheese money, but the old man looked at her kindly from his brown wrinkles, and refused to take it.

"I can't do anything for you in return, Captain Bob," she said.

He touched his grandson with his hand.

"Your father turned back his feet from death," he answered simply.

For a time Margaret was able to forget all dread and live in the summer. She lived, however, like the bee, full of her labors, and not like the grasshopper, churring and skipping in the stubble. There was much to be done, but nothing to be faced, at least not now, at least not while the leaves were green and the game plentiful, at least not during these days that were still so warm, when the birds were still busy with their final broods, and had not yet thought of the south.

One August day Margaret paddled across the pond with the Indian women to gather blueberries and raspberries on the

moors that covered the low hills. At noon she happened to find
herself alone with Molly Molasses, sitting in the shade of a rock.
Their birch-bark baskets were heaped with berries and the wind-
less air smelled heavily of the sweet fern growing all about them.
It was a sleepy time. Drowsily, Margaret watched a sea gull veering over the wigwams at the pond's edge, and across its barely
ruffled waters her eyes lingered with pleasure on the low, strong
outlines of her father's cabin, and caught the slow motion of the
cows feeding in the pasture beyond it, with Daisy's bright yellow
and white plainly visible among the green of grass and alders.

Drowsy with warmth and the sweetness of the air and the
buzz and hum of insects, Margaret leaned back against the
stone, her eyelids lowered, scarcely conscious of the old Indian
woman near her. She could never remember afterwards what
it was that suddenly gave her a feeling of something about to
happen, of a mysterious force approaching. Perhaps it came
from the great shadow swinging along the ferns and then stopping as though something hung poised above them; perhaps
it was some change in Molly Molasses that Margaret felt. Her
sleepiness vanished; tense and silent she turned to see what her
companion was doing.

Molly Molasses had risen to her feet and moved swiftly to
a low rock that rose a little out of the fern. There she stood,
turning her face upward into the full heat of the sunlight. She
was chanting, not very loud, and above her an eagle circled on
wide straight wings, his white head and tail now in shadow, now
dazzlingly bright in the sun as he veered, lazily, mightily, circling
nearer and nearer about the head of the chanting squaw.

Margaret watched breathlessly, with the myths of the olden
times vaguely stirring in her mind, of young Ganymede borne
away from the meadows by the eagle to be the cupbearer of the
gods, and of Odin throned among the storm clouds with eagles
at his feet. This great bird, too, had the air of being a messenger
from the heights of heaven, so proudly and serenely did he float
in the burning air, and Molly Molasses was transfigured in the

communion she held with the creature of the sky. No longer was she a rather pathetic old woman in a shapeless calico dress and beaded moccasins, with a dirty sun-bonnet hanging down her back. Now her clothes became no more than coverings to her. Some power surged up through her out of the earth to meet the power circling above her in the air. Feet planted firmly on the rock, body vigorous and straight against the blue, face for the time grown young again in the ecstasy of the moment and the light flooding down upon it, Molly stood chanting upward to the veering bird above her, whose dark wings' stretch measured not less than the height of a tall man.

Then, as the girl watched the great magic before her, the eagle drifted away as silently as he had appeared and the power went out of the air, and left only a summer hillslope, and an old squaw who had ceased her chanting and stood with bowed head and hands a little spread, palms downward, as though she were returning back to the earth the force which the earth had lent her.

Margaret again grew aware of dress and bonnet, of wrinkles and dulling hair. Once more it was Molly Molasses who stood before her, and reached down to pick up a single white feather caught in the sweet fern at her feet. She put it thoughtfully into the pouch at her neck where she carried her charms, muttering to herself something which the girl took to be incantations, and then returned to the shadow where they had been sitting with their berry baskets. Margaret noticed that she walked almost as though she had been blinded by the sun's glare, and when the girl spoke to her she did not seem to hear, but sat like a stunned person, whose spirit has been driven out of the body, and must be given time once more to return and take up its seat among the members.

So Margaret waited. This explained, then, why old Molly was always treated with such respect by the younger squaws and even by the men. She had power of some sort over the elements; she was in some mysterious relation to the unseen forces. Margaret, who loved beauty and order and courage, who loved people and birds and flowers, had thought always of any communication with the unknown as a thing of dark shadows, filled with the secrecy of Endor and deep voices rising from the ground. But this had taken place in the fullest sunlight, in an ecstasy of fragrant air and hot calm.

"This is what Father meant when he said that life had many mysteries and interplays of forces of which we never guess," she thought. And although the thing was new to her mind, she did not try to belittle or explain away what she had seen. Her thought stretched to encompass this new beauty of an old woman and a bird. She would never look eastward from her cabin windows again without thinking of this noonday hillslope and of the shadow of wings moving in a ring about Molly Molasses.

She started, surprised by the old woman's voice.

"It is good," she said, "eagle coming when you here."

RECOLLECTIONS OF GOVERNOR
JOHN NEPTUNE OF THE PENOBSCOTS

by

GIDEON T. RIDLON, SR.

When I was a lad, possibly 10 years of age, a family of the Penobscot Indians came to the high tableland above the Saco and were encamped for several weeks in an oak grove known as Boulter's Woods. The visit of these descendants of the ancient Abenakis proved a great local attraction and the camp was the nucleus around which the palefaces assembled from the near by village and outlying farms for miles around.

The family consisted of Lieutenant Governor John Neptune, one of the most intelligent and distinguished of the Maine

From the *Portland Sunday Telegram* (Portland, Maine, 1910).

Indians, and his two daughters, mighty big women, Mrs. Newell and Mrs. Mitchell, both of them young, also a papoose, Johnny Mitchell, then a little fellow who insisted upon running away after the white people who visited the encampment. Possibly there were others of the tribe present, Newell Lyon and some of the oldest sons of Mrs. Newell, but I am not sure about the number.

"Governor Neptune," as he was called, was the most picturesque and attractive figure in the group. He was a person of commanding presence, being of good stature and of enormous circumference at the equatorial region. He was probably a full blooded Indian and of the genuine "copper color" so characteristic of the American aborigines.

Recollections of this remarkable man as I was so early impressed by his personality have inspired me to institute such research as might disclose some authentic record of his long life, amongst the books and documents of the Maine Historical Society, and my inquiry was rewarded by some very interesting references to his career; but I was surprised to find so little concerning the remnant of this race so long inhabiting our State.

I found mention of Lieutenant Governor John Neptune in connection with negotiations by the Massachusetts government, through commissioners, for the relinquishment by the Indians at Old Town of an extensive territory of their eastern lands, a policy of the white men ever since their settlement in America, when he sat in the council with other chiefs of his tribe to hear what the representatives of the General Court had to say and to offer for the Indian's concession. In the report of this meeting at the village on Old Town Island, John Neptune's portraiture represents him as wearing a scarlet coat, or robe, ornamented with silver brooches and beads, and that he was "a chief of commanding figure, of great dignity of manners and extensive influence among his tribe." Also as "a noble looking son of the forest." At this council Orsong Neptune and Captain

Francis, who was a remarkably intelligent and well informed Indian, were the speakers. As peace offerings the commissioners presented the chiefs with pieces of scarlet broadcloth and silver breast-plates, upon which were engraved the arms of the State of Maine, and these tokens of the good will (?) of the white man's government "were received with great exhibitions of pleasure."

On the 19th of September, 1816, John Neptune was publicly and ceremonially inducted into office as lieutenant governor of the Penobscot tribe of Indians according to their ancient custom. The chiefs and twenty Indians from the Passamaquoddy and St. John tribes were present to assist, all dressed in Indian fashion, neat and becoming. A great tent had been pitched. Neptune and the chiefs had seats near the door upon a platform. He was clad in a coat of scarlet broadcloth with silver brooches, collars, arm clasps, jewels and other ornaments. Upon a square blue cloth was exhibited a crescent medal twice the size of a dollar, emblematically inscribed with curious devices and suspended by a ribbon a yard in length, knotted at the ends. The spectators admitted were seated upon a platform covered with blankets. After the presentation of belts of wampum and a short address by the sagamore, he advanced and suspended the medal as the badge of investiture about John Neptune's neck.

These ceremonies were followed by cordial salutations expressive of great friendship and loyalty, a dance in which the squaws took part and a feast at which two fat oxen and a variety of vegetables were served, and all present, Indians and whites, were invited to partake. These services and festivities consumed more than three hours. The office was to be holden for life, and henceforth John Neptune was known as "Governor Neptune."

Let me now present Governor Neptune as I saw and heard him. He was squatting upon his feet, "Indian fashion," under a widespreading oak, in a pile of basket-stuff and shavings, smoking his pipe as he skilfully shaped the piece of ash he was

dressing with his bent knife, holding it upon his knee. He was clad in a loose frock and breeches. His black hair was long and fell heavily upon his broad shoulders. His upper garment was clasped at the neck by a large silver brooch. Mrs. Newell and Mrs. Mitchell, his daughters, were sitting near him weaving the bright colored ribbons of wood into baskets, merrily chatting and laughing, probably at the expense of their white visitors, while papoose Johnny, was at play near by.

Now, John Neptune was a great hunter and a good storyteller, and he fairly revelled in his dramatic descriptions of some of his adventures with wild beasts in the north woods of Maine. I recall with vividness the story of his encounter with an enormous black bear upon a branch of the Penobscot while on one of his hunting excursions. He said: "Me young man then, an' mighty strong." He was passing down the stream early in the morning, drifting noiselessly down the current in his canoe under the shadow of the overhanging hemlocks when he was startled by a growl and saw a big bear upon the bank. He seems to have been without any firearm for he paddled to the shore and attacked bruin with his tomahawk. As he began his account of this adventure, he was busy with his knife, but becoming very much excited as he proceeded, and springing to his feet, he seized a small axe that lay near to demonstrate with. He said: "When me go near him the mighty big bear he stand up an' snap his teeth an' snort an' come at me; so I keep off so he no reach me with his claws to hug; but when he get pretty near I put the hatchet in between his ears an' it come out down here"; meanwhile demonstrating with the axe and with his left hand upon his head and at his throat.

I shall never forget the appearance of the old chief as he described this fight with the bear. His looks and movements startled me. His face became animated, his black eyes shot fire and his whole form became visibly agitated as he lived over again this dangerous adventure with the savage beast; and he wielded his axe with the vehemence of one in some desperate struggle. I was young then, a mere lad, and my impressionable mind caught the dramatic picture with ineffaceable tenacity, and there it has remained for half a century, sharp and clear.

12. Katahdin: "The Forest Sinai of the Abenakis"

HENRY THOREAU CLIMBS THE MOUNTAIN

[1846]

by

HENRY D. THOREAU

IN THE night I dreamed of trout-fishing; and, when at length I awoke, it seemed a fable that this painted fish swam there so near my couch, and rose to our hooks the last evening, and I doubted if I had not dreamed it all. So I arose before dawn to test its truth, while my companions were still sleeping. There stood Ktaadn with distinct and cloudless outline in the moonlight; and the rippling of the rapids was the only sound to break the stillness. Standing on the shore, I once more cast my line into the stream, and found the dream to be real and the fable true. The speckled trout and silvery roach, like flying-fish, sped swiftly through the moonlight air, describing bright arcs on the dark side of Ktaadn, until moonlight, now fading into daylight, brought satiety to my mind, and the minds of my companions, who had joined me.

By six o'clock, having mounted our packs and a good blanket-

From *The Maine Woods* by Henry D. Thoreau (Ticknor & Fields: Boston, 1864).

ful of trout, ready dressed, and swung up such baggage and provision as we wished to leave behind upon the tops of saplings, to be out of the reach of bears, we started for the summit of the mountain, distant, as Uncle George said the boatmen called it, about four miles, but as I judged, and as it proved, nearer fourteen. He had never been any nearer the mountain than this, and there was not the slightest trace of man to guide us farther in this direction. At first, pushing a few rods up the Aboljacknagesic, or "open-land stream," we fastened our batteau to a tree, and traveled up the north side, through burnt lands, now partially overgrown with young aspens and other shrubbery; but soon, recrossing this stream, where it was about fifty or sixty feet wide, upon a jam of logs and rocks,—and you could cross it by this means almost anywhere,—we struck at once for the highest peak, over a mile or more of comparatively open land, still very gradually ascending the while. Here it fell to my lot, as the oldest mountain-climber, to take the lead. So, scanning the woody side of the mountain, which lay still at an indefinite distance, stretched out some seven or eight miles in length before us, we determined to steer directly for the base of the highest peak, leaving a large slide, by which, as I have since learned, some of our predecessors ascended, on our left. This course would lead us parallel to a dark seam in the forest, which marked the bed of a torrent, and over a slight spur, which extended southward from the main mountain, from whose bare summit we could get an outlook over the country, and climb directly up the peak, which would then be close at hand. Seen from this point, a bare ridge at the extremity of the open land, Ktaadn presented a different aspect from any mountain I have seen, there being a greater proportion of naked rock rising abruptly from the forest; and we looked up at this blue barrier as if it were some fragment of a wall which anciently bounded the earth in that direction. Setting the compass for a northeast course, which was the bearing of the southern base of the highest peak, we were soon buried in the woods.

We soon began to meet with traces of bears and moose, and those of rabbits were everywhere visible. The tracks of moose, more or less recent, to speak literally, covered every square rod on the sides of the mountain; and these ainmals are probably more numerous there now than ever before, being driven into this wilderness, from all sides, by the settlements. The track of a full-grown moose is like that of a cow, or larger, and of the young, like that of a calf. Sometimes we found ourselves traveling in faint paths, which they had made, like cow-paths in the woods, only far more indistinct, being rather openings, affording imperfect vistas through the dense underwood, than trodden paths; and everywhere the twigs had been browsed by them, clipped as smoothly as if by a knife. The bark of trees was stripped up by them to the height of eight or nine feet, in long, narrow strips, an inch wide, still showing the distinct marks of their teeth. We expected nothing less than to meet a herd of them every moment, and our Nimrod held his shooting-iron in readiness; but we did not go out of our way to look for them, and, though numerous, they are so wary that the unskillful hunter might range the forest a long time before he could get sight of one. They are sometimes dangerous to encounter, and will not turn out for the hunter, but furiously rush upon him and trample him to death, unless he is lucky enough to avoid them by dodging round a tree. The largest are nearly as large as a horse, and weigh sometimes one thousand pounds; and it is said that they can step over a five-foot gate in their ordinary walk. They are described as exceedingly awkward-looking animals, with their long legs and short bodies, making a ludicrous figure when in full run, but making great headway, nevertheless. It seemed a mystery to us how they could thread these woods, which it required all our suppleness to accomplish,—climbing, stooping, and winding, alternately. They are said to drop their long and branching horns, which usually spread five or six feet, on their backs, and make their way easily by the weight of their bodies. Our boatmen said, but I know not with how much truth, that their horns are apt to be gnawed away by vermin while they sleep. Their flesh, which is more like beef than venison, is common in Bangor market.

We had proceeded on thus seven or eight miles, till about noon, with frequent pauses to refresh the weary ones, crossing a considerable mountain stream, which we conjectured to be Murch Brook, at whose mouth we had camped, all the time in woods, without having once seen the summit, and rising very gradually, when the boatmen beginning to despair a little, and fearing that we were leaving the mountain on one side of us, for they had not entire faith in the compass, McCauslin climbed a tree, from the top of which he could see the peak, when it appeared that we had not swerved from a right line, the compass down below still ranging with his arm, which pointed to the summit. By the side of a cool mountain rill, amid the woods, where the water began to partake of the purity and transparency of the air, we stopped to cook some of our fishes, which we had brought thus far in order to save our hard-bread and pork, in the use of which we had put ourselves on short allowance. We soon had a fire blazing, and stood around it, under the damp and sombre forest of firs and birches, each with a sharpened stick, three or four feet in length, upon which he had spitted his trout, or roach, previously well gashed and salted, our sticks radiating like the spokes of a wheel from one centre, and each crowding his particular fish into the most desirable exposure, not with the truest regard always to his neighbor's rights. Thus we regaled ourselves, drinking meanwhile at the spring, till one man's pack, at least, was considerably lightened, when we again took up our line of march.

At length we reached an elevation sufficiently bare to afford a view of the summit, still distant and blue, almost as if retreating from us. A torrent, which proved to be the same we had crossed, was seen tumbling down in front, literally from out of the clouds. But this glimpse at our whereabouts was soon lost, and we were buried in the woods again. The wood was chiefly yellow birch, spruce, fir, mountain-ash, or round-wood, as the Maine people call it, and moose-wood. It was the worst kind of traveling; sometimes like the densest scrub oak patches with us. The cornel, or bunch-berries, were very abundant, as well as Solomon's-seal and moose-berries. Blueberries were distributed along our whole route; and in one place the bushes were drooping with the weight of the fruit, still as fresh as ever. It was the 7th of September. Such patches afforded a grateful repast, and served to bait the tired party forward. When any lagged behind, the cry of "blueberries" was most effectual to bring them up. Even at this elevation we passed through a moose-yard, formed by a large flat rock, four or five rods square, where they tread down the snow in winter. At length, fearing that if we held the direct course to the summit, we should not find any water near our camping-ground, we gradually swerved to the west, till, at four o'clock, we struck again the torrent which I have mentioned, and here, in view of the summit, the weary party decided to camp that night.

While my companions were seeking a suitable spot for this purpose, I improved the little daylight that was left in climbing the mountain alone. We were in a deep and narrow ravine, sloping up to the clouds, at an angle of nearly forty-five degrees, and hemmed in by walls of rock, which were at first covered with low trees, then with impenetrable thickets of scraggy birches and spruce trees, and with moss, but at last bare of all vegetation but lichens, and almost continually draped in clouds. Following up the course of the torrent which occupied this,—and I mean to lay some emphasis on this word up,—pulling myself up by the side of perpendicular falls of twenty or thirty feet, by the roots of firs and birches, and then, perhaps, walking a level rod or two in the thin stream, for it took up the whole road, ascending by huge steps, as it were, a giant's stairway, down which a river flowed, I had soon cleared the trees, and paused on the successive shelves, to look back over the country. The torrent was from fifteen to thirty feet wide, without a tributary, and seemingly not diminishing in breadth as I advanced; but still it came rushing and roaring down, with a copious tide, over and amidst masses of bare rock, from the very clouds, as though a waterspout had just burst over the mountain. Leaving this at last, I began to work my way, scarcely less arduous than Satan's anciently through Chaos, up the nearest though not the highest peak, at first scrambling on all fours over the tops of ancient black spruce trees (Abies nigra), old as the flood, from two to ten or twelve feet in height, their tops flat and spreading, and their foliage blue, and nipped with cold, as if for centuries they had ceased growing upward against the bleak sky, the solid cold. I walked some good rods erect upon the tops of these trees, which were overgrown with moss and mountain cranberries. It seemed that in the course of time they had filled up the intervals between the huge rocks, and the cold wind had uniformly leveled all over. Here the principle of vegetation was hard put to it. There was apparently a belt of this kind running quite round the mountain, though, perhaps, nowhere so remarkable as here. Once, slumping through, I looked down ten feet, into a dark and cavernous region, and saw the stem of a spruce, on whose top I stood, as on a mass of coarse basketwork, fully nine inches in diameter at the ground. These holes were bears' dens, and the bears were even then at home. This was the sort of garden I made my way over, for an eighth of a mile, at the risk, it is true, of treading on some of the plants, not seeing any path through it,—certainly the most treacherous and porous country I ever traveled.

> "Nigh foundered on he fares,
>   Treading the crude consistence, half on foot,
>   Half flying,"

But nothing could exceed the toughness of the twigs,—not one snapped under my weight, for they had slowly grown. Having slumped, scrambled, rolled, bounced, and walked, by turns, over this scraggy country, I arrived upon a side-hill, or rather side-mountain, where rocks, gray, silent rocks, were the flocks and herds that pastured, chewing a rocky cud at sunset. They looked at me with hard gray eyes, without a bleat or a low. This brought me to the skirt of a cloud, and bounded my walk that night. But I had already seen that Maine country when I turned about, waving, flowing, rippling, down below.

When I returned to my companions, they had selected a camping-ground on the torrent's edge, and were resting on the ground; one was on the sick list, rolled in a blanket, on a damp shelf of rock. It was a savage and dreary scenery enough, so wildly rough, that they looked long to find a level and open space for the tent. We could not well camp higher, for want of fuel; and the trees here seemed so evergreen and sappy, that we almost doubted if they would acknowledge the influence of fire; but fire prevailed at last, and blazed here, too, like a good citizen of the world. Even at this height we met with frequent traces of moose, as well as of bears. As here was no cedar, we made our bed of coarser feathered spruce; but at any rate the feathers were plucked from the live tree. It was, perhaps, even a more grand and desolate place for a night's lodging than the summit would have been, being in the neighborhood of those wild trees, and of the torrent. Some more aerial and finer-spirited winds rushed and roared through the ravine all night, from time to time arousing our fire, and dispersing the embers about. It was as if we lay in the very nest of a young whirlwind. At midnight, one of my bedfellows, being startled in his dreams by the sudden blazing up to its top of a fir tree, whose green boughs were dried by the heat, sprang up, with a cry, from his bed, thinking the world on fire, and drew the whole camp after him.

In the morning, after whetting our appetite on some raw pork, a wafer of hard-bread, and a dipper of condensed cloud or waterspout, we all together began to make our way up the falls, which I have described; this time choosing the right hand, or highest peak, which was not the one I had approached before. But soon my companions were lost to my sight behind the mountain ridge in my rear, which still seemed ever retreating before me, and I climbed alone over huge rocks, loosely poised, a mile or more, still edging toward the clouds; for though the day was clear elsewhere, the summit was concealed by mist. The mountain seemed a vast aggregation of loose rocks, as if some time it had rained rocks, and they lay as they fell on the mountain sides, nowhere fairly at rest, but leaning on each other, all rocking stones, with cavities between, but scarcely any soil or smoother shelf. They were the raw materials of a planet dropped from an unseen quarry, which the vast chemistry of nature would anon work up, or work down, into the smiling and verdant plains and valleys of earth. This was an undone extremity of the globe; as in lignite we see coal in the process of formation.

At length I entered within the skirts of the cloud which seemed forever drifting over the summit, and yet would never be gone, but was generated out of that pure air as fast as it flowed away; and when, a quarter of a mile farther, I reached the summit of the ridge, which those who have seen it in clearer weather say is about five miles long, and contains a thousand acres of table-land, I was deep within the hostile ranks of clouds, and all objects were obscured by them. Now the wind would blow me out a yard of clear sunlight, wherein I stood; then a gray, dawning light was all it could accomplish, the cloud-line ever rising and falling with the wind's intensity. Sometimes it seemed as if the summit would be cleared in a few moments, and smile in sunshine; but what was gained on one side was lost on another. It was like sitting in a chimney and waiting for the smoke to blow away. It was, in fact, a cloud-factory,—these were the cloudworks, and the wind turned them off done from the cool, bare rocks. Occasionally, when the windy columns broke in to me, I caught sight of a dark, damp crag to the right or left; the mist driving ceaselessly between it and me. It reminded me of the creations of the old epic and dramatic poets, of Atlas, Vulcan, the Cyclops, and Prometheus. Such was Caucasus and the rock where Prometheus was bound. Aeschylus had no doubt visited such scenery as this. It was vast, Titanic, and such as man never inhabits. Some part of the beholder, even some vital part, seems to escape through the loose grating of his ribs as he ascends. He is more lone than you can imagine. There is less of substantial thought and fair understanding in him than in the plains where men inhabit. His reason is dispersed and shadowy, more thin and subtile, like the air. Vast, Titanic, inhuman Nature has got him at disadvantage, caught him alone, and pilfers him of some of his divine faculty. She does not smile on him as in the plains. She seems to say sternly, Why came ye here before your time? This ground is not prepared for you. Is it not enough that I smile in the valleys? I have never made this soil for thy feet, this air for thy breathing, these rocks for thy neighbors. I cannot pity nor fondle thee here, but forever relentlessly drive thee hence to where I am kind. Why seek me where I have not called thee, and then complain because you find me but a stepmother? Shouldst thou freeze or starve, or shudder thy life away, here is no shrine, nor altar, nor any access to my ear.

> "Chaos and ancient Night, I come no spy
> With purpose to explore or to disturb
> The secrets of your realm, but . . .
> .   .   .   .   .   .   as my way
> Lies through your spacious empire up to light."

The tops of mountains are among the unfinished parts of the globe, whither it is a slight insult to the gods to climb and pry into their secrets, and try their effect on our humanity. Only daring and insolent men, perchance, go there. Simple races, as savages, do not climb mountains,—their tops are sacred and mysterious tracts never visited by them. Pomola is always angry with those who climb to the summit of Ktaadn.

According to Jackson, who, in his capacity of geological surveyor of the State, has accurately measured it, the altitude of Ktaadn is 5300 feet, or a little more than one mile above the level of the sea, and he adds, "It is then evidently the highest point in the State of Maine, and is the most abrupt granite mountain in New England." The peculiarities of that spacious table-land on which I was standing, as well as the remarkable semicircular precipice or basin on the eastern side, were all concealed by the mist. I had brought my whole pack to the top, not knowing but I should have to make my descent to the river, and possibly to the settled portion of the State alone, and by some other route, and wishing to have a complete outfit with me. But at length fearing that my companions would be anxious to reach the river before night, and knowing that the clouds might rest on the mountain for days, I was compelled to descend. Occasionally, as I came down, the wind would blow me a vista open, through which I could see the country eastward, boundless forests, and lakes, and streams, gleaming in the sun, some of them emptying into the East Branch. There were also new mountains in sight in that direction. Now and then some small bird of the sparrow family would flit away before me, unable to command its course, like a fragment of the gray rock blown off by the wind.

I found my companions where I had left them, on the side of the peak, gathering the mountain cranberries, which filled every crevice between the rocks, together with blueberries, which had a spicier flavor the higher up they grew, but were not the less agreeable to our palates. When the country is settled, and roads are made, these cranberries will perhaps become an article of commerce. From this elevation, just on the skirts of the clouds, we could overlook the country, west and south, for a hundred miles. There it was, the state of Maine, which we had seen on the map, but not much like that,—immeasurable forest for the sun to shine on, that eastern stuff we hear of in Massachusetts. No clearing, no house. It did not look as if a solitary traveler had cut so much as a walking-stick there. Countless lakes,— Moosehead in the southwest, forty miles long by ten wide, like a gleaming silver platter at the end of the table; Chesuncook, eighteen long by three wide, without an island; Millinocket, on the south, with its hundred islands; and a hundred others without a name; and mountains, also whose names, for the most part, are known only to the Indians. The forest looked like a firm grass sward, and the effect of these lakes in its midst has been well compared, by one who has since visited this same spot, to that of a "mirror broken into a thousand fragments, and wildly scattered over the grass, reflecting the full blaze of the sun." It was a large farm for somebody, when cleared. According to the Gazetteer, which was printed before the boundary question was settled, this single Penobscot County, in which we were, was larger than the whole State of Vermont, with its fourteen counties; and this was only a part of the wild lands of Maine. We are concerned now, however, about natural, not political limits. We were about eighty miles, as the bird flies, from Bangor, or one hundred and fifteen, as we had ridden, and walked, and paddled. We had to console ourselves with the reflection that this view was probably as good as that from the peak, as far as it went; and what were a mountain without its attendant clouds and mists? Like ourselves, neither Bailey nor Jackson had obtained a clear view from the summit.

Setting out on our return to the river, still at an early hour in the day, we decided to follow the course of the torrent, which we supposed to be Murch Brook, as long as it would not lead us too far out of our way.

THE LEGEND OF PAMOLA

by

REV. EUGENE VETROMILE

The Penobscot Indians believed that an evil spirit, called Pamola (he curses on the mountain)—resided, during the summer season, on the top of Mount Katahdin—(the greatest of mountains.) They offered sacrifices to him to appease him, so that he should not curse them, or otherwise injure them. Although they hunted and fished in the woods and lakes around Mount Katahdin, yet they never attempted to go on the top of that mountain, in the assurance that they would never be able to return from that place, but be either killed or devoured by the evil spirit Pamola. They pretended to have seen this spirit on the top of the mountain on several occasions while hunting or fishing around it. It was but till late, that they have attempted to ascend that mountain. It is not long since that a party of white people desired to go on the top of Mount Katahdin, and took some Indians to accompany them as guides. The Indians escorted them to the foot of the mountain, but they refused to go further, fearing to be either killed or devoured by Pamola. No persuasion from the party could induce them to proceed further; on the contrary, the Indians tried to dissuade the party from ascending the mountain, speak to them of this evil spirit, and how many Indians had been killed or devoured by him, and that no man ever returned, who dared to go on Mount Katahdin. The Indians, however, were prevailed upon to wait for the descent of the party, who, in spite of the remonstrance of the Indians, ascended the mountain by themselves, without guides. They

From *The Abenakis and Their History* by Rev. Eugene Vetromile (James B. Kirker: New York, 1866).

were quite surprised to see the party back, as they entertained no hope of their return, believing with certainty that they had been killed or devoured by Pamola.

It would not be improper to give a brief episode of the Indian tradition concerning this evil spirit Pamola, residing upon Mount Katahdin—a mountain famous amongst the Indians of Maine—a tradition, which is believed by the Indians unto this very day. They relate that several hundred years ago, while a Penobscot Indian was encamped eastward of Mount Katahdin in the autumn hunting season, a severe and unexpected fall of snow covered the whole land to the depth of several feet. Being unprovided with snow shoes, he found himself unable to return home. After remaining several days in the camp, blocked up with drifts of snow, and seeing no means of escape, he thought that he was doomed to perish; hence, as it were through despair, he called with loud voice on Pamola for several times. Finally, Pamola made his appearance on the top of the mountain. The Indian took courage, and offered to him a sacrifice of oil and fat, which he poured and consumed upon burning coals out of the camp. As the smoke was ascending, Pamola was descending. The sacrifice was consumed when this spirit got only half way down the mountain. Here the Indian took more oil and fat, and repeated the sacrifice, till Pamola arrived at the camp, and the Indian welcomed him, saying: "You are welcome, partner." Pamola replied: "You have done well to call me partner; because you have called me by that name, you are saved, otherwise you would have been killed by me. No Indian has ever called on me and lived, having always been devoured by me. Now I will take you on the mountain, and you shall be happy with me." Pamola put the Indian on his shoulders, bid him close the eyes, and in few moments, with a noise like the whistling of a powerful wind, they were inside of the mountain. The Indian describes the interior of Mount Katahdin as containing a good, comfortable wigwam, furnished with abundance of venison, and with all the luxuries of life, and that Pamola had wife and children living in the mountain. Pamola gave him his daughter to wife, and told him that after one year he could return to his friends on the Penobscot, and that he might go back to the mountain to see his wife any time he pleased, and remain as long as he wished. He was warned that he could not marry again, but if he should marry again, he would be at once transported to Mount Katahdin, with no hope of ever more going out of it. After one year the Indian returned to Oldtown and related all that had happened to him in Mount Katahdin, and the circumstances through which he got into it. The Indians persuaded him to marry again, which he at first refused, but they at last prevailed on him to marry, but the morning after his marriage, he disappeared, and nothing more was heard of him; they felt sure that he had been taken by Pamola into Mount Katahdin, as he had told them.

This fact filled the Indians with consternation, and they conceived a great fear for this evil spirit, yet a young Indian woman constantly persisted in refusing to believe even in the existence of Pamola, unless she saw him with her own eyes. It happened one day, that while she was on the shores of the lake Amboctictus,[1] Pamola appeared to her and reproached her with her incredulity. He took her by force, put her on his shoulders, and after a few moments' flight, with a great whistling of wind, they were in the interior of the mountain. There she remained for one year, and was well treated, but was got with child by Pamola. A few months before her confinement, Pamola told her to go back to her relations, saying that the child that was to be born of her would be great, and would perform such wonders as to amaze the nation. He would have the power to kill any person or animal by simply pointing out at the object with the fore finger of his right hand. Hence, that the child was to be watched very closely till the age of manhood, because many evils might follow from that power. But when the child grew

---

[1] Amboctictus is a lake near Mount Katahdin, on the southwest side. It appears that this lake was consecrated to Pamola.

up he would save his own nation from the hands of its enemies, and would confer many benefits to the people. If she should be in need of any assistance, she had nothing to do but to call on Pamola in any place she might be, and he would appear to her. He warned her not to marry again; because if she should marry again, both she and the child would at once be transported into Mount Katahdin for ever. He then put her on his shoulders in the same manner as he had done in taking her up to the mountain, and left her on the shore of the lake Amboctictus. She returned to Oldtown, where she related all that had happened to her, and also that she had seen, in the mountain, that Indian, of whom I have made mention above.

The child was born, and she took great care of him. She called several times on Pamola, who always made his appearance to her. When she wanted any venison, either into the woods or in the river, she had but to take the child, and holding his right hand, she stretched out his fore finger, and made it point out to a deer, or moose, and it at once fell dead. So, also, in a flock of ducks, she made the child's first finger single one out of the flock, which likewise fell dead. The child grew, and he was the admiration and pride of all.

It happened one day, that while he was standing at the door of the wigwam, he saw a friend of his mother coming. He announced it to her, and at the same time, with the first finger of his right hand, he pointed at him, and the man immediately dropped dead. This fact caused great consternation, not only in the mother of the child, but also in the entire tribe, who looked on him as a very dangerous subject among them. Everybody fled from his company, and even from his sight. The mother called on Pamola, and related to him what had happened, and also the fear and consternation in which she and the entire tribe were. Pamola told her that he had already warned her to watch the child, because the power conferred on the child might produce serious evils. He now advised her to keep the child altogether apart from society till the age of manhood, as he might be fatal with many others. The Indians wanted her to marry, but she refused on the ground of it being forbidden by Pamola, who was her husband, and in case of marriage, she and child both would be taken up Mount Katahdin. However, the Indians prevailed upon her, and she married, but in the evening of the marriage-day, while all the Indians were gathered together in dancing and feasting for the celebration of the marriage, both she and the child disappeared for ever.

This is, of course, a superstitious tale, made up by the prolific imagination of some Indians, yet we can perceive in it some vestiges of the fall of the first man, in having transgressed the command of God, and how it could be repaired only by God. We can also trace some ideas of the mystery of the Incarnation of the Son of God in the womb of the Blessed Virgin Mary, mixed with fables, superstitions, and pagan errors. The appearance of God to Moses in a burning bush upon Mount Horeb, may be glimpsed in Pamola appearing to the Indian on Mount Katahdin, and so forth; yet these are but conjectures.

13. Maine Winter

THE SNOWSTORM

by

LELAND HALL

HE HAD hardly closed the door behind him when he came back again.

"It's snowing," he said. "Look!" And he held out his arm for them to see the fine snowflakes caught in the wool of his sleeve.

His mother was still sitting up with Florence. Rufus had gone to bed.

"It's begun to snow, mother."

"I thought I heard the wind moaning, son. Is everything shut up good out to the barn?"

"I'll take a look round."

Florence went to the door and looked out after him. The lamp flared and smoked in the sudden wind.

"Heavens, May!" she said, "if it comes on bad however shall we get home?"

The door of Ad's room had been open all day to let in warmth from downstairs. His bed was made with white sheets, the first he had slept in since his absence, and his mother had thoroughly warmed a nightgown for him. Notwithstanding the long day and these comforts at the end of it, he could not go to sleep. The

---

Reprinted from *They Seldom Speak* by permission of the author, Leland Hall. (Harcourt, Brace & Co.: New York, 1936).

moaning of the wind rose to a shriller note, and sudden gusts shook the window in its frame and hurled snow like fine shot against the glass. Little by little the rattle of the window was muffled in a packing of snow. Through the repeated assaults of the gale and the shuddering of the house, the sound of Rufus's snoring came faintly and monotonously from another room. In the darkness of his own room Ad's open eyes found nothing to see; when he closed them the brightness of Carrie's face shone before him. However deep the snow fell, he could go easily to see her the next day on his new snowshoes. He was impatient for the night to pass. He wanted to talk to Carrie about the future, about how he could free himself from the routine of the stable and find a more active and varied work. There was the hauling for Ezra Sayles. He could have a talk with Carrie about that, several talks with her, since the snow would hold Rufus here two or three days more than he had planned. Ad felt that now, when he could not sleep, would have been a good time to talk with her; no doubt she would have lain awake with him and they could have planned together.

The bang of a door downstairs startled him from his reverie. It must be the kitchen door which the wind had burst from its feeble latch. He drew on a pair of socks and felt his way down the dark stair. His mother was before him in the kitchen with a lighted lamp. He made fast the door and bolted it, then swept up the snow which had blown in and threw it in the sink.

"No need for you to come down, Ad," she said. "I am used to looking out for the place."

"I hadn't gone to sleep, mother."

Ad closed the door to the stairway from which a cold draught blew.

"Have you kept the fire going, mother?" he asked, for a fire was in the stove and the kitchen was soon warm again.

"I've been out once or twice. I always have it on my mind. Sit down a minute; I'll warm you a glass of milk and that will make you sleep."

She was in her wrapper now, with Joe Ranco's fur-lined moccasins on her feet.

"Did the storm keep you awake, son?"

"No, mother. I was thinking."

"I was thinking, too. It's funny, but since your father died whenever the storms blow I feel he is safe out of it. When I was a girl and the storms blew, my mother and I tried not to think; now the howling wind makes me think of my own father. I see him on his ship as I never saw him before. And what were you thinking about, son?"

"About what's ahead, mother; about what I'm going to do."

"That's right and proper. You've done well till now. Your father would have been pleased, and I'm thankful every day for what you've done for me, though you're only a youngster. Yet you'll be twenty soon; I can hardly believe it. I had been married most a year at your age and Rufus was on the way. I keep wondering if you've found a nice girl in Eldridge, one you'd like to settle down with; but that's none of my business."

"Why should I settle down, mother?"

"It's just a need we all feel sooner or later. It's just natural. You don't want to be working for yourself all the time, or even for your mother. Then there's children; you'd be fond of children, son."

"Do you think I ought to get married, mother?"

"It's easier to start young."

"I wonder—I wonder," said Ad, "if that's what I was thinking about upstairs."

He drank half his warm milk.

"If the storm keeps up, Ruf can't get away for awhile, mother."

"We'll be cosy here, though I hope Florence won't worry about the children."

He drank the rest of his milk and looked at his mother. He could not say how she had changed. The white hair made a difference, even more difference now she was in the familiar wrapper than it had made when he had first seen her, with the dress and the beads round her neck. Her eyes were no longer brimful of something that had abounded in her.

"If I married would you come to live with us, mother?"

"No, son. You know that well."

"You don't lack for company here?"

"There's too many running in all day."

"Does—does Carrie come over to see you?"

"She's in and out like a swallow in the barn. She's a nice girl, with a will of her own and smarter than most, though she has a lot to learn, as it seems to me. But then, what young folks haven't?"

May picked up the glass her son had drunk from and rinsed it at the sink.

"See how the snow is piling on the windows," she said, "and see it blow in under the door."

She took a newspaper from the woodbox and folded it in narrow strips with which she stopped the crack under the door. Ad, preoccupied, put more wood in the stove and mechanically adjusted the draughts.

"It's most three o'clock," said his mother, "and it's Christmas day. Go to bed and sleep like a good boy. I've a token for you in the morning."

From his bed Ad heard the kitchen clock strike three. Rufus's snoring still came steadily through the noise of the storm. He drowsed away, half dreaming, not of Carrie and the bright look on her face, but of the little old trunk from which his mother had brought him curios to play with during his long illness, and of a string of wooden beads his grandfather had brought back from Mexico for May, his little daughter.

At six he awakened to hear Rufus descending the narrow stair into the kitchen. It was still black night and still the house shuddered in gusts of the wind. By the light of his lamp he saw that his window was completely banked with snow.

Down in the kitchen Rufus was pushing with all his might to force his feet into an old pair of his father's rubber boots.

"Jed will never get here this morning," he said, "and I might as well go out and get the milking done."

"No telling how it's drifted," said Ad. "Better let me go ahead on my snowshoes."

He took a lighted lantern and his snowshoes to the narrow porch outside the kitchen door. The snow had lodged against the railing and prevented high drifting before the door itself and the length of the porch; and kneeling in comparative shelter Ad attached his snowshoes by the light of the lantern. But just outside the porch a four-foot drift threw back the lantern light, and above it blew the stinging wind, with incessantly streaming volleys of snow cast from the invisible heavens or torn from the surface of the drift. When Ad, having managed to break into the drift, stood in his snowshoes on the top of it, the wind nearly wrenched the lantern from his hand. One way he could not hold his face against the storm; the other he looked into swirls as impenetrable as fog. The lantern lit but one step at a time.

Bearing to the left, he felt his way towards the walls of the buildings that must be there, and plodded along them past the closed barn door, which he would not venture to open by lantern light, to a smaller door which let into the cowshed; and here reaching below the level of the snow, found with his hand the hook which locked it. But he could not pull the door open against the snow; and leaving it locked, he fought his way back to the house, half bent against the wind.

"We'll have to wait till it's light, Ruf," he said. "No use now."

By seven there was a gray light out of doors. He got to the barn door and worked it open enough for him to get down through it into the barn. It was warmer than outside. One of Ruf's horses whinnied. The cows were undisturbed. At the back of the barn was a door giving into a work room, where, over the bench, he found the old pair of snowshoes his father had always hung there; and with these he fought his way back to the house again. The third time Rufus followed him, with a milk pail.

"Can you get the big cans out, Ad?"

"Guess so, Ruf."

He had to dig out the big cans from the stakes on which they had been set, but once he had got them free, driven by the wind they rolled over the snow before him.

Tranquil within the kitchen May prepared a breakfast for them; and after this had been cleared away, Florence stuffed the goose and sewed it up for the oven.

"Let's go for the pump, now," said Ad to his brother, and against the bitter odds of the storm they cleared the pump in the barnyard and managed to carry in water to the stock. They could not, however, open the hen-house door; and since the trap had been dropped before their run, it seemed for a while as if the shut-in fowls must go hungry. But Ad, to whom the storm sounded a challenge he could not for a moment let pass, remembered a skylight in the roof of the henhouse. He cleared this and dropped down feed for the creatures within.

At last, with nothing more at home to satisfy his restlessness, he set off across the field in the blinding rage of the snow and fought his way on his snowshoes to the Parkers'. The children saw his feet pass outside above the level of the window-sill, and ran from their toys in mixed fear and wonder to join their parents and Carrie in the kitchen.

"There's someone coming!" they cried.

Ad was not disappointed in Carrie's welcome. By day her eyes shone at him even brighter than by night, and she marvelled at his energy and his daring. But she had little time to talk with him now, and he sat in a chair and watched her busy with the cooking, while the two little girls sidled up to him and fingered his face.

There was a covered way from the Parkers' house to their barn and Andrew had not had to fight to get to his milking. But he had to lug water out from the kitchen.

Before he left Ad had a word with Carrie.

"Notice I've got your muffler on? Never felt the cold at all, and the snow couldn't get down my neck. Maybe I'll come over again this afternoon."

"Oh, I hope you will. It's awful being shut in the house all day, isn't it?"

"I can't stand it," Ad replied, and with a twinkle in his eyes: "Wait and see if I do this afternoon."

The fat goose Florence had brought was deliciously cooked. They had apple sauce with it, and potatoes, and mashed turnip; and afterwards a mince pie and cider to drink with it. The talk ran on family affairs. So it had always been in Ad's recollection; and though he felt near to his mother and believed she felt really nearer to him than to the older children, still when they talked thus he felt as if he did not belong to the family at all. And there was talk about Ad's having lent money to Spence, just as if it had not been Ad who had lent it, or Ad's money he had lent.

Ad was already back at the Parkers' in the early afternoon, and it was while he was there that the wind dropped and the dull clouds pushed off with their snow into the darkness of the east. For a moment before it set, the sun shone clear. A level rayless light lay on the still snow, half white, half blue in shadow over the country. Carrie stood at the window, and caught in the sunshine, seemed more to face the dawn than the even approach of night. Yet as Ad watched her, the shadow crept up across her breast, across her shoulders, across her face. Then only her hair gleamed.

"The storm is over," she said, "and you'll be going tomorrow."

"That depends on the roads," he said. "Perhaps we can't break through for a day or so."

"When will you be coming back?"

"I haven't gone yet," he said. "I thought I'd ask you something first. What do you say we get married?"

"When?"

"Next summer."

"I was so afraid you wouldn't ask me before you went back," she said.

With his arms tight round her, he knew he held a treasure worth more than a bit of fun; and he would not let go even when Annie called from the kitchen.

THE SOUND OF THE POND ICE

by

HENRY BESTON

Our house stands above a pond, a rolling slope of old fields leading down to the tumble and jumble of rocks which make the shore. We do not see the whole pond but only a kind of comfortable bay some two miles long and perhaps a mile or so across. To the south lies a country road, a wooded vale, and a great farm above on a hill; across and to the east are woods again and then a more rural scene of farms and open land. It is the north, and as I set down these words the whole country lies quiescent in the cup of winter's hand.

Last night, coming in from the barn, I stood awhile in the moonlight looking down towards the pond in winter solitude. Because this year winds have swept the surface clean of early snows, the light of the high and wintry moon glowed palely upwards again from a sombre, even a black fixity of ice. Nothing could have seemed more frozen to stone, more a part of universal silence.

From *Northern Farm, A Chronicle of Maine*, copyright, 1948, by the author, Henry Beston. Reprinted by permission of Rinehart & Company, Inc., publishers.

All about me, too, seemed still, field and faraway stand of pine lying frozen in the motionless air to the same moonlit absence of all sound. Had I paused but a moment and then closed the door behind me, I probably would have spoken of the silence of the night. But I lingered a longish while, and lingering found that the seeming stillness was but the interval between the shuddering, the mysterious outcrying of the frozen pond. For the pond was hollow with sound, as it is sometimes when the nights are bitter and the ice is free from snow.

It is the voice of solid ice one hears and not the wail and crash and goblin sighing of moving ice floes such as one hears on the wintry St. Lawrence below the Isle of Orleans. The sounds made by the pond are sounds of power moving in bondage, of force constrained within a force and going where it can. The ice is taking up, settling, expanding, and cracking across though there is not a sign of all this either from the hill above or from the shore.

What I first heard was a kind of abrupt, disembodied groan. It came from the pond . . . and from nowhere. An interval of silence followed, perhaps a half note or a full note long. Then across, again from below, again disembodied, a long, booming, and hollow utterance, and then again a groan.

Again and again came the sounds; the night was still yet never still. Curiously enough, I had heard nothing while busy in the barn. Now, I heard. Neither faint nor heavy-loud, yet each one distinct and audible, the murmurs rose and ended and began again in the night. Sometimes there was a sort of hollow oboe sound, and sometimes a groan with a delicate undertone of thunder.

As I stood listening to the ice below, I became aware that I was really listening to the whole pond. There are miles of ice to the north and a shore of coves and bays, and all this ice was eloquent under the moon. Now east, now west, now from some far inlet, now from the cove hidden in the pines, the pond cried out in its strange and hollow tongue.

The nearer sounds were, of course, the louder, but even those in the distance were strangely clear. And save for this sound of ice, there seemed no other sound in all the world.

Just as I turned to go in, there came from below one curious and sinister crack which ran off into a sound like the whine of a giant whip of steel lashed through the moonlit air.

My old friends and neighbors, Howard and Agnes Rollins, used to tell me that the ice often spoke and groaned before a big storm. I must watch the glass and the wind and the northeast.

THE WATERS OF EARLY SPRING

by

HENRY BESTON

It has always been our custom to take a little stroll before we put the house to bed, merely going to the gate and back when the nights are hostile with a bitterness of cold. Now that nights more mercifully human have come with the slow and dilatory spring, we go beyond the gate for perhaps a quarter or even half a mile, walking with miry feet down the farm road and through a sound of many waters.

Tonight under a faintly hazy sky and through a light wind one can feel but not hear, the winter is flowing downhill towards the still frozen and imprisoned pond. Out of the forests and the uplands a skein of rills is pouring, the small streams now seeking their ancient courses, now following an hour's new runnel along the darkness of a wall.

So heavy is the hayfield soil, and so matted down with living roots below and thick dead grass above, that little earth seems to be lost anywhere, and for the moment there is no runnel trying to make its way across ploughed land. But I have had my troubles in the past.

If the opening music of the northern year begins with a first trumpet call of the return of light, and the return of warmth is the second great flourish from the air, the unsealing of the waters of earth is certainly the third. As we walked tonight in a darkness from which a young moon had only just withdrawn, the earth everywhere, like something talking to itself, murmured and even sang with its living waters and its living streams.

Between us and the gate, a torrent as from an over-flowing spring, half-blocked by a culvert heaved by frost, chided about our feet, and making another and smaller sound found its way downhill again in the night. Farther on, where woods close in to one side and the ground is stony and uneven, there tinkled out of the tree shapes and the gloom a sound of tiny cascades falling with incessant flow into a pool together with the loud and musical plashing of some newborn and unfamiliar brook.

Cold and wet, the smell in the spring air was not yet the smell of earth and spring. No fragrance of the soil, no mystery of vernal warmth hung above the farmland, but only a chill of sodden earth, water, and old snow. I knew that if I cared to look, I could find to the north of weathered ledges in the woods such sunken, grey-dirty, and gritty banks of ice as only the spring rains find and harry from the earth.

Yet spring somehow was a part of the night, the miry coldness, and the sound of water, a part of this reluctance of winter to break camp, a part of these skies with Sirius and Orion ready to vanish in the west. The long siege was broken, the great snows were over and gone, the ice was coming down from above tide-water in the current of the great rivers, and the colored twigs of the trees were at last awake.

Walking homewards towards the farm, now listening to the sound of water, now forgetting it as we talked, we both could see that much of the pond was surfaced with open water above its floor of ice. At the foot of our own hayfields a cove facing south and east showed in liquid and motionless dark, whilst beyond, and again above the ice, lay puddles and seas whose reflected quiet of starshine was a promise of the open water soon to come.

Across the pools, at the great farm on the hill, a light suddenly went out. Our own windows shone nearby, but we did not enter, so haunted were we both by the sense of the change in the year and the continuous sound of waters moving in the earth.

When we at length entered the house, using the side door and its tramped over and muddy step, we found ourselves welcomed by something we are very seldom aware of summer or winter— the country smell of the old house.

All old farms, I imagine, have some such rustic flavor in their walls; country dwellers will recognize what I mean. A hundred and fifty years of barrelled apples, of vegetables stored in a field-stone cellar, of potatoes in the last of the spring, of earth some-where and never very far, of old and enduring wood and wood-smoke, too, and perhaps the faintest touch of mould from things stored long, long ago in a bin—all these and heaven knows what other farmhouse ghosts were unmistakably present in the neat room with its lamp and books. The cold and humid night had stirred the house as well as ourselves: it had its own rustic memories.

Elizabeth presently brought in two slices of apple pie and two glasses of cold milk, and for a first time I did not bother to build up the fire.

THE NORTHERN LIGHTS

by

JOHN RICHARDS

I thought above a distant hill I saw
The lights of some great city, where her lamps
Glowed on a low-hung cloud, but as I gazed,
A shaft of silver fire grew and gleamed
As though some Titan slowly raised his spear.
And all the while the night grew luminous,
And ghostly lightnings played across the sky.
As when a king reviews his thousand knights,
They, horse to horse, stirrup to stirrup, stand
And brandish high bright blades that catch and throw
Flashes of noonday fire, so all the North
Burns like a battle-front with silver arms,
While from on high Vega enthroned surveys
The silent armies of the Arctic night.

From *Songs of a Schoolmaster* by John Richards (Rumford Press: Concord, N. H., 1948). By permission of the author.

14. The Forest and the Loggers

CRUISING THE PRIMEVAL WOODS

by

JOHN S. SPRINGER

IT IS a peculiarity of the white Pine that the trees are given to associating together in clusters or families. It is now a rare thing to find a sufficient quantity of timber in one of those clusters to meet the demands of a team during the usual period of hauling, which is about three months.

Twenty-five or thirty years ago, large tracts of country were covered principally with Pine-trees. Those tracts seemed purposely located in the vicinity of lakes, large streams, and rivers; a winter's work could then be made contiguous to improved portions of the country, which rendered little previous exploration necessary. But the woodsman's ax, together with the destructive fires which have swept over large districts from time to time, have, so to speak, driven this tree far back into the interior wilderness. In fact, the Pine seems doomed, by the avarice and enterprise of the white man, gradually to disappear from the borders of civilization, as have the Aborigines of this country before the onward march of the Saxon race.

The diminished size and number of these Pine communities,

From *Forest Life and Forest Trees* by John S. Springer (Harper and Brothers: New York, 1856).

near the borders of civil and agricultural abodes, added to the fact that this tree has been pursued to wild and unknown forest regions, renders exploring expeditions previous to the commencement of a winter's campaign absolutely indispensable, at least to insure success. This labor is performed, more or less, at all periods of the year; but, perhaps, the more general and appropriate time is found to be during the earlier part of autumn. The work of exploring is often performed during the winter, while the crews are on the ground, in camp. The difficulty of traveling through deep snows is overcome by the use of the snowshoe, which enables the wearer to walk upon the surface of the untrodden snow.

When the business of timber-hunting is deferred until autumn, the following method is practiced: Two or three men accustomed to the business take the necessary provisions, which usually consist of ship-bread, salt pork, tea, sugar, or molasses; for cooking utensils, a coffee-pot or light tea-kettle, a tin dipper, sometimes a frying-pan, a woolen blanket or two for bed-clothes, and an ax, with gun and ammunition; all of which are put on board a skiff, if the exploration is to be on the St. Croix, or on a bateau if on the Penobscot River, with two sets of propellers, setting poles for rapids, and paddles to be used on dead water.

With these slight preparations, away we 'start; now making our way up the main river, then shooting along up the less capacious branches; sometimes performing a journey of two hundred miles far into the interior, in those solitudes which never before, perhaps, echoed with the tones of the white man's voice. The locations for our nightly encampments are selected in time to make the necessary arrangements for refreshment and repose, before the darkness shuts down over the dense wilderness that surrounds us. Selecting a proper site near some gushing spring, or where a murmuring streamlet plays along its romantic little channel, we pitch our tent, which formerly consisted of a slender frame of little poles, slightly covered on the top and at each end with long boughs, the front entirely open, before which burns the watch-fire, by whose light the deep darkness of a forest night is rendered more solemn and palpable.

In some instances a large blanket is spread over the frame; and when there are good reasons to expect rain, we haul our boat up, turn it bottom side up, and crawl beneath it, this proving a sure protection from the falling rain or dew. Of late, small portable tent-coverings are used, which prove very convenient.

Next the evening meal is prepared. Here the tea is thoroughly boiled, in the coffee-pot or tea-kettle, over the little fire. A thin slice of salt pork is cut, and, running a sharp stick through it, it is held over the fire and roasted, being withdrawn occasionally to catch the drippings on a cake of pilot or ship bread. This is a good substitute for buttered toast, the roasted pork making an excellent rasher. Sometimes we ate the pork raw, dipping it in molasses, with some relish; and though the recital may cause, in delicate and pampered stomachs, some qualms, yet we can assure the uninitiated that, from these gross simples, the hungry woodsman makes many a delicious meal. After pipe devotions (for little else ascends from forest altars, though we have sometimes heard the voice of prayer even in the logging-swamps), we throw our weary limbs upon our boughy couches to seek repose in the slumbers of night.

Sometimes our slumbers are disturbed by the shrill whooping of the owl, whose residence is chosen in those lonely solitudes of dense woodlands, where this ghostly watchman of the night makes the wild wood reverberate with the echo of his whoo-ho-ho-whah-whoo! which is enough, as one has observed, to frighten a garrison of soldiers. Few sounds, I am certain, so really harmless in themselves, awaken such a thrill of terror, as it breaks suddenly upon the ear during the stillness and loneliness of the midnight hour.

Arriving at length upon or near the territory to be explored, we haul our bateau safely on shore, and turn it bottom upward. Then, dividing our luggage into parcels, and making use of our blankets for knapsacks, we begin to traverse the wild forests, unfrequented except by the stately moose, the timid deer, the roaming black bear, and other wild animals of less note, whom we frequently disturb in their solitary haunts.

When it is necessary to obtain views from low lands, the obstructions are overcome by ascending the highest trees. When an ascent is to be made, the Spruce-tree is generally selected, principally for the superior facilities which its numerous limbs afford the climber. To gain the first limbs of this tree, which are from twenty to forty feet from the ground, a smaller tree is undercut and lodged against it, clambering up which the top of the Spruce is reached. In some cases, when a very elevated position is desired, the Spruce-tree is lodged against the trunk of some lofty Pine, up which we ascend to a height twice that of the surrounding forest.

From such a tree-top, like a mariner at the mast-head upon the "look-out" for whales (for indeed the Pine is the whale of the forest), large "clumps" and "veins" of Pine are discovered, whose towering tops may be seen for miles around. Such views fill the bosom of timber-hunters with an intense interest. They are the object of his search, his treasure, his El Dorado, and they are beheld with peculiar and thrilling emotions. To detail the process more minutely, we should observe that the man in the tree-top points out the direction in which the Pines are seen; or, if hid from the view of those below by the surrounding foliage, he breaks a small limb, and throws it in the direction in which they appear, while a man at the base marks the direction indicated by the falling limb by a compass which he holds in his hand, the compass being quite as necessary in the wilderness as on the pathless ocean.

A camp having been established and the arrangements made, serious indications of winter appear in cold, freezing nights and light falls of snow. It is now about time to look for the arrival of the team and extra hands. This event we anticipate with as

much interest as voyagers are wont to feel when they meet
upon the ocean after several months at sea. Letters and newspapers are expected, and, when received, perused with avidity.
New acquaintances are to be made, new tools to be examined,
and everything foreign, however insignificant, is an object of
interest.

What is called a team is variously composed of from four to
six, and even eight oxen. During the months of November and
December, after the ground and swamps are frozen, and early
snows fall, our team is attached to a "long sled," loaded with
provisions, tools, &c., accompanied with a new recruit of hands.
Leaving home and the scenes of civilization, slowly we move
forward to join those who had proceded us to make preparations
for our reception. After several days' journeyings, putting up at
night at places erected and supplied for the convenience of such
travelers, and at suitable distances on the route, we finally reach
our new home. Our arrival is no less agreeable to ourselves than
welcome to our comrades. But there are incidents scattered all
the way along, and seldom do we perform such a journey without experiencing something worth relating.

On one occasion, late in the fall, we started for our winter
quarters up river. We had traveled about one hundred miles,
passing along up the military road, then south upon the Calais
road to Baskahegan Lake, which we were to cross, our camps
being on the opposite side. We reached the borders of the lake
late in the afternoon. The ice was not so thickly frozen as was
anticipated, so that the practicability of crossing seemed exceedingly problematical. Having been long on the way, we were
anxious, if possible, to arrive in camp that night. The shores
of the lake were so swampy that it was deemed impracticable
to perform the route around it, and it was finally determined
to make an effort to cross upon the ice. We had twelve oxen,
which were disposed of in the following order: the lightest yoke
of oxen was selected and driven in yoke before to test the
strength of the ice, and, in case the loaded teams should break

through, to be used to pull them out. These were our reserve. The next in the line of march was a pair of oxen attached to a sled, with hay, &c. Next in order was a four-ox team; these were also attached to a sled, loaded with hay and provisions; and, finally, to bring up the rear, still another four-ox team, with a loaded sled—all of which were strung out at suitable distances, to prevent too much weight coming upon any one point, thus rendering our passage more safe. The word was given, when we all moved forward, intending first to gain a point which ran out into the lake, covered with a thick, small growth. The ice cracked and buckled beneath our feet at every step. Proceeding in this way, we gained the point in safety. It had by this time become late, and the last rays of the setting sun gilded the tops of the towering pines, which peered far up in the air above the surrounding forest.

The night was very cold, and the wind swept up the lake with a penetrating chill, which made us button up our garments closely to prevent its too ready access to our bodies. Having gained the point in safety, we were emboldened to set forward again upon the main body of the lake, which was yet to be crossed. Here the ice seemed less capable of sustaining our weight than in the cove, which, from its protected position, had probably congealed sooner than the main lake, which was more exposed to the action of winds.

Here the ice gave more alarming indications of its incapacity to hold us. We had not proceeded more than three fourths of a mile when the hindermost team broke through, sled and all, which was very naturally accounted for, as the teams which preceded cracked and weakened the ice. The alarm was given along the line, when the other teams stopped; and while we were preparing to extricate those already in, the next team of four oxen dropped in also; and finally they were all in at once, except the reserve pair. Had they kept in motion, probably the foremost teams might have escaped; but, upon stopping, the ice gradually settled, when in they went. There we were on that bleak spot, with the shades of night fast settling down upon us, and ten oxen struggling in the benumbing waters: business enough, thought we.

Standing upon the edge of the ice, a man was placed by the side of each ox to keep his head out of the water. We unyoked one at a time, and, throwing a rope round the roots of his horns, the warp was carried forward and attached to the little oxen, whose services on this occasion were very necessary. A strong man was placed on the ice at the edge, so that, lifting the ox by his horns, he was able to press the ice down and raise his shoulder up on the edge, when the warp-oxen would pull them out. For half an hour we had a lively time of it, and in an almost incredibly short time we had them all safely out, and drove them back upon the point nearly a mile. It was now very dark. We left our sleds in the water with the hay, pulling out a few armsful, which we carried to the shore to rub the oxen down with. Poor fellows! they seemed nearly chilled to death, while they shook as if they would fall to pieces.

We built up a large fire, and, leaving the principal part of the crew behind to take care of the oxen, I, with several of the hands, started to find, if possible, the camps, where were waiting those who had been previously engaged in making arrangements for the winter. This was esteemed by some rather risky, as it was getting very dark, and we did not know exactly which way to shape our course. But the prospect seemed gloomy and uninviting to remain upon that bleak point all night, and, besides, we wished the assistance of the camp's crew in taking our teams over next day. Delay was not to be thought of. We therefore started. A squall of snow came up when we were midway across, which completely bewildered us, and we became divided in opinion as to the proper course to steer. Tenacious of my own views, I resolved to pursue the course which appeared to me right, when the others consented to follow. Finally, after several hours of hard travel, we gained the shore, not far from the road which led back to the camp, about half a mile distant in the woods. We were here, again, puzzled to know whether the camp lay at the right or left. Settling that matter by guess, as Yankees often do other things, we traveled along by the shore about one fourth of a mile, when, to our great relief, we came to the road, up which we passed, and reached the camp a little after midnight, hungry and fatigued. We found our comrades snugly quartered and soundly sleeping. Refreshing ourselves with hot tea, bread, and beef, we turned in and slept until daylight, when, after breakfast, all hands started to rejoin those left behind. We were with them in a few hours. Poor fellows! they had had a pretty uncomfortable season, not one moment's sleep during the night, and scantily provided with food, while the oxen fared harder still. We succeeded in getting out of the ice all but one load of hay, which we left behind. Not venturing to cross directly, we now followed round the lake, close in shore, and finally reached our winter quarters in safety, and without further accident.

The task of taking oxen on to the ground every fall is very considerable, especially when we go far into the interior, as we frequently do nearly two hundred miles. This labor and expense is sometimes obviated by leaving them in the spring to shift for themselves in the wilderness and on the meadows, where they remain until autumn, when they are hunted up. During their wilderness exile they thrive finely, and, when found, appear very wild; yet wondering, they seem to look at us as though they had some lingering recollection of having seen us before. It is often very difficult to catch and yoke them; but, with all their wildness, they evidently show signs of pleasure in the recognition.

THE FLOWERING OF A LUMBER TOWN

by

STEWART H. HOLBROOK

The rock-maple floors of Bangor's two hotels showed the impress of a thousand and more calked boots, and the proud plank sidewalks of the young city were deeply holed by rivermen's shoes, too, and splintered as well. For Bangor in Maine was to be the very first of the great lumber towns and in some respects the greatest of them all.

Conditions were perfect to turn the trick. Unwatered rum cost three cents a glass, a glass was a dipperful, and a thirsty logger helped himself with the tin dipper that was chained to the open barrel. And down Exchange Street, a piece, two rather pretty ladies had rented a house and put up a small sign announcing "Gentlemen's Washing Taken In"—a genteel and harmless euphemism. No chamber of commerce was needed to make Bangor; the lodestones were there already and talk in a hundred bunkhouses, back in the deep timber, would take care of the advertising.

Coordinating conditions also were magnificent. North from Bangor, and drained by the river that turned her sawmills, there stretched two and one-half million acres of black and wonderful timber. Once he saw it, the scene gripped the fancy of young Henry Thoreau, a-visiting here from Concord, down in Massachusetts.

There stands the city of Bangor (he wrote in 1846) like a star on the edge of night, still hewing at the forest of which it is

built, already overflowing with the luxuries and refinements of
Europe and sending its vessels to Spain, to England, and to the
West Indies for its groceries—and yet only a few ax-men have
gone up-river into the howling wilderness that feeds it.

A howling wilderness it was. The tall black spruce was dwarfed
by the towering white pines that rose up, straight as masts and
light as cork, close to two hundred feet above the ground. How
far north of Bangor ran this forest, no man knew. Some said it
reached to the Pole itself; everybody said it would last forever.
It would take a small war and two pretty stirring orations by
Dan'l Webster to learn where the Yankee pine left off and the
Canuck pine began.

Through this vast forest ran the Penobscot, with all its lakes
and tributaries, in season a swift-moving highway down which
with no power other than brawn and a peavey the forest could be
brought to mills and tidewater at Bangor. It was a tempera-
mental highway, difficult to manage in spite of dams; but manage
it they did and for a full century sharp-shod men walked fair
down the middle of it on bobbing logs.

Fifty miles south of town, down the deep Penobscot, was the
open sea. The tides in the river were remarkably high, and the
deep-sea skippers liked the port of Bangor, for here they could,
at low water slack, fill their casks easily from over ship's side
and find the Penobscot water fresh and saltless, though in time
it came to have the flavor of pine in it.

A numerous fleet, Bangor-built and Bangor-owned, carried
lumber from here to the world and brought back rum, and
molasses and sugar to be made into more rum to get more logs to
make more lumber to trade for more rum. It was all a perfect
cycle from the lumbermen's viewpoint, while from that of the
practicing logger—the man who used the ax and saw—Bangor
was nothing less than Paradise. Booze, bawds, and battle with
roistering loggers—there was really nothing else in life, except
timber, and that was handy by. Bangor set the classic pattern

that would follow the timber line West to the Pacific shore, distant by three thousand miles, one hundred years, and two trillion feet of lumber.

God indeed smiled on the rising lumber capital of the world, and He caused one of His apostles to name it. The citizens of the humming town on the Penobscot wanted a town charter, in 1791, so they drew up a highly official and legal application. The name of their new home in the forest, they decided, should be Sunbury, which handsome name was inscribed in the application and the document turned over to the Reverend Seth Noble to carry to Boston, where the Great Seal and the governor's signature might be put upon it.

The Reverend Seth Noble was a local divine whose voice was such that it could be, and often was, heard above the drone of four hundred and ten saws and the combined howls of wolves and loggers on carouse. But the Reverend Seth cared little for the chosen name, which smelled of paganism. He erased it and inserted in a neat round hand the name by which his favorite hymn was known in the old hymnals, "Bangor."

The name fitted Bangor, Maine, and so did the hymn itself, although the loggers probably did not realize how well:

> Hark from the tombs a doleful sound;
> Mine ears attend the cry—
> Ye living men, come view the ground
> Where ye must shortly die.

And die they did, up there in the gloom of the two million acres of tall black stuff—when a sudden waft blew a tall pine the wrong way; when there was the sickening slump in a mile-long landing of logs before they rolled Death over a man; or, the whiskered Old Fellow with the Scythe might hold off, jokingly, until the logs were fair in the stream, then strike you down into the white boiling water of the Ripogenus, on the west branch. Death always stood just behind the logger and very close to the riverman.

That's why loggers lived the way they did. Death might come out of the trees above, with the merest whisssh of warning, or it might wait in the form of a watered rock, just around the next bend in the river. . . . Little wonder they pounded on the white pine bars of Bangor's groggeries and yelled for another drink all around.

The early years of Bangor saw only moderate progress. The first settler hewed out his home there in 1769, and within a year the first of a long line of sawmills was going. But Bangor didn't get its town charter for two decades, and the first ship with a Bangor house flag didn't go down the ways until 1811. Shortly thereafter, and suddenly, there came a brief era of speculation.

Indians, white hunters, and even a few land-lookers had long told of the mighty trees in the vast forests of the Penobscot. These tales finally permeated to the populous cities of Portland and Portsmouth and even to metropolitan Boston and Philadelphia, where lived men of vision and substance. Good pines that were handy to streams, they knew, were already becoming scarce along the Connecticut, the Saco, and the lower Androscoggin and the Kennebec. Late in the eighteenth century men of means began buying Penobscot timber.

The District of Maine—there was no State of Maine until 1820—was happy to be shut of its timberland. It disposed of much of this by grants to colleges and academies and to soldiers of the Revolution; and it sold even more through lotteries. Money was hard to come by, for the provincial governments. Timberland not only was worthless, it was in the way. You had, as they said, to let daylight into the swamp before corn and potatoes would grow.

So the buying and granting went on. William Bingham, a wealthy Philadelphian, sent a timber cruiser on a voyage through the woods of central and eastern Maine, and then Mr. Bingham bought, for twelve and a half cents an acre, a goodly slice of Maine for himself. In one hunk Mr. Bingham purchased

2,107,396 acres of white pine and spruce in which no ax, save it be an Indian's stone tomahawk, had been heard.

It is beyond the minds of men today to conceive of two million acres of virgin timber in one solid block, owned by one man. For more than a century afterward a horde of loggers hacked away at the Bingham Purchase, driving part down the Kennebec, part down the Penobscot; and of a winter's work one logger would say to another that he had been working on the Kennebec Million, or the Penobscot Million.

There were many lesser but still large purchases, too, and Bangor soon became the scene of a land speculation that would be matched only in the Far West of later years. This was only proper, for the Penobscot country was really New England's last frontier, the only frontier in America where men moved from West to East to reach it.

In 1835 land brokers' offices crowded the saloons and "gentlemen's washing" houses all along Exchange Street, and they ran like the water-front sawmills—all day and all night. Timberland that had brought six and twelve cents an acre a few years before was now changing hands at six dollars, eight dollars, and even ten dollars. Fast courier lines, a sort of Pony Express, were set up between Bangor and Boston. Smooth gents formed the somewhat diaphanous Bangor Lower Stillwater Mill Company, obviously more interested in lots than in mills, and staged a combination auction-banquet, the latter presided over by a caterer from New York. Champagne was poured from original bottles into washtubs, and all invited to belly-around and drink hearty. Fortunately, for the amazed loggers, this affair was held in June, when the drive was in and a man was handy—and thirsty.

The wildcatters turned over $127,000 in timberlands that day, and the loggers who would later cut the timber got ory-eyed on free champagne.

The speculation boom, of course, soon burst, but actual logging along the Penobscot was just getting a good start, for men of action had come along with the men of vision. Railroad construction had been pushed twelve miles upriver as early as 1836, to reach Oldtown and Orono. Its rails were wood, with scrap iron spiked along the top, and its locomotive had been made in England by Stephenson himself. The redoubtable General Sam Veazie bought this road and started out to make it go.

General Veazie, while perhaps the most aggressive* of the early Bangor lumbermen, was quite typical. He soon built or bought control in nineteen mills at Oldtown, thirteen more at Basin Mills, and still twenty more in his own town of Veazie, which town he got a friendly legislature to set aside for him. The general thought it would be nice, and efficient, to elect men from his own company payroll to fill the rather important offices of tax assessors.

As early as 1825 the legislature had granted a charter to a company† formed to collect the great mass of logs of mixed ownership that floated down from the woods and to segregate them for the various mills at and between Oldtown and Bangor. General Veazie bought this franchise and ran things in his own way, possibly to his own advantage, for there was hell a-popping and much fighting about logs until the other lumbermen got the State to appoint a three-man commission to handle affairs at the Penobscot log boom.

But Veazie was not alone in his aggressiveness. There was Jefferson Sinclair, a great figure to whom many gave the credit for starting the boom idea in the first place. There was Moses Giddings and old Arad Thompson, individualists from 'way back, and the Pearsons, the Lumberts, the Bruces, and a score of others, all of them up on their hind legs and r'aring to go. Among them, and aided by just such aggressive and prehensile logging operators in New Brunswick, they brought about what to this day in Maine is referred to as the Aroostook War.

The "war" took its name from the then vaguely bounded country known as The Aroostook. The international boundary

* On occasion even boss lumbermen engaged in fisticuffs over logs.
† The Penobscot (log) Boom Company.

was as yet undetermined, but not so were the intentions of the Bangor logging operators and timber owners. They wanted all that great straight pine, come hell and high water, and they charged that the New Brunswickers were jumping the claim and cutting in Maine woods.

The State of Maine sent its land agents up to investigate. They discovered many rafts of logs, allegedly cut in Maine timber, being floated down the Aroostook River and into New Brunswick. They seized some of the rafts, only to have the Blue Nosers[3] cut them loose under cover of darkness. There was considerable hullabaloo, during which oxen were seized and stocks of wild hay burned. Among the actual loggers on both sides a heap of assault and battery took place, some of it naturally running to mayhem, through the loss of ears in combat.

Now the logging operators and timber owners set up a howl that was articulated through the Maine legislature loud enough to reach Washington, D. C. But Washington moved too slowly to suit long-memoried folk whose towns and cities—aye, and whose camps and sawmills—had been burned by the British a few years before. In 1839 Maine loaded some old brass cannon onto oxcarts and scows and sent militia north to man Forts Kent and Fairfield.

Some excellent sniping was done back and forth with ball and cap rifles, but the artillery did not go into action. Sir John Harvey and Lord Ashburton had come forward as peacemakers for Great Britain, and General Winfield Scott and Dan'l Webster acted for the embattled Bangor lumbermen. The Webster-Ashburton Treaty (1839) setting the present boundary, was the outcome, and the Maine troops returned to their homes.

With the Aroostook Question officially settled, both Penobscot and New Brunswick lumbermen continued to poach upon each other's preserves, but the only actual fighting done was carried on by the loggers themselves, who enjoyed it hugely,

---

[3] Citizens of the Maritime Provinces of Canada.

never allowing it again to become an International Incident but keeping it alive for local amusement and practice.

With comparative quiet restored along the border, Bangor went into the years of its glory. Williamsport, Pennsylvania, would later cut more lumber than Bangor. Saginaw and Muskegon in Michigan would cut more boards in a month than Bangor did in a year; and, in time, a single sawdust plant would rise on the Columbia River in the Pacific Northwest that could cut twice as much lumber as all of Bangor's four hundred and ten saws. Yet the fame of the Penobscot city became so great that no less than ten other Bangors were founded, hopefully, on the loggers' and lumbermen's trek South and West. A number of things contributed to this lustrous shining of Thoreau's star on the edge of night.

Bangor was the first city of size whose entire energies were given to the making and shipping of lumber and to the entertainment of the loggers who cut the trees. Then, too, it is from Bangor's canny and inventive men that stems so much that has been found sound and practicable throughout the years. And lastly, there were the sure-footed lads óf Bangor who, spring after spring, walked two hundred and more miles on heaving logs straight down the middle of the Penobscot. These men made such a name for themselves, by their agility on a moving log and by their foolhardy courage anywhere, that west of Bangor a Penobscot man came to be known as a Bangor Tiger—quick of foot and ready for battle.

Good as they were, the Bangor Tigers, like loggers elsewhere, lacked a forthright tool for driving the timber down rivers. For a century past, rivermen had got along the best they could with a tool as primitive as a stone ax. It was a swing dog, in its then most modern form, and a pretty poor rig it was. Around a short pole, some four feet long, hung an iron collar to which was attached a hook, or dog, for the rolling of logs. It was awkward, and dangerous, for the dog would move up and down and sidewise. Thus the dog was not always "there" when wanted, and a man giving a good quick heave on the staff might find himself flopping headlong over the log and into the stream. Rivermen cursed it, and it sent many of them into the water, not to rise until a million feet of logs had passed over them. Then they ceased to worry about swing dogs. But Bangor inventors didn't.

One afternoon in the spring of 1858, Joseph Peavey, a blacksmith of Stillwater Village, near Bangor, lay on his stomach in the old covered bridge that crossed the Stillwater branch of the Penobscot. Through a crack in the floor he was watching the efforts of a crew of rivermen below him to break a big jam of logs.

Old Peavey watched a while, and listened while the rivermen passed blistering remarks about the goddamn so-and-so swing dogs. Then, as he afterward told, the Big Idea came, like a shaft of sudden sunlight through a hole in a covered bridge. Peavey jumped up, shouting a blacksmith's equivalent of "Eureka!" and ran as fast as he could to the Peavey blacksmith shop. Here he directed his son Daniel how to make a rigid clasp to encircle a cant-dog staff, with lips on one side. These lips were drilled to take a bolt that would hold the hook, or dog, in place, allowing it to move up and down but not sidewise. Below the bulge in the cant-dog handle Daniel placed graduated collars of iron which added greatly to the strength of the handle. Then, as a piece of crowning genius, old Joe had his son drive a sharp iron spike into the end of the rig. . . . Thus the tool was born that would in years to come roll untold billions of feet of logs into the many rivers that run between the Penobscot and the Pacific, and from Hudson's Bay to the Gulf of Mexico.

Old Joe Peavey's last name would soon be known wherever logs were rolled, though the greatest single invention in the technology of logging would bring him no fortune.

Peavey got William Hale, noted Penobscot river boss, to try out the new tool. Hale pronounced it the soundest rig ever put in the hands of a calk-booted man. So Joe Peavey made a drawing of it and set out on foot for Bangor and the post office, with the intention of getting it patented. On the way he stopped to see a blacksmith friend in Orono.

Joe Peavey liked a glass of Medford rum, sometimes two glasses. His Orono friend poured liberally and old Joe, his stomach warm, displayed the plans he was sending to the patent office. This called for another round of rum, and so on. When Joe awoke next morning and shook the fog out of his old gray head, drawings and application for a "Patent Cantdog," not a peavey, were on their way to Washington, submitted by the Orono blacksmith.

But regardless of first patents, the Peavey family went into the business of making the tool Joe had invented, and the fourth generation of them are at it today, in Brewer, just across the Penobscot from Bangor. The name had long been admitted to dictionaries and is a generic term applied by woodsmen to all cant dogs. Not one logger in a thousand today knows whence and how came its name.

Joseph Peavey didn't stop with the riverman's tool. He is credited with the Peavey hoist, for pulling stumps and raising the gates of dams, and with the hay press, by which loose hay could be baled into small tight wads for transportation into the logging camps.

The idea of a large sorting boom to handle logs for many mills has already been mentioned. It was devised at Bangor in 1825, and was copied later on the Hudson, the Saginaw, the Mississippi, and other streams in the West.

Bangor men invented the Bangor Snubber, a machine for regulating the speed of sledloads of logs on steep hills, and the log-branding ax, or hammer, was a product of Bangor, and it is the logger's one concession to Art.

A log with no owner's mark on it and floating down the public highway of a river is anybody's log, so the practice of branding logs came early in the industry. Before the Bangor invention of a branding ax, men who had to be marvels with an ax cut the owner's mark in the ends of the logs. These marks, by necessity of the tool used, had to be a grouping of straight lines. They ran to what were called, Dart, Double-dart, Diamond, Crowsfoot, Anchor, Short Forty, Long Forty, and such.

With the branding ax, its face a steel pattern of the brand's design, lumbermen could allow their imaginations free rein. Log brands have run to wondrous patterns since then, and include Derby Hats, Wine Glasses, Beerkeg-bungs, Aeolian Harps, and Hearts and Flowers. Thus did inventive Bangor devise an outlet for the long-suppressed artistic urges of logging operators.

During the period 1830-1860, sawmills grew and multiplied along the Penobscot. Bangor doubled, then redoubled its population to seventeen thousand. Ships for lumber came so thick that on many days small boys could walk across the harbor from Bangor to Brewer on their decks. The channel to the sea once got so full of heavy pine slabs that Army dredges had to come to clear it, making it even deeper; and monstrous great ships, like the graceful "Belle of Bath" and the staunch "Phineas Pendleton," could dock at Bangor with room to spare underneath the keel.

Below and above Bangor, the river was never empty. From the mills clustered at Oldtown and Orono came long rafts made of sawed lumber floating down to the docks, to be taken apart, board by board, and stowed in the holds. Log rafts, too, some of them half a mile long, came into Bangor for sawing in the city mills. As for men in calked boots—they simply swarmed over everything and everywhere.

Out on a Bangor street one sniffed the air and found the perfume of pine in it. In the shops one smelled rum and molasses. It was pure affinity. Lumbermen sweetened the loggers' beans and tea with molasses; they made it into rum for the loggers' entertainment. And the logger, he put the pine dust in the air.

The big lumbermen built mansions all along State Street in Bangor, where some of the houses still survive. These first lumbermen were lusty fellows and they, too, set a pattern. It was a pattern that has been dimmed by the passage of time and dimmed again by the efforts of their scandalized descendants, but it is tolerably clear—and fascinating.

Most of these big lumbermen would drink Madeira, to be polite, when they entertained at home, but they liked Medford and West Indies rum, which they drank in vast quantities. They were kind to dumb animals, their favorite being the fast and tireless Morgan horse. These they imported from Vermont for themselves and their mistresses, whom they kept in semiregal style, if compared with the Spartan life enjoined on the young men and women of the Bangor Theological Seminary.[4]

Nor was the calk-booted proletariat without its entertainment. Quite early in Bangor's life the Devil himself took possession of much of the property centering around Haymarket Square, on the west side of town, and held its own securely until the timber line had moved west to Michigan. It was here, on Harlow Street, that the noble Fan Jones built and operated her justly famous Skyblue House.

Fan Jones was a woman of wide vision, looking both landward and seaward. There was a huge chimney on the outside of her place and this she caused to be painted sky blue, the blue of the brightest sky ever seen. It was never allowed to fade, but was repainted twice a year, brighter and more lovely each time. And this chimney was so placed that its heavenly color served as landmark for women-hungry loggers coming downriver from the woods, and as a promise of snug harbor to the sailors coming upriver. If a man got lost in Bangor, whether by land or by sea, it was no fault of Fan's; and she did very well by this public-spirited service.

Haymarket Square came to harbor a score of hellholes where grog and other vice abounded. It was a fitting subject, close to hand, on which the young divines of the theological seminary could practice calling down God's curse. Yet Satan had so well fortified it that in 1911, when Bangor suffered the worst fire in its history, the flames ate up five churches, a school, a bank and

---

[4] The Seminary derived much of its early support from lumbermen.

dozens of homes of the pious, but left the Haymarket with not so much as a blister of paint on its scarlet lights.

Bangor and the Penobscot did not reach the peak of lumber making and shipping until 1872, yet their importance in the lumber industry had faded a full decade before. By the time of the First Battle of Bull Run the bulk of Maine's white pine forests had gone through the saws, and Michigan, the next white pine stronghold, was the lumber colossus. A heap of spruce would go down the Penobscot just as some of it does in 1938— in tiny, four-foot sticks—but most of that spruce has gone into the chippers and digesters of pulpmills, to be regurgitated as long rolls of paper on which to print comic strips.[5]

SPRING FLOOD ON "BANGOR RIVER"

by

BEN AMES WILLIAMS

With the approach of the time when the ice might be expected to go out of the river, the spring break-up gradually pushed Mexico and Oregon and the tariff and all such remote affairs out of the minds of Bangor men. The lumbering crews were emerging from the woods, and they reported an unprecedented amount of anchor ice in the river, six to eight feet deep almost everywhere, while in some places here on tidewater the ice was thirty feet thick. A succession of unusually low tides in the

The selection from Ben Ames Williams' *The Strange Woman* is used by permission of, and arrangement with Houghton Mifflin Company (Boston, 1941).

[5] In a small neat park, near Bangor's fine library, is a group of statuary, "The Last Drive," depicting three calk-booted figures, two of them with peavey in hand. It is the work of Sculptor Charles E. Tefft and is the only mark left to indicate that Bangor was once the greatest lumber city on earth.

lower river had left this mass for the most part undisturbed, and a well which had been dug near the piers of the Bangor-Brewer Bridge found fourteen feet of ice there, most of it solid. The snow blanket in the woods was heavy, and warm rains, melting that snow overnight, would almost certainly produce a dangerous freshet.

On the seventeenth of March the rain began, turned to snow and then to sleet and then to snow again, and finally to rain once more. Word came from Old Town that the rising water there was beginning to break the two or three feet of blue ice which covered the river, and bring it down to jam at every narrow sluice. By the twenty-fourth of the month the jam filled the river solidly from above Old Town to within two miles of Bangor. A small channel was open from the foot of the jam to the bridge, and ice-pokers were at work loosing big blocks and freeing them in this channel, so that they might pass harmlessly away.

But on the twenty-sixth a thundershower came down the valley, with wind and heavy rain. Elder Pittridge, sprawling in his chair in the corner of McNeill's Tavern, heard dimly through the alcoholic fog which obscured his senses the reports from each newcomer, and a man fresh from Old Town, shouting his news, had for a while the attention of them all.

"They're getting hell up there," he cried, "and worse to come! The new ice slides under the old 'till it hits bottom. River's full of it, so no water can get through; and it's rising all the time. Bridges are gone a'ready, and if the jam don't draw tonight, the mills will float right off their foundations."

McNeill said positively: "She won't draw tonight. There's a high run of tides, water in my cellar right now. That'll hold her back!"

"By God, she'd better!" the other insisted. "Or half the mills in Old Town and Stillwater will come down-river by morning."

But the jam did not draw, and the rain continued. Up-river above the jam, the water rose thirty feet higher than its normal level. The Basin Mills at Old Town, lifted off their foundations, floated off and packed into the jam; the City Mills followed them.

"And that means we can't get the winter's cut sawed this year," McNeill announced. "Half of it will rot, or be lost. They'll have to hold it up-river, anywheres they can."

There was still debate as to whether flood conditions would hit Bangor. Above the wharves the river was a mass of ice, rising higher than the usual level of the water, locked and motionless. Elder Pittridge, half-sobered by the excitement in the air, Saturday morning walked out on the bridge to look upstream. The ice above the bridge was a tumbled chaos, in which the pressure of the water, exerting tremendous force, caused constant small upheavals. Blocks of ice as big as a cart might be squeezed upward between two others, rising slowly to their full height above the level of the jam before toppling on their sides. The air was full of a grinding, groaning noise; there was a rumbling and a squealing everywhere in the ice mass; and the men and boys watching from the vantage of the bridge stood in a silent wonder at the sight.

A small section of the upper jam broke away and came with a ponderous slowness downstream, carrying with it the wreckage of the City Mills. It struck the ice immediately above the bridge with a terrific concussion, and fragments were thrown up in huge sheets and piles, some of the smaller flying clear to fall upon the mass and shatter with explosive sounds. The bridge on which Elder Pittridge stood shuddered under that shock; and instantly the water followed till—checked again by the jam above the bridge—it began to overflow the banks on either side.

The people on the bridge had scattered before the approaching impact, running either way; but Elder Pittridge stayed where he was not caring how soon death reached for him. On the Brewer side where a line of houses fronted the water he saw the flood pouring into windows, saw women and children running for safety from those houses to the higher land; and almost indifferently he turned that way in an automatic move to help them. But before he reached the other end of the bridge, he saw that those in the houses must have escaped, so he turned back.

On the Bangor side, the sudden rising water had begun to sweep away lumber piled on the wharves awaiting shipment; and some of the wharf buildings were already shifting as the rising water lightened them to the floating point. By the time he reached the Bangor end of the bridge, scores of men were at work moving lumber back from the encroaching flood, carrying furniture and smaller objects out of the houses and buildings which the water had already reached. Elder Pittridge joined them, working with a desperate and driving energy, working as zealously as though these were his own possessions here in peril. He labored all that day, tirelessly, as long as there was light to see, rejoicing that in this common effort his help was welcomed. The waters of the Stream, backed up by that portion of the jam below its mouth, began to overflow the low ground on both sides of its banks. Before dark the buildings between the Stream and Exchange Street were flooded; but at dark the situation was no worse, and the jam was under increasing pressure with every hour that passed. When it should give way, unless it packed again in the narrows at High Head, the flood would pour down-river to the Bay.

So with darkness there was for a while some respite, and men had time to snatch a bite to eat; but Elder Pittridge did not seek food. He waited by the river above the Bangor end of the bridge, listening in the darkness for the first sounds that would indicate the jam was moving. The night was almost warm, the stars hidden, the air filled with misty haze rising from the ice. There were torches and lanterns everywhere in the watching crowd, and bonfires here and there around which men, wet and weary from their exertions during the day, huddled to await what was to come. But the light from these penetrated only a little distance; the river itself was hidden in hazy darkness.

It was almost midnight when there came in the constant grumbling and complaining of the ice a new note; a shrill and ominous sound. Elder Pittridge heard himself shouting: "There it draws!" The cry ran along the margin of the flood and up through the city; and a clamor of church bells began, every bell clanging out the warning. From the banks it was impossible to see what was happening; but the roar from the river was deafening. He heard the splintering crash as one section of the bridge was carried away; and then the tail of the jam, loosened and lifted by the steadily rising water, spread out to brush along the banks as it moved downstream. The crowds fled, drawing back from its encroaching advance, shouting and screaming in the darkness; and Elder Pittridge heard the scrape and slither and thump of lumber piles dissolving into their component parts as the ice ground planks to splinters or the water swept them away.

When the tail of the jam passed below the bridge, the water which thrust it on began to fall to lower levels. He followed the receding flood, gauging by it the movement of the jam—unseen in the darkness—in the river below. He came down toward the lower ground along the Stream, the water withdrawing before him till it was no more than eight or ten feet above its normal level; but then suddenly he felt it around his feet, and almost at once, before he could take a backward step, it had risen to his knees.

He knew what that meant. The jam had stopped again, packing in the narrows at High Head; and the combined waters of the river and the Stream, piling up behind it, rose with incredible speed. All along the margin of the flood, others had been as quick as he to guess the truth; and a general shout of many men and the shrill cries of women filled the night, and people everywhere fled blindly to safety. The grinding roar of the ice, tumbling and cracking as it wedged solidly in the narrows below the town, was even at this distance deafening; and the mighty river, draining rain and melting snow off seven thousand square miles of wilderness, rammed that ice plug hard home till it was an impenetrable dam rising from the river bed high above the normal level of the water. Barred thus from escape to sea, the flood banked high and then recoiled; and like a herd of stampeding cattle which begins to mill and then to spill in every direction, it overflowed the banks on both sides, and it came in swirling torrents and eddies, with hissing, sucking sounds that were terrifying in the steamy blackness of the pitch-dark night, surging up across the low flats along the east bank of Kenduskeag Stream.

LUMBER CAMP: MODERN MOOD

by

LOUISE DICKINSON RICH

Some winters we have lumber camps in here. Nobody has to have the general nature of a lumber camp described to him. Literature and the movies have done that quite adequately. They haven't shown, however, what it means to be neighbors to a lumber camp; to have as the boon companions of one's four-year-old son a bunch of the hardest and toughest teamsters, sawyers, border-jumpers and general roustabouts that ever came down a tote road; to find that one is suddenly confronted with a choice of stopping talking or learning an entirely new language—a language consisting of such terms as "bucking up on the landing," "sluiced his team" and "shaking out the road hay." Being what I am, I chose to learn the new language.

I also had to learn to differentiate between a day man, a stump cutter, and a member of a yarding crew. A day man gets paid by the day and does whatever the boss tells him to. He may

From *We Took to the Woods*, copyright, 1942, by Louise Dickinson Rich, published by J. B. Lippincott Company.

cut firewood, swamp out roads, pile up brush and tops, anything. A stump cutter is an individualist. He works alone, felling his own trees, limbing them out, sawing them up into four-foot lengths, piling the pieces neatly for the convenience of the scaler, and getting paid by the cord. He's usually pretty good. That's why he works alone. He can make more money that way than he could at day rate or by pooling his ability with that of someone else. Sometimes, however, he's hard to get along with and no one else will work with him. A yarding crew consists of three men and a twitch horse. One of the men cuts down the trees and limbs them, one drives the twitch horse, dragging—or "twitching"—the entire trunk of the tree to a cleared space called a yard, where the third man saws it up with a buck saw and piles it. A good yarding crew can cut and pile an awful lot of wood in a day.

Besides these classifications of woodsmen, who comprise the main population of the camp and who sleep in a long low bunkhouse, there are several specialists. There's the boss and the straw boss, who have their own little shack, not because they feel exclusive, but because the men like to sit around their bunkhouse in the evening and bellyache about the weather, the food, the administration of the camp, or the way the trees grow, or any one of a thousand other things. The presence of authority would put a definite damper on this favorite of all indoor sports. And while talk is cheap, like other cheap things—air and water, for example —it is invaluable. A man who has cursed the boss all evening to his confreres is almost always a man who goes to bed feeling at peace with the world, and who wakes up ready to put out a good day's work. So the boss lives in his own little hut, dropping over occasionally to join in the poker game that runs continually from supper to bed-time and all day Sunday.

In another little hut, known as the Office, live the clerk and scaler. The scaler, as his name implies, scales the wood for the men. That is, he estimates with the aid of a long marked rule called a scale rule the quantity each man cuts, keeps a record of the scale for the landowners, and reports each man's cut to the clerk, who pays the man accordingly. The clerk keeps the camp books, pays the men, orders supplies, tends the wangan—the little store where tobacco, candy, clothes, saw-blades and axes are sold—and runs the punch board, which is always a part of the camp picture. The clerk and scaler are men of at least some education, and I think they enjoy living alone, because they like to sit up nights and read, and in the bunkhouse lights have to be out at nine o'clock.

Behind a partition in the kitchen, which is also the dining-room, and which is by law a separate building, live the cook and his cookees, or helpers. They don't mingle much with the rest of the camp. They're too busy, for one thing. For another they have their discipline to maintain. If arguments start they're apt to start in the dining-room. That's one reason why no talking is allowed in the dining-room, aside from simple requests to pass the butter, please. And I mean "please." I've eaten a lot of meals in lumber camps, and I've been amazed at the prevalence of "please" and "thank you." I wish my own family were always so punctilious. The other reason for no talking is that the cook doesn't want the men dawdling over their meals. A large percentage of our woodsmen are Canadian Frenchmen, and they can't talk without gesticulating. This means they would have to put down their tools and stop eating, which would slow up the meal considerably. The cook contends that they can do their talking somewhere else. All he wants them to do is eat and get out, so his cookees can get on with their dishes.

Somewhere high on the social scale comes the blacksmith. He sometimes lives with the boss, sometimes with the clerk, and sometimes with the men, depending on his type. He makes the sleds that are used to haul the wood, keeps the horses shod, repairs tools, and is usually an amateur veterinary besides. He and the feeder—woods for stableman—are responsible for the health of the horses, but if anything beyond their ability arises, they take the responsibility of calling a real vet. The feeder waters and feeds the horses, cleans the stable, and keeps an eye on the pigs. Every lumber camp has five or six pigs. They are brought in in the fall, cute little tricks with curly tails, fed all winter on the tons of excellent garbage that are the inevitable by-product of catering to a hundred men or more, and sent out in the spring to be slaughtered. By that time they are simply enormous.

Every lumber camp also has cats. In the fall the cook brings in a cat to keep the kitchen free of mice and the stable free of rats that come in in the bales of hay. It is always a female cat. If I didn't know our Tom, I'd be inclined to believe the flat statement of an old friend, Beatty Balestier—yes, Kipling's brother-in-law, but he'd kill you if you mentioned it. Beatty told me once when I was trying to locate a tom kitten, "There's no such thing. All cats are female cats, and all kittens are the result of immaculate conception." My observation of lumber camp cats inclines me to believe he had a tenable argument there. But be that as it may, by spring every lumber camp within a radius of ten miles of us has at least a dozen cats—the original and three litters. All the kittens, regardless of their mother's complexion, are black and white. No wonder Tom is such a smuggy.

When a lumber camp first moves in, all the men look alike to me. They're all big and tough-looking and most of them need a shave, which they won't get all winter. They all dress more or less alike, in layers of shabby sweaters and shirts, ragged pants, and wool caps. They all walk along the road with the same swagger, carrying their axes and saws over their shoulders, swearing at their twitch horses, and dropping their eyes upon meeting me. After a while I begin to get them sorted out and those that I meet regularly I start speaking to. The first time I do this the same thing always happens. The man starts obviously, raises his eyes to look at me, looks all around to see if by any chance I mean a couple of other guys, and looks back at me. Then his face lights up in the warmest and friendliest of smiles, and he answers. If he can't speak English, he answers in French or

Russian or Finnish. It doesn't make any difference. We both know what we mean:—"Hello, stranger. I'll never get to know you very well. We haven't much in common, but we're both here on this snowy road, with the woods all around us. Stranger, I wish you well." They do wish me well, too. Lumberjacks have a reputation, I know, for being brawlers and roisterers and general trouble-makers, and I guess when they are on the Outside, with their systems full of rot-gut, they often deserve this reputation. But I have never met a lumberjack in the woods who didn't treat me with complete respect and friendliness— and I've met a lot of lumberjacks. What they do Outside, I neither know nor care.

15. The Rescue

by

FANNIE HARDY ECKSTORM

A FORGOTTEN story, a nameless hero.

Who the man was no one knows, except that he was a Spencer. This in no way distinguishes him; it is but saying, in other words, that he was a riverman, and begs the question of his identity, the Spencers being not a family, but a tribe. We might guess that his name was Elijah, and guess aright most likely; but this is nothing by which he could be discriminated, for every Spencer who was not named something else was named Elijah.

What sort of a Spencer was he? That is just what the story refuses to tell us: good or bad; honest or knavish; lettered or illiterate; a sober thrifty, useful citizen, or the most worthless ever spawned in Argyle, all that we know for a certainty is that he had in him the right stuff of heroes. For out of all the rescues that I ever heard of, this is the one which had in it the least of bravado and the most of determined courage, the one which the man who started out to make it might have given up with good excuse at any point, and yet that he seems never to have thought of giving up for a moment, but fought through in the face of incredible obstacles.

His reward? To be forgotten so entirely that no one knows his name. Almost is the deed itself passed out of memory. I

From *The Penobscot Man* by Fannie Hardy Eckstorm (Bangor, Maine, 1924). Reprinted by courtesy of Miss Charlotte W. Hardy.

heard it fifteen years ago from Reed McPheters, when we were encamped close by where it happened, and in all the years since, asking this one and that one who has spent his life upon the river, I found no one who knew the tale. It sounded all straight, they said, but they had never heard of it, and there were so many Spencers; they couldn't guess which one this was. I despaired of ever learning more, when at last I was directed to the brother of one of the men engaged. He certified to the main points and added new details. This is the story, built up from both accounts; it may be accepted as not far from the facts.

It happened up near Fowler's Carry, where now is the city of Millinocket. Whose wildest dreams ten years ago would ever have fabled a modern city springing up within the fastnesses of that forest? For more than sixty years, the only house between Little Schoodic and Chesuncook had been the Fowler homestead on the lower end of the carry. There or near by there, for fifty-four years, up to the year 1884, when they sold it to Charley Powers, who in turn sold the land to build a city on, no one but Fowlers had ever lived on Fowler's Carry. They were pioneers among a race of pioneers and watermen of superlative excellence. It did not hurt the pride of any man to hear it said that, between the Lower Lakes and Medway, the Fowler boys could do on the river what no other men dared to do. Everybody was free to admit that much. "Those Fowler boys," as Mrs. McCauslin said to Thoreau so long ago as 1846, "are perfect ducks for the water." As well they might be, brought up in the woods with no neighbors within miles, and never a high-road except in winter but such as was afforded by a wild and frothing river, rushing down over endless rapids and falls.

At the time of this story, the two brothers Frank and John Fowler, with their families, were living in the old homestead on the carry. To understand at all this story, it is needful to bear in mind the lay of the land; for this man Spencer had to swing around a circle of not less than nine miles before he could accomplish what he started out to do, namely to rescue four

men who were in great peril on the Gray Rock of Island Falls.
The difficulty is that Fowler's, unlike all the other carries of
the West Branch, does not skirt the river-bank, but is, or was,
a cross-country road from water to water, cutting off a great
bend in the river. To one looking up the river from the Forks
at Medway, it is as if he held a sickle left-handed, with his
thumb stuck straight out where he grasped the handle. At the tip
of the blade, like a plum upon the point of the sickle, would
be Quakish Lake; the curving steel would be the West Branch
of the Penobscot, tearing down a rocky course, some hundred
and fifty feet of fall in about four miles; the handle, with the
knuckles around it, would be Shad Pond, and the outstretched
thumb would be Millinocket Stream coming in from the north.
Now Fowler's Carry ran from a point about two miles up
Millinocket Stream to a point about a fourth of a mile below
Quakish Lake at the tip of the sickle. The carry was called two
miles long, which in Maine always means abundant measure,
and yet it was a far shorter portage than would have been required in following the river with all its falls: first, as one
leaves Quakish, Rhine's Pitch of about ten feet; then Island
Falls of two miles of very strong water with a heavy fall,—
twenty feet in twenty rods in one place,—and Grand Falls, a
mile long, with the Grand Pitch, twenty feet perpendicular,
just before the river enters Shad Pond. Fowler's, undoubtedly
chosen by the Indians ages ago as the shortest and best route
from lake to lake, did not go near the river; in most places it
was from two to more than three miles away from the river.

It was the very last day of April, 1867, when Scott and Rollins turned out their logs from the boom on Quakish Lake.
Theirs was not the main West Branch Drive, but a private drive,
which got into Quakish much earlier and was worked along by
a single boat's crew of seven men. That is why no one knows
about the matter; for if the success of a jest lies in the ear of
the hearer, much more does the memory of a heroic deed depend
upon the eyes of the spectator. But in this case had there been

onlookers, they never would have permitted Spencer to do what he did; they would have insisted upon helping, and so would have spoiled the story.

The last of April—seven men working on the logs at Quakish, one of them a Spencer. One who knows the place and the season has to stop and think about what it brings back to him,—crisp air; freezing nights; snowdrifts in the shaded hollows, and patches of dark ice, covered with hemlock needles, among the black growth; the chittering of red squirrels chasing each other and the pleasant conversation of chickadees consulting where to dig their nest. The round-leaved yellow violet is out then, even so far north as that, and the brown-winged Vanessa butterfly. How they endure the freezing nights no one knows, but for weeks now, fuzzy black-ended brown caterpillars have been crawling around on the snow. The bees are nosing about the woodpiles, their heads close to the sappy ends of the sticks, and the little flies that dance like tiny sprites in the golden light of sunset are treading up and down on air in their bewildering mazes. Out in the fields the sheep sniff the earth, and the cattle bite it for a relish; the ploughed land lies in furrows, wet and rank to the nostril, a wholesome smell—for one must remember again that spring comes late to these northern clearings. Leaves there would be none upon the hard wood; but the red maple might be blossomed like coral and the poplar beginning to fringe itself with silvery tassels, while birch and alder showed their corded catkins of twisted bullion and the "pussies" on the willows were large enough fairly to be called "cats," and were alive with bees. The squawbush would have lost something of the scarlet lacquer of its stems, and the big marsh willows would be less golden in their twigs. Already the partridges would have quit their diet of birch and poplar buds and be feeding on the shrubby willows in the lowlands, or foraging for the green leaves of last year's clover and goldthread. Already the fish-hawk would be at work at Shad Pond, carrying sticks to repair his family homestead, while up at Quakish, his natural enemy and bully, the great bald eagle, might be whiling away his idle time in honest fishing from his old station on a broomstick.

One never knows the idyllic charm of our northern woods who has not seen them in April, when it is all a feast of birds and buds and waking life. Midsummer does not compare with this. This month belongs to the birds and flowers; but most of all to the robin. I cannot tell this story without giving the robins the place which I know they must have had in it,— great husky fellows, as red as blood in the lifting between showers that made a golden sunset, sitting high in the treetops and splitting their throats with their rain-carol, singing in jubilance at being back again, glad to find once more the corner of the earth that they were born in, and trolling forth such lusty music that all their pertness and swagger and pilfering of a later date is forgiven in advance. Of all the birds of springtime, I would like best to be the robin just getting back to his old home; for it is brave and blithe and bonny that he is, and he is April to all of us in the far north.

So here there must have been robins, cheerful in the face of all weathers, singing their best when the skies are lowering and the mist drives down the lake. For whatever may be the joys of April at its loveliest, it would seem that this was a bad one. There are evidences in the story that much rain had fallen and was still falling, else why such a rapid rise of water after the most of the snow was gone and the river should have been quieting down to the ordinary driving-pitch? Quakish, then, instead of a sapphire lake girdled with the green of spruces, must have been gray and mist-enshrouded, the nights warmer than on fairer days, and the days alternations of misty sunshine and smart showers of finely sifted rain,—a whole week of wet weather that melted the snows in the woods, that overfilled the bogs, that left all the mosses green and spongy, overflowing in little streams which trickled down all the tiny runlets, and that dripped from the mossy cedars leaning out over Quakish, funereally draped in gray-green moss,—good weather enough for robins, who love the wet, but not such good weather for men driving logs.

The trouble, so Reed said, was in turning the logs out of the boom in Quakish too early. Just what that means is doubtful, if it does not imply long-continued rain, which would swell the river rapidly and make the work of driving the logs more difficult and dangerous than ordinary. Whatever it means, the very first thing, they got a jam on the old Gray Rock just below Rhine's Pitch and about a quarter of a mile above the head of Island Falls. It was a middle-jam, which is the worst to pick, and they had only a single boat's crew to take care of it. Scott, who was one of the head men of that drive, went down to Fowler's at the lower end of the carry at once, and offered the two brothers, John and Frank, fifteen dollars a day to go up and handle boats and do general work. That was the first day of May, and that very day Frank Fowler had gone up to Big Smith Brook to work for Fowler and Lynch. We hear no more of Scott in this story; it seems likely that, without going back to his men at all, he hastened out to Medway, twelve miles away, to pick up a crew there, and that he did not get back again till the story was over.

Meantime there were but seven men to look after that jam and whatever logs of theirs were running free. They had but their one boat, which it would never do to risk, and so they must have worked short-handed, some on the jam, the rest along the shore keeping the boat by them, ready to rescue the others if anything happened. The water must have been terribly rough then, and one who knows what to listen for in imagination can hear the hiss of the great boils and the bursting of the bubbles in the long white foam-streaks striping the waves which went rushing past, running deep and wicked. Out there in the scuds of rain, one who knows what to see can see once more the piled-up middle-jam and the four men upon it, red shirts and peavies, pulling and prying and pushing to loosen one by one the great jackstraws under their feet and send them darting down the rushing river,—precarious work, this, to pry out the foundations under your feet when you know that there is nothing beneath but water running at a race-horse rate, and below, two miles of dangerous falls.

How long the men had been working on that jam, why Spencer and the others started to take them off, at what time of day the catastrophe happened, neither account satisfactorily determines. Reed understood that the jam hauled suddenly, and left only about twenty logs upon the rock, with the four men on them. Frank Fowler, who should know if any man does, says otherwise, that the jam did not start till some time in the night. Even without the authority of his statement, this would be the better reason; for the former situation is too thrilling by half for a real event, and instead of urging Spencer on to such desperate efforts would, by making it hopeless from the start, have left him nothing to labor for. It seems most probable that the larger half of the crew had been working on this jam since Scott left them the day before (for it is now the second day of May, 1867), the other three resting or working near the boat, to be ready in case of accident; that the time must have been not far from six o'clock, the old-fashioned sun-time, which came a half hour later by the light than the railroad standard of to-day; and that it was now approaching supper-time, and the boat was coming out to take the men off. For it could not have been dark enough to quit work at that season, even of a lowery or a rainy day; but the river-driver's supper hour is seven o'clock, and as these were but a single boat's crew, too few men to carry a cook and separate wangan, they must leave the logs long enough before dark to cook for themselves. It seems likely that it was, as the men would say, "just about half-past hungry time," and the men on the jam saw with pleasure the boat, with Spaulding, Moores, and Spencer in it, dropping down to take them off. Perhaps the rain held up a little and the yellow of the sunset behind the rain-cloud showed through it, and the robins in the treetops all along the shore were singing, to be seen but not to be heard above the tumult of the water.

"Pretty birds them be to sing," the men might have remarked, leaning on their peavies, "and awful nice in pies." It may sound materialistic, but why is it not better that a robin should be good in a pie as well as out of it? They were willing enough to give him credit for his music, but supper was what was in their thoughts. And here were Spaulding and Moores and Spencer letting the boat down, two with their poles, one at the oars, intending to drop her into the eddy below the jam. Then the four men would tumble in, three of them would take an oar apiece, the boy would sit aft on the lazy seat, and back they would go to camp-fire, supper, and bed.

Two of those men were doomed to make their bed in a different place that night; and but for a miracle, the like of which I never heard of happening, all seven of them would have been there before morning.

It was but a step more to safety in the eddy, when snap went the stern-pole, and around the boat swung broadside to the current. Before they could straighten her with paddles she was swept down upon the head of Island Falls. She struck a rock, cracked open, and overset, all in the same instant. Quick? A driving-boat is built to act quick; that is her special virtue. There were now three men and a wrecked boat in the water of Island Falls, and four men on a jam in the middle of the river, powerless to save them. If the initial disaster was quick, the final one was to the spectators a prolonged agony. Two of their mates they saw drowned outright, and for the third there was no hope. There were they, four wet, hungry, shivering men, a moment before so near to blankets, supper, and fire, now abjectly miserable on a log-jam in mid-river, no one knowing of their plight, rain falling, night coming fast, the river rising, the jam they were on already beginning to feel the freshet and grow uneasy, their own danger imminent, and their hearts wrung by seeing a catastrophe which they could have in no wise prevented.

They were hungry, cold, wet, miserable, disheartened men, in peril of their lives. Did the robin still sing in the treetops? Then they damned his unseemly levity, and in the same breath wished they had the pie he was made for.

Two men were drowned outright, and so have nothing further to do with the story. No doubt they were as good men as any of those saved, as good watermen, perhaps, as Spencer was; but it was their fate to lose their lives, not to give them away. Moores was found about a month later down at Jerry Brook, and there was buried. Spaulding was not discovered till some time in September, under a log where the old mill-pond was, down at Medway, sixteen miles below where he was drowned. 'T is only a sample of what all river-stories are like; in almost all some one loses his life, and no one thinks of him afterward except the family, that sets one less chair at table, and a few mates here and there, who date their stories by the year such and such a one was drowned.

Meantime Spencer, on whom everything depends, is at the mercy of a raging flood on the head of Island Falls. There are two miles of this tumultuous water, but the River helped him. All watermen know—indeed, any one may observe the same thing by watching even a gutter-current—that all swift water has a pulse-beat; nominally its waves are stationary, but every now and then there comes a larger one, swelling quick and high with a sudden throb, quite different from the ordinary stationary wave. No sooner had Spencer been thrown into the water than one of these great waves took him and lifted him fairly up on the bottom of his overturned boat. It was slippery with wet pitch; it was narrow; it had no keel; he could not have held on at all, bucking and rearing as it did, reeling and rocking, as its long points, bow and stern, ploughed under the great boils, had not the boat when she turned over hit a rock so hard as to split one side open. He got his fingers into the crack, and it nipped them there.

We have four men on a middle-jam waiting to be drowned,

two below drowned already, and the seventh man with his fingers caught fast in the crack in a crazy old boat that—upside down, banging into him, overriding him, slatting him against rocks and logs, half drowned with spray and rushing waters, half stunned with being beaten against boat and rocks, his fingers crushed and aching cruelly—towed him the whole two miles down Island Falls. "And if that wa'n't something of an experunce, then I don't never want to have one happen to me!" says the woodsman, who can appreciate better than any amateur what it must mean.

It takes a good deal to drown a Spencer. There is a story current about four Spencers and four Province men, a Mattawamkeag crew, going out in 1870 to pick a jam on the upper pitch of Piscataquis Falls. When they saw how bad the water was, two of the Spencers leaped out of the boat and got ashore again; the other two Spencers and the Province men were carried over the falls. The Spencers were all right in the water, of course; they expected to arrive somewhere. Old Lute swam ashore about half a mile below, with his T. D. pipe still in his teeth. He emerged like Neptune, and shook the water off all ready for some more river-driving. Some bystander, a little curious, inquired where he had come from. He answered that he was "right down from Piscataquis Upper Pitch," and he guessed "them four Bluenoses that was in the boat with him was all drownded by that time!" He was right, too. The Spencer whom he did not worry about got ashore on the boat.

This Spencer was dragged down through Island Falls. Just as he reached the point where he did not care to travel much farther because below were the Grand Falls and Grand Pitch, which nothing can go over and live, the boat struck a wing-jam so hard that the crack gaped and let his fingers out. Then the boat went off and left him; for all this time the boat had been holding him rather than he holding the boat. As he was being carried past the jam, he threw one arm over a log, and another of those great pulse-beats of the river came, as before, and lifted him clear up upon the jam. Reed had heard that at just this moment the jam hauled, that he fell in between the logs as they were moving, grasped two of them, threw himself out upon them, and ran ashore over the tumbling, moving mass. This is requiring too much breath for even a Spencer. Any man, after being dragged through Island Falls the way this one had been, ought to have been grateful enough for the help of that great wave to lie there on the logs, sick and giddy and aching, till he got the water out of him and the woods stopped spinning around him, the noise of the river became a less deafening roar, and he could see the trees and logs in their natural color instead of just the black shapes of logs and trees.

It was getting quite dusk beneath the trees, and here was he, a battered and disabled man, alone on the river-bank, two miles below his comrades in distress and four miles at least from Fowler's, nothing for him to do but to get his legs under him and limp along the best he could to Fowler's Carry. John and Frank would go up and take the men off, and all would come out right.

The water was very strong; it was rising fast; to lose a moment would not do, for no one could tell how soon, under such a pressure as that, the jam on the Gray Rock might give way. He scrambled up, hobbling painfully, perhaps putting his fingers to his mouth to ease them, for they were raw and bloody and still white at the ends from the pinching they had received in the old boat's side; the split board working back and forth had maimed them cruelly. Then he set off down the drivers' path past Grand Falls. There was a boat down below the Grand Pitch, and it was easier, if not shorter, to go by water than to go through the woods, if, indeed he was landed on the left bank at all, which the story does not say. He walked and he ran and he hurried hobbling for a mile, when he reached the place where the boat was. Then he rowed down Shad Pond for a mile, and then poled up Millinocket Stream for two miles more. It must have taken him an hour at least since he was

washed ashore below Island Falls, and it was now on the edge
of darkness, the time when the robins are flying with sharp
peeps and queeps, jetting their tails and talking about going
to bed, for the robin is rather late about his hour of retiring.

At Fowler's landing Spencer hauled his boat up ashore
enough to hold her, and then toiled up the hill to the house.
He was very much done out. However, he could get the Fowler
boys to go over with their boat, and he would have no more
worries. He was hungry, too. A woodsman's appetite is not a
fickle fancy for victuals, to be lost or forgotten just because he
has had some strain upon his nerves. Perhaps, as he dragged
himself wearily up the hill in the dusk, he smelled that most
appetizing of all the smells of springtime, the odor of smoked
alewives roasting before an open fire. He could see in fancy
the row of golden-sided fishes, standing on their heads before
the bed of coals, as they leaned against the tongs laid across the
fire-dogs and gave forth, when they cracked open, a smell so
savory that no one who cannot remember smelling it in damp
April weather can dream how good it is. Spencer quickened his
steps, always supposing that he actually did smell it, for, where
the story is silent, conjecture has the right to wander.

He went up to the log-house, finished within and without
with rifted cedar, and appeared before the women within like
an apparition. It was long after supper; they were finishing the
last of the supper-dishes, and the delicious odor was only from
the refuse of the feast smouldering upon the coals. He was disappointed, more so than he would have cared to own. He had
been planning on being asked to supper, and had anticipated
his enjoyment of his share.

"Where's John and Frank?" he asked abruptly, stopping in
the doorway, a big, black bulk in the gloaming.

"Lord! how you scared me!" cried one of the women.

"Didn't mean to, mum," was his weak apology, leaning
against the door-jamb; he knew that he was faint as well as
hungry. "Where's John and Frank?"

"Milking," said John's wife.

"Up Big Smith Brook; went up yesterday," said Frank's wife, each one answering for her own.

He dropped into a seat with a groan.

"Why, what's the matter?" asked one of the women kindly. "You do look all beat out! No hat, and—land sakes! you're wet to the skin! Here, draw up close to the fire and get het up. What have you been doing of?"

Whether she had ever seen him before made no difference, the cordiality of those pioneer homes being too real for any formality. She drew him up to the fire and bade him rest. "What's the matter now?" she asked. There was always something the matter on those falls.

"Just ben runnin' Island Falls on the bottom of a boat," said he. His fingers almost made him wince when he got them near the fire.

She was a pioneer woman, and could think and act promptly. "Here, Billy and Ann,"—or whatever were the names of the first children she could catch,—"just you run out to the barn and tell your father to come right in; there's been a boat swamped up on Island Falls."

"What become of the others?" she asked, turning to the man.

He did not like to say it too bluntly.

"Ther're where they won't get out till they are taken out, I guess, mum," he answered.

She stood and plaited the hem of her apron. "How many?" she asked.

"Two—there was three of us in the boat. The other four's out on the jam on the old Gray Rock, if so be she ain't hauled yet."

The other woman had stood silent beside her sister-in-law. "And only you and John to do it; and you so used up! How can you ever?"

"Got to," said he.

There is never any fun in being a hero. This man didn't look

the hero either, just a worn-out, tired, used-up man, with hair
all tossed and tangled, a stoop in his shoulders, a crook in his
back, and every rag upon him steaming before the fire. His
hands he held down between his knees; he did not wish to
have the ladies see them; they were not presentable.

These were women who knew what to do for a man. Already
one of them had poured hot water on fresh tea leaves, while the
other stooped and stood a herring up against the andiron bar,
close to the coals.

"You ought not to, mum," said the man; "I ain't got time
to eat; we've got to git right off; there ain't no time to eat."
It was a feeble remonstrance. He wanted that alewife; the sight
of it put more heart into him than anything else could have done,
and to sit and sip his tea and watch that broil would, he felt,
make a new man of him.

"You've got plenty enough time to eat," said one of the
sisters-in-law, both hospitably busy with laying plates and tea-
things and bringing out the food in store. "It's too bad you
are too late for regular supper; things don't taste so good cold,
but we'll warm up the biscuit, if you don't mind them a little
crusty." No doubt the table was spread with other seasonable
food: cold buckwheat cakes, perhaps, with the richest and
sweetest of maple syrup, made from their own trees, and spicy
dried-apple sauce, as brown as mahogany, flavored with nutmeg
and dried orange peel, a delicious spring dainty, or custard pie
without stint of eggs, and thick, soft gingerbread, such as woodsmen love best of anything,—"the odds and ends," as no doubt
the ladies said, but food enough and good enough for any one;
for these frontier homes were places where there was no lack
of good fare, and where no one was allowed to pass without
the invitation to partake it.

"Just you rest easy," said the sisters, caring for him. "John has
got the boat to see to, and to get the drag down to it, and to
yoke up the oxen. You can't help a bit more than the children
can till it comes to getting the boat on; then maybe it will take

the whole of us, she's so big and heavy. You wait till you are called for and get rested; you'll need all the strength you've got when the time comes." So well did they perform their part, that before the boat was ready he was fit to do his share in helping John Fowler.

Meantime John Fowler was losing no minutes. He understood what his wife meant when he had come in with the foaming milk-pails and she had laid her hand upon his arm. It was: "Must you go, John?"—not dissuasion, but wifely concern.

All he said—for he knew that it meant some desperate under-taking—was, "How many? Where are they?"

A rescue is an obligation on all rivermen. While a chance re-mains it is not to be given up, no matter what it costs. "Drown ten men to save two," is the unwritten code of the River. The way in which this has been lived up to is one of the explanations of the willingness of the men to go into all sorts of hard places: they know that if human skill can do it, they are to be saved. Once when two men were adrift on the logs at Piscataquis Lower Pitch, six boats' crews, thirty-six men in all, leaped into their boats and ran the falls to save those two. It was mad folly for them to do it all at once, for the water was terribly rough; but they did it. Sebattis Solomon, good waterman as he was, almost lost his life in the attempt; for a leaping log knocked him out of his place in the bow, and had he not come up like a cork and thrown himself into his boat before his own midshipmen knew that he was out of it, he would not have lived to perform more deeds of water-craft.

This rescue on Island Falls was one of peculiar difficulty; for it must be made long after dark, in the worst of water, with only two men to handle a great Maynard boat whose crew should have been six men, four at the least. It required the most care-ful preparation for all emergencies. Everything must be pro-vided at the outset. There were poles and paddles to be put into the boat, an axe, a rope, perhaps some dry kindling for starting big bonfires along the shores to light up the river; and there must be torches of birch-bark wound on slender poles to stick up in the boat, lighting more fully the track by which she traveled. Then the boat was too large and heavy for two men to launch, so rollers must be provided, that the pitch might not be scraped off on the rocks in getting her afloat. Then everything within the boat must be lashed in place, that on the rough trip across the carry nothing essential should be lost out. Finally, John Fowler must get on his driving-boots and must hitch up the cattle. Last of all, when the drag was ready and Spencer stood beside it with two of the children, one carrying a lantern, it now being full dark, John Fowler had to go back again to get a little bottle of matches, perhaps to say good-by to his wife. To every one else those men seemed the same as saved already because he had started to do it, but he and she might have felt the flutter of uncertainty.

So, with the children leading, to light the road with the lantern, to tend the fires, and, if accident were to be piled upon accident that day, as sometimes happens, to bring back home the news of it, they set off up the hill and across the rocky pasture now growing up to pine bushes, with the oxen going at as brisk a pace as was good for either boat or cattle. Ahead the children danced and trotted, their swinging lantern a mere blur upon the misty night. Then came the oxen on the run, John Fowler giving them the gad, while Spencer tried to keep the boat upright. The old drag smashed and bounced on the great gray rocks embedded in the carry road, the boat was tossed more ways than if she were running the roughest water, and in spite of their lashings, the things inside her clattered and clashed. There was the jangling of chains, the shouting to the cattle, the creak of drag and boat, the rattle of the gad on horns and yoke, the racket of the poles inside the boat as they urged that cavalcade along, not sparing their speed. It was two miles to go, over as rough a road as a man cares to walk by daylight unencumbered, and then the off-set down to Rhine's Pitch. Half an Hour? Well, if they did it in half an hour, that was quick time; the miles in that region are good measure, and the bounces and jounces are thrown in besides.

Meantime there had been four men sitting on a jam out in the middle of the river. Nothing more is known about them. Being merely dummies in the story, whose whole office was to permit themselves to be rescued, no one has thought to preserve their names. Nor would they care themselves if we invent whom we will to take their places.

There were, let us say, a boy of eighteen, off on his first drive, qualifying for the West Branch; an old soldier who would have "seen her through," had not a minie ball through the lungs mustered him out at Gettysburg—a lean, gaunt man, always chirk and active, with a straggling, thin beard, the type of many a veteran whom we used to see when the war was over; and there was Tom Smith of Oldtown, which is no libel, for it used to be reported of the Tom Smiths of Oldtown that they named them Long Tom and Short Tom and Chub Tom, and then they began and numbered them, and they numbered them up to sixteen. This one was Tom Smith number sixteen and a half, the beginning of a new series of Tom Smiths, and not at all a bad sort of fellow; he was probably dark, with curly hair, and having been brought up in Oldtown, had never believed that it was going to be his luck to be drowned. The last was a short, thick-set, swarthy man, part Inman, who sat silent and smoked. He had nothing to say; he did nothing; he seemed to have no nerves; but in a nook as well protected as any from the drive of the rain and the spray of the river, he sat with his hands in his pockets and pulled at his old pipe, facing death without the quickening of a pulse beat. That was partly because he was a man approaching middle-age, who had been on the river long enough to learn that if a man is born to be drowned, a mud-puddle in the road is deep enough to do it, and if he isn't born to be drowned, the whole Penobscot River cannot keep him under long enough to save him from his natural fate; so there is no use in worrying over what is going to happen to you, even if you do find yourself in a tight place. That is the philosophy of the River. All brave men are fatalistic; the only objection to fatalism is when it is stupid.

But it is no comfortable situation to be where these men were, in a night of rain and mist, out on a pile of logs with the river rushing on all sides, so that it makes one giddy to see the white streaks racing past, like looking out of a train window in the dark at the lane of light which travels beside it,—to be there without fire or food or extra garments, and from hard and heating labor suddenly to have to sit down in a cold spring rain and wait for hours, with nothing to think of but the uncertainty of their fate and the horror of what they had seen. The boy took it hard; silently, of course, for stoicism is the custom of the river, and no one here likes to admit that he has any feelings; but this was the first time he had ever seen any one drown, and horror of it shook his nerves, and made the night seem full of noises; he was twice as chilly as he had been, his teeth chattered, and he did not like an old horned owl which kept hooting along the river-bank, audible above the rushing of the water.

What had become of Spencer, they did not know. They had seen him thrown up on the boat by the great wave; he stood a chance, that was all. If he were lost, they were doomed. It was only a question of time before that jam would be carried away by the rising water. Tom Smith took out his pocket-knife, and reaching down among the logs, began cutting into the side of one. It was not dark then, only full dusk, and the rain had given way to mist.

"What doing, Tom?" asked the soldier.

"Getting spruce gum," replied Tom Smith.

But the man who asked the question was not deceived: one does not look for much spruce gum on a pine log; Tom Smith had been cutting a water-line where he could feel it after dark with his fingers, and judge by the rising of the water when that jam would haul. Then he shut his knife, and put it in his pocket.

"Find any gum, Tom?" inquired the ex-soldier.

"Nothin' good for anything," replied Tom Smith; "that log was all rossy[1] anyway." Then he went dumb again.

The ex-soldier understood the situation. He had the boy on his mind, too; for he had seen enough of raw recruits under fire for the first time, and he did not believe that it helps a man's after-career to let his courage sink too low the first time he is facing peril. One has to see men die more or less, was his notion, and the right thing to do is to think that it is not at all unnatural: it does not follow that one's own turn is coming next. He began telling stories, funny stories, of times when there was nothing to eat and some one sneaked off with the best of the general's dinner, and his mess that day fared all right; of times when in hard places men were supremely comical and kept the others laughing with their drollery; of times when men did such great things that only to hear of them was to applaud,—stories like that of Major Hyde and the Seventh at Antietam, and of Chamberlain at Little Round Top. He had been—where had he not been?—at First Bull Run, at Williamsburg, Chickahominy, Fair Oaks, Antietam, Fredericksburg, Chancellorsville, Gettysburg. At Gettysburg he saw—and then he stopped to cough.

"Quite a cough," said Tom Smith.

"Keeping that to remember Gettysburg by," replied the veteran, wiping his forehead; "sometimes when I'm damp it comes on a little to 'mind me of old times."

It did not sound like a cough which river-driving would help to cure; but in that gaunt, thin-faced man with the straggling beard there was a power of grit. Just at present, instead of fretting because he could not get hot tea and warm blankets, he was taking upon himself to be the life of the little group upon the old Gray Rock.

"Oh, cheer up, sonny," said he to the boy; "don't you take it

---

[1] Rossy, a very old word, used of shaggy-barked trees, chiefly of hard wood trees, like swamp maple; but sometimes also of scurfy or scaly barked soft woods. It applies only to the loose, outside bark, which is often called ross.

to heart so much; like's not they are all snug somewheres; takes a deal of killing to use a man up, especially an able man at his trade. They'll all come hypering back bime-by when they get 'em another boat; you wouldn't believe what a man can go through and not be hurt a bit; why, I knowed a man"—

Meantime Tom Smith was consulting his water-line.

"Gettin' some more of that same kind o' gum?" asked the soldier.

"Yes," said Smith gloomily. His line was half an inch under water in about an hour, he calculated. At that rate the jam could not hold together till morning. Three inches more, he reckoned, and she would haul. Already the water sobbed and chuckled higher among the timbers, and one of the big pulses of the river would send it spouting up through the chinks in the centre of the mass where before the water had been almost still. The jam lifted around the edges, too, when one of these big fellows came hurrying past. Of course there are plenty of youths who never saw anything but a millpond, who will be assured that, had they been there, they would just have caught hold of the biggest log they could find and have serenely floated down to safety: it wouldn't have worried them any, because they always can see easy ways out of sinking ships and burning buildings and dangers which they never experienced. To such a riverman would reply: "Our boys ain't onto them smart tricks o' yourn with logs, but when you try to l'arn us how, don't start in on a middle-jam on Island Falls." Tom Smith and the others who were used to the business saw nothing to do but to wait for the end of things right where they were.

"Just the same sort of gum as before?" the old soldier had bantered, trying to get his information lightly.

"And it ain't no good sort, I can tell you," responded Tom Smith bitterly.

The old horned owl on the shore whooped again.

"Blame a owl!" said Tom Smith.

The soldier kept right along with his story, "the awfuliest comical story that ever was about a man that got his head shot clean off; something I seen myself."

His stories had more to do with sudden death than some would think in keeping with their surroundings; but all tales of the river are tragic. These men did not mind mere tragedy. Under their environment, to talk of drowning would not have been etiquette, but there was something almost cheerful in hearing about a man to whom nothing worse happened than getting his head cut clean off with a cannon-ball.

The horned owl hooted again.

"Darn—a—owl!" said Tom Smith, in so ladylike a way that it took off all the objections to strong language. He had to say something. He did not like the hollow mockery of that great voice in the dark that cried, "Oh, who, who, who are you?" He wasn't going to be anybody by tomorrow morning, if Spencer had been drowned with the rest and that water kept on rising half an inch or more an hour; he did not care to be reminded of the fact.

The ex-soldier coughed again, a racking spasm of coughing. River-driving in rainstorms and sitting out all night on middle-jams did not seem to be the sort of health-cure best adapted to a man who has had a minie ball through his lungs. Yet as soon as he could take his hands away from his side where he had pressed them, he began talking again, telling how he once made three men prisoners when he had nothing but an empty rifle; how when he was a vidette he used to trade tobacco with the enemy's outposts; how that first day at Gettysburg, the day before he got this, an old fellow in a high-crowned hat and a long-tailed blue had fought all day with the Seventh Wisconsin, and was a blame good shot, too; how at Yorktown, Old Seth of the Berdan Sharpshooters had captured one of the enemy's largest guns, and declared that if they would only bring him victuals enough, he could keep that gun till the end of the game, because not a man could get near to serve it while he had his bead on them. The man had seen life for three years, and there rose in him such a fountain of unquenchable vitality that no vicissitude nor danger could make him feel that he was not going to keep right on living; drown him on Island Falls if need be, and he would turn up somewhere else all alive and kicking, just as when they killed him in the army he had come out a river-driver. He did not worry about that cough even.

"Sometimes coughin' won't kill ye half so quick as ye wisht it would," was his cheerful philosophy.

"This old jam is heavin' now," cried the boy, clutching his arm.

"Don't ye be 'feared o' that, sonny," said he, as cool as ever; "you've ben gettin' the water in your head, hearin' the rush of it so long; it's just makin' you dizzy to see them white streaks racin' past; you'll feel a big ram-dazzlefication when this here raft pulls off'n the old Gray. When I was sharpshootin' down in"—

The old horned owl hooted again sepulchrally and near: "Oh, who, who, who are you?"

"Damn a hoot-owl!" cried Tom Smith, not mincing matters. A loon and a hoot-owl were two birds which he had no use for, always glad to see a man get into trouble.

"And the mock-birds down south," went on the soldier, coughing worse, but bringing himself back to his self-imposed task, for he was intending to talk till the jam broke, just to keep that youngster's courage up—"and the mock-birds so sweetly singing"—

"Hist! hark! I hear 'em comin'!" said the silent man. He had not spoken for almost two hours now.

They listened and could hear John Fowler shouting to his cattle; then they saw the misty glow of the lantern; then Spencer on the shore put his hands to his lips and gave a whoop that scared the hoot-owl out of competition.

Yes, they were all there.

That was good news, and it made the rescuers all the livelier at their work. It was not long before great fires were blazing on the shore, lighting the green wall of forest along the river-bank and the white scrolls of foam upon the water, and turning golden all the haze above the trees. The children fed them with dry brush from near at hand, and with every addition to the fires the blaze threw up an eruption of bright sparks and diffused an orange glare upon the blackness of the night. Then the great Maynard boat was rolled down to the water's edge and made ready, the blazing torch was stuck up in the peak of the bow, and, John Fowler in the bow, Spencer in the stern, they started to drop her down from the eddy below Rhine's Pitch.

The men on the jam saw her coming with breathless eagerness. Supper, fire, and bed were drawing just so much nearer to them every time that the ringing, iron-shod poles telegraphed above the rush of the waters a foot, a yard, a rod of distance lessened. The silent man rose and knocked the ashes out of his pipe. He put his hands to his lips. "Take the left of the big rock; don't try her inside!" He had been studying to some purpose, and now he came to the fore and helped to direct the boat, as dropping her cautiously, feeling their way inch by inch, partly by the light of the blazing torch, glaring red on the misty night, but more by that marvelous knowledge of the river which with the Fowlers was almost an instinct, Fowler and Spencer picked their way in the darkness among the rocks in the rising flood on that wild river.

The men on the jam hardly dared to look, for fear that even John Fowler might not be able to get down safe, and when they saw the boat go below them striving to make her turn and come up in the eddy, and the torch-light dim because it was burning down, they did not breathe for expectation that just as Spaulding's pole had snapped, so Spencer's would break on the same spot and leave them in despair. Then Fowler knocked the shaggy cinder from the top of the torch with his pole; the light blazed bright again; the boat loomed nearer; the flame leaped, and John Fowler swung her side against the jam.

Small time they lost in clambering in, four chilled and weary men of excellent cheerfulness. Then Spencer took the bow and gave the stern to John Fowler, that he might have the place requiring greatest skill, and they polled her back in safety to the eddy below Rhine's Pitch.

Four very wet and weary men tumbled ashore, and a Spencer more done-out than any of them. It is hard work to be a hero; he did not think of anything but going to bed. Some brief but not fulsome thanks were passed, no doubt, some credit for great water-craft was bestowed, and then John Fowler drove his oxen home, the children walking beside him with their lanterns.

At the river-drivers' camp the rescued men were thinking of supper. The boy was used up; he had crawled into the spreads and lay shaking in an ague there, because, even covered up head and ears, he could not help seeing things. The silent man took an axe, and the chip-chop of it off one side showed that he was cutting firewood. Tom Smith was getting potatoes out of a bag. The ex-soldier, bent over a little pile of birch-bark and whittlings, was starting a fire. No doubt he was thinking of Moores and Spaulding, for as he worked he sang softly,—

> " 'We're tenting to-night on the old camp-ground,
>   Give us a song to cheer.' "

Tom Smith, who, when he first landed, had given three great sighs of relief and then had begun to swear,—softly, very deliberately, entirely without animus, like the gentlest summer rain falling upon a roof, just repeating over and over everything which he could remember,—had turned his whole attention to supper.

"Boys," he said, "I've just earned fair a front seat in heaven for not swearing for the three damnedest long hours that ever was tooken out of a man's mortal life; but I'd swap even off with any man who would give me a roasted potato."

> " 'Many are the hearts that are weary to-night,' "

chanted the old soldier, paying no attention to anything but his fire and his own thoughts.

Just then, in the distance, far off, a horned owl hooted.

A conscious smirk drew across Tom Smith's face, and he clapped his hand upon his mouth. "Oh hell, I forgot," he murmured like a child who has been caught; "take it all back ag'in—'Damn a owl'—that's so; but p'raps they might give me a seat some'ers way back next the door."

The old soldier did not hear him at all; he was keeping on with his song, and had come to the refrain of it:—

> " 'Tenting to-night,
> Tenting to-night,
> Tenting on the old camp-ground.' "

Lots of times before, too, the other fellows had been taken, and he had been left.

No other man but one of the Fowlers could have made that rescue; everybody will tell you that. But who else could have done what Spencer did? The water rose that night and carried the jam away. A little less persistence on his part, a little less stubborn courage, a little more thought for his own safety, a little more disregard for other men's, and four men more would have been added to the total of the casualties of the river. That Spencer man came very near being a hero. Only he was not the fresh, sleek, well-groomed young fellow of books, who never gets wet, or tired, or torn; but just a rough, ragged, dirty, wrinkle-faced, sun-burned, utterly dragged-out man, with lame arms and sore fingers and bruises from rough treatment, the sort of man you pass on the street-corners, spring and fall, and speak of as belonging to the "lower class."

Pray, who knows where St. Peter is going to put you and me and the Spencers when he calls us up by classes and ranks us by the work done in this world? Will only reading and writing and arithmetic count? or will he demand some proof of pluck, persistence, and generous action? It is likely enough that St. Peter knows by name even all of the Spencers, and for such a deed as this may award his highest honors, something not bestowed upon the nameless ones who make up the "cultured masses."

16. The Maine of Living Memory

COAST CHILDREN OF THE EIGHTEEN NINETIES

by

MARY ELLEN CHASE

THE heavy toll which change and progress inevitably take as they make their inroads is today nowhere more evident than along the coast of Maine. In the smaller towns and villages even the grass-grown ruins of docks have been destroyed; in the larger, shipbuilding except for the construction of pleasure craft or of an occasional steamship, has virtually ceased. The five- and six-masted schooners, which add a touch of romance to populous harbours like Portland, have floated, rotting, untenanted, and useless, for more than several years. Square-riggers are no more. The lithe and beautiful yachts, which cruise idly from Kittery to Eastport or catch the sun on their brass and mahogany as they lie at anchor about Mount Desert or in Camden harbour, speak all too eloquently of the new industry which feeds and clothes the coast. Maine, once secure in her integrity, depends largely for her livelihood, at least so far as her coast life is concerned, upon

From *A Goodly Heritage* by Mary Ellen Chase. Copyright, 1932, by Henry Holt and Company, Inc. (New York, 1932).

the capital of those who seek her shores during the summer months.

In the nineties this was not yet so. True, the tide of the new prosperity had already crept into the spacious harbours about Mount Desert and Casco. Bar Harbor already knew its millionaires and Old Orchard its many sojourners. But the smaller, more land-locked villages still kept much to themselves, their carpenters building only an occasional cottage for strangers, their small hotels, boardinghouses, and homes entertaining only a few "rusticators." Blue Hill, now deservedly one of the most notable resorts of the coast, knew then neither golf-links nor club-house, neither estates whose clipped lawns sloped to the shore nor Chicago and Cleveland financiers who had money in plenty to spend. And Blue Hill children, although they were occasionally shy before city boys and girls with more stylish clothes and more urbane speech, had the village and the coast for their own.

We knew the manifold excitements of coast life, major and minor. We knew even then the drama of incoming vessels, waiting beyond the Narrows in the outer bay for the tides, tacking up the snug inner channel to anchor just off the harbour island or to tie up at the wharf to unload their provisions for the village stores and to load the staves and larger lumber for their outgoing. The names and the rigging of these craft were as familiar as the words in our spelling-books and far more welcome: "The Gold Hunter," the "Mildred May," the "John W. Stetson." We knew, occasionally, the inexpressible excitement of the arrival of a "foreign ship" from Barbados, manned by strange, swarthy men with bright handkerchiefs around their necks, and in their mouths unintelligible sounds. Once, indeed, as we of our family sat one September evening with our lessons around the dining-room table, such a dark face above such a handkerchief appeared in our open window, its owner muttering outlandish words and gesticulating with tattooed arms and hands.

My mother in her perturbation and terror well-nigh threw the lighted lamp at our caller, who, as we discovered upon the hurried arrival of my father, wanted only to know the way to the "medicine house." It was days before we recovered from our fright and more days before we ceased to be the centre of an envious group at school.

We knew and cherished with no little covetousness the stories of the "traders," which had gladdened the hearts of children of an earlier generation. A trader was a vessel from Boston or New York which earned the livelihood of its captain, or perchance of its owner, by carrying annually into the smaller harbours of the coast every kind of ware imaginable and selling its multifarious cargo at prices which the village stores could not meet. Blue Hill children of the sixties and seventies had waited months for the arrival of this floating junk-shop, scanning the sea from every hill and headland for an unfamiliar sail. According to the older people among us, its captain was invariably an accommodating soul, who was not in the least averse to interpreting as coin of the realm any stray bits of old iron, in exchange for which he would proffer oranges and great Boston apples, gorgeously striped candies, dates, figs, and nuts. Moreover, he carried in his hold, for those who had been most thrifty and parsimonious of their small savings, doll buggies and pop-guns, and for the despair of fathers and mothers, who could be lured to the wharf, bolts of cloth and shiny new shoes with voluptuous and alluring tassels.

Sometimes in those days, we understood, still with envy that progress had cheated us of so much greater excitement, Blue Hill had supplied her own traders. An obliging captain, with a weather eye out for his own pocket, sailing light from Boston or New York, Philadelphia or Norfolk, would gladly undertake the filling of commissions in those centres and bring home a sundry cargo. My aunt, a child of the sixties, told us on her infrequent visits the engrossing tale of a new bureau which she procured in this romantic fashion. At the age of six she had pieced together a bed-quilt by the "over and over" method, sewing together innumerable squares and triangles of calico, keeping as she did so the reward for her enterprise and perseverance ever before her eyes. Scanning critically for weeks each distant sail, she at last espied the "Merchant" ploughing through the waters of the outer bay. For hours she waited at the wharf until the tide should be sufficiently favourable for a landing and saw at last her bureau ready for unloading on the quarter-deck. Once again as a reward for industry or virtue (perhaps for both, for in those days, as in our own, they were well-nigh inseparable) she was allowed the fulfilment of great longing. This time, impelled no doubt by her seafaring heritage, she made the choice of a trunk which came after long weeks of waiting by way of another ship, "The Python."

These shopping sea-captains must, indeed, have been men of gregarious instincts and of great good nature. A slip of paper much torn and obviously incomplete, dated in 1859, gives a partial list of commissions to be fulfilled and suggests the arduous undertaking of the purchaser:

For J. Candage, a hoss harness

For Messrs. Holt, Horton, Candage, & 3 Hinckleys tobaco, both chewing & smoking

For J. C.—a new hat, my own size with 2 cravats & ties

For the minister, one cane, snake's head prefered, not to cost over $1

For Silvester C., a good quantity nails, all sizes, & 12 brass handles

For Coggin family, to invest $20 in white flour & raisins, also nuts of sorts, also toys such as marbles, tops, & a book of pictures

For Miss Clara Wood, stuff for weding dress with threads & silks for sewing same & white lace for triming

For Mrs. Duffy, 1 bolt flowered calico at lowest price, blue & white prefered, also buttons, also wools for knitting socks in bright shades, also pink roses for bonet brims

For Horton boys, 2 large pocket knives

For H. Henderson, 6 steel traps suitable for rabits or foxes

For little Osgood girl, a doll with black hair, blue eyes, big as possible for $1

For Mrs. Grindle, one singing bird in cage, for the church gift.

Even we in the nineties knew at first hand something of this sort of supply and demand. When I was in the neighbourhood of twelve, my father, together with three other men of the village, bought a quarter share in a two-masted schooner called "The Gold Hunter." Rumour had it that their act was largely one of charity since the captain and owner had fallen on evil days by the decline of the coast trade. But whatever its cause, the effect brought delighted satisfaction to four large families. "The Gold Hunter" was summarily dispatched to Boston with divers commissions to be accomplished by her relieved captain, and we waited with atavistic feverishness for her return.

Perhaps her cargo, when after a fortnight she again drew to the wharf, was less romantic than those of former days. I am sure, however, that it gave no less thrill. We children of the four families concerned, and we were many, watched with fascination the unloading of barrels of flour, sacks of grain, kegs of molasses and vinegar, cans of pilot bread (that invincible cracker!), bags of oatmeal—all the manifold sorts of provender which were to prove the staples for the men and beasts of our large and respective households during a long winter. We watched, too, the wet line on the black hull of "The Gold Hunter" as it increased in width from her steady rising out of the water during the steady disembowelling of her dark, musty hold.

Most remarkable of all her goods in those relatively fruitless days were crates of oranges, two kegs of white grapes, packed in sawdust, and—most wonderful to relate!—a huge bunch of bananas in a long, slatted frame. It may seem impossible today to wax romantic over a bunch of bananas! But in that huge frame standing on "The Gold Hunter's" deck, behind those masses of brown, tropical grass, were concealed far more than bananas, delectable and desirable as they were in themselves. Therein among those unripe, green protuberances, of whose snug members we caught now and then a baffling glimpse, lay a prestige and a pre-eminence among our fellows which in all the years that have passed I have never been able to recapture. My father had bought the bananas as a surprise. We were all excessively fond of them, but since they were tacitly recognized as an indulgence and since the price of them in the village store, at least of enough to supply our family, was prohibitive, we had never completely satisfied our desire.

The acknowlr 'gment of our supremacy over all the other children in town began as soon as the bananas had been lifted from their frame, cleared of their wiry grass, and hung from a beam in our cellar. Visible from the entrance of our bulkhead, they immediately attracted a crowd of spectators. There was hardly a school-less hour, indeed, for a space of three days, when half a dozen pairs of eyes were not gazing in wonder and envy down those stone stairs. We children meanwhile managed our exhibition by sitting on the open bulkhead doors, swinging our legs and dilating upon our possession with suitable and, I fear, complacent comments.

The culminating moment in this daily-enacted drama occurred one noon when my father, upon inspection of the great ungainly bunch, suggested that we cut the yellowest. That he contemplated any distribution never once occurred to any of us, neither to exhibitors nor to spectators. We watched him procure a box, mount it, and draw his jackknife from his pocket. I can yet feel the stilling of my heart when he handed down to me, who waited below with out-stretched apron, five, six, eight, twelve bananas, when he proposed that we should treat our friends. From that day to this I have never been able to regard a banana with the supercilious stare of the cultivated mind and eye. The munificence and magnanimity of my father, the opulence and distinction of us as a family, remain, always to be evoked by any chance sight of that humblest and ugliest of fruits.

(2)

The minor and usual excitements of coast life were legion. In the nineties there were still among us old sea-captains, barometers of sky and sea, who, in addition to telling us chimerical tales, instructed us in the mysterious ways of weather. We learned to predict the ominous secrets of winds that backed, of restless gulls flying inland, of mare's-tails swishing their milky white across the heavens, of still, cloudless days. We knew what to expect of spring tides, always cherishing the hope that on a March full moon boats would be torn from moorings and lumber floated from the town wharves. We knew when smelts were most likely to "run," coming in great shoals from the outer ocean on night tides in April and May and seeking the tidal streams for spawning. On such nights we went to bed at sundown to be called at three o'clock by my father. Armed with all the pails and baskets of the house, we walked a mile through the darkness to the most favoured brook. The tide was out, and the smelts were foiled and trapped in their tardy return to wider water. Their silver backs and white bellies, as in thousands they hurried pell-mell down the shallow stream, gleamed in the light of our lanterns; and we gathered them in our cold hands by hundreds, filling great baskets full and perhaps, when the miracle was accomplished and we gazed upon our catch, feeling a surprise and exhilaration not unlike that of the boy of the Galilean picnic who began his exciting day with but three small fishes.

The offerings of the sea in the ebb of springs were always more momentous than those of ordinary tides. Shells were more plentiful and often more rare. Wreckage strewed the shores of the outer bay, logs and beams which not infrequently held within their golden brown sides bolts of iron caked with salt. These meant inimitable driftwood fires and were always carried high up the beach and left to dry among the vetches and the lavender. After a spring tide there was also much high talk of treasure and no little search for it. We lived, indeed, on a coast that at once invited and nurtured such fancies. Not far from us lay the very island which was rumoured to hide within its sands the bulk of Captain Kidd's ill-gotten gains. Moreover, not so many years past, two boys who lived near us had been granted an experience, the equal of which few boys of any time or place could boast. Following an old foot-path through the woods during a storm, they had rested against a small boulder beneath a pine tree. One of them, idly kicking the soft mould at the base of the rock, caught the glint of metal, tarnished yet still bright enough to be distinguished against the black earth. They dug farther, with feet and with hands alike, to discover at last an iron pot half filled with gold coins—coins marked by strange designs and a stranger language. They proved to be French pieces of the seventeenth century, probably buried there, so the learned of our coast surmised, by escaping French traders and settlers of the nearby town of Castine when their fort was surprised and captured by the Dutch. What wonder that we scrutinized the wreckage of spring tides and dug now and again in likely coves or beneath giant boulders!

Yet another tale encouraged us to hope for dramatic possibilities even in the ploughing of a spring field. A fisherman not many miles distant had unearthed one May morning, while attempting to cultivate a hitherto barren half-acre, a large piece of copper, marked with unintelligible characters. Seeing in it a remedy for a leaking boat, he tacked it securely to the hull, to be told a few weeks later by summer visitors whom he took out for mackerel, that he had utilized for most practical purposes the corner-stone of a Jesuit chapel, dedicated to Our Lady of Holy Hope in the year 1609!

There was hardly a winter in the nineties when the ocean remained open. By January, sometimes even by Christmas, a great steel-like sheet of ice began to creep farther and farther out toward open sea. Then one cold morning we woke to find no water at all between our shores and those of Long Island, seven miles distant. This meant skating in plenty on the inner bay, and on the outer, once the cold had continued a full week, the laying out of a great track and horse-racing in open sleighs. Not even a launching, which we alas! had been born just too late to see from our own shores, could have been much more thrilling than these village gatherings on certain clear cold afternoons, the participants drawn from village barns, the bells jingling, a blazing fire at the starting-point by which we could warm ourselves with much laughter and many wagers on the horses of our choice.

Those long stretches of ice meant, too, the cutting and hauling of island wood. Oxen drew the creaking sledges which smelled of pine and fir, and obliging farmers encouraged us, once we had obtained our parents' consent, to ride out empty and to return on the top of the load or clinging to the broad runners. The white expanse stretched far and wide beneath a clear, cold sky. The islands were surrounded by rough, uneven boundaries where the tide had cracked and broken the ice, throwing up jagged slabs and cakes around their edges. Wraiths of blue mist rose from the muzzles of the oxen above the icicles clinging to their hairy throats; the creaking of the sledges was now and then supplemented by the booming of the ice as the moving water far beneath it raised or lowered the great solid mass. The climatic changes, even of thirty years, have robbed the coast children of today of no higher adventure.

More suddenly even than it had come, the great sheet of ice broke up and moved seaward. Suspicious gleams of pale blue appeared here and there on a warm, windy morning in March or early April; sullen and explosive muttering punctuated the air. Then with the full outgoing tide the cakes of ice began to move, jamming and hurtling one another, sometimes being thrown into the air by the pressure beneath. Adventuresome boys of parents more careless than our own occasionally tried the risky experiment of crossing the inner bay by jumping from one to another if perchance the break-up occurred on a Saturday. If it happened on ordinary days, it must be intermittently watched from the schoolhouse windows, which on one side faced the sea, but which were placed so high in the wall as to be barely accessible even to the most ambitious vision. The difficulty of keeping one's mind and eyes upon one's books on such a morning was intense.

Tuesdays, Thursdays, and Saturdays in spring and summer were fish-boat mornings. By seven o'clock on days when the tide served, Captain Andrew Cole had sailed from the outer bay, having far earlier hauled his trawl. The young representatives of each family table gathered at the wharf, not reluctant to wait their turn while the green water slapped at the piers and the gulls were certain of full stomachs. A five-pound haddock, cleaned and scraped, could be bought for fifteen cents, the black stripe down his silvery sides guaranteeing wary purchasers against the despised hake, which no Maine connoisseur of fish could tolerate. There were clams, too, dipped from a sodden tub at ten cents a quart measure and, upon occasion, tinker mackerel in ravishing shades of blue and green, so cheap that two dozen might be bought without greatly diminishing the family pocketbook.

There were clams to be dug from the mud flats, many bare feet spotting them by the tiny jets of water which they spouted from their hiding-places. The backaches produced by heavy clam-hoes in tough mud were always less painful than those engendered by piling wood or cultivating garden rows of potatoes or beans! We baked them by building fires of driftwood beneath flat rocks and laying the clams between layers of wet seaweed. Nearly every summer these clambakes took on a co-operative character participated in by the village at large. On these occasions our elders chartered a schooner in the harbour large enough to consider a hundred persons a mere handful. We sailed then to Long Island, laden with foodstuffs sufficient for any ordinary siege, and spent the day on wider, sandier shores. The dinner served on such village picnics tested the gastronomic capacities of the community and could hardly be excelled by any eighteenth century repast. Lobsters and clams, broiled and baked, fish in chowders, hard-boiled eggs, sandwiches and doughnuts, fresh cakes, turnovers, and tarts, blueberry and apple pies, root beer, lemonade and coffee! What wonder that the sail homeward before a southeast wind was silent and that we trudged in families, still silent, up the village street, filled, among many other things, with a sleepy content!

(3)

Beyond all these tangible influences, the coast itself, and the very fact that we lived upon it, placed its intangible mark upon our minds. Secure though we were in our safe haven, we knew full well that the sea was treacherous and insecure. Something of the same shrewd, patient wisdom must be the heritage of prairie children or of those dwelling by great rivers, who are born to scent disaster in rising winds and waters. Few of us of my generation will ever forget that tragic November night when the Boston boat went down with all on board. Reared on tales of shipwreck and suffering upon oceans near and far, we were not surprised by the hardships which every winter brought within our knowledge. We read or were told of lighthouse children drowned by falling into fissures of the rock, of a woman who tended a great lamp through a three days' storm while the body of her husband lay in the lighthouse sitting-room. We knew of outlying islands beset with starvation in an especially bitter winter, of mailboats foundered in high seas. Is it too much then to believe that there crept into our minds earlier than into the minds of most children a sense of the inevitability, not only of suffering but of endurance as well, that we grew, perhaps unconsciously and insensibly, to look upon sorrow not as an individual, concrete matter but rather as a mighty abstraction, necessary and common to all human life? An easier, more

fortified age may well question such an assumption; but few
who were born to a seafaring heritage and few who knew
coast life even a quarter of a century ago will doubt it.

THE ICE TRADE ON THE KENNEBEC

by

ROBERT P. TRISTRAM COFFIN

The shopkeepers of Hallowell and Gardiner and Augusta had
watched the January weather like hawks. They thumbed their
ledgers and shook their graying temples at the lengthening
columns of debit. The doctors had their eye on the sky as they
felt of their lank wallets. Twenty miles deep each side of the
river, farmers in small story-and-a-half farmhouses eyed their
grocery-store thermometers at the side door, and bit more
sparingly into their B.L. plugs. They chewed longer on their
cuds too. In the kitchen, the wife was scraping the lower staves
of the flour barrel. The big bugs in the wide white mansions
along the river looked out of their east or west windows at
crack of day to see the state of the water. Teachers in school
grew short with their pupils who confused Washington's crossing of the Delaware with Clark's fording the fields around
Vincennes. The mild weather continued. The river rolled on,
blue in its ripples. Shopkeepers got short with their wives.

Then a sharp blue wind came up out of the northwest, the mer-
cury in the thermometers tumbled. The pines roared on into the
dark, the stars snapped in the sky like sapphires. Good weather
for future soldiers, Napoleon once remarked. Napoleon be
hanged! So thought the farmers along the Kennebec, who were
up in history as much as they were down in their pork barrels.

There were enough small pairs of pants running around their farms already. What they needed was nights to breed that life-giving ice which would keep the small thighs in the trousers going. Good freezing nights for starting the crop of the water.

The cold spell was a real one. Farmers had to beat their arms each side of their buffalo coats. Next sundown the wind fell. It got still as a pocket. You could hear the stars sputter over the valley. The shopkeepers sat sipping their evening's lime juice and gloated over their newspapers. "The Hudson Valley: continued mild weather, southerly winds, higher temperatures and showers for next week." It was a different story up here in Maine. The kitchen windowpanes had white ferns at their corners. A knife handle would have to be used on the water bucket in the morning. Down Hudson, up Kennebec! In the morning, there were no more waves running on the river. The water looked like a long, dark looking glass dropped between the hills. In a hundred sheds the grindstones were humming.

Then next day the January thaw came. Teachers went all to pieces as early as Wednesday in the week. Doctors used the whip on their horses as they clattered over the steaming ruts. Shopkeepers did not throw in the extra pilot bread but tied up the bags and bit off the twine. The big bugs behind the Ionian porticoes put aside the *Annals* of Tacitus and took down the *Magnalia Christi Americana* of Cotton Mather and Jonathan Edwards's *Sinners in the Hands of an Angry God*. Small boys lost their tempers and kicked the jackstraws their bachelor uncles had whittled out in the shape of oars and eelspears all over the floor. Farmers sat down to Indian pudding without any salt hake to season it off.

Young Timothy Toothaker decided not to ask Susannah Orr a certain question until mayflower time or later. And he stopped spooling new rungs for her future bed.

The thaw lasted eight days. Somebody saw a robin. He didn't get any vote of thanks from his neighbors. A body could see his dead grandmother in such fog as there was. The graybeards by the barrel stove in Ephraim Doughty's grocery store at Bowdoin Center shivered in their shoes. Ephraim had said earlier in the evening, as he looked out at the weather glumly, "Open winter, fat graveyards." Active Frost cheated at checkers and got caught. Wash Alexander drank up all his wife's Peruna.

The only consolation in Kennebec County was the newspaper. It said it was raining all up and down the Hudson, from Saratoga to Staten Island.

February came in murky. But the trotting horses on the Kennebec barns swung round at last and headed north: the thermometer went below zero and stayed there. Everybody began to breathe again, and the grindstones started singing.

The Kennebec was gray glass again, next dawn and next and next. It grew blacker as the days went by. In the third night the drums began, a single stroke, now and then, low bass and far away, rolling and reverberating along the hills. Next morning there were white cracks on the dark drumhead to show where the drumsticks had struck. All at once, at four o'clock, the whole stretch of the river below the Augusta falls blossomed out with children in bright scarves, just out of school. A thousand young farmers and townsmen ground bark, cut figure eights, and yelled themselves hoarse at Ring-Leavo. Fat boys of six on their first skates stared wide-eyed at the green water weeds hanging still and going down into fearful darkness under their toes. At night bonfires ran down the river from bend to bend. Flame answered flame from Skowhegan to Swan Island. Everybody but those in slippers and those in the cradles was out on the ice. And next afternoon the horses had taken to the new ice highway that connected all the Kennebec towns. Men flew along behind them, mountains of robes in narrow sleighs. Their big mustaches smoked, and their breaths clung to them like mufflers straining out behind. Women swept past, little crepe bonnets cocked over the left eye and eyes like jets and blue diamonds. The ice was marked off into lanes, the racing sleighs came out. Horses came up the river, neck and neck, the flowers of their breaths festooned each side of them like garlands hung from high head to high head. Whips cracked, and shouts sent out long echoes each way. The chipped ice shone like splinters flying from a rainbow. Young men had young arms around waists of only eighteen inches, and young people started off on the road to matrimony on the thinnest of bright steel shoes.

But back up on the farms the men were grinding their picks. Women were laying out armfuls of gray socks with white heels and toes, piling up the flannel shirts, packing up bacon and ham and sausage meat and loaves. Boys were oiling harness and polishing the glass sidelights of headstalls. Chains were clinking, and sleds were being piled with blankets and bedding and victuals and extra whiffletrees, cant dogs, picks, and feed for the horses.

Down along the river the doors stood open in the big ice-houses, with sides lined with sawdust, that for months had been shut in silence except for the sharp, thin music of wasps. Men were clearing out old roughage and rubbing the sections of track free of rust. Machinery was being oiled. Gouges and scrapers were being looked over and assembled by the river's side.

The preachers and everybody else in Gardiner and Richmond, Hallowell and Dresden, went to bed that night praying for the snow to hold up and the red blood in the glass to stay down in the ball where it belonged. The river of Henry Hudson was still liquid as it went under the Catskills and down by the walls of the Palisades. God was in his heaven!

In the clear dawn next day, along a hundred roads that led down to the Kennebec, farmers were trudging, mustaches hanging down to the woolen mufflers like the tusks on the walrus. Brown mustaches, golden ones, black ones, gray ones, and white. But every one in front of a man. And behind them streamed their wealth, on its own feet. Tall, sinewy sons, out of school for good and on the doorstep of manhood and marriage, horses with hides like scrubbed horse chestnuts, big of hoof and billowy of muscle, fattened on corn, sharp shod, with long calks of steel that bit into the frozen ground. Here you could reckon up a man's prosperity in solid, tangible things, as in the days of Jacob and Laban. Goods with the breath of life in them. Like Job's. The richest man was one who had nine or ten strong men to follow the swing of his creasing trousers in ringing, ironed shoes. Or three or four spans of horses with the morning star in their foreheads and the music of steel under their feet. So the wealth of the Kennebec came down to the harvest of Maine's best winter crop in the eighties.

Tramps, even, were coming. And all the black sheep of a hundred faraway pastures, beyond Maine, were swinging off the sides of freight cars in the chill gray of the morning. Drifters from far beyond New England.

The men crowded into the river lodging houses of Hallowell and Gardiner, Pittston and Dresden. They unloaded and stowed their dunnage in their temporary homes for the next few weeks. They armed themselves with picks and gougers and saws. Each man had his favorite tool tucked under his quilted arm. They descended on the cold harvest floor with horses and sons in a great host.

Then the field of the harvest was marked off for the game of wealth to be played there. Men walked with gougers tracing the line their narrow plows made straight as a die across the river. After them came the horse-drawn gougers cutting a deeper double furrow. Another army of men took up the game at right angles to the others, crisscrossing the wide fields. And then the sawyers came, slow with their loads of shoulder muscle and woolen shirts. They set in their saws and began the cutting of the gigantic checkers from the checkerboards on the hard Kennebec. The men stood to their work with both hands on the handles each side of their long tools, going down, coming back, fifty men keeping time as they ate into the stuff that meant their life, bed, and board, and fodder for their cattle. It was a sight to see the gates-ajar mustaches swinging like pendulums, gold and dark, and the breath in them changing to icicles as they worked. Every so often the picks spoke, and the sawed lines lengthened ahead of the sawyers. Noon saw a dozen checkerboards marked out on the river. One notable fact about the tools of the ice industry on the Kennebec is this: they were the only tools that were good enough to remain unchanged from the beginning of the industry to the end of it.

Then the workers went to the shores and ate their cold ham and bread and broke the crystals in the top of their jugs and drank the sluggish milk. They built fires to toast their thick soles and sat on the leeward side chewing their quids of tobacco in the heat and haze of the smoke that made the tears run from their eyes. Fathers and sons broke into cakes and frosty doughnuts the wives and mothers had made. Apple pie with splinters of ice.

The afternoon saw the first great checkers of ice lifted from the checkerboards. With heaving of cant dogs and picks, the square crystals came up into the splendid sunshine, sparkling like emeralds shading to azure in their deep hearts, with sections of whole rainbows where the edges were flawed. Layer on layer of brightness, layers of solid winter to go into the hot heart of summer in faraway cities and scorching lands. Long canals opened up into dark water, and men poled the cakes down to the ends where other men caught them with cant dogs as they came, hoisted them up on the ice, slued them to the runways. Chains clanked, the hooks bit into them, and up they flashed along the high lines of steel and plunged into the icehouses.

Inside, men caught the thunderng cakes and switched them, this one to the right, this to the left, to their places. The walls of cakes rose gradually, aisles of air spaces left between the walls of solid crystal. The workers here were in their shirt sleeves. They were the youngest of the men, sons more often than fathers. Their work made them glow inside like cookstoves. The sweat ran down their faces. They stood by the cataracts of ice and flung the bright streams each way, stepping as in a dance to keep clear of a blow that would shatter their bones. The work was like the thunder of summer in their ears, thunder all day long. And the house filled up with the cakes. Square cakes piled as even as the sides of a barn, true and deep blue in the steaming dusk. The men walked between walls of Maine's cold wealth.

And the steel-bright days went by. No thaws or rain came to erase the grooves in the checkerboards. The icehouses were filled to their eaves and the last tier roofed in the aisles between the cakes. Roughage was heaped over all. The doors were closed and sealed.

That year the Hudson did not freeze over till March. The betting of the Maine farmers had been three to one against its doing so. They won their bets. The rival river, the only rival the clear blue Kennebec had among the rivers of earth, had lean-kine stalls along its banks that year of our Lord. The Lord had been good. The Kennebec ice farmers heaped great towers of the harvest outside their houses and covered them with spruce boughs and sawdust, for extra measure. The Knickerbocker Ice Company lost nothing. For they owned most of the icehouses along both the Hudson and the Kennebec. All ice was ice to them. The Kennebec crop was better than the Hudson, in fact, for the water in the Maine river was clearer and purer. Kennebec ice stood at the head of all ice. It was the Hudson ice cutters who lost. But if Peter was robbed, Paul was paid. The Kennebec farmers went back to their hens and heifers with wallets stuffing out their trousers and their sons' trousers, after the $4-a-week lodging and eating bills had been paid. The grocers canceled whole tomes of ledgers. The schoolteachers kept their patience right up to "Horatius at the Bridge" in the Friday afternoon's speaking. New barrels of pork and flour came home to the high farms on the whistling runners of the horse sleds. And barrels of halibuts' heads and broken-bread. Active Frost stopped moving his checkers when his foeman turned to take a shot at the spittoon. And Timothy Toothaker asked the question when he brought his Susannah the first bunch of mayflowers. They were married and setting up housekeeping on new pine floors and in the spooled maple bed before the catkins were gone from the popples.

The geese were coming back early, up along Merrymeeting, that same spring, before the middle of April. And in late April that best day of all the spring on the Kennebec came, when the first boat arrived, the Boston steamer, with the star on her smokestack and her whistle tied down all the way from Swan Island to the Cobbosseecontee, waking the dead and the hills with her news of spring at last. There was not a church bell in the five towns that wasn't ringing. Women in bombazine waved handkerchiefs. School was let out for the day, and the hills were alive with children.

May saw the ice ships arrive and tie up at the docks. The ice-houses opened their doors. The Kennebec crystals came down the runs, slithered across the decks of the four-masters and into the holds. When a number of the old hulls were loaded, which had once breasted the waves on the underside of the world, white under thunderclouds of sail, a tugboat steamed down-river on a neap tide, dragging the old veterans of the Atlantic back to the Atlantic again, below Popham.

And down in New York and Philadelphia prosperous citizens were getting down their ice-cream freezers. Children in Richmond and children under the shadow of the Blue Ridge were running starry-eyed behind high carts with letters frosted and dripping with icicles. The letters on those carts spelled "Kennebec Ice." And deep in Alabama and Mississippi pickaninnies ran with pieces of Maine's finest river in their black palms and heaven in their eyes. Farther south, the crystals of Maine touched the fruit of the Caribbees. Far down off the Horn and up the other side, ships with bones bred in Maine forests carried the Maine treasure to the Pacific. Trains plowed through the dusty cornlands of Nebraska and on to the Rockies, carrying Maine ice. And a whole nation knew the taste of the clear Kennebec. Half the world, too, England and France, and Holland.

But all that was in the twilight days of wooden ships, when Maine women still kept their neat houses moving around the world. That was when the wizards had not wakened new secrets out of electricity and steel. That was in the eighties and nineties.

Now the Kennebec icehouses are rotting and falling back into the earth. Their interiors are taken over by the wasps and the mice. The old piers are sinking into the water. No ship comes up in tow of a tug through the first leaves of May. School keeps week after week, and there are no bells ringing out to greet the steamer that leads up the spring. The gougers and saws are rusted half away.

For the Kennebec crystals, last harvest of Maine's finest river, have joined the white pine and the spruce, the sturgeon and shad and salmon. The end is elegy. The day of natural ice is done. New men, outside New England, bring their sons in their strength to the work of refrigerating homes and factories. And the small farmhouses, back from the river, that once housed great numbers of young men and boys, are full of empty rooms where the swallows bring up their young, or they have only a few children who work at their tasks and never need turn their heads toward the river, where the strength of their fathers lay and their fathers' lives.

The other day my good Kennebec friend whose great house looks up the river and down, over a twelve-foot hedge of spruce, took me out and showed me the tools of the ice harvesters. They were dark with rust and covered with cobwebs. They had joined the flint arrows and the bows that once bent to bring life to the men along the ancient Kennebec. When we were coming back we passed a strange depression in the woods, grown up with lusty spruces. It was the refrigerator men of my friend's house used a hundred fifty years ago. It was the ruins of the earth cellar where they had stored their vegetables in summer and winter, to keep them from heat and cold. It was the Kennebec refrigerator his ancestors and mine learned how to make from the Indians when they drove them away into the everlasting dark from the bright blue river. That refrigerator was a ruin, and the Kennebec was as young and lusty as ever as it hurried toward the sea. Someday our own sons' far great-grandchildren may find among the timbers of my friend's house the rusted shards of the electric refrigerator that serves the house today. And the Kennebec will be going down to the sea, as young and as fresh and blue as ever.

AN OLD SEACOAST MANSION

by

SARAH ORNE JEWETT

I do not know that the Brandon house is really very remarkable, but I never have been in one that interested me in the same way. Kate used to recount to select audiences at school some of her experiences with her Aunt Katherine, and it was popularly believed that she once carried down some indestructible picture-books when they were first in fashion, and the old lady basted them for her to hem round the edges at the rate of two a day. It may have been fabulous. It was impossible to imagine any children in the old place; everything was for grown people; even the stair-railing was too high to slide down on. The chairs looked as if they had been put, at the furnishing of the house, in their places, and there they meant to remain. The carpets were particularly interesting, and I remember Kate's pointing out to me one day a great square figure in one, and telling me she used to keep house there with her dolls for lack of a better playhouse, and if one of them chanced to fall outside the boundary stripe, it was immediately put to bed with a cold. It is a house with great possibilities; it might easily be made charming. There are four

From *Deep Haven* by Sarah O. Jewett (Houghton Mifflin Company: Boston, 1877).

very large rooms on the lower floor, and six above, a wide hall
in each story, and a fascinating garret over the whole, where
were many mysterious old chests and boxes, in one of which
we found Kate's grandmother's love-letters; and you may be
sure the vista of rummages which Mr. Lancaster had laughed
about was explored to its very end. The rooms all have elaborate
cornices, and the lower hall is very fine, with an archway dividing
it, and panellings of all sorts, and a great door at each end,
through which the lilacs in front and the old pensioner plum-
trees in the garden are seen exchanging bows and gestures. Coming from the Lancasters' high city house, it did not seem as if we
had to go up stairs at all there, for every step of the stairway is
so broad and low, and you come half-way to a square landing
with an old straight-backed chair in each farther corner; and
between them a large, round-topped window, with a cushioned
seat, looking out on the garden and the village, the hills far inland, and the sunset beyond all. Then you turn and go up a few
more steps to the upper hall, where we used to stay a great deal.
There were more old chairs and a pair of remarkable sofas, on
which we used to deposit the treasures collected in our wanderings. The wide window which looks out on the lilacs and the
sea was a favorite seat of ours. Facing each other on either side
of it are two old secretaries, and one of them we ascertained to be
the hiding-place of secret drawers, in which may be found valuable records deposited by ourselves one rainy day when we first
explored it. We wrote, between us, a tragic "journal" on some
yellow old letter-paper we found in the desk. We put it in the
most hidden drawer by itself, and flatter ourselves that it will be
regarded with great interest some time or other. Of one of the
front rooms, "the best chamber," we stood rather in dread. It is
very remarkable that there seem to be no ghost-stories connected
with any part of the house, particularly this. We are neither of
us nervous; but there is certainly something dismal about the
room. The huge curtained bed and immense easy-chairs, windows, and everything were draped in some old-fashioned kind

of white cloth which always seemed to be waving and moving about of itself. The carpet was most singularly colored with dark reds and indescribable grays and browns, and the pattern, after a whole summer's study, could never be followed with one's eye. The paper was captured in a French prize somewhere some time in the last century, and part of the figure was shaggy, and there in little spiders found habitation, and went visiting their acquaintances across the shiny places. The color was an unearthly pink and a forbidding maroon, with dim, white spots, which gave it the appearance of having moulded. It made you low-spirited to look long in the mirror; and the great lounge one could not have cheerful associations with, after hearing that Miss Brandon herself did not like it, having seen so many of her relatives lie there dead. There were fantastic china ornaments from Bible subjects on the mantel, and the only picture was one of the Maid of Orleans tied with an unnecessarily strong rope to a very stout stake. The best parlor we also rarely used, because all the portraits which hung there had for some unaccountable reason taken a violent dislike to us, and followed us suspiciously with their eyes. The furniture was stately and very uncomfortable, and there was something about the room which suggested an invisible funeral.

There is not very much to say about the dining-room. It was not specially interesting, though the sea was in sight from one of the windows. There were some old Dutch pictures on the wall, so dark that one could scarcely make out what they were meant to represent, and one or two engravings. There was a huge sideboard, for which Kate had brought down from Boston Miss Brandon's own silver which had stood there for so many years, and looked so much more at home and in place than any other possibly could have looked, and Kate also found in the closet the three great decanters with silver labels chained round their necks, which had always been the companions of the tea-service in her aunt's lifetime. From the little closets in the sideboard there came a most significant odor of cake and wine whenever one opened the doors. We used Miss Brandon's beautiful old blue India china which she had given to Kate, and which had been carefully packed all winter. Kate sat at the head and I at the foot of the round table, and I must confess that we were apt to have either a feast or a famine, for at first we often forgot to provide our dinners. If this were the case Maggie was sure to serve us with most derisive elegance, and make us wait for as much ceremony as she thought necessary for one of Mrs. Lancaster's dinner-parties.

The west parlor was our favorite room down stairs. It had a great fireplace framed in blue and white Dutch tiles which ingeniously and instructively represented the careers of the good and the bad man: the starting-place of each being a very singular cradle in the centre at the top. The last two of the series are very high art: a great coffin stands in the foreground of each, and the virtuous man is being led off by two disagreeable-looking angels, while the wicked one is hastening from an indescribable but unpleasant assemblage of claws and horns and eyes which is rapidly advancing from the distance, open-mouthed, and bringing a chain with it.

There was a large cabinet holding all the small curiosities and knick-knacks there seemed to be no other place for,—odd china figures and cups and vases, unaccountable Chinese carvings and exquisite corals and sea-shells, minerals and Swiss wood-work, and articles of vertu from the South Seas. Underneath were stored boxes of letters and old magazines; for this was one of the houses where nothing seems to have been thrown away. In one parting we found a parcel of old manuscript sermons, the existence of which was a mystery, until Kate remembered there had been a gifted son of the house who entered the ministry and soon died. The windows had each a pane of stained glass, and on the wide sills we used to put our immense bouquets of field-flowers. There was one place which I liked and sat in more than any other. The chimney filled nearly the whole side of the room, all but this little corner, where there was just room for a very comfortable high-backed cushioned chair, and a narrow window where I always had a bunch of fresh green ferns in a tall champagne-glass. I used to write there often, and always sat there when Kate sang and played. She sent for a tuner, and used to successfully coax the long-imprisoned music from the antiquated piano, and sing for her visitors by the hour. She almost always sang her oldest songs, for they seemed most in keeping with everything about us. I used to fancy that the portraits liked our being there. There was one young girl who seemed solitary and forlorn among the rest in the room, who were all middle-aged. For their part they looked amiable, but rather unhappy, as if she had come in and interrupted their conversation. We both grew very fond of her, and it seemed, when we went in the last morning on purpose to take leave of her, as if she looked at us imploringly. She was soon afterward boxed up, and now enjoys society after her own heart in Kate's room in Boston.

There was the largest sofa I ever saw opposite the fireplace; it must have been brought in in pieces, and built in the room. It was broad enough for Kate and me to lie on together, and and very high and square; but there was a pile of soft cushions at one end. We used to enjoy it greatly in September, when the evenings were long and cool, and we had many candles, and a fire—and crickets too—on the hearth, and the dear dog lying on the rug. I remember one rainy night, just before Miss Tennant and Kitty Bruce went away; we had a real drift-wood fire, and blew out the lights and told stories. Miss Margaret knows so many and tells them so well. Kate and I were unusually entertaining, for we became familiar with the family record of the town, and could recount marvellous adventures by land and sea, and ghost-stories by the dozen. We had never either of us been in a society consisting of so many travelled people! Hardly a man but had been the most of his life at sea. Speaking of ghost-stories, I must tell you that once in the summer two Cambridge girls who were spending a week with us unwisely enticed us into giving some thrilling recitals, which nearly frightened them out of their wits, and Kate and I were finally in terror ourselves. We had all been on the sofa in the dark, singing and talking, and were waiting in great suspense after I had finished one of such particular horror that I declared it should be the last, when we heard footsteps on the hall stairs. There were lights in the dining-room which shone faintly through the half-closed door, and we saw something white and shapeless come slowly down, and clutched each other's gowns in agony. It was only Kate's dog, who came in and laid his head in her lap and slept peacefully. We thought we could not sleep a wink after this, and I bravely went alone out to the light to see my watch, and, finding it was past twelve, we concluded to sit up all night and to go down to the shore at sunrise, it would be so much easier than getting up early some morning. We had been out rowing and had taken a long walk the day before, and were obliged to dance and make other slight exertions to keep ourselves awake at one time. We lunched at two, and I never shall forget the sunrise that morning; but we were singularly quiet and abstracted that day, and indeed for several days after Deephaven was "a land in which it seemed always afternoon," we breakfasted so late.

As Mrs. Kew had said, there was "a power of china." Kate and I were convinced that the lives of her grandmothers must have been spent in giving tea-parties. We counted ten sets of cups, beside quantities of stray ones; and some member of the family had evidently devoted her time to making a collection of pitchers.

There was an escritoire in Miss Brandon's own room, which we looked over one day. There was a little package of letters; ship letters mostly, tied with a very pale and tired-looking blue ribbon. They were in a drawer with a locket holding a faded miniature on ivory and a lock of brown hair, and there were also some dry twigs and bits of leaf which had long ago been bright wild-roses, such as still bloom among the Deephaven rocks. Kate said that she had often heard her mother wonder why her aunt never had cared to marry, for she had chances enough doubtless, and had been rich and handsome and finely educated. So there was a sailor lover after all, and perhaps he had been lost at sea and she faithfully kept the secret, never mourning outwardly. "And I always thought her the most matter-of-fact old lady," said Kate; "yet here's her romance, after all." We put the letters outside on a chair to read, but afterwards carefully replaced them, without untying them. I'm glad we did. There were other letters which we did read, and which interested us very much,—letters from her girl friends written in the boarding-school vacations, and just after she finished school. Those in one of the smaller packages were charming; it must have been such a bright, nice girl who wrote them! They were very few, and were tied with black ribbon, and marked on the outside in girlish writing: "My dearest friend, Dolly McAllister, died September 3, 1809, aged eighteen." The ribbon had evidently been untied and the letters read many times. One began: "My dear, delightful Kitten: I am quite overjoyed to find my father has business which will force him to go to Deephaven next week, and he kindly says if there be no more rain I may ride with him to see you. I will surely come, for if there is danger of spattering my gown, and he bids me stay at home, I shall go galloping after him and overtake him when it is too late to send me back. I have so much to tell you." I wish I knew more about the visit. Poor Miss Katherine! it made us sad to look over these treasures of her girlhood. There were her compositions and exercise-books; some samplers and queer little keepsakes; withered flowers and some pebbles and other things of like value, with which there was probably some pleasant association. "Only think of her keeping them all her days," said I to Kate. "I am continually throwing some relic of that kind away, because I forget why I have it!"

There was a box in the lower part which Kate was glad to find, for she had heard her mother wonder if some such things were not in existence. It held a crucifix and a mass-book and some rosaries, and Kate told me Miss Katherine's youngest and favorite brother had become a Roman Catholic while studying in Europe. It was a dreadful blow to the family; for in those days there could have been few deeper disgraces to the Brandon family than to have one of its sons go over to popery. Only Miss Katherine treated him with kindness, and after a time he disappeared without telling even her where he was going, and was only heard from indirectly once or twice afterward. It was a great grief to her. "And mamma knows," said Kate, "that she always had a lingering hope for his return, for one of the last times she saw Aunt Katherine before she was ill she spoke of soon going to be with all the rest, and said, 'Though your Uncle Henry, dear,'—and she stopped and smiled sadly; 'you'll think me a very foolish old woman, but I never quite gave up thinking he might come home.' "

WINTER BIRDS ON APPLEDORE

by

CELIA THAXTER

It is exhilarating, spite of the intense cold, to wake to the brightness the northwest gale always brings after the hopeless smother of a prolonged snow-storm. The sea is deep indigo, whitened with flashing waves all over the surface; the sky is speckless; no cloud passes across it the whole day long; and the sun sets red and clear, without any abatement of the wind. The spray flying on the western shore for a moment is rosy as the sinking sun shines through, but for a moment only,—and again there is nothing but the ghastly whiteness of the salt-water ice, the cold, gray rock, the sullen, foaming brine, the unrelenting

From *Among the Isles of Shoals* by Celia Thaxter. (Houghton Mifflin and Company: Boston, 1884).

heavens, and the sharp wind cutting like a knife. All night long
it roars beneath the hollow sky,—roars still at sunrise. Again
the day passes precisely like the one gone before; the sun lies
in a glare of quicksilver on the western water, sinks again in
the red west to rise on just such another day; and thus goes on,
for weeks sometimes, with an exasperating pertinacity that
would try the most philosophical patience. There comes a time
when just that glare of quicksilver on the water is not to be
endured a minute longer. During this period no boat goes to or
comes from the mainland, and the prisoners on the rock are cut off
from all intercourse with their kind. Abroad, only the cattle
move, crowding into the sunniest corners, and stupidly chewing
the cud; and the hens and ducks, that chatter and cackle and
cheerfully crow in spite of fate and the northwest gale. The
dauntless and graceful gulls soar on their strong pinions over
the drift cast up about the coves. Sometimes flocks of snow-
buntings wheel about the house and pierce the loud breathing
of the wind with sweet, wild cries. And often the spectral arctic
owl may be seen on a height, sitting upright, like a column of
snow, its large, round head slowly turning from left to right,
ever on the alert, watching for the rats that plague the settlement
almost as grievously as they did Hamelin town, in Brunswick,
five hundred years ago.

How the rats came here first is not known; probably some old
ship imported them. They live partly on mussels, the shells of
which lie in heaps about their holes, as the violet-lined freshwater shells lie about the nests of the muskrats on the mainland.
They burrow among the rocks close to the shore, in favorable
spots, and, somewhat like the moles, make subterranean galleries,
whence they issue at low tide, and, stealing to the crevices of
seaweed-curtained rocks, they fall upon and dislodge any unfortunate crabs they may find, and kill and devour them. Many
a rat has caught a Tartar in this perilous kind of hunting, has
been dragged into the sea and killed,—drowned in the clutches

of the crab he sought to devour; for the strength of those shell-fish is something astonishing.

Several snowy owls haunt the island the whole winter long. I have never heard them cry like other owls; when disturbed or angry, they make a sound like a watchman's rattle, very loud and harsh, or they whistle with intense shrillness, like a human being. Their habitual silence adds to their ghostliness; and when at noonday they sit, high up, snow-white above the snow-drifts, blinking their pale yellow eyes in the sun, they are weird indeed. One night in March I saw one perched upon a rock between me and the "last remains of sunset dimly burning" in the west, his curious outline drawn black against the redness of the sky, his large head bent forward, and the whole aspect meditative and most human in its expression. I longed to go out and sit beside him and talk to him in the twilight, to ask of him the story of his life, or, if he would have permitted it, to watch him without a word. The plumage of this creature is wonderfully beautiful,—white, with scattered spots like little flecks of tawny cloud,—and his black beak and talons are powerful and sharp as iron; he might literally grapple his friend, or his enemy, with hooks of steel. As he is clothed in a mass of down, his outlines are so soft that he is like an enormous snowflake while flying; and he is a sight worth seeing when he stretches wide his broad wings, and sweeps down on his prey, silent and swift, with an unerring aim, and bears it off to the highest rock he can find, to devour it. In the summer one finds frequently upon the heights a little, solid ball of silvery fur and pure white bones, washed and bleached by the rain and sun; it is the rat's skin and skeleton in a compact bundle, which the owl rejects after having swallowed it.

Some quieter day, on the edge of a southerly wind, perhaps, boats go out over the gray, sad water after sea-fowl,—the murres that swim in little companies, keeping just out of reach of shot, and are so spiteful that they beat the boat with their beaks, when wounded, in impotent rage, till they are despatched with an oar or another shot; or kittiwakes,—exquisite creatures like living forms of snow and cloud in color, with beaks and feet of dull gold,—that come when you wave a white handkerchief, and flutter almost within reach of your hand; or oldwives, called by the native scoldenores, with clean white caps; or clumsy eider-ducks, or coots, or mergansers, or whatever they may find. Black ducks, of course, are often shot. Their jet-black, shining plumage is splendidly handsome, set off with the broad, flame-colored beak. Little auks, stormy-petrels, loons, grebes, *lords-and-ladies, sea-pigeons, sea-parrots, various guillemots, and all sorts of gulls abound. Sometimes an eagle sweeps over; gannets pay occasional visits; the great blue heron is often seen in autumn and spring. One of the most striking birds is the cormorant, called here "shag"; from it the rock at Duck Island takes its name. It used to be an object of almost awful interest to me when I beheld it perched upon White Island Head,— a solemn figure, high and dark against the clouds. Once, while living on that island, in the thickest of a great storm in autumn, when we seemed to be set between two contending armies, deafened by the continuous cannonading of breakers, and lashed and beaten by winds and waters till it was almost impossible to hear ourselves speak, we became aware of another sound, which pierced to our ears, bringing a sudden terror lest it should be the voices of human beings. Opening the window a little, what a wild combination of sounds came shrieking in! A large flock of wild geese had settled for safety upon the rock, and completely surrounded us,—agitated, clamorous, weary. We might have secured any number of them, but it would have been a shameful thing. We were glad, indeed, that they should share our little foothold in that chaos, and they flew away unhurt when the tempest lulled. I was a very young child when this happened, but I never can forget that autumn night,—it seemed so wonderful and pitiful that those storm-beaten birds

---

* harlequin ducks; *histrionicus histrionicus* H. B.

should have come crying to our rock; and the strange, wild chorus that swept in when the window was pried open a little took so strong a hold upon my imagination that I shall hear it as long as I live. The lighthouse, so beneficent to mankind, is the destroyer of birds,—of land birds particularly, though in thick weather sea-birds are occasionally bewildered into breaking their heads against the glass, plunging forward headlong towards the light, just as the frail moth of summer evenings madly seeks its death in the candle's blaze. Sometimes in autumn, always in spring, when birds are migrating, they are destroyed in such quantities by this means that it is painful to reflect upon. The keeper living at the island three years ago told me that he picked up three hundred and seventy-five in one morning at the foot of the lighthouse, all dead. They fly with such force against the glass that their beaks are often splintered. The keeper said he found the destruction greatest in hazy weather, and he thought "they struck a ray at a great distance and followed it up." Many a May morning have I wandered about the rock at the foot of the tower mourning over a little apron brimful of sparrows, swallows, thrushes, robins, fire-winged blackbirds, many-colored warblers and flycatchers, beautifully clothed yellow-birds, nuthatches, catbirds, even the purple finch and scarlet tanager and golden oriole, and many more beside,— enough to break the heart of a small child to think of! Once a great eagle flew against the lantern and shivered the glass. That was before I lived there; but after we came, two gulls cracked one of the large, clear panes, one stormy night.

The sea-birds are comparatively few and shy at this time; but I remember when they were plentiful enough, when on Duck Island in summer the "medrakes," or tern, made rude nests on the beach, and the little yellow gulls, just out of the eggs, ran tumbling about among the stones, hiding their foolish heads in every crack and cranny, and, like the ostrich, imagining themselves safe so long as they could not see the danger. And even now the sandpipers build in numbers on the islands, and the young birds, which look like tiny tufts of fog, run about among the bayberry-bushes, with sweet, scared piping. They are exquisitely beautiful and delicate, covered with a down just like gray mist, with brilliant black eyes, and slender, graceful legs that make one think of grass-stems. And here the loons congregate in spring and autumn. These birds seem to me the most human and at the same time the most demoniac of their kind. I learned to imitate their different cries; they are wonderful! At one time the loon language was so familiar that I could almost always summon a considerable flock by going down to the water and assuming the neighborly and conversational tone which they generally use: after calling a few minutes, first a far-off voice responded, then other voices answered him, and when this was kept up a while, half a dozen birds would come sailing in. It was the most delightful little party imaginable; so comical were they, so entertaining, that it was impossible not to laugh aloud,—and they could laugh too, in a way which chilled the marrow of one's bones. They always laugh, when shot at, if they are missed; as the Shoalers say, "They laugh like a warrior." But their long, wild, melancholy cry before a storm is the most awful note I ever heard from a bird. It is so sad, so hopeless,—a clear, high shriek, shaken, as it drops into silence, into broken notes that make you think of the fluttering of a pennon in the wind,—a shudder of sound. They invariably utter this cry before a storm.

Between the gales from all points of the compass, that

> " 'twixt the green sea and the azured vault
>   Set roaring war,"

some day there falls a dead calm; the whole expanse of the ocean is like a mirror; there's not a whisper of a wave, not a sigh from any wind about the world,—an awful, breathless pause prevails. Then if a loon swims into the motionless little bights about the island, and raises his weird cry, the silent rocks re-echo the unearthly tone, and it seems as if the creature were in league with the mysterious forces that are so soon to turn this deathly stillness into confusion and dismay. All through the day the ominous quiet lasts; in the afternoon, while yet the sea is glassy, a curious undertone of mournful sound can be perceived,—not fitful,—a steady moan such as the wind makes over the mouth of an empty jar. Then the islanders say, "Do you hear Hog Island crying? Now look out for a storm!" No one knows how that low moaning is produced, or why Appledore, of all the islands, should alone lament before the tempest.

MAINE ISLANDS IN THE DAYS OF SAIL

by

W. H. BISHOP

Middleton took steamer for Rockland—an all-night's voyage on a tossing sea. He met with no notable adventure there except the view of a couple of patent-medicine William Tells, who shot apples from each other's heads with genuine rifles, only for the purpose of drawing a crowd to buy their wares. He embarked again, under its half-circle of rude stone and timber limekilns, faintly smoking, like a row of sacked fortresses of the date of the Merovingians, and was soon sailing among the more important islands of the archepelago of Penobscot Bay. He saw at Dix Island and North Haven the quarries of granite of which government custom-houses and post-offices are built, and at Vinalhaven more quarries, where an enormous obelisk for a soldiers' monument was being chiselled out. And so he came down to the outermost of the group, the Isle au Haut, pronounced locally Isle of Holt.

These islands were larger and bolder, and repeated in charming blue knolls all around the horizon the distant Camden

From *Fish and Men in the Maine Islands* by W. H. Bishop (Harper and Brothers: New York, 1885).

Mountains and Blue Hills themselves on the main, but had in shape the general character of those he had just left. They were cut into innumerable long coves in the direction of their greatest length, from north-east to south-west.

"I have half a mind to invent a legend," said he, "that when the manitou of coasts was getting up this topography, he drew his fingers through the mud, with the idea of a graphic imitation of the fringe on his hunting jacket, wiggled them about a little, and let it stand."

An occasional tide-mill, turned each way by ebb and flow, is found on these deep coves. The grist from them is said to be of a better quality than from the steam-mills, being less heated in the process. But the coves are much more turned to account as natural traps for fish. Weirs of sticks and brush, with a single entrance left, are set across them, and the entrance is closed at high tide, imprisoning whatever has passed in. The bottom is almost bare at low water. Middleton heard of famous catches of mackerel, shad, and black-fish, which had been headed off and driven in by a cordon of boats, and stranded on the mud when the tide had gone out. One of his informants said he had thus made fifty dollars in a single day.

The principal channel among the islands was generally termed the Thoroughfare. And—whatever had happened to justify it— the prefix "burnt" was very common. He came, on the Isle of Holt, to Burnt Thoroughfare, and presently, on Deer Island, to Burnt Cove, and not far away was the small island of Burnt Coat. He crossed by a charming untravelled road, so faintly traced as to be like the mere fading vision of a road, over the flank of a mountain, to the outer shore. On the mountain was a lake, giving ice of such clearness in the winter, according to the boast of a native, that you could see to read through twenty-two inches of it, not only as well as, but better than, without it. He held that it had actual magnifying properties.

There was at the Isle au Haut a rude timber assembly hall, with an excellent dancing floor, erected in a spruce grove by the sparsely scattered inhabitants for their social purposes. There were no horses, and when one of the few Isle au Haut cattle found itself by chance in company with horses on the mainland, its agitation was described as something remarkable. Sheep were kept; the principle crops were turnips, hay, and wool. There was an enormous fish as the vane of the meetinghouse. The minister had just then suddenly gone insane. It *did* appear an uninteresting society, Middleton decided, in endeavoring to supply himself with a reason for this; so he had himself set across in a cat-boat—a sail of six miles—to Green's Landing, on Deer Island.

Great granite bowlders occupied all the most desirable building sites at Green's Landing, and the houses of the residents took what remained. Here were some small quarries in bankruptcy. Blocks of mortgaged granite, a great rusted pair of wheels, and a broken crane stood about with a melancholy air, which the signs of two rival music halls near together, "Green's Eureka" and "Eaton's Olympic," could not counterbalance. Miniature islands, with a cedar or two on each, lay on the skirts of the shore, out in the Thoroughfare, as they were apt to do almost everywhere. In misty effects, or in the evening, they seemed like some rakish craft at anchor there. There were other reefs wholly bare, the round dark bulk of which impressed one at night like clumsy marine creatures. You almost expected to hear them snore, and see them take an occasional roll over.

It would not be fair, he found, to infer excessive hilariousness on the part of the residents from the two halls in so small a place. However it might have been in more prosperous times (from which descended traditions of "calico parties," panoramas, and even an "Uncle Tom's Cabin" company, which brought along its own properties in its own sailing craft), they were rarely used now for anything more lively than religious meetings. The islanders were, in fact, of a decided seriousness. Though it happened that even their pastors—one for instance wore earrings, had been a fisherman, and was now a store-keeper, and postmaster as well—were frequently obliged to unite business with their sacred functions for support, the concerns of the small meeting-houses, Seventh-day Baptist, Close-communion Baptist, and Adventist, were the strongest preoccupation of all.

It was a seriousness that seemed to bear a certain ratio to the remoteness of the place from the world at large. On far-away Monhegan, an island of one hundred and twenty-five people, without a post-office or any regular connection with the mainland, the theological tendency seemed all-pervading. No dancing or other profane amusements, no Olympic or Eureka halls, there. The extreme of social gaiety was known as a "Sing." This was was the singing of Moody and Sankey's hymns by the women, with the aid of a cabinet organ, while the rough men stood about in the door-ways as spectators. Middleton heard there the loungers, seated on the barrels at the store of an evening, discuss "free grace" and the "higher life" with all the animation of a question of politics or the scandalous chronicles of a neighborhood.

And yet there now took place on Deer Island an incident of quite an opposite bearing. Middleton set it down to a sort of discouraged listlessness belonging to a place in the very un-American condition of not looking forward to becoming immediately the greatest or only something or other of its kind. Deer Isle was one of the Maine towns which, instead of increasing, annually declined in population. It had now some hundreds less even than in 1860. It formerly owned as many as three hundred sail of vessels; now it was much if it had a score. Nobody bubbled over with the story; it was a state of things not well worth talking about, but, after a while, from some store-keeper, with plenty of leisure on his hands, leaning in his doorway whittling a stick, or some veteran in the shadow of deserted wharf and fish houses falling to pieces of their own weight, the story came out.

The profits of vessel fishing had declined year by year. The government first cut down the nominal rating of tonnage to

English measure, and then took off a bounty of four dollars a ton it had been accustomed to pay by way of encouragement. The old folks had got through going to sea, the young folks did not want to go; it became difficult to get crews, and so the vessels were sold out.

Why did not the young folks want to go? The "pogy" business, the quarries, and the rise of lobstering, all held out more favorable inducements to remain ashore. Depression in time overtook these pursuits of the shore also. The "pogy" business was the catching of porgies and menhaden for their oil. Every resident along the shore had his press—not unlike a ciderpress in its general effect. But then, attracted by the profits of the trade, swift steamers were fitted out by Rhode Island capitalists to cruise with seines; numerous regular factories put up, to such purpose that the porgy was presently all but annihilated.* This particular year he came no more. The quarries were bankrupt, as has been said; but this was a purely local Deer Island matter, while the complaints about fishing were universal. Lobstering, too, which had once paid a steady man four and five dollars a day, was reduced by competition to a matter of a dollar a day, and no more.

But to the incident. The insane minister of the church at Isle au Haut was at present on this island, running at large, harmless enough, but full of pitiably wild projects. He was heard preaching to himself late at night in the lonesome woods; he was continually going down to cool the fever of his iron-gray head, that yet bore traces of scholarly thought, by washing it in the edge of the water. Then he would fancy that he must build a great hotel on Thurlow's Hill with the mortgaged granite, and would hurry, hurry, hurry, cruelly, all day long, without a moment's intermission, from the shore to the upland and back again. These performances could hardly be viewed with unmixed sympathy, and excited the laughter of the young folks.

---

* A like destructionist policy, carried on during the same years, cleared the sturgeon out of our rivers. H. B.

On Sunday night he was allowed to hold a service in Green's Eureka Hall. His audience was made up chiefly of young fishermen, hands from the lobster factory, and quarrymen, or ex-quarrymen, girls, in a kind of uniform of sailor hat and plaid shawl folded close around them, with some children, who took the ceremonies seriously. Their conduct, on the whole, was remarkably good. The disturbance was confined to some unnecessary stalking in and out, completely from one end of the room to the other. The demented preacher affected indignation at this, but was in reality well pleased at having an audience at all, and an opportunity to imitate, with a hundred vagaries, the ceremonies with which he had once been so familiar. Outside stood Isaacson—a cheap-John, who had opened a stock of second-hand clothing for ladies and gentlemen in a disused fish-house on the wharf—and an itinerant doctor, who made the round of the islands twice a year, in his own cat-boat, to cure complaints, awaiting him since his last coming. These two exchanged anecdotes at the expense of all religion, as well as this caricature of it, and seemed to amuse themselves vastly.

Deer Island, eleven miles long, is next in size to Mount Desert, which is fourteen. It is cut up into extraordinary shapes by its coves. There are peninsulas almost gone, and others, over Oceanville way, gone entirely, so that if you crossed to them at ebb tide, it was necessary to wait for the next in order to come back. There were boulders in plenty at one end; good farming land—with a faint reflection in the buildings upon it of the fashionable prosperity of its not very remote neighbor Mount Desert—at the other. The hamlet of Burnt Cove was fairly typical of its kind. It consisted of a score of white houses thinly scattered around an inlet, a chilly white meeting-house on a hill, with no wisp of shade near it, a few gray fish buildings along the water's edge, two wharves on one side of the inlet and one on the other, and three battered schooners lying at anchor. They were waiting for their crews, gone ashore for the haying. One was a "pink-stern" * trading boat. This term, which was once probably "peak-stern," indicated a peculiar high-pooped build which made it the most picturesque of the various kinds of craft encountered. She was fitted out with a miscellaneous stock of goods, and cruised from island to island, often stopping where there was but a single family or individual, and picked up the threads of an infinitesimal commerce to be reached in no other way.

There were some bits of unique ruin on the shore at Burnt Cove. A footway leaning against the sagging gable end of a fish-house, to which was affixed part of the beak of a ship, tottered to its fall. Débris of the kind peculiar to such a settlement—old lobster-traps, broken yawls and dories, spars, a cast-off "pogy" press, unhooped tubs and barrels—had been piled upon an old wharf, till, what with this and its sapping by the tides, its back had broken, and it had gone down to lie among the black sea-weeds. Near by, a dismounted brass gun, brought back by some adventurous person from a wreck at the Magdalen Islands, lay in the grass, while under the window of a cabin was a broken yawl, through the gaps in which grass and flowers had grown up with a charming effect.

In the interior, from point to point, would be found weather-beaten school-houses, and by each school-house a few graves. The inscription "drowned" was frequent on the slabs, tantalizingly void of the further particulars.

"It reminds one too much," said Middleton, "of the inquisitive person with the new acquaintance whose thumb was missing. 'Do tell me how it came about?' said the inquisitive person.

" 'On one condition, that you shall ask no other questions.'

" 'Agreed.'

" 'Very well, it was bit off.' "

The old-time well-sweep was common; there were pasturing sheep among the boulders; on the top of granite, apparently the most sterile, grew mosses, filled with a hardy small cranberry. Middleton accepted with a fine resignation—for their owners—

* the once familiar "pinkie" H. B.

the straitened circumstances which compelled many nice old farm-houses to be left in the landscapes in their pleasing tones of weather-beaten gray and long unrenovated Indian red.

Within the houses the women yet drive the spinning-wheel, and a spinning match took place at one of the school-houses during his stay. It is the bold, large wool-wheel, at which the figure stands, in so much more striking a pose than sitting Gretchen at her flax-wheel. He entered more than once, under cover of the convenient request for a glass of milk, to watch such a figure spinning by a kitchen door, into which fell an angular bar of sunlight, and through which were visible the blue hills and the sea.

It was the islander who was both farmer and fisherman, as a person uniting in himself the two most ancient and honorable occupations, that aroused in Middleton the principal interest. Such a one could not take the trips of two to three weeks with the seiners of the coast fleet; still less could he go the long voyages of the bankers, to the bays of L'Escaut and Chaleurs, to Greenland, and even, as sometimes happens, to the coasts of Iceland, for fresh halibut, where they join the fleets of Northern France, the Netherlands, and Scandinavia. He must attend his lobster-traps; set weirs for herring, menhaden, alewives, and mackerel; keep drag-nets and trawls; perhaps, if favorably located, make a specialty of supplying bait to the fleet, which, now that this must be fresh and kept iced, is often in great straits for it. Between times he runs out to sea for a day or two in his cat-boat, his "Hampton boat," or his jigger. The cat-boat, it appeared, was the better sailer, since the more canvas in a single sail the closer into the wind; but the Hampton boat—a modified pink-stern, with shoulder-of-mutton sails on its small masts—was the "abler," that is to say, better qualified to stand the exigencies of all sorts of weather. The jigger, however, a small schooner of perhaps forty feet long by ten feet beam, with a considerable hold, and a cabin with four bunks, a table, and a rusty sheet-iron stove forward, seemed the most available for general purposes, whether for taking a haul of fish, "smacking" a load of lobsters, wood, or ice, or hawking a load of apples at retail to ports where they were a rarity.

A professional "dragger" carried nearly a mile of nets. They were straight, and not very deep. The fish was meshed in them by the gills. Thus by the regulation of the size of the mesh only picked fish need be taken, while the great purse seines of the fleet take everything, destroy at every haul a value nearly equal to what is saved, and tend towards rapid extinction of the fish. Middleton was told that they have already reduced the average size.

The trawl was another engine of formidable havoc, against which there was equal complaint. It is the method in use among the bankers, except on George's, where the tide runs too swift for anything but lying to an anchor, and hand-lining over the side. The purse seine and the trawl are two methods of taking fish *par excellence;* the former for the mackerel, the latter for all the others of greater size. When Middleton saw a trawl, he found that it was a long cord with hundreds of baited hooks fixed at intervals upon it. It was sunk so as to rest on the bottom, buoyed at both ends, and left there. A trawler kept great numbers of these lines neatly coiled in tubs, and set them one after another. After a sufficient lapse of time, he went back to the first, and "underran" it, that is, drew up one end, passed it over his boat, taking off the fish, and baiting the hooks anew, and paid it out at the other side just as he had taken it in. The method pursued by the bankers was to carry twelve or fourteen dories, which were put out when the fishing ground was arrived at, with two men in each, provided with tubs of trawls at discretion.

It was the sun-cured salt-fish that was the favorite article of diet in the islanders' households, while very little account was made of the fresh. The young people had some merry customs of their own with it. They represented that if a certain particularly salt strip in the centre, called the "dream line," were eaten before going to bed, the girl or the young man one was to marry would be indicated by appearing in a vision and handing a glass of water to appease the thirst.

The island farmer appeared to have certain advantages over him of the main-land in one way, while he was at a disadvantage in another. When the wind was to the eastward, the fog, generated out to sea where the Gulf Stream touches the polar current making down from Baffin Bay, was blown thick upon him, while ten miles back from shore there was little trace of it. On the other hand, the "steam of the water," as he called it, melted the snow and mitigated the severity of his winters.

His ground froze up about the first of December, and thawed out for cultivation about the first of May. There was no winter sowing. The principal crop, as in the State of Maine in general, was hay. The Deer Island farmer thought it would be worth double all the others put together. Next in importance came potatoes and barley. He got from one hundred and fifty to two hundred bushels of potatoes and thirty to forty of barley to the acre. He had corn and wheat as well; but the sunshine to yellow his corn was often lacking, and though the yield of wheat was or could be made from thirty-five to forty bushels an acre, with the most careful bolting it would hardly make white flour, and was not as good as cheap Western. He put on his lands a top dressing of the refuse from the lobster factories, and also flats' mud, which he found excellent.

Two of his routine operations were especially novel to our visitor. He owned little outlying islands, which he devoted either to hay or the pasturage of sheep. In mild seasons the sheep ran at large there the year round, as untamed as the wild goats of Robinson Crusoe. At other times they must be brought off in the autumn, to be sheltered through the winter, and returned in the spring. These transfers, made in boats of moderate size across straits of half a mile, a mile, and even more in width, and the bringing of the hay in the same way, piled high upon a deck around the mast, instead of in the familiar farm wain, had many odd and pleasing aspects.

On "a good bitin' day" the farmer was apt to be off to sea in hot haste, leaving work on shore to the old men and boys, and even to the girls. One day Middleton saw a slender young woman swinging a scythe in a grass lot under the tuition of a Nestor leaning on a crutch, who rather severely scolded her for swinging it uphill, instead of following the slope of the ground.

The remark was common that in these times a living could not be got from either the land or the water alone. As far as his land operations were concerned, the islander esteemed that he conducted them in the usual way. He had the modern improvements; he attended the meetings of a farmers' club at Blue Hill, exhibited prize turnips at the county fair at Ellsworth, and would have promptly repudiated the idea of having any "manners and customs," different from those of people in general, or which could be a source of curiosity and entertainment to anybody.

Monhegan is still accurately described in the words of Captain John Smith, who came to it on his cruise in the year 1614: "A round, high isle, with little Monanis by its side, betwixt which is a harbor where our ships can lie at anchor." He made a garden here, he tells, "on the rocky isle, in May, which grew so well it served for salads in June and July."

There is a white light-house on the back of the round, high isle. Half way up the hill towards it, from a fringe of gray fish-houses at the water's edge, climbs the weather-beaten little settlement, in which all the habitations of the island and its whole population are concentrated. The school-house is at the top of the buildings. Then comes a space of débris of igneous rock like the scoriae of a volcano, the color of ploughed ground, on which is railed off a bare little graveyard, visible from all directions.

The little harbor was speckled with small boats when Middleton came in, and the schooner *Marthy*, which "smacked" fish regularly to Portland, and a freighter, going in to Herring Gut to be painted, were lying there at anchor. The small boats were tied to the tall stakes, more common as the Bay of Fundy is approached, with crosses on the top, which at low tide give the appearance of some melancholy marine graveyard too.

It is not a common kind of harbor. It is a deep channel between Monhegan and Menana (as Monanis is now called), open at the outer end, and partly closed at the inner by a rugged black ledge called Smutty Nose. On Smutty Nose is reared a tall pole, part of a tall pole, part of a disused apparatus for communications between the light-house and the keeper of the fog-whistle on Menana, which has the air of a jury-mast rigged as a signal of distress. In south-east gales a formidable surf drives in through the passage, and it is then by no means so agreeable a place of anchorage. In a wild night of rain, wind, and pitch-darkness of 1858, the whole contents of the strait, fourteen fishing vessels, besides the flotilla of boats, were piled upon Smutty Nose in a mass.

There was a shark's forked tail nailed to the principal spile of the wharf, as hawks are nailed, by way of warning, to farmers' barn-doors. The fish-houses had a warm yellow lichen, such as grew also on some of the high cliffs of the outer shore, on the weather side. Over the doors of some of them, by way of decoration, were name-boards picked up from castaway boats, as the "Rescue," or "Excalibur." The principal activity centered around two little sand beaches, the only ones on the island, which would be set down, by a voyager coming to it as a new land, as quite of the ideal and providential sort.

The greater part of the male population, stalwart, rawboned men in flannel shirts, well-tanned canvas jackets, and big boots, came down to meet him. When they had gratified their curiosity about the new-comer, they went back, and threw themselves down at the top of the first rise of the slope, among the houses, in the nonchalant attitudes which were their normal condition when the fish were not schooling. A philosophic, bearded man from the main-land, come to pass the summer here, was calking his boat, drawn up on the stocks near by, and joined in their gossip. Occasionally one of them took up a battered telescope, which always lay there in the grass or against the neighboring wood-pile, and swept the horizon for indications of fish.

Monhegan was the most remote and primitive of all the Maine islands. It had no direct communication with the main-land, and no post-office. Such mail as came to it was brought over by some casual fishing-boat from Herring Gut, where it had accumulated. The bearer, sitting on a rock or the gunwhale of a boat on one of the little beaches, distributed their letters to the group flocking around him, from the old newspaper in which he had tied them up for safe-keeping. There were plenty of sheep, but little agriculture, no roads, nor use for any except to haul a little wood from the other end of the island in winter. In this service cows as well as the few oxen were put under the yoke.

There were hollyhocks, camomile, and dahlias in some of the small door-yards, but these could not redeem the shabbiness of a growth of white-weed,* knee-deep along all the straggling paths of the hamlet, to which no one had public spirit enough to take a scythe. Though but a mile long, the centre and eastern end of the island had still the most virgin and savage air. Gorges containing the whitened bones of ancient cedar-trees, with wet morasses barred the way. The low, thick, resinous groves, too, were impenetrable, except for some dark burrows like lairs where the sheep had gone through. Long gray moss, like the drift of some deluge, hung from the branches of the spruces; but the carpet was of an over-luxuriant, vivid kind, more suggestive —though starred with scarlet bunch-berries—of death and decay than even the graveyard on the slope.

Had Middleton met there in his ramblings the crew of Captain Smith, or Dixey Bull the pirate—the same who once sacked

---

* the white daisy H. B.

Pemaquid fort with sixteen renegadoes, and who was opposed to hard drinking, but said, "When others have prayers, we'll have a song or a story"—he thought he should hardly have been surprised. One day, thinking this, and how their doublets and trunk-hose and slouch hats must have had the archaism pretty well taken out of them by the severe knocking about in their voyages, and at any rate could not be more incongruous with the landscape now than in the year 1615, out of the bushes came three highly renegado-looking fellows, with their cabin-boy, marching single file and carrying long staves. They were unknown—for this was at a time when he had personal cognizance of everybody on the island—and they were so grim and weather-beaten as to their countenances, and so faded in their attire, marching on in unbroken silence, and disappearing again into the bushes, that had the leader cried, "Off with his head!" and sworn with a dozen antiquated oaths that he was Dixey Bull in person, he could hardly have had a keener suspicion of it.

Now such a suggestion of the marvellous as this should really be left at this point to stand as one of those inexplicable things that from time to time baffle all the researches of modern science, but it may be better on some accounts to say that a further inquiry into the movements of the mysterious renegadoes revealed that they were part of a schooner's crew, who had come ashore over High Head for a stroll.

Such landings, in an idle time on the sea, were not uncommon. It was in this way that a crew landed, one remarkable occasion, at Menana to play a game of ball. The skipper, in chasing the ball as they played, came full upon a glorious pot of money in a crevice of the rocks. Unwilling to divide with the rest, he concealed his discovery till all had gone off to the schooner. Taking then a trusty man, he returned to secure it. But, alas! he could find no trace of it now, search as he would. He sat down at last on the high rocks of Menana, and cried like a child with rage and despair at losing this unique opening to golden fortune. Nor has the pot of money ever been found to this day.

If it *should* be found, Middleton wished it might be by the plucky fellow in charge of the steam fog-whistle on Menana. The fingers of this man's hand were once so mangled in his machinery that they had to be amputated. He ran his whistle for an hour after the accident—till the light-keeper could cross over to his relief—sailed then, a half-day's journey in a light wind, to Herring Gut, took a team from there to Tennant's Harbor, got himself comfortably shaved while waiting for the surgeon, and then had the amputation performed.

Monhegan had a glorious open out-look, somewhat too rare in the other Maine islands, where impertinent satellites, of which the map gives little idea, are continually cropping up to destroy the desirable effect of space. From an elevated point Middleton could follow the sea all around, and shoreward a distant blue island or two lay on the high-lifted horizon like clouds over the tops of the pines. But he liked most to lie on the brim of the outer cliffs, the High Heads and White Heads, that rose one hundred and fifty feet straight from the angry breakers, and look off upon the wide ocean expanse, scattered with sails as if with a flight of butterfly moths. Timid groups of sheep looked on with curiosity at him from the vantage ground of neighboring hillocks. He was often the companion here of the lookout, watching for the schooling of fish in the interest of the nonchalant group on the grassy bank below.

17. The Rote*

by

GEORGE S. WASSON

WE COUNTRY doctors, in particular, are likely to have strange experiences, yet what is certainly the most singular episode of my practice might as easily have fallen to the lot of one in almost any walk of life. Many attempts have been made to explain the affair; I myself was nearly worn out at the time in the same vain endeavor, though now content to let it rest among the mysteries before which, chaff who will, sages and fools alike stand helpless as babes.

It was the second autumn after I had hung out my shingle in the remote northern seacoast village of Killick Cove, and an unusually tempestuous season it proved. There were early and heavy falls of snow, but a series of pelting eastern rainstorms ensued, and at Christmas time the tawny yellow of the landscape was only here and there accentuated by wasted patches of white, pierced with stiff brown reeds and grasses.

Throughout the place people shook their heads, and spoke ominously of the "Green Christmas," though, in face of nature's peculiarly drear and sad-colored aspect at the time, the term seemed much of a misnomer. Under a long continuance of

From *Home From the Sea* by George S. Wasson by permission of Mildred C. Wasson. (Houghton Mifflin Company: Boston, 1908).

* The sound along the coast made by the ocean as it tumbles ashore: Old English and Coastal Maine. H. B.

strong easterly winds, the sea outside remained so rough as to hamper greatly the fishermen and lobster-catchers, who chiefly made up the population of the little town; indeed, it seemed that for weeks my ears had been filled day and night with the unceasing jarring rumble of the rote.

The day before Christmas was especially disagreeable and depressing. Fierce rainsqualls alternated with flurries of wet snow, and the fast increasing boom of the close-bordering sea began to have a noticeable effect upon the nerves. Then, too, the tossing bell-buoy on the Hue and Cry ledges, seldom silent, on this dark afternoon sent its mournful tones vibrating inland upon the salty gusts with dismal iteration.

I lodged at the time in a small house on the principal street of the straggling village, my office being, in fact, nothing less than the hitherto inviolable best room of the widowed owner. On this day the home-like sounds of dish-washing after dinner still issued from the adjacent kitchen, when a mud-bedraggled open wagon stopped at the front gate. Though the rain had then ceased to a great extent, the driver was fully encased in oilskins; and, as he advanced through the matted grass to the seldom used front door, I recognized him as Shubael Spurling, a fishing skipper living in a distant section of the town, known as the Number Four District. This time my services were sought for a valuable cow, whose ailment baffled local talent completely; and with slight delay we were wallowing through the mud and puddles of the lonely road leading to Number Four.

A dreary ride at best, it was especially so under the watery skies of this stormy afternoon. For some miles there were no trees, and, as I say, constant rains had given the wind-swept country a most cheerless and sodden appearance. Coming as I had from a quiet town in the interior, where wind was almost unheeded, where stately elms lined the broad streets, and a peaceful river flowed through long reaches of fertile intervale, this for some time seemed to me, indeed, a barren and desolate land. Here, in rocky Killick Cove, the great salt sea was always overwhelmingly in evidence. The talk of the people was chiefly of wind and weather, of fishing craft and their crews, and hairbreadth escapes. The rude little wooden weather-vanes, so common throughout the village, were closely watched from dawn to dark, and the wind never varied in direction or force without much ensuing discussion of the change and its effect upon absent fishing boats.

But it was the ever-present sound of the sea which made the greatest impression upon my bucolic mind; day and night, summer and winter, always the ceaseless rote of the sea, like the breathing of some great monster it seemed to me; sometimes very low and faint in the village, but still always noticeable in some degree, and at times jarring every window in the town with its thunderous rumble.

At the top of a rocky ridge called Harbor Hill, directly behind the settlement, Skipper Shubael stopped his horse, and for some moments closely scanned the great extent of leaden sea, already thickly flecked with rushing whitecaps. Believing, as did many others, that the present long-continued "spell of weather" was about to culminate in a heavy gale, an aged uncle of his, he explained to me, had started early that morning in his small schooner for a distant fishing ground known as "Betty Moody's Garden," hoping to save from damage a number of trawls set there some days previous. Several sail of vessels were in sight from the hilltop, staggering under shortened canvas toward the cove from various directions, but Shubael soon declared positively that his uncle's little pinky schooner, Palm, was not among them.

After this, the road plunged abruptly into a dense, heron-haunted swamp of alders and cat-tails, with, here and there, gloomy-looking hackmatacks raising their drooping forms against a pale gray sky blurred by hurrying masses of scud from the sea. Then followed a dreary extent of rain-soaked pasture, thickly strewn with huge granite boulders, among which the narrow road wound its way, between moss-grown stone walls. Stray sheep bleated forlornly as they fled at the wagon's approach, and the hoarse cawing of innumerable crows rose above the rote's distant booming.

For some distance here the road was especially bad, and in bumping too roughly over a protruding ledge, one of the wagon springs gave way. This caused much delay, but with assistance from the nearest house we were at length enabled to proceed again slowly. Rain was then once more driving in slanting torrents before the ever-augmenting gale, and, with darkness already settling down, I foresaw anything but a pleasurable return over the rough route.

A short distance farther, emerging from a thick growth of birches, the leaves of which formed a sodden cushion under the dripping wheels, the road again dropped with appalling steepness into a deep gully, and crossed a turbulent brook by a rude bridge built of treenail-riddled oak plank from a wrecked vessel. As the stiff-kneed old mare cautiously braced herself for the steep descent, furious gusts of chilling wind blew up the ravine, laden with the heavy odor of kelp, apparently direct from the sea. My ear also caught the repeated tones of a bell, and, like a deep bass to the brook's noisy babble, came again with startling distinctness to the sullen rumble of the rote. I at once asked Skipper Shubael how it was that we got these sounds so plainly, at such a distance inland.

"Well, there you, doctor," he said; "it does appear as though we'd come close anigh the shore again, and no mistake. You'll 'most always git the rote good and plain here to this hollow, for all it's a plumb three mile back to the shore, the straightest course ever a man can lay. Someways or 'nother, this hollow fetches the sound up along, kind of tunnel-fashion like, I cal'late. If only it hadn't turned to and shut in so thick-a-fog and rain again, you could sight straight down through the hollow from here, and see it breaking a clear torch on the Hue and Cry, I'll warrant! Seem's though I seldom ever knowed the sea to make faster than what it has since morning; and Lord knows, it was rough as a grater before, so there's quite a few of us ain't made a set for a week's time. This wind breezens on at every hand's turn now, and I wisht I could know for certain whether Uncle Pelly made out to pull them trawls of hisn, out there on the 'Garden' to-day. That's where he lives to; that little reddish-colored house up there, front of them fars,* with the big ellum handy-by. The old sir picked him a real sightly place to build, didn't he, though?"

"Why, yes," I said; "but it has always seemed strange to me that so many of you fishermen should have located so far inland, away from your work."

"Oh, well," the skipper said, as we began to ascend the opposite bank of the gully, "it was the old-seed folks that turned to and built clean away in back here, to commence with. All the way ever I heard it accounted for is they growed so sick and tired of fog and salt water, that, come to git forehanded enough to build, they was possessed to strike in back here fur's ever they could. I think's likely they figured that, come to quit going altogether, they'd love to set and take their comfort to home, and have green stuff growing close aboard of 'em for all the rest-part of their stopping. Folks changes 'round, though. You take it this day o' the world, and a place in back here amongst the far trees ain't worth a red. The women-folks in particular don't like up this way; they'd lievser be down to the Cove, where there's gos-sup-talk going on to make it kind of lively like. But take Uncle Pelly, he likes tiptop when he's home; the thing of it is he ain't home no great. He's going on eighty, and has swore off fishing no end already, but you let mack'rel commence to mash off here, or let haddick strike anyways plenty in the fall i' the year same's they done a spell ago, and the old sir is just as fishy as ever. I tell him he'd full better lay back now, and take some peace of his life, but wild hosses wouldn't hold him home soon's ever he takes a notion to go.

"He's got it worked down consid'ble fine, too, the old sir has. You take it out abreast of his place there on the aidge of the

---

* old-fashioned Maine for "firs." H. B.

hollow, and you'll get the rote double and thribble as plain as what we do here. As fur back as I can remember, it's always been his way to take a walk down acrosst his field there to the aidge of the hollow every morning reg'lar, so's to stop and listen for the rote a spell. Nobody else knows exactly how he works it, but seem's though someways or 'nother he makes out to tell whether or no it's going to be a day outside. That sounds kind of queer like, but it's seldom ever he misses his cal'lation.

"There's always some rote in that hollow, you see, no matter if it's the dead of summer time and stark calm, and Uncle Pelly, he cal'lates to make a set to the east'ard or west'ard, according to whichever way he gits the rote the plainest. He cal'lates to keep well to wind'ard in room of to loo'ard, you see, allowing the rote tells him it's liable to breezen up and overblow, especially soon's ever the weather grows catchy in the fall o' the year. Folks can laugh all they want; there's something to it, just the same. I never knowed the old sir to stub his toe any great yet, without it was to blow a sail or two off'n him, and he's been going out of here rising of sixty year now."

It was nearly dark when we came upon a cluster of houses, in few of which, however, were any signs of life visible. Shubael remarked that but a baker's dozen or so remained in all the once populous Number Four District, and that most of these would be glad to sell at any price. Directly after he pointed out the lights of his own dwelling, beyond question also "sightly," but standing fully exposed to every bleak wind, on the very top of the highest rocky hill in the township of Killick Cove. Just opposite, dimly discernible in the gathering gloom, rose the bulky form of the meeting-house and its stunted belfry, like the neighboring schoolhouse of Number Four, long closed for lack of population to support it; "a couple more of our old has-beens," was the skipper's brief comment as we turned in at his barnyard.

I soon ascertained without surprise that the unfortunate cow, rather than the difficulty from which she suffered, had already yielded to the unique treatment adopted. Meantime the storm steadily increased, until, returning nearly in its face being thought out of the question, I accepted the hospitalities of the house over night. But for me, at least, little sleep was possible in the distracting turmoil raging about the building until near daybreak. In the furious blasts several blinds banged themselves from their fastenings with ear-splitting crashes; a loose sash of my window rattled abominably, and pelting floods of rain beat with constantly increasing violence against the small panes, till, forcing entrance, it dripped steadily from the narrow sill on the braided rugs of the floor. Later in the night, changing to sleet, it beat upon the glass like a sand-blast, until succeeded near dawn by the muffled swirl of plastering snow.

Next morning, under a thick coating of ice, the trees cracked sharply in the then waning gale, as we started to return in a borrowed wagon, with wheels clogged by muddy snow and leaves. When nearly abreast of the small house in which Shubael's uncle Pelatiah Spurling, lived, two men were met bearing homeward pails of water drawn from a well in the adjoining field. They first spoke of the unequaled fury of the storm, and then, after condoling with Skipper Shubael over the loss of the cow, inquired whether he had seen or heard anything of his uncle before leaving the village the day before.

While one was yet speaking, the tall, angular figure of a white-bearded old man appeared from behind a clump of alders in the field close by. He wore a short jumper of faded blue frocking, with the oilskin sou'-wester and high red boots of the local fishermen. In one hand was a wooden water bucket, and, with head sharply inclined against the still boisterous wind and drizzle, he slowly followed a well-worn path toward the spring.

"There he goes now, this minute!" Shubael exclaimed. "Hullo, there, Uncle Pelly, you!" he shouted. "Keep her off a point or two! Guess you must had an all-day job of it yesterday, and no yachting trip, neither, was it?"

Apparently not hearing these words, however, the old man plodded steadily on. At the well-curb he left his pail, and continued across the spongy field in the direction of the hollow.

"The old sir grows deef right along, now'days," one of the men said.

"Yes, he doos so," the other assented. "My woman, she was speaking of it only the last time he was in home there. All the way you can make any talk along of him now'days is to get close aboard on the port side. I'm glad, though, he give his hooker sheet, and come back yesterday before this breeze o' wind took holt so spiteful. But he must got in consid'ble late, for I was home all the afternoon myself, and never see no sign of him coming up along before night-time."

"I guess likely they made a long day of it fast enough," said Shubael. "The old sir allowed he cal'lated to pull them trawls if it took a leg. By good rights they had no call to go out yesterday, anyways. You can't take and jump the old Palm into a head-beat sea same's you could forty year ago, and, to tell the truth, I'm plaguy glad the old man see when he'd got enough, and pointed her for the turf in some kind of season. Just you take and watch him a minute, doctor! He's dropped his bucket there to the well, so's to lug home a turn of water when he comes back along, same's usual. There, you, now he's got hisself all placed in just the right berth to hearken to the rote. Godfrey mighty! seem's though I'd seen him doing that very same act since I was the bigness of a trawl-kag!"

Leaning slightly forward, with one hand raised to his ear in an attitude of rapt attention, old Skipper Pelatiah Spurling stood listening under the gnarly limbs of a great oak, at the verge of the hollow, his long, white beard fluttering to one side in the strong sea wind.

"Unless he's very deaf, he ought to hear that rumble this morning," I said. "What do you suppose he expects to learn just now?"

"That's hard telling," one of the men laughed. "I've lived nigh neighbor to him the heft of my life, and ain't never fathomed this rote business yet. There's no rubbing it out, though,

that somehow or 'nother, from the way she sounds up through
the hollow there, the old sir will 'most generally give you the
correct almanac for quite a little spell ahead!"

Shubael then spoke of waiting to learn from the old man his
experience of the day before, but, as I was now growing somewhat anxious to reach my office again, he postponed the inter-
view until a later occasion.

At the top of Harbor Hill we once more held up for a moment
to view the wild scene that suddenly opened before us. Seaward
a dense bank of fog still hung close over the madly heaving
waters. From under this gray shroud of mist enormous cockling
surges constantly rushed, and, charging upon the land in endless
columns, tore themselves to pieces on the jagged, kelp-grown
ledges in a broad fringe of seething foam and high-leaping spray.
Half a mile off-shore, where the black heads of the dreaded Hue
and Cry ledges now and then appeared in a mass of tumbling
breakers, the blood-red bell buoy danced the maddest of horn-
pipes, now buried from sight completely, and now flung reeling
headlong on the crest of some great, on-rushing sea, its frenzied
clang at times pealing loud above the rumbling rote. Suddenly,
somewhat farther to the left, a mountainous, darkling billow
seemed to gather others to its mighty self, and, rearing a ragged
outline high above the misty horizon, broke in a wildly careering
smother of snow-white foam, fully an acre in extent. An instant
later came a thunderous report that shook the very ledges beneath our feet.

"Set-fire!" cried Shubael. "Now you've heard him talk, doctor!
That was Old Aaron that up and spoke just now, and you might
stop here to this Cove a long spell and not hear the likes again!
It's seldom ever hubbly enough for Old Aaron to break, but
when he doos take the notion, then all hands best stand from
under!"

Saying which, in his excitement Shubael leaned far over the
dashboard, and surprised the mare into a temporary trot by sev-

eral blows with the reins. Half way down the hill an old man, bent nearly double, came hobbling from his door to hail us.

"Make out to sight 'em, Shu?" he called.

"Sight what?" the skipper asked, stopping short.

"Why, the sticks of the wrack. Ain't you heard tell? They say there's some little hooker lays sunk off there somewheres, betwixt Old Aaron and the main, with just her mastheads showing."

"There wa'n't ary spar showing out there two minutes' time since, that I'll make affidavy to!" Shubael declared. "I guess likely no wrack won't hang together long when Old Aaron breaks same's he done just now, anyways!"

"That's what I says to 'em myself," the old fellow piped. "I told 'em he broke once at low-water slack last night, too, but they all allowed I dremp it."

"Your hearing is full better than the most of us now, Skipper Tommy!" Shubael called, as we drove on toward the village.

Nearly abreast of the bellowing Hue and Cry breakers, the road skirted a strip of coarse shingle beach, lying between glistening, spray-swept ledges, which reflected the pale sky in countless shining pools. Here the towering, white-crested seas hurled themselves in far-reaching floods of seething brine that swept the snow from long stretches of the road, leaving in its place great windrows of fragrant rock-weed and kelp. Scattered groups of people conferred at the tops of their voices, and intently watched the churning waste of breakers off-shore. Women in hooded shawls pulled children back from the steep, gullied beach; mongrel curs raced to and fro among the long, stranded kelps, barking frantically at each breaking sea; and overhead the gulls wheeled, shrilly screaming.

We saw at once that something unusual had happened. Shubael Spurling drove straight to the nearest squad of men, prominent among whom he recognized a young fellow frequently going on shares in old Skipper Pelatiah's little schooner. Although uncommonly heavily clad in thick coat and knit muffler, this young man struck me at once as looking pinched and cold.

"What about this wrack business we hear tell of? Where doos she lay to?" Shubael demanded immediately.

"She give up only just a short spell since," the young man said. "The mastheads was showing all the morning off here, nigh in range with the bell."

"What one d'ye call her?" asked Shubael earnestly.

"Why, the old Palm, of course," said the other. "She's all the one to get picked up this time, so fur as ever I know."

"Palm be jiggered!" Shubael exclaimed irritably. "Shut up your tomfoolery, and talk some kind of sense, will you! The Palm come in last evening, to my knowing."

"My God, skipper! don't you really know yet?" the white-faced young fellow cried. "We was running her for home last night, and wearing nothing only a close-reefed foresail, with the sheet chock to the rigging at that! It blowed a livin' gale o' wind, and was shut in just as thick-a-snow outside as ever you see it in God's world. We made a grain too fur to the east'ard, and Old Aaron up and broke on us fit to pitchpole the ablest big Georges-man that ever sailed out of Cape Ann! It piled aboard all of ten foot deep over the stern, and wiped the five of us off'n her clip and clean—"

"Godfrey mighty, you!" broke in Shubael, his face flushing in downright anger; "I cal'late you'll do, young feller, by the jumping Judas I do, now! You'll make out to hold your end up, every time. Let me just tell you what; you'd full better hire right out for one of these play-actors, in room of heaving away your time going haddicking out of here no longer! Next thing, maybe you'll be telling us how all the rest-part but you was drownded, won't ye?"

For answer, the young man swallowed hard, and nodded his head.

"Oho, I thought likely," said Shubael, with a grim smile. "All goners but you, every mother's son of 'em, you claim! Kind of rubbing it in, to take and lose the whole kit of 'em that way, wa'n't it? Maybe, now, you wouldn't mind just telling of me how comes it Uncle Pally is home there to Number Four this same Christmas mornin'!"

"How comes what?" the other asked, in a puzzled way.

"I say, while you're at it, turn to and tell us how it was that the old sir never passed in his checks, too, in this 'ere scand'lous bad scrape of yourn!"

"Old man Pel'tiah Spurling stood to the tiller hisself the time that sea hove us nigh end over end," the young fellow said solemnly, while Skipper Shubael stared him in the face, angry and incredulous. "After we was all washed off'n her, him and me was all the ones to catch hand-holt again. Him and me gripped holt of the weather rail till she went out from under, and the very last words ever the old sir spoke he says like this, 'I been going out of this Cove risin' seventy year now, and this is the first time ever God A'mighty shut the door plumb in my face when it come night-time!' The next secont a master great comber fell atop of us, and I never knowed another living thing till they fetched me to in Cap'n Futtock's store over here."

"John Ed Grommet!" spoke Shubael Spurling sternly; "if ever I wanted to take and pick me the biggest reg'lar built, out and out, A No. 1 liar that ever yet drawed the breath of life to this Cove, I wouldn't have fur to seek, now, sure's ever the tide ebbs and flows! I cal'late you've got the nerve to stand right up in your boots with some fool-lie on your blame' tongue it 't was the day of judgment; but by the Lord, I want you should understand this time good and plain that I see Uncle Pel'tiah home there not two hours' time since! I see him and passed the time o' day along of him, too, and what's more, the doctor here seen him, and Jason Kentle, and your own cousin, Thomas Grommet, they seen him the very same time, going down acrosst his mowin' field to the hollow. Leave it right direct to you, doctor, if that ain't God's own truth I'm telling!"

But before I could speak a great shout broke from the men behind us, and turning quickly, we saw a tangled mass of wreckage borne in at racehorse speed upon the crest of an immense combing sea. A luminous, greenish light flashed for an instant through the great, toppling wave, and, as it fell with deafening roar upon the resonant shingle, the body of Skipper Pelatiah Spurling was pitched head-long in a wild rush of hissing foam, almost at the feet of his relative.

18. Enter the Summer Visitor

THE EIGHTEEN NINETIES AT BAR HARBOR

by

F. MARION CRAWFORD

THE first impression made by Bar Harbor at the height of its season upon the mind of one fresh from a more staid and crystallized civilization is that it is passing through a period of transition, in which there is some of the awkwardness which we associate with rapid growth, and something also of the youthful freshness which gives that very awkwardness a charm. The name of Mount Desert suggests, perhaps, a grim and forbidding cliff, frowning upon the pale waves of a melancholy ocean. Instead, the traveller who crosses the bay in the level light of an August afternoon looks upon the soft, rolling outline of wooded hills, on the highest of which a little hotel breaks the sky-line, upon a shore along which villas and cottages stretch on either side of a toy wooden village, which looks as though it were to be put away in a box at night, and upon the surrounding sea, an almost landlocked inlet, in which other islands, like satellites of Mount Desert, are scattered here and there.

As the little steamer draws up to her moorings the groups of people waiting on the pier stand out distinctly, and the usual types detach themselves one by one. The clusters of hotel-runners

From *Bar Harbor* by F. Marion Crawford (Charles Scribner's Sons: New York, 1894).

and expressmen are lounging listlessly until they shall be roused
to clamorous activity by the landing of the first passenger; in
knots and pairs, those serenely idle people of all ages, who, in all
places and seasons, seem to find an ever-new amusement in
watching the arrival of trains or boats, are as deeply interested
as usual; the inevitable big and solemn dog, of nondescript breed
and eclectic affections, is stalking about with an air of responsibility.

And yet the little crowd is not quite like other gatherings on
other piers. Girls in smart cotton frocks are sitting in shining little village carts, with grooms at their horses' sleek heads, wedged
in between empty buck-boards that look like paralyzed centi-
pedes, the drivers of which wear clothes ranging from the livery
of the large stables to the weather-bleached coat of the "native"
from Cherryfield or Ellsworth, who has brought over his horse
to take his share of the "rusticator's" ready money during the
short season. There are no hotel omnibuses, no covered traps of
any kind, as becomes a holiday place where winter and rough
weather are enemies not meant to be reckoned with; everybody
seems either to know everyone else, or not to care if he does not,
and there is an air of cheerful informality about the whole scene
which immediately makes one feel welcome and at home.

In order not to be behind every self-respecting town throughout the Western world Bar Harbor has a Main Street, which
plunges violently down a steep place toward the pier, and which
is beautified for a short distance by a mushroom growth of tents
and shanties, the summer home of the almond-eyed laundryman,
the itinerant photographer with a specialty of tintypes, and the
seller of weary-looking fruit, of sandwiches that have seen better
days, and temperance drinks of gorgeous hues. Plymouth Rock
also vaunts its "pants" and young ladies are recommended to
grow up with Castoria.

Then comes the more necessary shops—the tinsmith's, at
whose door a large bull-terrier benevolently grins all day; the
tailor's where one may study the fashions of New York filtered

through Bangor; the china shop, where bright-colored lamp-shades spread themselves like great butterflies in the window, and the establishment of Mr. Bee, the locally famous and indispensable provider of summer literature, and of appropriate alleviations for the same, in the shape of caramels, cigarettes, and chewing-gum. Directly opposite stands a huge hotel, apparently closed or almost deserted, but evidently built in the years when the gnawing tooth of the national jig-saw grievously tormented all manner of wood-work, a melancholy relic of an earlier time when, as "Rodick's," it was almost another name for Bar Harbor itself.

No lover of Bar Harbor has been found bold enough to say that Main Street is pretty; and yet, between ten and twelve o'clock on a summer's morning, it has a character, if not a beauty, of its own. Alongside of the "board walk," which takes the place of a pavement, the buckboards are drawn up, waiting to be hired; in some of them, often drawn by four horses, are parties of people, consisting usually of more women than men, as is becoming in New England, already starting upon one of the longer expeditions, and only stopping to collect a stray member or to lay in a stock of fruit and sugar-plums. Farmer's carts, with closed hoods like Shaker sunbonnets, are on their rounds from one cottage to another, meandering through the crowd, and driven with exasperating calmness by people who sit far back in their little tunnels, and cannot possibly see on either side of them to get out of anyone else's way. Then there are all sorts of light private traps, usually driven by women or girls bound on household errands or visits, and psychologically unbalanced between their desire to speak to the friends who meet them on foot, and their anxiety lest they should be forced to recognize the particular acquaintance on whom they are just going to call.

Along the board-walk there is a row of little shops, some of them scarcely larger than booths, the proprietors of which perch like birds of passage, pluming themselves in the sunshine of the brief season, and taking flight again before the autumn gales. In one window a lot of Turkish finery looks curiously exotic, especially the little slippers, gay with tassels and embroidery, turning up their pointed toes as if scorning the stouter footgear which tramps along outside. Another shop is bright with the crude colors of Spanish scarfs and pottery; in another, Japanese wares manage to keep their faint smell of the East in spite of the salt northern air, and farther on you may wonder at the misplaced ingenuity of Florida shell jewelry, and be fascinated by the rakish leer of the varnished alligator.

By one of the contrasts which make Bar Harbor peculiarly attractive, next door to these cosmopolitan shops there still thrives one of the indigenous general stores, where salt fish are sold, and household furniture and crockery, and the candy peculiar to New England stores and New York peanut stands, which keeps through all vicissitudes a vague odor of sawdust, and where you may also buy, as was once advertised by the ingenious dealer, "baby carriages, butter, and paint."

Should you wish to give a message to a friend without the trouble of writing a note, the chances are more than even that you will find him or her any morning on the board-walk, or in the neighborhood of the post-office, for as there is no delivery at Bar Harbor, and as the mails are often delayed, there is ample opportunity to search for an acquaintance in the waiting crowd. Here also congregate the grooms in undress livery, with leather mail-bags slung under one arm, who have ridden in from the outlying cottages, and who walk their horses up and down, or exchange stable notes with their acquaintances; sailors from private yachts, usually big, fair Scandinavians; mail orderlies from any men-of-war which may happen to be in port; boys and girls who do not find the waiting long, and all that mysterious tribe of people who look as if they could not possibly receive a dozen letters a year, and yet who are always assiduously looking out for them. As usual, the post-office is a loadstone for all the dogs in the village, and as there are many strangers among them, of all breeds and ages and tempers, walking round and round one another with stiff legs and bristling backs, unregenerate man is kept in tremulous expectation of a dog-fight as free as any in Stamboul. But somehow the fight rarely comes off, though the resident canine population has become fearfully and wonderfully mixed, through the outsiders who have loved and ridden away. One nondescript, especially, is not soon forgotten, a nightmare cross of a creature in which the curly locks and feathery tail of the spaniel are violently modified by the characteristic pointed breastbone and bandy legs of a dachshund.

Wandering through the streets of the little village one is struck again and again by the sharp contrast between what may be called the natural life of the place and the artificial condition which fashion has imposed upon it. In some of the streets almost every house is evidently meant to be rented, the owners usually retiring to restricted quarters at the back, where they stow themselves away and hang themselves up on pegs until they may come into their own again. Here and there a native cottage has been bought and altered by a summer resident, and over the whole there is the peculiarly smug expression of a quarter which is accustomed to put its best foot foremost for a few months of the year. But in the back lanes and sidestreets there are still the conditions of the small New England community, in which land is poor and work is slack during the long winter, so that although there is no abject poverty in the sense in which it is known to cities, there is also little time or inclination for the mere prettiness of life.

An element of the picturesque is supplied by an Indian camp, which used for years to be pitched in a marshy field known as Squaw Hollow; but with the advent of a Village Improvement Society certain newfangled and disturbing ideas as to sanitary conditions obtained a hearing, and the Indians were banished to a back road out of the way of sensitive eyes and noses. They claim to be of the Passamaquoddy tribe, speak their own language, and follow the peaceful trades of basket-weaving and moccasin-making, the building of birch-bark canoes. Their little

dwellings—some of them tents, some of them shanties covered
with tar-paper and strips of bark—are scattered about, and in
the shadow of one of them sits a lady of enormous girth, who
calls herself their queen, and who wears, perhaps as a badge of
sovereignty, a huge fur cap even in the hottest weather. She is
not less industrious than other "regular royal" queens, for she
sells baskets and tells fortunes even more flattering than the
fabled tale of Hope. Some of the young men are fine, swarthy,
taciturn creatures, who look as though they knew how to put a
knife to other uses than whittling the frame of a canoe; but one
does not feel tempted to rush upon Fate for the sake of any of
the dumpy and greasy-looking damsels who will soon become
like their even dumpier and greasier mothers.

The whole encampment is pungent with the acrid smoke of
green wood, and many children—round, good-natured balls of
fat in all shades of yellow and brown—roll about in close friendship with queer little dogs, in which the absence of breed pro-
duces a family likeness. It is curious to see in the characteristic
work of these people the survival of the instinctive taste of semi-
savage races, and the total lack of it in everything else. The designs cut on the bark of their canoes, the cunningly blended
colors in their basket-work, are thoroughly good in their way;
but contact with a higher civilization seems to have affected
them as it has the Japanese, turning their attention chiefly to
making napkin-rings and collar-boxes, and to a hideous delight
in tawdry finery, which is fondly, though distantly, modelled on
current American fashions.

Bar Harbor drinks the cup of summer standing. In mid-April
the snow may lie six feet deep, and before the end of October
long icicles are often hanging on the north side of the rocks,
while even in August the northern lights shoot up their quiver-
ing, spectral spears from the horizon to the Zenith. Some fierce
days of heat there are in July, but on the whole the temperature
is decidedly arctic, especially to one accustomed to a less rigorous
climate. In New York we are used to having the kindly fruits of

the earth brought to us long before their natural season, and it
sounds strangely to be told at Bar Harbor that the first garden
strawberries may be looked for about the fourth of July, and
that June lilies will bloom early in August; but such trifles only
give one a feeling of chasing the summer, as climate-fanciers
follow the spring, and are certainly not to be reckoned as griev-
ances.

THE DIFFERENCE

by

ELIZABETH PARSONS

For Amy, the voyage every summer held the same excitement,
and every fall the return trip carried its own desolation. In June,
on the trip east on the big steamer, it was always the noisy sailing from the city that filled her with delight—adventure coupled
with the knowledge that she was going to the place she liked best
in the world. The clatter of trucks and wagons, the El rattling
by overhead, the shouts of the drivers and dock-hands and the
occasional roar of a steamer, the haste, the dirt blowing up off
the cobblestones in the harbor wind, the scramble in the long
shed with porters, luggage, and other passengers: it was all wonderful. Wonderful too was the slow passage across the red-
carpeted gangplank on to the steamer with its familiar smell
of varnish, cooking, and rubber on the stairs, the polite progress
through the crowd to the proper staterooms, the long warning
whistle, and the officer calling along the decks and saloons, "All
ashore that's going ashore! All ashore that's going ashore!"

This was what Amy waited eight, nine months of the year for

—this was, for her, all the adventure and romance that could possibly exist, and each year it had been miraculously repeated ever since she had been old enough to sense it. The long, heavenly summer lay ahead, sunny and gay, and this was the proper way to get to it; all this superb haste, din, and thronging of holiday-makers and freight-carriers was exactly right. Everything she hated was left behind; ahead was only the country of her choice, and all the marvelous frenzy of departure seemed a celebration and a thanksgiving. All the year she remembered how it would be when, after the night spent in the tiny, white-painted cabin, she woke to find the ship moving along very close to the shore that rose straight up in the sunlight out of the clear green water, with an occasional village gathered at a cove and a lighthouse, dazzlingly white, ringing its bell in greeting from a wooded point.

Now and then Amy thought of something that Brian, her little brother, had said once when someone had asked him what he liked best in the world. Bending over to scratch his knee he had said—defiantly, in case it might sound silly—"To wake up and see the sun shining on the State of Maine." There *had* been a little titter from the questioner—"How *darling* of you, Brian dear"—and Brian had examined his knee very closely. But Amy wished she had thought of that herself; she felt just that way too, and she ought to have been the first to say it.

Waking in her bunk, she would scramble up to open the varnished venetian-blind shutter and look out at the green steep shore and the bright water trembling in the early morning calm. All winter she would think of that moment that was to come, when she would kneel on the round-seated chair and put her head out into the soft air and the agonizingly brilliant sunlight. She did not let herself think ahead to the return journey in September, familiar and vivid though that was, too. She knew very well what that was like—the quiet leave-taking in the fall. Then, when the steamer sailed back to the city, it sailed from a river village, and the ship and the passengers were composed and phlegmatic and businesslike as though they too felt that this was no time for rejoicing, and the less fuss the better. Then, only a few people glumly trod the red carpets of the saloons or stood along the rail wrapped in coats against the afternoon breeze and watched the shores slide by. This was the end of the warm days, the end of the picnics, the sailing, the long days spent fishing on the heaving bay, the grinding of surrey wheels on clam-shell driveways and the smell of nasturtiums along tennis-court fences. Gone for another year were the fresh-cleaned sneakers drying on the window-sills, the sand in the fibre matting of bedroom floors, the cheeping of goldfinches that dipped over the hayfields, and the mourning of bell buoy and lighthouse on foggy nights. Why should anyone be gay now? The muffled backs of all the passengers said the same thing: "Well, that is over—so soon." At the towns where the steamer stopped, everyone stood silently watching the freight being loaded; at each town it grew colder as afternoon settled into evening, and finally at the last stop it was pitch dark, with bright reflections wriggling in the black water, and anchored ships lying all around, their lights small against invisible shores. Then the steamer turned and left Amy's country, heading out to sea with a rush of phosphorescent water trembling under the straight white bow—but Amy did not know that; she was asleep by then, for she was not allowed to sit up after eight-thirty. The last thing she always remembered of the fall journey was the noise of the little chain in the shiny copper wash-basin in the corner of her stateroom rattling and rattling with the vibration of the engines.

When Amy was eleven, she began to make plans for running away to sea, and the summer she was thirteen she fell in love with one of the crew on the steamer *Brewster* on the trip to the eastward. Of course she had been in love several times before— oh, lots, and very badly each time, too—but this was something quite different. It was unsuitable, in the first place, and there was something else about it that prevented her from telling even

Helen, her best friend, and it was terribly, really thrilling and romantic to fall in love with somebody who, though he did work on a steamer and not a full-rigged ship or even a coaster, at least did go to sea.

The first time Amy saw him, he was standing coiling a line in the *Brewster's* bow, with his back to the wind so that his light hair was blown forward over the top of his head. He was slight and quite pale, with freckles, and he looked very grown-up to Amy—seventeen or eighteen, anyway—and his blue jersey had *Brewster* sewed on in small white letters across the back. He made his line fast to the rail and as he turned he saw Amy, and her heart dropped into her stomach. She noticed that his eyes were set a little slanting in his head, and that they were grey. Then he slid quickly over the rail, and was gone down the ladder.

Amy rushed through supper and, avoiding her family, was on deck early as the gloom spread across the sea. The trailing gulls cried, and the lonely feeling in Amy's insides settled down heavily as she hovered, a thin little thing in a Peter Thompson coat, about the ship's bow. There was no one on deck but the lonely lookout, standing with his hands in the pockets of his pea-coat, a solitary and dream-like figure. Amy was found and sent off to bed, where she cried at the heartlessness of a fate that caused her to love unrequited; and though always before she had been fond of this mysterious time of day at sea, now she thought there was nothing so dreary as a ship rushing through the dusk. But she felt a little excited, too, remembering she had been through all this before—though this seemed, somehow, different; just how, she did not know.

In the morning, while the *Brewster* lay unloading at a small wharf, Amy watched the men shoving the freight up the gangway and into the shed and, as the tide was low, shooting down again very fast with their empty trucks into the hold. It was a hot morning, glaring bright. Amy stood with the other passengers, listening to their talk with an eye out for the boy in the blue jersey. And there he was!—trotting out from the hold, trundling his truck up the steep gangway and disappearing into the building on the wharf; then out he came at a run, dodging a man coming up by a hair's breadth, so that the man shouted, "Watch it, Lewis!" and tipped his truck to get out of the way. So that was his name—Lewis. Amy said it in a whisper. After a while, on one of his runs out of the wharf, he looked up quickly and saw her. The next time he gave her a fleeting smile. Amy moved away, suddenly alarmed.

On the trip back in the fall, Lewis was still there, and Amy, who had loved him happily all summer and lain awake every night making up stories about him and herself and the schooner they would have together, met his eye once or twice and felt scared and thrilled when he smiled at her. But he did not speak to her. She slipped away from her parents several times to look for him, but she did not find him.

All winter he was in her mind. She wrote about him voluminously in her journal, she drew pictures of him, she made countless disguised "L's" all through her school books. Half the time she knew he couldn't possibly have noticed her, and the rest of the time she was sure he thought about her as much as she thought about him. He was the hero of every book she read; he was the one person in the world who understood her perfectly, so that even in the midst of tears she would say to herself, "Lewis would know how it is," though that was apt to make her cry more still. He was with her in every emergency—when she went to have her teeth straightened, when Helen fell out of a tree and nobody knew for a while how badly she might be hurt, when she had to make a five-minute recitation on "The Oregon Trail" at school. He was her solace and her grief; she had certainly never been in love so badly before. In fact, this time she did not tell Helen anything about it, though in the past she had been given to boasting to Helen, who never seemed to have any romances to amount to anything—or at any rate not in comparison with Amy's.

Summer came again, and again it was time for the trip east. Amy's father wrote to engage staterooms for the family, and the blow fell at lunch a few days later.

Brian said, "What cabins have we got on the *Brewster* this year, Father?" And his father answered, "We've got them on the *Bridgeton* this year. The *Brewster* was full every trip that week."

"I don't like the *Bridgeton* so well," said Brian. "We've been on the *Brewster* so much more."

"I don't see any difference, myself," said his father. "They're built just alike. They both even have "B" stamped on their butter-pats."

Brian was silent, scraping his fork around the inside of his baked potato skin.

Amy said, "Excuse me," to her mother, and running upstairs she locked herself in the bathroom, dropped on the floor and pressed her head hard against the cold rim of the bathtub, shaken with anger and sorrow. This was absolutely the end of it all— she would never see Lewis again, he would forget her, and all because her father hadn't written early enough for reservations. Furiously she banged her fists on the tub, tears running down her face, hating her father, her mother, everybody. After waiting all winter to see him, thinking of him every second, waiting to see him in the summer—now everything was *ruined*. What could she do? Wildly she began to plan. She would run away; she would pretend she was sick the day they were to leave so they would have to go on another day and somehow she would see that they got on the *Brewster;* she would steal the tickets from her father's desk and write the steamship company herself, making up some story so the passage would be changed. . . . But even as she planned, with tears falling fast, she knew it wouldn't be any use—nothing would be any good. Things were as they were, and there was nothing you could do about it.

It was the first time in her life she had thought that.

It was an overcast September afternoon when the *Brewster* sailed from the river port. Amy saw him just as the boat was leaving the wharf, standing coiling a line just as she had first seen him. She waited by the rail, feeling a little sick, not quite looking at him after the first moment. All the months seemed now to have been no time at all; yet there was a freezing difference about him, for she had thought of him too much. He finished his coil, and turned and saw her. For a minute he looked at her, and then he smiled, surprised, and as though he was glad to see her, and for the first time he spoke to her. He said, "Hello, kid," and coming over to her he swung a leg across the rail and sat perched there. They looked at each other solemnly for longer than they knew; then Amy turned away without answering.

But after supper she could not keep away from the ship's bow, so she walked along the saloon, conscious of the people sitting in the red plush chairs and the stewardesses with their jingling keys, and opened a sliding door to the deck.

Lewis was standing almost exactly outside, and he moved quickly to shut the door for her. He had on his blue jersey and a small dark-blue cap with a shiny visor. They both said "Hello," and Lewis lit a cigarette and they leaned their elbows on the rail and looked down at the tumbling water. They were both uncomfortable.

"Have you been on the *Brewster* all this time?" Amy asked, and Lewis said, "Yes, off and on, but I'm leaving in the fall. I've got me a job on a boat going South. I only worked on her summers while I was in school. Now that's over, so I'm off."

The ship was running into fog, and the pale gloom closed in around them. It was almost dark, and the lights along the deck came suddenly on, making the mist deeper and giving a theatrical look to the deck. Amy had nothing to say; his strangeness chilled her. She wished now that she had not seen him again—no, not that, but still she wanted to get away from him. He was older, harder, than she remembered, and he was better in her thoughts than here beside her, the cigarette between his fingers, the damp air darkening his hair below his cap. She could not bear never to see him again, yet she was unhappy with him now.

"I wondered what happened to you," said Lewis suddenly. "I used to wonder about you some, believe it or not."

"Did you?" cried Amy breathlessly.

He nodded, smiling down at the water. "I wanted to speak to you before but I thought you'd think I was kind of fresh—but today you surprised me, so I just did."

"I thought about you some, too," said Amy, embarrassed. Her mouth felt dry, and she began to be afraid one of her family might come along and discover her. The sea swished and curled below them, and swirls of foam streamed off into the dark. The ship was rolling now, slowly, creaking a little, hung with fog-drops that gathered and ran off and gathered again. Desolation lay heavily on them both. Suddenly the fog-whistle blew, a long aching blast so full of forlornness and foreboding that it seemed to give voice to their own uneasiness.

"What's your name?" asked Lewis finally.

She said, "Amy. I know yours is Lewis. I heard a man call you that once when you were unloading at Warren's Landing." Again they were silent.

"Well, I've got to go," he said, straightening up, and tossing his cigarette off into the mist. "They give you hell if they catch you with a passenger. And besides—" But he let the sentence rest there. "So long, Amy." Quickly he put his hands on her shoulders, holding her still; his eyes, slanting and grey, searched her face—asking for something, it seemed to her, and a little mocking . . . Frightened, she did not move.

"Good-bye, Amy," he said again, and raised her chin with his forefinger.

Oh, cried Amy passionately, inside herself, *don't go! Don't leave me!*

But she only said stiffly, "Good-bye," and her voice was lost in another lingering, yearning wail from the whistle.

He gave her a little pat on the shoulder and quickly ruffled her hair, his hand running cold and hard against her cheek. Then he was gone, just as she turned swiftly, without thought, to him.

In the stillness after the whistle's blast had died away the *Brewster* rolled low, trembling, into the waves, and the rail was gritty with cinders and wet under Amy's hands as she stood looking out at the dark.

19. Farming Country

THIS GREEN FIELD

by

ELIZABETH COATSWORTH

This green field is the masterpiece
Of many hands. Here you may know
Backs strained and thighs and wills were bent
And sweat poured out to make it so.

Cut, cleaned, and tended, now it lies
Docile to man, while he stands near,
But let him turn, and it will slip
Into the thicket, like a deer.

OXEN

by

CHARLES DUNN, JR.

Oxen, lying in their stalls dozing contentedly through the winter
night. One of them heaves his huge body sideways. His wide horn

From *Country Poems,* copyright, 1931, 1942, by Elizabeth Coatsworth. Used
with the permission of The Macmillan Company.
From *Cloudman Hill Heritage* by Charles Dunn, Jr. (Marion E. Dodd:
Northampton, Mass., 1939).

strikes the smooth stanchion to which he is fastened by a tie-chain which clinks musically. One of his mates wakens and begins to rise, hind quarters first, then, unfolding one knee at a time, he stands upon his feet and stretches. Every muscle of his sixteen hundred pound carcass is taut and a quick blast from his nostrils relieves the pressure of air in his mighty lungs. There is a prickly, itchy sensation of his skin—Spring is approaching, and he and his mates will be shedding the thick woolly coat of hair that has kept them warm through the cold months, since the fall ploughing was finished, and the year's supply of firewood was drawn from the woodlot on the east end of the farm.—Also it is morning. A great star is shining through the east window of the ox-barn and a faint tinge of daylight is showing across the snow-covered fields. Very soon the Farm Boy will be lifting the latch and coming into the feed-floor where a great pile of clover hay lies ready for the morning foddering. The oxen are all on their feet at the sound of his footsteps crunching the frozen snow. They utter lowing sounds and rattle their tie-chains as he hangs his lantern on a snap-hook at the end of a chain, suspending it away from any contact with hay or straw. Great forkfuls of the fragrant hay are piled into the cribs, and hungry mouths are munching at bovine breakfasts. Half an hour and the hay has been consumed. A box on trucks with "provender" is wheeled along the cribs and each ox is given his portion of ground grains. After the breakfast in the household, the Farm Boy (he is a husky youngster of twenty years) will come to the ox-barn again to give the oxen water and yoke one pair of them to an ox-sled, break a road around the barn and get out the smoke-house, which has been laid up on skids for a whole year since the annual supply of hams was cured and smoked a year ago.

Yes, it is Spring. The ox in his stall knew it when he arose, stretched himself and felt his winter coat of hair begin to loosen. The tie-up door swings open, a stately pair are loosed from their tie-chains and step clumsily out into the sharp morning air. The Farm Boy follows them, the yoke and bows under his left arm, the goad-stick in his right hand. He leans the yoke against the barnyard fence and removes one of the bows. He walks up to "Broad," the "off" ox, places the U-shaped bow under his neck, leads him to the yoke and fastens the bow in its place with a bow-pin. Removing the other bow he holds it in his right hand, lifts the end of the yoke in the other hand and says: "Wo-hoish 'Buck,' come under!" The command is at once obeyed. Buck steps up by the side of Broad, the yoke and bow are fastened on his neck, and the pair are ready for their work. Such patience and submission are to be found in no other work animal of the Northern countries. Perhaps the Farm Boy, who had been attending the Academy at the village during the Winter Term, remembered his Latin; how the conquered people that followed the chariot of Caesar on his return to Rome were made to "pass under the yoke" in token of their submission.

And now the big barnyard gate swings wide as the Farm Boy with a wave of his goad-stick and a brief "Wo-hoish" starts toward the ox-sled, followed by his team. The off ox steps across the sled-tongue, and they range up side by side while the end of the sled-tongue is slipped through the yoke-ring and the iron clevis-pin drops into place. A log-chain is hooked just above the yoke-ring and the other end of the chain made fast to the iron hook on the top of the tongue-roller of the sled and—"Wo-hoish Buck, haw Broad"—a ton and a half of ox-beef is thrust against the bows and yoke.—Nothing happens. The heavy sled remains stationary. Ah, the steel sled-shoves are frozen fast by sub-zero nights to the snow beneath them. A direct pull fails to loosen them. So: "Back Buck, haw Broad here!" with a wave of the goad-stick across Buck's face and a swing across Broad's back, there is a powerful left swing of the sled-tongue and a sidewise motion of the sled which wrenches the runners loose from the snow, and everything is moving. Around behind the big barn there has been no track for all winter. Snow, however, is not very deep there, for the wind eddying around the big building has blown a lot of it away. Two feet, perhaps, remained; but oxen can wallow, how they can wallow! Pulling out the clevis-pin and unhooking the chain from the yoke, leaving the sled standing, the Farm Boy, taking a shovel, marked out two tracks through the snow leading out around and coming back alongside the smoke-house. Then the oxen in response to his "Wo-hoish! Come on boys!" followed him around two or three times, crushing down the snow until a good track was made for the sled which, presently, was halted alongside the smoke-house. Just then the tall form of the Farmer, wearing a gray home-spun frock, cap and mittens, appeared around the corner of the barn. "Want any help, Sonny?" he shouted against the wind. "No, sir, I can handle it all right."

"Better shovel out a cross-haul, and let the cattle tip it over with a chain and slip-link."

So the chain was passed around the smoke-house; the slip-link adjusted; the oxen unhooked from the sled and faced out at right angles to the sled-rails, standing in the cross-haul while the Farm Boy made the chain fast to the yoke-ring. "Now you 'gaels'" (addressing the oxen) "just you go about four steps an' stop when I say, whoa. If you pull that smoke-house clear across the sled I won't get it loaded in a month of Sundays." "Wo-hoish easy—just a step—Whoa!"—and over came the smoke-house square on top of the sled. The chain and slip-link bound it securely to the sled-rails, and away they went around the barn and to a low cairn of fieldstone at a little distance from the buildings, so there would be no danger from fire. The Farmer had been busy with his snow-shovel and the sled was backed down to the cairn—the smoke-house up-ended over it, ready to receive the hams and strips of bacon that had been in the curing-pickle for weeks. Here they would brown and get a smoky flavor in a smoldering smudge of green birch chips and sawdust, carefully tended by the Farmer himself. Then the Farmer, looking up at the March sun, said: "It's noon, Sonny. Give 'em a drink and tie 'em up. I've put a foddering of hay in their cribs."

And so the Farm Boy, having finished his forenoon work with

his oxen, rushed into the farmhouse kitchen, gave his hands and face a cold water wash at the sink, slicked his hair at the mirror by the window, and sat down to a dinner of pork sausage, boiled potato, mashed turnip, cucumber pickles, steamed brown bread and butter, and several cups of tea with pumpkin pie, and a slab of home-made cheese. How good it all tasted and how he did eat!

THE FIELDS IN SPRING

by

GLADYS HASTY CARROLL

"I hope you'll plant a good lot of them Kentucky Wonders," Jen said. "That's the best bean, I believe, ever I cooked."

"I'm saving seven rows for them," her father answered. "And poles all cut for them to run on, too."

"Lowe's Champion is fine, though, for a bush bean."

"You can't beat Lowe's Champion much, I always said."

Jen stopped in the shed to reach into the bags of seed potatoes her father had been quartering through the last week. They were withered and spongy, but in them she could see the hard, pinkish-brown fruit that they would bear. From this bag would come the round, red Pine Brooks Seedlings, and from those bags the Early Rose, long, crisp white potatoes with pink eyes. The Shaws like the Early Rose the best of all. But somewhere here there was seed for the Late Rose, too, and the Green Mountain, and the Gold Coin. It made an interest in the winter to try one kind and then another, to boil this and bake that, to see which kept its flavor and texture best and made good eating in the spring. "What potatoes are these?" Mark Shaw would ask. "I got them in the arch," Jen would say. "They're the Gold Coin. Gold Coin's a good potato." But they liked the Early Rose best, for all around.

"Did you save any seed of them big potatoes ma brought down from Kezar Falls that time?" Jen asked, hearing her father behind her.

"I planted them yesterday," Mark Shaw said. "I let Ed have some too. We don't want to let them run out. Nobody else ever raised that kind around here."

He loaded two of the bags and some wooden measures and a hoe on his wheelbarrow and called to John. Jen stood in the shed door and watched them go across the yard and through the bars and up over the hill. None of the other children had ever been so faithful as John to the spring work, not one; John had something in him. It might not be that he helped much this year, but it was good for him to get the feel of the sun on his back and the loose dirt under his feet; and next year this time he would be six, and after that, seven.

"The ground is covered with dandelions," thought Jen. "I must get me a knife and pail and dig a good mess for dinner."

She liked to walk through the grass in the morning, and reach down into the roots of things, tenderly and gratefully, to get food that cost nothing and was fresh and damp with dew. There was nothing better than wild greens in the spring.

Toward the middle of May, Margaret spent a Saturday in the field with Ed. It was not usual in Shaw women to work out-of-doors, but Margaret had insisted and Ed indulged her. Down under the hill not even the chimney tops of their house were visible to them, nor the ridgepole of their barn. It was almost as if they had no buildings, but were a peasant couple travelled out to the solitude of their own plot of land. The lilac bushes by the fence were budded and the plum trees in full bloom. Strawberries had blossomed all along the edges of the ploughed piece. A bobolink sang in the marsh. Margaret walked first, in a short plaid gingham dress with no sleeves, dropping corn, and Ed followed, dropping beans. She could feel him, tall and steady, behind her. Sometimes he spoke. "There goes a bluebird. See him? Over the hill now." After a few rows he set down his pail of beans and began covering what they had planted, with the crisp sound of metal moving the soil. "Tired, puss?" he asked her. She shook her head but he put his arm around her while they stood for a minute resting, and she leaned against him. "No, Ed. Just happy." Ed grinned. This was life as he liked it, everything simple and in its place.

They ate their lunch in the shade of a walnut tree on the side hill. Margaret had brought biscuit with home-cured ham between, hard-boiled eggs, and cake, and sweetened tea in glass bottles. When they had finished, Ed lay with his head in Margaret's lap and she fingered his thick, damp hair, smoothing it back from his forehead where his hat had stuck it down. She felt at ease with him out here, more than she did in the house, much more than before they had been married. She knew him now, and all his ways, and how to please him; it was not always easy to do, but she knew how. Ed lay relaxed, his hand unthinking against her, his mind wandering over this which stretched out for acres on all sides of his body and which belonged to him. He felt the sticks and stones under his shoulders, but they were not so hard as they would have been to another; they were his. He felt the softness of the grass, too, and knew that it would grow, that he would fill his barn with it by and by and the yellow sides of Jersey cows become sleek and round.

"Sing me something, why don't you?" he asked.

Margaret flushed.

"Somebody might hear," she said. "I couldn't."

"Say one of your poems then."

"Oh, I couldn't."

He lifted himself on his elbows and grasped her wrists.

"Say one!"

She said the first lines she could think of.

"The lark's on the wing,
The snail's on the thorn—"

At the end she added, "I'm not sure that's right, Ed!"

"It's good enough," Ed said. "I know what it means. That's what it's for, I guess, as much as anything else."

"I guess so, " Margaret answered shyly.

It was good to have Ed speak of poetry. She sat looking down at him, feeling him heavy and hot beside her, and wondered how women told men when there were going to be children, and what men did then. She had never talked with Mil of such things, for Mil had a bitter, shame-faced way about them, and all that Margaret knew she had read in books. It did not say in the books how a woman told her husband she expected to have a child, especially when she was not sure. Except in story books where the wife whispered, "I think I'm going to have a baby, darling. Are you glad?" Margaret could not speak to Ed like that; she would feel queer. The word "baby" had too silly a sound to be said to Ed, and she never called him "darling." To Ed it would have to be told as if it did not matter; but it did, and so she could not say it at all. She did not mind. To-day she was not in the least afraid. She felt strong and capable out here. Bearing another Shaw would be a fine thing to do. If he came as she expected she could bring him into the field next spring, and let him lie on a blanket in the sun while his father planted corn and beans in hills and covered them. She felt proud now that he had happened so soon; she must be a natural mother.

"Well," said Ed. "This won't do the planting."

She walked back beside him to the piece and they worked steadily. She would be careful, she thought. She would eat the right things. She would nurse her baby and keep him pink and round. Her children would never go as Mil's went so much, with dirty hair and uncut nails and ragged stockings; she was thinking already of more than one, of a boy, and a girl, and another boy.

"I can finish it Monday, if the weather's fine," Ed said. They stood looking back over what they had done. Margaret wondered if even now the kernels she had planted in the morning might be beginning to stir. If the soil was good they ought to be, she thought proudly. They went up the hill side by side, Ed pushing the wheelbarrow. The grass was tall enough to brush Margaret's ankles as she walked. Carefully they followed the track they had made coming down, not to leave two paths. The sun set in a burst of color as it had the night before and would the next night. It was a stretch of clear weather just now. A whippoorwill sang in the lilac bush.

COON HUNT

by

E. B. WHITE

There were two dogs with us the night we went coon hunting. One was an old hound, veteran of a thousand campaigns, who knew what we were up to and who wasted no time in idle diversions. The other was a puppy, brought along to observe and learn; to him the star-sprinkled sky and the deep dark woods and the myriad scents and the lateness of the hour and the frosty ground were intoxicating. The excitement of our departure was too much for his bowels. Tied in the truck, he was purged all the way over to Winkumpaw Brook and was hollow as a rotten log before the night was well under way. This may have had something to do with what happened.

It was great hunting that night, perfect for man and beast, a fateful night for coon. The stars leaned close, and some lost their hold and fell. I was amazed at how quickly and easily the men moved through the woods in strange country, guided by hunches and a bit of lantern gleam. The woods hit back at you if you let your guard down.

We were an odd lot. A couple of the men were in coveralls—those bunny suits garage mechanics wear. One old fellow had been all stove to pieces in a car accident; another was down with a hard cold and a racking cough; another had broken two ribs the day before and had been strapped up that afternoon by a doctor. He had killed the pain with a few shots of whisky and the spirits had evidently reminded him of coon hunting. This fellow had a terrible thirst for water all during the night and he had a way of straying off from the main party and hugging the water courses where he could kneel and drink when the need was great. We could sometimes follow the progress of his thirst in the winking of his buglight, in some faraway valley. After a bit he would rejoin us. "I'm drier'n a covered bridge," he would say disconsolately.

I felt a strong affinity for the puppy because he and I were the new ones to this strange game, and somehow it seemed to me we were sharing the same excitement and mystery of a night in the woods. I had begun to feel the excitement back in the kitchen of the farmhouse, where the hunters had gathered, dropping in and standing about against the walls of the room. The talk began right away, all the cooning lore, the tales of being lost from three in the morning until six, and the tricks a coon would play on a dog. There was a woman in the room, wife of the owner of the old dog, and she was the only one for whom the night held no special allure. She sat knitting a huge mitten. Mostly, the hunters paid no attention to her. Only one remark went her way. One of the men, observing the mitten, asked:

"Gettin' that man o' yours ready for winter?"

She nodded.

"I should kill him before winter if he was mine—he's no good for anything else," the fellow continued, pleasantly.

The woman raised a grudging smile to this sure-fire witticism.

She plied the needles without interruption. This obviously was not the first time she had been left at home while men and dogs went about their business, and it wasn't going to be the last time either. For her it was just one night in a long succession of nights. This was the fall and in the fall the men hunted coon. They left after sundown and returned before sunup. That was all there was to that.

The best coon country is always far away. Men are roamers, and getting a long way from home is part of the sport. Our motorcade consisted of two vehicles, a truck for the dogs and owners, and a sedan for the hangers-on, lantern-bearers, and advisory committee. The old dog jumped into place the minute he was let out of the barn; the puppy was hoisted in and tied. The two of them sat on a pile of straw just behind the cab. The man with the broken ribs got into the sedan. Nobody seemed to think it was in the least odd that he was going coon hunting, to walk twelve or fifteen miles in rough country. He said the adhesive tape held everything O. K. and anyway, he said, the only time his chest hurt was when he breathed.

We advanced without stealth, the truck leading. The headlights of our car shone directly in the faces of the dogs. The old dog leaned back craftily against the sideboards, to steady himself against the motion. He half closed his eyes and was as quiet on the journey as a middle-aged drummer on a way train. The pup crouched uneasily and was frequently thrown. He would rare up and sniff, then crouch again, then a curve would throw him and he would lose his balance and go down. He found a hole in the sideboards and occasionally would press his nose through to sniff the air. Then the excitement would attack his bowels and he would let go all over everything—with some difficulty because of the violent motion of the truck. The old dog observed this untidiness with profound contempt.

We got away from the highway after a while and followed a rough back road up into some country I had never been into. At last we got out and let the old hound go. He went to work instantly, dropping downhill out of sight. We could hear his little bell tinkling as he ranged about in the dim valley between us and a night-struck lake. When he picked up a scent, suddenly his full round tones went through you, and the night was a gong that had been struck. The old dog knew his business. The men, waiting around, would discuss in great detail his hunting and would describe what he was doing off there, and what the coon was doing; but I doubted that they knew, and they just kept making things up the way children do. As soon as the hound barked tree, which is a slightly different sound than the sound of the running, we followed his voice and shot the coon.

Once the dog led us to an old apple tree in an almost impenetrable thicket, and when the flashlights were shined up into the topmost branches no coon was there. The owner was puzzled and embarrassed. Nothing like this had ever happened before, he said. There was a long period of consultation and speculation, all sorts of theories were advanced. The most popular was that the coon had climbed the apple tree, then crossed, squirrel-like into the branches of a nearby hackmatack, then descended, fooling the hound. Either this was the case or the dog had made an error. Upward of an hour was spent trying every angle of this delicious contretemps.

The puppy was held in leash most of the time, but when the first coon was treed he was allowed to watch the kill. Lights from half a dozen flashlights swept the tree top and converged to make a halo, with the coon's bright little sharp face in the center of the luminous ring. Our host lethargically drew his pistol, prolonging the climax with a legitimate sense of the theater. No one spoke while he drew a bead. The shot seemed to puncture first the night, then the coon. The coon lost his grip and landed with a thud, still alive and fighting. The old hound rushed in savagely to grab him by the throat and finish him off. It was a big bull coon; he died bravely and swiftly, and the hound worked with silent fury. Then the puppy, in leash, was allowed to advance and sniff. He was trembling in every muscle, and was all eyes and ears and nose—like a child being allowed to see something meant only for grownups. (I felt a little that way myself.) As he stretched his nose forward timidly to inhale the heady smell of the warm coon the old hound, jealous, snarled and leaped. The owner jerked back. The puppy yelped in terror. Everyone laughed. It was a youngster, getting burned by life— that sort of sight. Made you laugh.

After midnight we moved into easier country about ten miles away. Here the going was better—old fields and orchards, where the little wild apples lay in thick clusters under the trees. Old stone walls ran into the woods, and now and then there would be an empty barn as a ghostly landmark. The night grew frosty and the ground underfoot was slippery with rime. The bare birches wore the stars on their fingers, and the world rolled seductively, a dark symphony of brooding groves and plains. Things had gone well, and everyone was content just to be out in the small hours, following the musical directions of a wise and busy dog.

The puppy's owner had slipped the leash and allowed his charge to range about a bit. Nobody was paying much attention to him. The pup stayed with the party mostly, and although he was aware of the long-range operations of the older dog, he seemed to know that this was out of his class; he seemed timid of the woods and tended to stay close, contenting himself with sniffing about and occasionally jumping up to kiss someone's face. We were stepping along through the woods, the old hound near at hand, when the thing happened. Suddenly the puppy (who had not made a sound up to this point) let out a loud whoop and went charging off on a tangent. Everybody stopped dead in surprise.

"What goes on here anyway?" said somebody quietly.

The old hound was as mystified as the rest of us. This was a show-off stunt apparently, this puppy trying to bark coon. Nobody could make it out. Obviously there was no coon scent or the old dog would have picked it up instantly and been at his work.

"What in the devil?" asked somebody.

The puppy was howling unmercifully as though possessed. He charged here and there and came back along his own track passing us at a crazy mad pace, and diving into the woods on the other side of the trail. The yelps sounded hysterical now. Again the puppy charged back. This time as he passed we could see that he had a queer look in his eye and that his movements were erratic. He would dive one way at a terrible clip, then stop and back off as though ducking an enemy, half cringing; but he kept putting up this terrible holler and commotion. Once he came straight at me. I stepped aside and he went by screaming.

"Runnin' fit," said his owner. "That's the trouble. I can tell now by the way he acts. He's took with cramps in his bowwils and he don't know anythin' to do 'cept run and holler. C'mon, Dusty, c'mon, boy!"

He kept calling him softly. But Dusty was in another world and the shapes were after him. It was an eerie business, this crazy dog tearing around in the dark woods, half coming at you, half running from you. Even the old dog seemed disturbed and worried, as though to say: "You see—you will bring a child along, after his bedtime."

The men were patient, sympathetic now.

"That's all it is, he's took with a fit."

Dusty charged into the midst of us, scattering us. He stopped, bristling, his eyes too bright, a trace of froth at his mouth. He seemed half angry, half scared and wanting comfort. "Nothing much you can do, he'll run it off," they said.

And Dusty ran it off, in the deep dark woods, big with imaginary coons and enormous jealous old hounds, alive with the beautiful smells of the wild. His evening had been too much for him; for the time being he was as crazy as a loon. Someone suggested we go home.

We started moving up toward the cars, which were two or three fields away over where you could see the elms black against the sky. The thought of home wasn't popular. A counter suggestion was made to prolong the hunting, and we separated off into two parties, one to return to the cars, the other to cut across country with the old dog and intercept the main body where a certain woods road met the highway. I walked several more miles, and for the first time began to feel cold. It was another hour before I saw Dusty again. He was all right. All he needed was to be held in somebody's arms. He was very, very sleepy. He and I were both sleepy. I think we will both remember the first night we ever went coon hunting.

THE FIRST AROOSTOOK POTATOES

by

PEARL ASHBY TIBBETTS

June came to Aroostook and made of it a paradise.

The shores of the river were garlanded with wild roses. Pink and fragrant they covered the dwarf bushes growing in the gravel on the water's edge, and extended all zigzag like the edge of hamburg lace in and out of the jointed grass.

Birds were everywhere. The woods, the roadside, the shores of the river, the lakes and the air were filled with the songs, the nests, and the flying wings of birds. For the migrating song birds this northern wilderness was journey's end. The waterfowl, ducks, geese and other web-foots in their spring pilgrimage first began to drop to earth and build nests. Only a small part of them, the impatient ones from each flock, yielded to the lure of the small mirror-lakes, while the majority went a little farther north into

From *Land Under Heaven* by Pearl Ashby Tibbetts (Falmouth Book House: Portland, Maine, 1937).

Canada. Woodcock, plover and partridges were numerous and nearly as tame as domestic fowl.

With the coming of spring Morris had built a shack of logs and moved to his own land. Johnny Parker was hard at work chopping trees for a mid-summer burning and James Ashton was left alone. Other young men had taken farms and some had their wives with them in their log camps.

His crop was planted among the stumps. Rows of vegetables of all kinds occupied one end of his burnt land. Then a patch of buckwheat and a strip of peas and oats. The peas and oats were sown together and when they grew, the oat stalks supported the pea vines and kept the grain off the ground. This was the way the farmers of Madawaska had learned from their forefathers, the Acadians.

Johnny Parker, true son of Ireland, declared that no crop was complete without potatoes and volunteered to go across the Line for some seed. At The Fort he hired William Kelley with his canoe and the trip was made by water, down the river, around the Falls and on down between the wooded shores to a small settlement. Here they bought three bushels of Early Blues for a round silver dollar. Nearly the last one in Johnny's pocket.

After a hazardous trip back, as the river was still swollen from melting snow in the woods, they reached The Fort with their precious load. Mr. Kelley was paid with one bushel and the other two were dragged home on a rude wooden sledge over the muddy trail by the exultant Johnny.

He presided at the ceremony of cutting the potatoes into sections and directing the others how to plant them. The ground among the stumps was dark and mellow. With a "nigger" hoe they turned back a narrow strip to a depth of six inches and in each hole placed the half of a small potato or a quarter section of a larger one.

The Early Blues were a long smooth potato with a bluish tint to the skin which became darker, almost a purple, at the seed end. These were the first potatoes ever planted in this country, destined fifty years later to be famous all over the world for the large quantity and fine quality of its potatoes.

As the men carefully placed one seed in each hole and packed the earth over them with the sole of their boot, Johnny made this prophetic remark, "Tuck the blue noses in well, me lads, and before many months we'll have a feast fit for a king." From the Irishman's remark came the nickname and with pride the inhabitants of New Brunswick to this day are called Bluenoses.

Ferdinand and some strangers called at the new settlement one day in midsummer. The strangers were United States surveyors and were about the business of marking the new boundary lines between the Dominion of Canada and the United States. The party consisted of two soldiers in uniform, half a dozen scouts, and two colored orderlies. James was digging a cellar for his new house when they appeared at his clearing.

Near his building site was a gigantic pine, one of the original King's Pines, for it bore on its massive side an arrow-shaped scar. Owing to a slight defect midway of the trunk, it had been rejected and left standing when the agents of the King had cut over the territory fifty years before.

Under this primeval giant the visitors drew rein and James, brushing some of the yellow soil from his clothing and hands, went to greet them. In a manner becoming the University Club, Ferdinand Armsden made the introductions.

"Mr. Lee, allow me to present Mr. James Ashton, formerly of Derbyshire, England. Mr. Ashton, this is Captain Robert E. Lee of Virginia, his first trip into our beautiful country, and we hope not his last."

It was Robert E. Lee of Virginia, tall young surveyor, who twenty years later was Commander-in-Chief of the Southern forces in the Civil War.

The grinning colored boys brought water from the brook and the men, in turn, drank from the dripping wooden bucket. The surveying party was to meet the British agents at The Fort. As they moved down the trail, they paused beside the burnt land field, with its new crop growing among the blackened stumps. To Ferdinand, who rode beside him, Captain Lee said:

"Like the greatest of all men, George Washington, I believe there is no victory like that of conquering the wilderness."

At the bend of the trail they turned to wave to the pioneer but he had again bent to his task of placing field stones in his cellar wall.

In early fall the surveyors finished their work and Ferdinand returned home. With enthusiasm he told of resurveying the Line between the two countries, and with a note of justifiable pride in his voice said, "With their modern instruments and all their skill, they found the original line run by Park Holland in 1820 to be right." No posts had been set during the first survey, but Ferdinand could recall locations and landmarks.

This time a six rod strip was cleared, the trees burned, and iron posts placed at intervals along the entire eastern boundary of the State, a distance of more than two hundred miles. Ten years later this cleared strip was covered with young spruce trees and from a bird's view point they may have looked like a width of green velvet carpet spread between two countries.

THE FOUNDING OF "NEW SWEDEN"

by

PEARL ASHBY TIBBETTS

With renewed energy the backwoods farmers pursued the fight for the railroad into their fertile country. Charters were granted by the State; whole townships of wild land given to promote the project; promises were made and contracts signed. Some unseen power, some trickery and chicanery still defeated the arrival of the much hoped for iron horse.

From *Land Under Heaven* by Pearl Ashby Tibbetts (Falmouth Book House: Portland, Maine, 1937).

Stephen had been content to stay at home for a few years after the war, to regain his health and help on the farm. But now he was becoming restless and looking around for something to do. No use to raise farm produce when the road to market led two hundred miles through the woods. A State surveyor came north looking for a crew of dependable woodsmen and native survey- ors, and Stephen hired with him.

The United States Consul to Sweden, William Widgery Thomas, was bringing a colony of Swedes to settle some of the wild land in the State.* "With the consent of the State of Maine and the will of the Lord, I will plant a colony here that will turn this wilderness into one of the fairest spots in America," said Minister Thomas. The surveying party was going up into the unbroken wilderness to make a location for the immigrants.

One hundred and twenty-five acres of trees were felled and the land cleared. Sixteen log houses were built on as many hundred acre farms. These cabins were well built and roomy. Each one was equipped with a stove and a few articles of necessary furniture. In the center of the clearing a plot of fifty acres was reserved and on this an enormous barn-like structure was built and called the Capitol.

Stephen was at home for a few days in the spring and was full of enthusiasm for the beauties and wealth of the land to be given the Swedes. "I hope they will appreciate their new homes," he said. "Nowhere could the woods be more lovely. Mile after mile of rolling hardwood ridges covered with a heavy growth of beech, birch, and sugar maple. There is plenty of black growth on the lowlands. Springs are gushing from the crests of the ridges, and the brooks are full of trout. Deer are everywhere, and the partridges are as tame as chickens. The soil is rich and deep, just waiting for the plow."

James Ashton smiled. "When I first looked over this beautiful country years ago, I felt that my wanderings were done. Each

---

* The Swedes arrived in the summer of 1870. H. B.

year I feel more satisfied with the land and more impatient for a chance to give it a fair trial."

Stephen said, "All the surveyors and men from 'outside' were amazed at the beauty of the country and the natural wealth of the forests. Before they came up here they thought that the place was a frozen wilderness, but they didn't mind the cold at all. They say it is a dry cold here, not like the seacoast where it is damp and penetrating."

Great plans were made for the arrival of the Swedes. The ship that brought them across the ocean would land them at St. John in New Brunswick and teams would bring them across the Province and into the State at The Fort. There they would be welcomed and from there proceed to their new homes.

The selectmen at The Fort appointed committees for the reception and entertainment of the arrivals. Word was sent to Catherine and Mrs. Bradley that they had been appointed with three other women from the Flannery settlement across the river to serve a dinner. Board tables were made in the public square with flag-draped poles at each corner. There were to be music and speeches of welcome.

The twenty-third of July dawned clear and fair and the country people for miles around gathered in the main street and along the road to the Line to see the new settlers. The members of the dinner committee had been cooking and collecting food for days and all was in readiness. The aroma from two large iron kettles hung over an open fire and, filled with steaming coffee, tantalized the nostrils of the expectant crowd. Dinner was to be served the immigrants and officials at the long tables and the folks from the settlements had brought picnic lunches. In back of every gig, wagon and oxcart was a basket, pail or pasteboard box bulging with food.

The long line of teams appeared and wound over the narrow, crooked road, past the iron post on the Boundary Line and into the United States. The procession was headed by a carriage containing Mr. Thomas and a Swedish guest. Twenty-five wagons and carts followed, filled with the half hundred men, women, and children and their worldly possessions.

To the backwoods children the blond and stalwart people in their foreign dress looked like beings from another world. The women wore small shawls over their heads and when these were slipped back, there were revealed on the nape of their necks huge pugs of hair, the color of molasses candy. Most of them wore rings in their ears. The men wore high-waisted trousers of gray wool and very short coats. They all wore wooden shoes. Many of them carried big loaves of black rye bread.

After the dinner, while the Minister was interpreting the speech of welcome, Neels and Lucy stood at the foot of one of the tables. A beautiful young girl was seated beside her mother near them and held a covered basket in her lap. Her blue eyes looked frightened and she spoke to her mother in a low voice.

It had been years since Neels had even thought in the language of his childhood and now he was surprised to find he could understand what she said. He leaned forward and answered in a few words of Danish. The mother looked startled but the girl seemed pleased. Lucy smiled at them and asked, "What did you say to them, Neels?" and he answered.

"The girl asked her mother if all these big woods around here were full of bears, and I told her not to be afraid."

Then they all laughed and Hilda opened the cover of the basket a few inches and showed them a yellow kitten. She had brought it all the way from Sweden!

The dinner was over and the procession moved up the long winding road that followed the river toward their new home. Stephen and two other young men stayed in the Swedish settlement for a few days to help the peasants get settled. In the fall Stephen went to teach a school in a room of the Capitol building and boarded with the parents of the young girl who had brought the yellow kitten from the Old Country. Her name was Hilda Jensen.

BAKED BEANS

by

JOHN GOULD

They tell me the Maine custom of beans every Saturday night comes from the awe the old folks held for the Sabbath. On Sunday you didn't cook anything, and a pot of beans left over from the night before fed the body without disturbing the soul. I do know that some other parts of New England, such as Vermont, take their beans any old time, and like them just as well, but they are open-minded enough to have stewed chicken on Saturday night. Stewed chicken, around here, is now strictly Sunday dinner fare, and we have retained the Saturday night beans without keeping the good Christian principle involved. As to Boston, all I know is that every year we send baking beans down that way, and they send back the next year and want some more, and I figure they must like them. They say it's hard to find a decent bean today in Boston, but that isn't so, because we sell a lot of beans down there.

Anyway, Great-grandmother's bean pot never missed a Saturday that I know of, and it always got a boiling out afterward with baking soda and was carefully set away on its own special shelf under the cupboard. Then we suddenly had no bean pot, and an aunt came up bringing a new one just out of the store. She said, "By the time the lad gets big enough to eat beans, this one'll be fit to bake some in." She knew what she was talking about. She knew the pores of a bean pot take on a mellowing that comes from weekly bakings. It takes barrels of beans, gallons of molasses, whole saltings of pork, bushels of onions, and months of blue moons to fire the quintessence into a good bean pot. The hand of the potter, whimsical as he may be, can't work this miracle in his kiln. It takes the loving care of a mother to pick and choose only the right beans, and the right kinds of beans. None of your midget pea beans by a long shot. Nobody ever found out how to brown a pea bean, and nobody around here ever cared about trying. Our beans at their best are Jacob's Cattle beans, and it isn't everybody ever heard of them. Some old fellow who knew his Bible named them. Laban's cattle were different from Jacob's, maybe you remember—Jacob's Cattle were ring-straked and speckled and spotted. And so is a Jacob's Cattle bean. Some may hold out for cranberry beans and such, but I believe a Jacob's Cattle is the prettiest dry bean of all. It comes about the size of a good kidney bean, and some say it is a cousin. Kidneys are not regular fare around here, nobody seems to like them steadily. But everybody bakes kidneys now and then, and no home ought to be without them.

Right straight along, most people use either soldier beans, with the little picture of a soldier on them, or the old-fashioned yellow eye bean. There is an improved yellow eye, which never seemed to me to be any great improvement, and I don't recommend them if you still have some seeds of the old-fashioned. We like to stick with Jacob's Cattle, and don't feel we go far wrong in doing it.

But even the beans aren't all-important. It takes hot hardwood fires over a long period of time, and none but the old and established families really get the best baked beans. And it helps to have other things in the oven at the same time—potato-yeast bread, punkin pies, sheets of caraway cookies, Johnny-cake, and all such as that.

So the catastrophe struck, and Saturday night before we moved into our new home we were impoverished to the extent of one useful and fairly well broken in bean pot. We started life anew, sort of, and brought into the new kitchen a brand, spanking new bean pot from the store, which was shiny and untarnished, and wasn't worth a cent. We began even, and I suppose succeeding generations can tell how old their house is by how good their beans are.

When we went to buy a bean pot, we found the latest thing out was a steel one, highly polished and looking like something fine. We didn't buy one, although the man said we wouldn't be able to tell the difference. That's all the man knew. And it isn't wholly because principle is involved. One day a man down at the village asked his wife why she couldn't bake beans as good as my wife's. She was sore about it, but every Saturday he would complain that his beans weren't as good as the ones he had up at our house. His wife finally asked my wife, and mine said, "It's the fire. You can't bake beans in an electric oven."

They find their sparkling electric range has a number of advantages our wood range can't boast, but it seems to us a fine stove in the kitchen is a poor substitute for good beans in the dining room.

So I'm not so sure we couldn't tell the difference between a crockery pot and a steel one. We didn't want to take a chance. If a steel bean pot bakes better beans than a stone one, all I can say is I don't want any better beans than come out of our traditional vessels.

Uncle Timothy used to despise the annual job of threshing beans. He did thresh them, but it was under protest. He called the flail a "poverty stick" on the grounds that nothing was worse than being so poor you had to thresh your own beans. We still thresh our beans by hand, although flailing, like scything, is somewhat a chore that dates you. The flail is two sticks joined with a swivel, and you swing one in an arc so the other comes down with a bang on the pile of bean vines on the floor. After you have hit the vines enough times, you have knocked the dry beans out of the pods, and you can pitch the vines away and leave the beans in a heap on the floor. They still have dust and chaff and a good share of dirt amongst them, but the wind blows around here often enough so we can winnow beans in time for any Saturday.

It is considerable fun to watch a novice swing a flail. He grasps the handle with malice aforethought, brings it back up, and over and down with strength and abandon. The idea is to lay the thumper out at full length on the floor. What he really does is fetch himself a smart wallop behind the left ear and set the shingles on the roof to yapping and jingling in a manner most amazing to hear. Those present, not being tuned to the symphony, carry him out in the open air, loosen his shirt, and wait to hear his first remarks. When mastered the flail is a useful instrument, and it doesn't take long to pound out the year's crop of beans. It makes a good job for rainy days, and if we had a power threshing machine we'd finish up the beans in no time and then have nothing to do in bad weather. But when the flail is in the hands of anyone but an expert it becomes a menace. Since threshing beans is best done with company, it is customary for two men to work at it, standing opposite each other in such a way that one man's flail comes down within inches of the other's nose. A miscue makes for uncomplimentary remarks, and a certain amount of noise which disturbs folks in the house. They tell me it sounds like a dull and heavy thud, but it seemed to me more like being inside a galvanized bucket someone has hit with a rock.

Anyway, really enjoyable beans are not a simple thing to prepare. They start in the spring with the planting, and follow along through the months. And the cooking itself is nothing you do quickly, at the last minute before eating time. Great-grandmother's recipe, which was hand-written in the old book that got burned, paid full tribute to the time required, for her recipe began, "Friday night pick over two cups beans . . ." It was never Tuesday, or Thursday—and it was always Friday. She regulated each Friday night by the number expected for Saturday night, so sometimes she used three cups, sometimes she filled the pot clear to the brim. The beans were put on the back of the stove to soak, and before bedtime the kitchen was rich with that beany smell so promissory and hopeful.

The recipe then skipped to Saturday morning about ten o'clock, and said, "Put a good-sized onion on bottom of pot. Put in beans. Add ½ cup molasses, tblsp. mustard, 2 tsp. salt, piece lean pork, cover with boiling water." Then Great-grandmother stoked the fire all day, kept water over the beans until the middle of the afternoon. In the middle of the afternoon she would let them boil a little dry, which browned them up good. After she thought they were dry enough, she would pour water on again, and the pot would sizzle, a cloud of steam would pour out in the room, and each and every bean would assume its rightful share of essence and power. It was, indeed, a pot of beans—but baking them is predicated on the individual bean. One hardbean can spoil a whole supper. The whole is no greater than any of its parts.

Perhaps you wonder how we happen to remember Great-grandmother's recipe when the book was burned. Great-grandmother wrote that when she was fourteen years old, and she probably never looked at it again. Our women bake beans, not from recipes, not from memory—but from instinct. Give them a box of wood, a bag of beans, a shelf of ingredients, and a pot worth using, and they'll wind up the week with a steaming bowl of baked beans well worth all the nice things I've said about them.

THE OUTLAW DOGS

by

C. A. STEPHENS

Not a little farm work still remained to be done;—our farm work, in fact, was never done. For a fortnight after our return from the camping trip, we were busy, ploughing stubble ground, drawing off loose stones and building a piece of "double wall" along the side of the north field. There was also a field of winter rye to be got in. The Old Squire was, moreover, preparing to re-embark in the lumbering business at certain lots of timber land which he owned up in the "great woods." Loggers would be hired for this work, however, for Addison, Halstead and I expected to attend the district school which was announced to begin on the Monday after Thanksgiving.

It was mostly dull, hard work now, all day long, and often we were obliged to husk corn, or dry apples, during the evening. The only amusement for a time was one or two husking parties, and an "apple bee" at the Murches'.

On the morning of the 30th of October we waked to find the ground white with snow; several inches had fallen; but it went off, after a day or two; the weather had grown quite cold, however. Ice formed nearly every night. The cattle were now at the barns, but the sheep were still running about the pastures and fields. On the night of the 5th of November the upper part of the lake froze over, as well as the smaller ponds in the vicinity. I found that the boys thereabouts knew how to skate, and was not long in buying a pair of skates, myself. I had much difficulty in learning to use them for several days; at length, I caught the

From *When Life Was Young at the Old Farm in Maine* by C. A. Stephens (The Colonial Press Inc.: Clinton, Mass., 1912).

knack of it, and felt well repaid for a good many hard falls, when at last I could glide away and keep up with Halse, Addison and Thomas Edwards, who skated well. Even Theodora and Ellen could skate.

For a week that fall Lake Pennesseewassee was grand skating ground. Parties of boys from a distance came there every evening and built bonfires on the shore to enliven the scene.

I think that it was the third day before Thanksgiving that eight of us went to the lake, at about four in the afternoon, to have an hour of skating before dark. We found Alfred Batchelder there in advance of us. As Alfred did not now speak to our boys, he kept a little aloof from us.

Near the head of the lake is an island and above it a bog. We had skated around the head of the lake, and keeping to the east side of the island, circled about it, and were coming down on the west side along an arm, some two hundred yards wide, where there was known to be deep water. We thought the ice perfectly firm and safe there, since that on the east side of the island, over which we had just skated, had proved so. All of us were at full racing speed, and Alfred was keeping six or eight rods further out, but parallel with us. Suddenly we heard a crash and saw Alfred go down. The water gushed up around him.

There was no premonitory cracking or yielding. The ice broke on the instant; and so rapidly was he moving that a hole twelve or fifteen feet long was torn by the sheer force with which he went against it. As he fell through, he went under once, but luckily came up in the hole he had made, and got his hands and arms on the edges of the ice, which, however, kept bending down and breaking off. The breaking and his fall were so sudden that he had not even time to cry out till he came up and caught hold of the ice.

Instinctively we all sheered off toward the west shore at first. Then came the impulse to save him. A peeled hemlock log lay stranded on the shore upon rocks, with about four feet of its length frozen in the ice. I remember rushing to this, to get it up and slide it out to him. Finding I could not wrench it loose with my hands, I kicked it with first one foot and then the other, and broke both my skates; but the ice held it like a vise. Then I started on my broken skates to find a pole; two or three of the other boys were also running for poles, shouting excitedly.

All the while Alfred was calling despairingly to us; every time the ice broke, he would nearly disappear under the water, which was deadly cold.

Addison who had first pulled off his skates, then thought of green alder poles. Running to the nearest clump, he bent down and hurriedly cut off two, each as large as a pump-brake. Before I was done kicking the peeled hemlock log, or Halse was back from his pole hunt, Addison had shoved one of the long alders out to Alf, who managed to clutch hold of it.

Addison had hold of the butt end, and Willis Murch, nearer the shore, had reached out the top of the second alder to Addison. The ice yielded somewhat and the water came up; but they all held fast. By this time the rest of us had cut more alders, one of which was thrust out to Willis; and then by main strength we hauled Alfred out and back where the ice was firmer.

It is doubtful whether we should have got him out of the lake but for this expedient; for the water was so cold and the wind so bitterly sharp, that he could not long have supported himself by those bending ice edges. His teeth chattered noisily when at length we hauled him ashore; Addison's, too! Both were wet through. We started and ran as hard as we could towards home. Two of us had to drag Alf at the start; but he ran better after the first hundred yards: and we were all very warm by the time we got him home.

It is often difficult to determine why the ice on some portions of a pond should be thin and treacherous, as in the above instance, while on other portions it is quite safe. Indeed, there is no way of determining except by cautious inspection.

I must do Alfred the justice to record that he came around

quite handsomely to thank Addison, and then asked his pardon for the hard words that he had used at Fair time.

The morning following is marked forever in my memory by an unexpected trip up to the "great woods"—the result of certain disturbing rumors which had been in circulation throughout the autumn, but of which I have not previously spoken, since they were confined mainly to a school district two miles to the east of the Old Squire's farm.

On that morning a party of not less than thirty men and boys, with hounds, was made up to go in pursuit of a pack of outlaw dogs which had been killing sheep and calves in that town and vicinity. As yet the flocks in our own neighborhood had not been molested, but there was no saying how soon the marauders might pay us a visit; and a public effort had been inaugurated to hunt the pack down and destroy it.

The history of these dog outlaws was a singular one and parallels in canine life the famous story of "Dr. Jekyll and Mr. Hyde." The fact that dogs do occasionally lead double lives—one that of a docile house-dog by day, and the other that of a wild, dangerous beast by night—is well established. In this case a trusted dog had become not only an outlaw himself, but drew others about him and was the leader of a dangerous band.

A farmer named Frost, three miles from us, began to lose sheep from a flock of seventy which he owned and which were kept in a pasture that included a high hill and sloped northward over rough, bushy land to the great woods. It was not the custom there to enclose the sheep in pens or shelters, at night. They wandered at will in the pasture, and were rarely visited oftener than once a week, and that usually on Sunday morning. Then either the farmer or one of his boys would go to the pasture to give the sheep salt and count them. This was the custom among the farmers in that locality, nearly all of whom owned flocks sometimes as small as twenty, but rarely larger than seventy-five, since sheep in New England do not thrive when kept in large flocks.

Farmer Frost was not the only one who had lost sheep at this time. Six other flocks were invaded, but his loss occurred first. His son Rufus, going to the pasture to salt and count the sheep on a Sunday morning, found that two ewes and a grown lamb were missing. Later in the day the partially devoured remains of the sheep were found in the pasture not far from a brook.

"Bear's work," the farmer and his neighbors said, although an old hunter who visited the spot pronounced against the theory. But a bear had been seen recently in the vicinity; and Monday morning the Frost boys loaded their guns for a thorough hunt. Two traps were also set near the carcasses, which were left as found, to lure the destroyer back.

The destroyer did not return; the traps remained as they were set; and the youthful hunters were unsuccessful in rousing a bear in the woods. But on the following Wednesday night a farmer named Needham, living a mile and a half from Frost, lost two sheep, the bodies of which were found in his pasture, partly eaten.

It chanced that Farmer Needham, or his son Emerson, owned a dog which was greatly prized. They called him Bender. Bender was said to be a half-breed, Newfoundland and mastiff, but had, I think, a strain of more common blood in his ancestry, for there was a tawny crescent mark beneath each of his eyes. Bender was the pink of propriety and a dog of unblemished reputation.

On this occasion Bender went with the farmer and his boys to the sheep pasture, and smelled the dead sheep with every appearance of surprise and horror. The hair on his shoulders bristled with indignation. He coursed around, seeking for bear tracks, and ran barking about the pasture. In short, he did everything that a properly grieved dog should do under the circumstances, and so far from touching or eating any of the torn mutton, he plainly scorned such a thing.

The boys took Bender with them to hunt bears, as their main reliance and ally, and Bender hunted assiduously. Three or four other dogs, belonging at farms in the vicinity, were also taken on these hunts. One was a collie, another a mongrel bulldog, and a third a large brindled dog of no known pedigree. Still another half-bred St. Bernard dog set off with the others, but on reaching the sheep pasture, where they went first to get the trail and make a start, this latter dog behaved oddly, left the others and slunk away home.

Some of the boys attributed this to cowardice, and he was hooted; others suspected Roke, for that was his name, of having killed the sheep. Suspicion against him so increased that his master kept him chained at home.

No bears were tracked to their dens, and none were caught in the traps, which were also set in the Needham pasture; but less than a week later another farmer, this time the owner of the mongrel bulldog, lost three sheep in one night. As previously, the sheep were found dead and partly eaten.

If Roke's alibi had not had a tangible chain at one end of it that night, his character would have been as good as lost; for his refusal to hunt with the other dogs and the manner in which he behaved while near the dead sheep, had rendered him a public "suspect." When near the carcasses he had growled morosely, and shown his teeth. When barked at by the other dogs, he had taken himself off.

A few nights afterward Farmer Frost lost two more sheep from his flock in the pasture, and the following night Rufus watched in the pasture with a loaded gun, quite without results.

About that time two or three others watched in their pastures. Some shut up their sheep. But the losses continued to occur. Within a radius of three or four miles as many as twenty-four sheep were killed in the course of three weeks.

None of the watchers by night or the hunters by day had, as yet, obtained so much as a trace or a clue to the animal which had done the killing. They came to think that it was quite useless to watch by night; the marauding creature, whether bear, wild-cat, or dog, was apparently too wily, or too keen-scented, to enter a pasture and approach a flock where a man was concealed.

Rufus Frost, who had watched repeatedly, then hit on a stratagem. First he cut off about a foot from the barrel of a shotgun, to shorten it, and then made a kind of bag, or sack, by sewing two sheep-pelts together. Thus equipped, he repaired to the pasture after dark, and joined himself to the flock, not as a watcher, but as a sheep. That is to say, he crept into the sheepskin bag, which was also capacious enough to contain the short gun, and lay down on the outskirts of the flock, a little aloof.

The sheep were lying in a group, ruminating, as is their habit, by night. Rufus drew a tangle of wool over his head, and otherwise contrived to pose as a sheep lying down. He assumed that when thus bagged up in fresh sheepskin, the odor of a sheep would be diffused, and the appearance of one so well counterfeited as to deceive even a bear. His gun he had charged heavily with buckshot; and altogether the ruse was ingenious, if nothing more.

Nothing disturbed the flock on the first night that he spent in the pasture, nor on the second; but he resolved to persevere. It was no very bad way to pass an autumn night; the weather was pleasant and warm, and there was a bright moon nearing its full.

He had kept awake during the first night, listening and watching for the most of the time; but he caught naps the second, and on the third was sleeping comfortably at about two in the morning, when he was suddenly set upon, tooth and nail, by what he believed, on first waking, to be a whole family of bears. One had him by the leg, through the bag, shaking him. Another was dragging at the back of the bag, while the teeth of a third were snapping at his face. Still other teeth were chewing upon his arm, and the growling was something frightful!

This was an alarming manner in which to be wakened from a sound nap, and it is little wonder that Rufus, although a plucky youngster, rolled over and over and yelled with the full power of his lungs.

His shouts produced an effect. First one and then another of his assailants let go and drew back; and getting the wool out of his eyes, Rufus saw that the creatures were not bears, but four astonished dogs, standing a few feet away, regarding him with doubt and disgust.

To all appearance he had been a sheep, lying a little apart from the others, and they had fallen upon him as one; but his shouts led them to think that he was not mutton, after all, and they did not know what to make of it!

Rufus, almost equally astonished, now lay quite still, staring at them. The dogs looked at each other, licked the wool from their mouths, and sat down to contemplate him further.

Rufus, on his part, waxed even more amazed as he looked, for by the bright moonlight he at once identified the four dogs. They were, alas! the highly respectable, exemplary old Bender, the collie Tige, the brindle, and the mongrel bulldog—all loved and trusted members of society. Rufus was so astonished that he did not think of using his blunderbuss; he simply whistled.

That whistle appeared to resolve the doubts of the dogs instantly. They growled menacingly and sprang away like the wind. Rufus saw them run across the pasture to the woods, and afterward, for some minutes, heard them washing themselves in the brook, as roguish, sheep-killing dogs always do before returning home.

But in this case the dogs appeared to know that they had been detected, and that so for as their characters as good and virtuous dogs went, the game was up. Not one of them returned home. All four took to the woods, and thereafter lived predatory lives. They were aware of the gravity of their offences.

During October and early November they were heard of as a pack of bad sheep-killers, time and again; but they now followed their evil practices at a distance from their former homes, where, indeed, the farmers took the precaution of carefully guarding their sheep. On one night of October they killed three calves in a farmer's field, four miles from the Frost farm. Several parties set off to hunt them, but they escaped and lived as outlaws, subsisting from nocturnal forays until snow came, when they were tracked to a den beneath a high crag, called the "Overset," up in the great woods.

It was Rufus Frost and Emerson Needham, the former owner of Bender, who tracked the band to their retreat. Finding it impossible to call or drive the criminals out, they blocked the entrance of the den with large stones, and then came home to devise some way of destroying them—since it is a pretty well-established fact that when once a dog has relapsed into the savage habits of his wild ancestry he can never be reclaimed.

Someone had suggested suffocating the dogs with brimstone fumes; and so, early the following morning, Rufus and Emerson, heading a party of fifteen men and boys, came to the Edwards farm and the Old Squire's to get brimstone rolls, which we had on account of our bees. Their coming, on such an errand, carried a wave of excitement with it. Old Hewey Glinds, the trapper, was sent for and joined the party, in spite of his rheumatism. Every boy in the neighborhood begged earnestly to go; and the most of us, on one plea and another, obtained permission to do so.

All told, I believe, there were thirty-one in the party, not counting dogs. Entering the woods we proceeded first to Stoss Pond, then through Black Ash Swamp, and thence over a mountainous wooded ridge to Overset Pond.

In fact we seemed to be going to the remote depths of the wilderness; and what a savage aspect the snowy evergreen forest wore that morning! At last, we came out on the pond. Very black it looked, for it was what is called a "warm pond." Ice had not yet formed over it. The snow-clad crag where the cave was, on the farther side, loomed up, ghostly white by contrast.

Rufus and Emerson had gone ahead and were there in advance of us; they shouted across to us that the dogs had not escaped. We then all hurried on over snowy stones and logs to reach the place.

It was a gruesome sort of den, back under an overhang of rocks fully seventy feet high. Near the dark aperture which the boys had blocked, numbers of freshly gnawed bones lay in the snow, which presented a very sinister appearance.

Those in advance had already kindled a fire of drift-stuff not far away on the shore. The hounds and dogs which had come with the party, scenting the outlaw dogs in the cave, were barking noisily; and from within could be heard a muffled but savage bay of defiance.

"That's old Bender!" exclaimed Emerson. "And he knows right well, too, that his time's come!"

"Suppose they will show fight?" several asked.

"Fight! Yes!" cried old Hewey, who had now hobbled up. "They'll fight wuss than any wild critters!"

One of the older boys, Ransom Frost, declared that he was not afraid to take a club and go into the cave.

"Don't you think of such a thing!" exclaimed old Hewey. "Tham's desperate dogs! They'd pitch onto you like tigers! Tham dogs know there's no hope for tham, and they're going to fight— if they get the chance!"

It was a difficult place to approach, and several different plans of attack were proposed. When the two hounds and three dogs which had come up with us barked and scratched at the heavy, flat stones which Rufus and Emerson had piled in the mouth of the cave, old Bender and Tige would rush forward on their side of the obstruction, with savage growls. Yet when Rufus or any of the others attempted to steal up with their guns, to shoot through the chinks, the outlaws drew back out of sight, in the gloom. There was a fierceness in their growling such as I never have heard from other dogs.

The owner of Watch, the collie, now crept up close and called to his former pet. "I think I can call my dog out," said he.

He called long and endearingly, "Come, Watch! Come, good fellow! You know me, Watch! Come out! Come, Watch, come!"

But the outlawed Watch gave not a sign of recognition or affection; he stood with the band.

Tige's former master then tried the same thing, but elicited only a deep growl of hostility.

"Oh, you can whistle and call, but you won't get tham dogs to go back on one another!" chuckled old Hewey. "Tham dogs have taken an oath together. They won't trust ye and I swan I wouldn't either, if I was in their places! They know you are Judases!"

It was decided that the brimstone should be used. Live embers from the fire were put in the kettle. Green, thick boughs were cut from fir-trees hard by; and then, while the older members of the party stood in line in front of the hole beneath the rocks, to strike down the dogs if they succeeded in getting out, Rufus and Emerson removed a part of the stones, and with some difficulty introduced the kettle inside, amidst a chorus of ugly growls from the beleaguered outlaws. The brimstone was then put into the kettle, more fire applied, and the hole covered quickly with boughs. And now even we younger boys were allowed to bear a hand, scraping up snow and piling it over the boughs, the better to keep in the smoke and fumes.

The splutter of the burning sulphur could plainly be heard through the barrier, and also the loud, defiant bark of old Bender and the growls of Tige.

Very soon the barking ceased, and there was a great commotion, during which we heard the kettle rattle. This was succeeded presently by a fierce, throaty snarling of such pent-up rage that chills ran down the backs of some of us as we listened. After a few minutes this, too, ceased. For a little space there was complete silence; then began the strangest sound I ever heard.

It was like the sad moaning of the stormy wind, as we some-times hear it in the loose window casements of a deserted house. Hardly audible at first, it rose fitfully, moaning, moaning, then sank and rose again. It was not a whine, as for pity or mercy, but a kind of canine farewell to life: the death-song of the outlaws. This, too, ceased after a time; but old Hewey did not advise taking away the boughs for fifteen or twenty minutes. "Make a sure job on't," he said.

Choking fumes issued from the cave for some time after it was opened and the stones pulled away. Bender was then discovered lying only a few feet back from the entrance. He appeared to have dashed the kettle aside, as if seeking to quench the fire and smoke. Tige was close behind him, Watch farther back. Very stark and grim all four looked when finally they were hauled out with a pole and hook and given a finishing shot.

It was thought best to burn the bodies of the outlaws. The fire on the shore was replenished with a large quantity of drift-wood, fir boughs and other dry stuff which we gathered, and the four carcasses heaved up on the pile. It was a calm day, but thick, dark clouds had by this time again overspread the sky, causing the pond to look still blacker. The blaze gained headway; and a dense column of smoke and sparks rose straight upward to a great height. Owing to the snow and the darkening heavens, the fire wore a very ruddy aspect, and I vividly recall how its melancholy crackling was borne along the white shore, as we turned away and retraced our steps homeward.

FROST IS ON THE BUNCHBERRY

by

ABBIE HUSTON EVANS

Cold cannot hurt this country huddled under hemlock;
It ekes out cover of a kind, what with spruce and fir
And threadbare birch and alder. This chill means snow;
But fields are ready for it, they are not caught napping
Though the sun goes wan now, skimmed over like the pools.

Frost is on the boxberry, on the hard-hit bunchberry,
Where Bokhara color darkens half the pasture.

From *The Bright North* by Abbie Huston Evans (The Macmillan Company: New York, 1938). Used by permission of The Macmillan Company.

Everywhere I look I see numbed small ones
Wearing bronze and dull maroon, like men enduring time.
Frost is on the matted grass at the edge of the alder-swamp.
And the young juniper, just taking hold,
Side-tilted, new-alighted, with a claw stuck in,
Shivers on the south slope.—How long till snow? How long?

At night the wind complains long in the narrow box
Of the raging airtight stove in the plain room.
Stars glitter round the chimney. How safe the low black barn is
Under the Dipper's handle, arched over like a wing.

MAKING THE SPRING

by

ROBERT P. TRISTRAM COFFIN

Before the fire, before the bread,
The drinking water comes ahead
Of all the bedrock things which keep
The farmstead well, from sleep to sleep.
Beds should head towards the north,
Bones be saved for next week's broth;
But water from a boiling-spring
Is underneath each living thing.

Here at the roots of the white pine
Beads of trickling water shine.
Take the shovel and begin.
Dig deep. Set half a hogshead in,
Bottomless but sound of stave,
Half the depth of a good grave.

From *One Horse Farm*, copyright, 1949, by Robert P. Tristram Coffin and
used by permission of The Macmillan Company.

Have the rim a hand's-breadth over
The pine spills, put the oaken cover
On with hinges of old leather
Against ambitious frogs and weather.
Put your shovel of gravel down.
When the spring overflows and brown
Water gives place to a crystal,
Have the boy who's sharp as a thistle,
Half wide freckles, the small boy-child
Who is half the woods and wild
As a young deer lie the first
On his belly and slake his thirst
With wide mouth against the shine,
So always your spring will taste of pine.

The cleaning of this essential thing
Will be the act that leads in Spring.
Before the bluets frost the glade
You will come with your long spade
And the quicksilver boys to clear
Your spring of pine spills of last year,
To delve the bottom till the round
Diamond bulges from the ground
And the dancing rainbow shows,
To let the small boy wet his nose
In the first drink that will wake
White violets and the enamelled snake.

20. Mirrors Held Up to Maine

MAINE SUNSHINE

by

KATHARINE BUTLER HATHAWAY

THERE were two things I noticed and marveled at in my new world. One of these was the sun and the other was the air. I had never seen a world so gilded and so richly bathed and blessed by such a benign sun as that world was by that sun. The sun seemed to pour down a lavish, golden, invulnerable contentment on everything, on people, houses, animals, fields—and a sweetness like the sweetness of passion. The sun had so much room to shine in there. It had the whole sky to shine in, and it had miles and miles of hills and woods, it had islands and rocks and boats to glisten on and soak into like oil. And it was thanks to the matchless air of that peninsula that such a flood of sunshine never became a burden. It always seemed exactly right, golden and voluptuous yet without weight. It was as if the air there were so buoyant that it always lifted up part of the weight of the sun's heat and kept it from ever falling too heavily on our shoulders. It was indescribable air. It made every day seem like a gala day. We never woke up to an ordinary humdrum morning.

I noticed these two things, the air and the sun, at my own house more than I had ever noticed them at the other end of the town. I imagined that the reason for this was that my house responded to sun and air more than most houses do. Sometimes it felt like a boat at anchor. There is that curious quality about all the little noises on a boat which makes them sound unmistakably boaty. The tapping of a rope against canvas, the squeak of a pulley, a voice or a footstep heard on a boat are different from the same sounds heard on land. They are magnified and yet softened by the sea air. All such little noises around my house struck me as having that same soft boaty sound. A clothespin dropped on the doorstep had it, and the rustle of a curtain in an open window sounded like a sail fluttering. When the window sill burned my fingers on a hot morning it was just as if I had touched the gunwale of a dory that had been lying in the sun for hours.

They were so compelling, the divine air and the brilliant sun on my doorstep and all around me as far as I could see, that I stopped thinking. They made thinking seem ridiculous. The thing that would have been the most natural thing to do was to change into a plant or a fruit tree, and I almost felt myself changing. There was no other way to express my thanks for all this, except to burst into leaves and flowers.

PURSUIT AT SEA

by

ELISABETH OGILVIE

The lobstermen on the Island suspect one family of pulling other people's traps, and arrange to have one of the sons followed and watched.

It sometimes happens that in mid-winter the wind lulls, the sun shines brilliantly for a week and goes down each night in a mad

From *High Tide at Noon* by Elisabeth Ogilvie (Thomas Y. Crowell Company: New York, 1944).

glory of fire; all day long the water is the color of sapphire and ultramarine, dark jade in the shallows, purple close to the rockweed-covered ledges. The gulls wheel in great circles over the spruce-crested islands that dream in the bay. In storm the islands are fringed with flying white spray, but in these periods of calm, they seem to float on the surface of the sea.

It's easy to find the buoys then, and from Grand Manan to Casco Bay the lobster boats are out, dories and peapods, scrubby little powerboats and big graceful ones like the "White Lady."

One of these rare weeks began the day after the visit to the Birds. For two days of this heaven-sent weather, George Bird and his sons didn't leave the harbor until most of the other boats had gone. On the third day, just as the Island was beginning to say, "By God, they knew we meant business—" on the third day Simon Bird went out before daylight and didn't come back until midafternoon.

The Island seethed. George and Ash were too scared to do anything but obey, but Simon was a different breed o' cats, for all he was a Bird. Somebody would have to tail him, the Island decided. On the beach, in the fish houses, in the store, over the pool table, the men talked it over. There were volunteers—Owen was one of them, but Nils was chosen. The Sorensens lived the nearest to the Birds, and Nils' room looked across the field and the lane so that he could see lights in the Bird kitchen when they were up early in the winter darkness.

When Nils came up to Stephen Bennett's house to tell them about his new job, he was quietly pleased. "Kind of like the idea of pestering Simon," he admitted. His eyes said nothing at all as they met Joanna's, but she felt the strong link of comradeship between them that had existed all through their growing-up. Nils hadn't forgotten, any more than she had; he would gain revenge for them both.

Now Nils was up every morning long before daylight, fixing his own breakfast and eating it by lamplight while the rest of the house slept above him; then he dressed in his heavy outdoor clothing and went out into the sharp cold hush before dawn, when the air stung his throat, and the stars burned with a white brilliance over the Island. Brigport was a long, crouched shape across the sound, like a sleeping animal. There was hardly a sound anywhere, except his own feet on the ground that creaked with frost. The wind died down sometimes in this last hour before daybreak, and the water on the rocks was like breathing. He walked down to the shore in this silence, keeping close to the fish houses and not walking on the beach stones.

When Jud Gray left the Island, he had sold his boat shop back to Stephen Bennett, who'd owned it first, and Marcus Yetton now had his shop at the farther end, which rose flush with the outermost end of the old wharf. This was where Nils went, threading his way among the hogsheads and traps like a shadow among shadows, his rubber boots uncannily noiseless; he never stumbled, or rolled a stone under his foot, or bumped against a hogshead. He waited, in the dark doorway of Marcus' place. The cold struck through his clothes; the water gurgled and bumped under the wharf, and the sky was pale over the Eastern End woods.

He never had to wait long before there was a faint rattle of beach stones, a bump against wood, a punt being slipped lightly down to the sea's edge; then the clink of oars in the oarlocks, and the whisper of water about the blades. The punt would glide past the end of the wharf, and Nils would wait a little longer until he heard, clear in the silence, the shipping of oars, the heavy clink of the mooring chain. Then the throttled murmur of Simon's engine, thrown back by the rocks as it passed them.

Nils could tell by the sound whether the boat turned to the east'ard or the west'ard when it left the harbor. Then, moving fast, he clambered down over the spilings to the beach and untied his own punt.

By now the winter dawn threw a paling light across the Island; the spruces were very black against the eastern sky, the world was drained of all color. On the water the wind was sharp.

There was a stiff chop in the rip tide at the harbor mouth. Nils' boat rode it steadily, responsive to his hand on the wheel. And when daylight was a reality, and not just a promise, he saw Simon ahead of him, bow pointed out to sea. If Simon looked back, he could see Nils.

Nils stayed behind him all day. Sunrise touched the sea with gold as far as he could look, and sometimes he had to narrow his eyes against the glare in order to see the tiny, dancing black speck that was Simon's boat. Simon roared to the east'ard, spray flying in a rainbow glitter from his bow, and Nils roared behind him. When Simon at last reached his string and began to haul, Nils cut off his engine and sat on the engine box, smoking, sheltered from the wind by the sprayhood, drinking hot coffee from his thermos jug. As the sun climbed toward the zenith, and struck up sparks of silver fire from the whole tossing, blue-green expanse, it was easier to watch Simon work along his string. The boat was at some distance, and Simon was only a minute dark figure moving back and forth in the cockpit, gaffing buoys with a venomous thrust, slamming the lobsters into the box, and throwing the traps overboard again as if it were Nils himself he had there, bound hand and foot and weighted down with a weir stone.

Perhaps there would be no sunshine, but snow on the wind, and foreboding black clouds driving across the sky, and a steadily roughening sea to wash over the decks, so that the boats would be iced before they reached home. But it was never too rough for Simon to go out, or for Nils to follow him. It became a strange, silent duel, with no signs of exhaustion on either side.

Simon didn't have reason to stay out all day when Nils trailed him so closely. Sometimes, to Nils' amusement, he invented side trips—apparently hoping to make Nils run out of gas. But Nils had prepared for this. He kept his tank filled, and two extra cans of gas in the cuddy. He was ready and willing to stay out all day—round and round the Rock, the boats wallowing in the wash from the steep shores of the ledge. The keepers and their families came out with glasses, to see what sort of hare-and-hound chase was taking place around their barren stronghold. Nils took off his cap and waved it at them, yelling greetings through the bitter-cold, sparkling air.

Nils' happy attitude, as if he were on a pleasure sail in the middle of summer, was usually too much for Simon. He would start for the Island. His boat was narrower in the beam than Nils', and when he reached Sou-west Point, where the red rock cliffs gleamed in the winter sunshine, half hidden in boiling surf, he skirted close to the ledges or between them, his engine wide open. He was tacitly daring Nils to follow him, but Nils was no fool. Eventually he must start for the harbor along the west side, and then Nils was with him again.

Simon wouldn't go to the car with his lobsters these days, not with Nils coming up alongside to shout cheerfully, "How they crawlin', Cap'n Simon?" No, Simon went straight to his mooring and gaffed up the buoy with a vicious thrust, and had reached the shore and disappeared before Nils rowed to the beach. Later, Simon would sell his lobsters.

The Island was laughing. They hadn't enjoyed anything so much for years.

"Simon knows they're laughing," Stephen told Nils one night. "Watch out for him. He won't take this forever."

THE CATCH OF THE HALIBUT

by

RUTH MOORE

The engine, barely ticking over, drove the boat ahead slowly. The ground-line of the trawl with its hundreds of baited hooks paid out steadily from the tub and disappeared astern. Hod guided it with deft rhythmic taps from a smooth tapered stick, lifting the loaded hooks over the gunnel and tossing them a little, so that they floated free and untangled away from the ground-line. For a moment they seemed to lie motionless on the water; then they sank slowly, the bait gleaming at first and growing dull as it went deeper into the water.

If you just looked at the top of the water, Donny thought, you wouldn't realize how deep it was. But that line, with the bait going deeper and deeper into the green, showed you how it really was.

The big swells, smooth as cream, lifted the boat without a ripple, passing under her soundlessly and letting her drop into their troughs with a smooth, sleepy, gliding motion. Donny thought for a while as the sun rose and made a strain against his eyes, and began to cook a rich fishy smell out of the bait, that he might be going to be seasick. But the feeling didn't get worse and after a while he forgot it.

They set nine tubs of trawl and then let the boat drift while they waited for the low-water-slack and had a mid-morning lunch. Then it was time to go back and haul the first trawl.

As they slid alongside the buoy and Hog gaffed it in, Donny felt a mounting excitement. Hod and Willie were excited, too, he could tell. The next few minutes would tell the tale.

If there were any fish on The Ridges today, the boat might go home with kidboards loaded down. Or the hooks might come up full of trash—sea-cucumbers and whore's eggs—or fouled up with something almost as worthless, like dogfish or skates.

"By gorry," Willie said suddenly, "I wouldn't swap my job, right now, for any other job you could name."

"I would." Hod grunted. He was hauling the trawl with wide sweeps of his big arms, his shoulders straining at the weight. "Go ahead and talk," he went on, grinning at Willie over his shoulder, "with me doing the work. You can haul the next one. Then you'll swap."

"Nup," Willie said. "Right now I feel like a harvester, a treasure-hunter *and* a gambler. Ain't I a cussed fool, though?" He leaned against the side of the coop, where he could watch the line coming aboard, and winked at Donny. "He feels the same way, only he wouldn't let on—not if he was t'ketch the solid-gold Old Man a the Sea, with eyes a diamonds."

"Right," Hod said. "Gambler, did you say, Willie? Have a look."

The first hooks were coming in, carrying nothing but some shreds of sea-flea chewed bait.

"H'm," said Willie, and said no more.

Looking down into the water, straining out over the side until Willie, afraid he would fall overboard, reached out and clutched the baggy seat of his oil-pants, Donny could see other bare hooks coming up in slow procession.

The entire trawl was empty, except for one lone skate, which Hod slatted off the hook so hard that its teeth, jawbone and all, came out and floated away, looking like somebody's set of uppers incongruously lost and bobbing around in the ocean.

"Too bad the' ain't no other way t'git one a them cussed things off a hook," Willie said thoughtfully.

"What would you do—ask him to spit it out?" Hod wasn't mad, only disappointed. He stowed the trawl under the stern by simply giving the tub a shove along the slippery platform with his foot. Actually, there wasn't any other way to get a skate off a trawl-hook.

The next trawl, which Willie hauled, was more of the same— empty hooks and sea-fleas—and the third one started out to be no different. Then, halfway up, the heavy ground-line took a sudden lunge into the sea. Hod tried to hold it, giving line slowly, and Willie, suddenly watchful, said in a low, excited voice, "Let him run, boy!"

He grabbed a bait-knife out of its leather sheath on the wash-board, and began as fast as he could to cut the hooks off the trawl. Donny thought he had never seen hands move so quickly.

But even with Hod paying out as little as he could, the line began to burn through his hands so fast that Willie couldn't catch the hooks. For a moment there was a flurry of flying line and gangions,* broad shoulders and backs and slipping rubber boots, and Donny, huddled into a corner of the coop to be out of the way, couldn't see what was going on. Then Willie stepped back. The neat coil of trawl that had been in the tub was nearly all paid out again. Hod had an ample length of it in his hand, but it seemed to be slack in the water.

"He gone?" asked Willie tensely. "He didn't hook you, did he?"

Hod shook his head. "I'm almost scared to start hauling," he said. "I can't tell if he's there or not." He began to take in steadily on the line, and as it came aboard Willie methodically cut off its hooks. The line stayed slack for what seemed to be a long time. Then suddenly it straightened out and cut through the water with a *z-zing*.

"No, by God, he ain't gone!" Hod shouted. He braced back and held the line, this time not having to bother about the hooks. Slowly he horsed it in, now gaining, now losing line, but in the end gaining more than he lost.

"Want a spell?" Willie asked, after a time.

Hod started to say something, but at that moment the line decided it was going back to the bottom of the sea, and back to bottom it went, grinding toughly between his clenched fists.

"Gorry!" Willie said. "No wonder the' warn't no ground fish on The Ridges today, with that feller around. What'd you think 't is, Hod?"

"Haul's like a halibut," Hod said, panting. "If it's a shark, it's a jeasly big one." He took a breather, holding the line taut, and then began to haul again. This time it came up more easily, yielding itself in a series of hard jerks and rushes.

"He's drownin' out some," Willie said. He picked up a stout-

---

* Gangions: the short, baited lines hanging from the main trawl line. H. B.

handled gaff and moved over to the gunnel beside Hod, peering anxiously down into the water. For a moment he stood watching. Then his whole body tensed up with excitement.

"By God, I can see him! It's a halibut bigger'n the top a Hazlett's Rock!" He went on talking, as if to himself, in a voice that was half whisper and half croon. Poising the gaff at the surface of the water, Willie said, "Easy, boy. E-e-easy, there. Let him run a little, haul up his head. Oh, you sonova, you great big beautiful sonova— Look out!"

Donny, unable to stand inaction any longer, slipped out of his corner and climbed to the roof of the coop. From there, lying on his stomach, he could look past Hod's shoulders and into the water. Deep down, swirling in the green-black light, he could see something that looked as big as the bottom of the ocean, now dark, now white, as it turned back and belly upward to the pull of the line.

"Dong him in," Willie crooned. "Git him up here just once where I can whang this gaft into his gills. Easy, there. E-e-easy. Dong him in!"

The flat monstrosity, feeling doom with the surface of the water, started down, and Hod lost twenty feet of line. He was breathing hard and the sweat was running down his face. He got the lost line back, felt it give a little. With a tremendous lash of bubbles and foam, the head of the halibut broke water.

"Put the gaft to him," croaked Hod, and Willie put the gaft to him, sinking it deep into the vulnerable soft gills. Together they heaved upward. The great gasping head appeared at the gunnel.

Creatures of different worlds, the three looked wildly into one another's eyes; then Hod freed a hand from the line, picked up a short heavy hardwood club that lay on the gunnel, hauled off and let the halibut have it, twice, in the middle of his thick triangular head. The big fish stiffened and momentarily ceased his lashing. In that interval, the men hauled the rest of him in over the side. Hod struck him again as the fins began to quiver and the tail, as large as a small table-top, started to drum on the boards of the platform.

"Jeepers!" Donny said, staring with awe at the dead fish. "Look at his head. It wouldn't go into a bucket!"

"Go nigh a couple of hundred pounds, I guess." Hod sat down, exhausted, and pulled the cotton gloves off his blistered and bloody hands. "I guess you and Don'll have to haul the next few tubs, Willie. I'm pooped."

"How'll you swap now, Hod?" Willie said slyly, "say with some fat man's got a nice shiny office desk t' set to?"

Hod grinned. "Haul your trawls, you old bait-bucket," he said affectionately. "Or it'll be midnight before we get home."

GRAVEYARD IN THE WOODS

by

ELINOR GRAHAM

As one thought catches another, before the mind can stop to organize a pattern, I think of the graveyard where Captain Merryman lies buried. It is lost in a new-grown forest of oak and pine. When he was buried there was no forest there. That patch of earth, once hallowed to receive the dead, is lost now in a growth of tall young trees. It takes a living man to keep the forest back.

This graveyard in the woods, of which I speak, where many forbears of our neighbors and our friends lie buried, is lost to living memory, and foxes make their dens inside the graves. I've seen the fox-holes, and I've seen a fox streaking down the field that leads to the graveyard. I was stealing lemon lilies when

From *Maine Charm String* by Elinor Graham. Used by permission of The Macmillan Company: New York, 1946.

I saw the fox. The lilies grow around a house long since burned down. All that remains is an apple tree, a large honeysuckle bush, some double narcissus and a field of lemon lilies.

Perhaps I should feel guilty about the lemon lilies, but I don't. At the time I boldly took my wheelbarrow and pushed it down Flying Point Road. Bold as brass, I was, with the shovel in the barrow for anyone to see. To my mind these houses on the Point belong to one another. It is appropriate that one should help another to a greater beauty.

The foundation stones around which the lemon lilies now run wild, was once part of a Rogers home. I thought it would be all right to take a clump or two from a Rogers house to grace the dooryard of a Merryman. The Rogerses and the Merrymans were friends. In the Revolutionary War period, when most men who could sign their names at all signed, "John Goodman, Yeoman," the forbears of the Rogerses and the Merrymans signed "Gentleman." That must have been a bond in far-off days.

I had dug up several clumps when I saw the red fox looking at me. He stood motionless, with his great bushy tail lifted. It is the only time I have ever looked a real live fox in the eye. Foxes look very human. I stood up suddenly, and he turned and dashed down the field toward the woods. I left my lilies and my shovel and followed. When I got into the gloom of the dense growth of oak trees, I almost turned back, for the underbrush was very thick. To the left of me was an opening where a granite ledge had forbidden trees to grow. There on the top of the ledge I thought I saw the fox again. It may have been my imagination. Just a blur of russet caught my eye. I turned and made my way to the clearing; and there it was, the graveyard in the woods.

The gravestones are all dark gray slabs about three inches thick. Most of the inscriptions are obliterated. I walked to where I could see a stone more deeply engraved than the rest. It had a dove of peace chiseled at the top. The dove was in flight and held the olive branch in its bill. Under it were the words,

"Capt. Stephen Merryman, 1758-1828," and a verse too badly eroded to be read; but I was glad to see my captain had lived his full threescore years and ten.

As I was looking at his grave, I became aware of the fox holes. There must have been five or six large dens. As I looked closer I was shocked and horrified to see that in one or two cases bones lay at the entrance to the dens. Chills ran through me, and then reason asserted itself. I realized they couldn't be the bones of the departed inasmuch as this was a graveyard in which no one had been buried in a hundred years.

We have another graveyard of more recent date. It is well tended. The neighbors organize a bee each summer; plant flowers, fill the urns, and lovingly care for the graves. There are rambler roses on the fences; and in the fall sugar maple trees light torches you can see for miles. So sumptuous is it that it starts my heart to beating like a riveting machine when I see its October glory. I'm no graveyard prowler, nor do I like the thought of my own body in the ground; but in a sentimental moment, I have said I should like to rest in our graveyard on Flying Point when the time comes when I must give up my hold on life. But the forgotten graveyard in the woods, that has been pre-empted by wild living things, is more of a challenge to the imagination. Now that I know more about it, I am glad that something as wild as a fox, and as wise, has dug with sharp claws into the earth that once was turned for Captain Stephen Merry-man.

THE MAINE GUIDE

by

LOUISE DICKINSON RICH

Here's the Maine guide. He wears what amounts to a uniform. It consists of a wool shirt, preferably plaid, nicely faded to soft, warm tones; dark pants, either plus-fours, for some unknown reason, or riding breeches; wool socks and the soleless, Indian-type moccasin, or high laced boots. He carries a bandana in his hip pocket and may or may not wear another knotted around his neck. But he must wear a battered felt hat, with a collection of salmon flies stuck in the band, and he must wear it with an air; and he must wear a hunting knife day and night; and he must look tough and efficient. If he has high cheek bones and tans easily, that is his good luck. He can then admit to part-Indian ancestry, accurately or not. Indian blood is an item highly esteemed by sports. Naturally he could do his work as well in mail-order slacks, or in a tuxedo, for that matter; but the sports wouldn't think so. Sports are funny.

"That fellow there," the sport is supposed to say, showing his vacation movies in his Westchester rumpus room, "was my quarter-breed guide. He's quite a character. Never had any education beyond the seventh grade, but I don't know anyone I'd rather spend a week alone with. That's the real test. He's a genuine natural philosopher. For instance, we were talking about the War, and he said—and I never thought of it this way before—." What the guide said he probably lifted from Shirer's book, but translated into Down East, it wouldn't be recognizable.

A few livid scars are a great asset to a guide. It doesn't matter

From *We Took to the Woods*, copyright, 1942, by Louise Dickinson Rich, published by J. B. Lippincott Company.

how he got them. Maybe as a barefoot boy he stepped on a rake. The holes make swell bear-trap scars, acquired one night up in the Allagash, when the thermometer was at thirty below and the nearest settlement was fifty miles away. Maybe he cut his hand peeling potatoes. It sounds much better to say a beaver bit him. Maybe he fell downstairs and gashed his forehead. When asked—and he'll be asked all right—he can tell all about his big fight with the lynx. They all make good stories to tell around the evening campfires.

Oh, those evening camp-fires! That's when the good guide gets in his dirty work. That's when he sows the seed for a re-engagement next year.

This is the set-up:—Supper—fresh-caught trout with bacon curls, potatoes baked in the coals and slathered with butter, a kind of biscuit cooked in a frying pan and resembling Yorkshire pudding, canned peas and fruit—is over. The sports, pleasantly stuffed and mildly weary from having "helped" paddle for ten or twelve miles, stretch out around the fire. Down on the shingle that natural philosopher, that real character, Bobcat Bill, washes the dishes. The water glows like bloodstained ebony in the leaping light, and the firs stand up behind, black and motionless. Back in the bush a fox barks and a deer crashes away from the scent of wood-smoke. All around lies the wilderness, dark and unknown and sinister. Inside the little pool of light is all that is left of the safe and familiar—the canoes drawn up on the shore, the piled packsacks and blanket rolls, the forms and faces of friends. A loon sends its lost-soul lament over the darkling water, and a shiver runs around the fire. Then Bobcat Bill strolls up from the lake, throws an armful of dry-ki* onto the blaze, and begins tossing blankets toward the group. In the flash of a buck's tail the old magic begins to work. The tight little fire-heated circle of fellowship is formed. We're all brothers here, united by our common cause against the power of the

* freshwater driftwood of dead trees and branches. H. B.

black beyond. We're all valiant, noble renegades from civilization's chafing bonds. We're dangerous and free!

The loon throws its blood-curdling cry against the mountains once more, and laughs its crazy laughter.

"Never hear one of them critters a-hollerin'," Bobcat Bill drifts easily into his act, "but what it 'minds me of one time I was lost up on them big caribou barrens across the lake. That's how I come by this here scar on my shoulder. Reason I was up in there, a feller had met foul play—"

I'm making guides sound like a bunch of frauds, and I don't mean to. They work hard and they're in a difficult position. Like all merchandisers, they're obliged to give the customer what he wants, and it's their tough luck that the customer wants adventure.

WOODSMAN'S HOMECOMING

by

HENRY MILNER RIDEOUT

A fortnight later day was breaking in the woods heavily, slowly, coming with effort through a chill smother of damp. It made itself felt more as darkness withdrawn than as light increased; morning seemed to have lost the way; and except for the sleepy chirping of a bird or two and a drip hardly begun among unseen branches, nothing promised that the world should ever wake again. A smell of last year's moldering leaves weighed down the wet obscurity. Not by sight but by slope underfoot and a guess that a whitebirch phantom was leaning where it ought to lean, Salem knew his ground. He was descending the northern side of Rum-Time Hill.

From *The Winter Bell* by Henry Milner Rideout (Duffield and Company: New York, 1922).

Halfway down, a sudden return of night overspread and told him that here stood the old hemlock. Salem halted and dropped on the grass his burden, a canvas bag holding load enough for a horse.

He parted the bushes on his right, walked straight in through black undergrowth for half a dozen paces, then stopped and took from his pocket a candle end, which he lighted.

"Still here."

At his feet shone a dark pool no wider or deeper than a bucket, reflecting the pointed flame and his finger tips, until a baby frog hopped in and went kicking down.

"All choked with leaves," thought Salem. "Used to be big as a barrel."

He placed the candle in a socket of moss and himself on a rock. Beside him on a withered sapling butt hung a ragged film of iron rust. This, when Salem put it there last, had been a tin cup.

"Nobody come since, prob'ly."

The pool, a spring known to Indians dead and gone, had given the hill its name when river drivers halted there to mix grog of Santa Cruz rum or Medford. Salem found it a pleasant thought, for the moment, that he could go in the dark to places which, now the old-time people were no more, other men could not find by daylight.

"Nobody here since."

He made a birch-bark dipper and drank. The water was cold, clear, living as ever. He sighed, in part with satisfaction, in part with regret.

The spring grew quiet. The frog reappeared later and clung to its margin, like a tiny scrap of puckered leather watching him with eyes. The candle burned steady and wore a faint halo in the mist. By its light Salem's face was that of a man who feared nothing behind him any more.

"Maybe I'll see her once or twice a year, when I go down."

For two weeks he had worked hard, earning money toward the supplies, the horseload in the bag. He had lacked time, ran his excuse—lacked courage, he knew in his heart—to return to her door until the day before yesterday, when no one answered his knock. He had not seen her after that night.

"Bawled like a baby," he thought.

But no, he was not ashamed. Doubt, ignorance or doubt, had kept him away. What could a man tell her, what could he have stammered to one who twice in his life had preserved his soul, reason, what you call it, from destruction?

"Round Christmas time, say, I'll try again."

He smiled, knowing well that he could not go without her so long.

"A lon'ly way of coming home, this is."

He had missed his other friends. A call at the captain's had brought forth only Mr. Cook, short-spoken, fidgety, and secretive: Captain Constantine was "got up and traipsed off a-fishin' somewheres, when he ought to known better." Kingcome, too, was gone from mill and boardinghouse without word left. Salem's good-byes had failed on every hand. He sat here very much alone in the night mist, by a forgotten well among rocks and trees.

"No good," he said aloud.

There was no pleasure, after all, in the things he knew best, in a gift like this of homing straight to places the most beloved. A choked spring; he would come with a spade one day and clear it: but a choked spring and a wafer of iron rust eaten through with holes, warned him what to expect. His cabin by the lake would be a dreary sight. He smelled the mustiness from here, felt in advance the peculiar melancholy that hovers in a dwelling re-taken by weeds and forest growth.

He rose. His fellow thinker, the infant frog, at once deserted him and went down quite cheerful, swimming with hind legs only. Salem blew the candle out and waded through leaves to his bag. It seemed heavier than before, the mist darker. At the foot of the hill he went stumbling, now in moss-grown corduroy road, now in stale water or cold, drenching grass that lined the hollows of thank-you-marms.

He made good speed, however, for Lambkill Heath, seen from another hilltop, stretched gray without form under a border of black woods, these in turn under starlight filling a sky the darkness of which had as yet no more than a greenish tinge. The lower stars quivered and shook, all but the morning star, hung aloft like a tiny though intenser moon.

"Getting nigh home."

Salem crossed the heath in a brightening vapor. When fir woods again solemnly inclosed him he could see the grass of the winter sled road which he followed.

"Here 'tis."

He had reached the lake near his own cove before sunrise. Dropping the bag, he sat down. Blackened granite rocks, their bases faintly striped with paler bleaching, huddled among reeds at a margin of brown water. Beyond lay nothing but mist, as far as the hills now edged with radiance where the great star dissolved. It was a cold scene to look upon, the air biting.

"A poor time to visit your house in ruin. For old time's sake, better start the day with a swim. Rouse your blood, too."

Salem stripped, and climbed down to a flat rock from which he had often plunged. That icy-looking smoke made a man blench, but he gathered himself, set his teeth, and dove.

He came up laughing, for the water was warm as new milk.

"I'd forgotten."

The smell of it, too, overcame him with remembrance, a frail sweetness blended of many hints—like green leaves crushed, or live trout, or willow bark just peeled—yet unlike them and without name, an exhalation from all forest roots and inland waters. He swam lazily, then floated on his back, watching the smoke curl upward, melt, and drift with patches of blue sky. A loon far away began to laugh.

From near by came a rippling sound as of some animal that

swam quietly; a deer, perhaps, crossing the lake before sunrise. Treading water, Salem looked about; but he could see nothing, and lay back to float. The smell of water lilies, fresh and clean as rain, drew by on the surface.

Afterward, rolling over with a splash, Salem buried his face, then raised it, to swim out. For a moment, while his eyes were dripping, he thought he saw in the mist a shadow likeness of Mary Prior's face pass in profile toward shore. It faded slowly as a cloud picture. Although Salem's eyes did not often play false, the illusion failed to startle him, for she had been in his head all the while. He buried his face again, went racing toward the farther shore, across deep water, turned at the edge of lily pads, and came racing back.

The sun warmed the grass and dried him, when at last he sat on shore by his bag. Dressing, he thought there came voices behind him, but listened and heard no more. A crow cawed somewhere among bright fluttering tops of poplar.

"Cook breakfast here and make tea?" Salem debated the question. "Or go up now and see the worst?"

It was better, he concluded, to have this forlorn part over with, and do his home coming while still in a glow. Salem jumped up and mounted the bank.

His house looked out at him from the deepest bend of the fir wall. It was not a ruin or overgrown, but stood there low and brown as ever, the door open, the chimney smoking. A yellow tent rose behind it.

"Someone's moved in. Some rascal's taken her over."

Salem drew near slowly. This might prove worse than what he had imagined. A hungry scent of bacon and coffee came out to greet him. And then, white, glossy, half awake, out came Sagamore—the Second, but like the First alive again—to yawn and stretch on his doorstep. The dog's collar shone in the sun.

"We thought you'd like to find your house ready," said a voice that he knew. "So we came and pitched our tent."

Mary Prior had followed her dog to the threshold. She stood

there smiling down at the wanderer. Indoors beyond her Salem caught a glimpse of Trapper's mother, Mrs. Kingcome, the little mother of a giant, who turned long enough from her cooking to throw him a brighteyed welcome and a wave of her fork.

"The men," said Mary, "are camping above, in the next cove. There they come now."

A birch canoe gilded with sunlight stole in through the reeds, two weighty figures ballasting her. Trapper flourished his paddle. Captain John Constantine held in air a pickerel that seemed longer than his arm, and bellowed so that the woods rang:

"How's that for breakfast?"

Salem called back an inarticulate hail, and turned.

"You don't object?" said the girl.

His face shone.

"Object? I—I want to break something!" he cried. "You folks—" He could not finish. "Why, then, we were! We were swimming in the lake together before sunrise!"

She was not so pale as he remembered her.

"Are you sorry," she asked, "not to have it all to yourself alone?"

THE HEADLESS MAN OF DAMARISCOVE ISLAND

by

HAROLD W. CASTNER

About the year 1895 or 1896, the U. S. Government recognized the need of a Life Saving Station on Damariscove Island. Federal funds were available and the work was begun. A man named Wilson, of Harpswell, contracted to build the foundations and had a crew of Italian workmen transported to the island. The

From *The Lincoln County News* (Damariscotta, Maine, 1947).

work was progressing when all of a sudden the workers became panic stricken and left in a hurry.

The details of this singular desertion of the island are recalled to this day by living witnesses. Other happenings there are touched with the same atmosphere of mystery, and it is not to be wondered at that many believe that there is some foundation for the strange tales told of Damariscove.

The island is rich in historical significance and can be classed with Monhegan in the earliest records of this area. These first records give the name in two parts as Damarill's Cove. As early as 1614 Captain John Smith recorded the island and mentioned it in his account as Damarill's Islands. This came about from the fact that at high tide the island is divided and in early times the northern part was called Wood Island. The historian Williamson mentions these islands as the Damariscove Islands. The origin of the name is quite probably due to the fact that the ownership of the group was claimed by a sailor, one Humphrey Damerill, who died in Boston in 1650. Some historians have conjectured that this same Humphrey Damerill might have been a member of the Popham Colony who made his way back to the coast of Maine after the return of the colony to England in 1608.

When Colonel David Dunbar induced so many Scotch emigrants to settle these parts in the second quarter of the eighteenth century, one Daniel Knight of Newburyport, or Salem, Massachusetts, was an interested listener. He was a man of education and wealth, and became interested in purchasing land in this vicinity. He was normally the wealthiest man in the area of what is now Boothbay. His first purchase was all of Damariscove Island, where he came and settled with his family of eight children. The youngest son was named Patishall Knight. He gave the boy this name in honor of Captain Richard Patishall, who had been a previous owner of the island after the death of Damerill. Captain Patishall was at Pemaquid on August 2, 1689, with his ship, when the Indians made a surprise attack. After subduing the fort they captured the Captain, appropriated his ship to their own designs and took him away captive. A story whose origins are lost in the past has reached our times that the Captain, becoming troublesome to his Indian captors, was killed by them, they then cutting off his head as a trophy. This was not an unusual act among the coastal Indians who in this way honored a particularly brave enemy. His body was then thrown into the sea, and it is said that his dog leaped after it and was seen no more.   One version of the story maintains that the headless body of the Captain and the body of the dog were washed ashore on the Captain's own island of Damariscove.   The curtain of history is drawn on any further mention of Captain Richard Patishall save for the note that Daniel Knight named his son after this victim of the wars. Patishall Knight was the great, great grandfather of the author, and father of Margaret Knight who married Deacon Nathaniel Chapman of Nobleboro.

When the Revolutionary War broke out, Daniel Knight moved his family to Pleasant Cove. Most of his family joined the patriots in open rebellion. This included Patishall and Daniel, Jr., who served throughout the war. During the war the island was practically deserted except for fishermen and some sheep who were herded there. It is an historical fact that after the English captain, H. Mowatt, had completely destroyed Falmouth, (Portland), on that bleak rainy October day in 1775, his next port of call was Damariscove Island where he commandeerd some sheep. Another story persists through the dim and incomplete records that an unruly prisoner on board was taken to the island and beheaded. Whatever other tragic legends and traditions have grown up about the island appear to have their origin in the beliefs of those who had some knowledge of the early events of the island's history.

When the Italian workmen arrived at Damariscove, they found that once the day's work was done, there was plenty of leisure time to while away. Part of this they spent listening to stories about the island. It was a belief of those living there that Captain

Patishall and his dog had for over two hundred years kept constant vigil over the isle, and the Italians, it would seem, were impressed by the sincerity of those who told them the story.

One balmy evening one of the Italians was strolling on the far reaches of the shore when he came upon a large log which had drifted in from the sea. He found it a convenient and comfortable place to rest, and sat down. He later came rushing into the camp terrified and excited. Perspiration was dripping from his forehead, and he recounted a horrible experience to all the Italians. He related that he had hardly seated himself on the log when he was approached by a headless man who informed him that he could not stay there. He was nearly exhausted from fright but described this horrible experience and the dress of the man with no head. This was immediately believed by all hands and without a moment's delay they all planned their escape from this terrible place, and no amount of argument would affect their decision. In the morning they had all departed and work was suspended for some time. It is an historical fact that this group of Italian workmen departed the island in great haste and as a result of this story of one of their number. There have been persistent reports of this headless man from other sources but the present author can find no documentary proof to substantiate them. Probably the most authentic report of actually seeing this headless man was the experience of Captain Chase. He was a man of education and not in the least superstitious. He was known as a "High Top" which means a man who has the reputation for repeatedly large catches of fish. He visited Damariscove often and solemnly declared that on one trip he saw the headless figure on the beach. Whether he did or did not may be disputed but the fact that he would not visit the island again is definite proof that he thought he did. This event gave great impetus to the belief as no one was held in higher regard than Captain Chase.

One man now living was a resident of the island for four years. He gave the author a vivid account of an experience which may interest the reader. He said he was then a young man of twenty-one, not superstitious and not afraid of ghosts. He had a bulldog, and this dog was the only one on the island. He tells of hearing on several occasions a repeated barking from the far end of the island, a barking so distinct and dog-like that he went several times in search of this possible other animal. But he was never able to find anything, and it must be added that he was always careful to check on the whereabouts of his own dog before going on the search. Many others have reported this same mysterious sound but no one has yet seen the ghost-dog of the island.

What the fate of brave Captain Patishall may have been, and whether or not his headless body washed ashore on his own island of Damariscove are matters which will forever remain unknown, but the traditions of the island still touch the imagination of the coast. The story of the headless figure in its antique dress followed by its phantom dog has come down to our own days, and interested visitors may still hear from living men the tale of the ghostly barking heard by night across the desolate and treeless rocks of the island, itself lost in the greater darkness of the seas.

NO MORE SEA

by

JESSIE WHEELER FREEMAN

Her name is Sabrina but folks called her Briny
And Briny was right for she took to the sea;
Man-shirted, scant-skirted, she'd handle a tiller
As neatly as most girls the spoon in their tea.

When she married Rufe Candage she laughed that 'twas only
Because he was captain and so she could go

From *Town Down East* by Jessie Wheeler Freeman (The Stephen Daye Press: New York, 1949).

On voyages with him. She'd brave out a tempest,
"O come now, I like it, this bit of a blow!"

But one voyage she missed, though she stormed and she pleaded:
Rufe wanted his son born proper on land;
So he left her when dawn was bright on the harbor—
She will never forget that last wave of his hand.

Sabrina is buying a house on the Mount Road:
This is the place for young Rufe and me;
No lonesomer here than wherever I'm living—
And it's far from the sight, and the sound, of the sea.

21. A "Duplicious" Incident

by

ARTHUR R. MACDOUGALL, JR.

THIS is Bill X's story. It isn't mine. I do not think that it proves anything, except that I was five or ten dollars ahead of my economic incompetency.

Dud and I were at the county seat. Turning the corner of Madison Avenue and Water Street, we met Mrs. X. You will observe that I am omitting the last name. Mrs. X is a large specimen. She is a mountain of protoplasm and a molehill of virtue.

Wasting no more than a glance at Dud, who squandered no more on her, she began a puffing, tearful story. Them nincompoop wardens had gone and put her Bill in jail ag'in. Jist what did they think she and Bill's misfortunate children could live on, while they had their vile revenge? Here it was, near to Chistmus, the birthday of Him who said suffer the little children to come unto Him, and consider the lilies of the field. And not one cent! Not a cent did she have to her name. And Pansy—that was the baby—was the cutest little angel! And Bill Junior, and Don, and Philander, and Frankie, and Narcissus, who was the next youngest girl, and Bob, and Georgie—they were all good children, even if their father warn't religious. And what was she (their mother) to do? Christmas was goin' to be like somebudy's funeral

Reprinted by permission of Coward-McCann, Inc., from *Where Flows the Kennebec* by Arthur R. MacDougall, Jr. Copyright, 1947, by Arthur R. MacDougall, Jr.

at their house instead of a Christian holiday. But there! She could stand all that, if she knew where the next meal was coming from. And she wished that I had been there at the court to hear them game wardens lie about poor, helpless, innersent Bill, who had been the victim of their evil, connivin' plot. She knew that I was not the man to watch justice miscarry. And . . . finally . . . would I lend her ten dollars to keep her dear ones alive a little while longer?

I knew Mrs. X. I knew Bill X. But there were the children, Pansy, Narcissus, and all the rest. Furthermore, they always looked half-clad and partially starved. Also, I did have ten dollars.

Mrs. X saw me weakening. Her hand was half out for the money, which, by the way, I had determined would be five dollars instead of the suggested ten.

"Jist a min-it," interposed Dud. "Did yer say Bill was in jail, Malty?"

"I certainly did. Don't you read the papers?"

"Sometimes I do; then ag'in I have spells when I rely on my neighbors. All I was comin' at was that maybe Mak an' me c'ud go over to the jail, where Bill's boardin' at the taxpayers' expense, an' have a good talk with him. Then if Mak figgered yer needed the money worse'n he does hisself, he c'ud see yer later."

Mrs. X was not pleased with Dud. Dabbling a last week's hanky at her eyes, she said, "I'd be awful glad to have our minister call on poor Bill, and Bill w'ud be, too, but I don't see what that has got to do with the fact that I hain't had no breakfast myself, an' I'm in a delicate condition and all—"

Dud addressed me. "Mak, let's go call on this feller townsman of ours. As fer Malty's breakfast, the town has to look after Bill's family while he's incarcerated."

Dud was right. When we had walked away from Bill's missus, Dud said to me, "I thought if yer had a few min-its to invest on your eddication, it w'ud be a good idea."

The Sheriff led us into the "boardinghouse" where Bill was "doing time."

"Howareyer, Bill?" said Dud. "The last time I seen yer, you was gang-hookin' trout off the spawnin' bed at East Carry Pon."

Bill replied that he was feelin' as well as c'ud be expected under the circumstances, but that he was as unhappy as a houn'-dorg tied to a manure-spreader.

"How did it happen to yer?" asked Dud.

"I am good an' sick of rehashin' it," grunted Bill. "Every time I open my mouth down here, somebody puts his foot in it. I told that cornseated jedge 'zactly how it happened, an' the durn cuss acted as if he figgered I was lying. When I git free, that's a man that don't want to cross my path, becuz if he does I'll kill him with my two hands."

"Bill always was a vicious talker," Dud said to me.

"See here, Dud, I wounded that buck erbout three o'clock in the afternoon. What man, except a lounge lizard in a red shirt, w'ud leave a deer to die a lingerin' death an' be et up by var-ments? Of course it got dark. It always does after the sun goes down. Was I to blame that I had a devil of a time comin' up with that buck? W'ud it have been kind to dumb animals if I had gone home, leavin' the poor innersent critter to bleed away his life a half inch at a time?

"Natcherly I had a flashlight. Nobudy but a tender-toed cityite w'ud git catched out after dark without some sort of a light. Do they expect a man to hedgehorg back in the pitch dark!

" 'Sunrise to sunset,' says that jedge. Don't the poor idgit know that them lawmakers down to Augusty can't regulate daylight an' dark? Now, see here, Dud, don't you always figger to have a light in your pocket when ye're huntin' ten er fifteen miles from home?"

"Aya, I do," agreed Dud, "but I don't ordinarily tote a six-cell light. Two batteries make plenty of light, when the weary hunter homeward plods, as the poet says."

"Huh. Them smart-faced lawyers tried to make a p'int of that; said that a six-celled flashlight looked 'spicious. But I told 'em, and that ornery jedge, too. Says I, 'One of them ten-cent flash-lights hain't no more use to a man in the dark than a firefly crawled under the Lord's bushel basket.' That's the very words I told them!"

"How much did they soak yer?" asked Dud.

Bill's eyes blazed. "They tried to collect a hundred dollars an' the costs of court. 'I won't pay it,' I told them. So here I be."

"Sure as preachin' yer are," said Dud. "Didjer ever hear erbout the time the game wardens tried to catch Elijah Dole?"

"Naw, an' I don't want to hear it."

"The int'restin' part of it was that they didn't catch 'Lijah. He was too smart for them."

"Be yer tryin' to incinderate that I hain't smart?"

"Elijah shot a moose," drawled Dud, ignoring Bill's question. "It was in closed season. The wardens got wind of it, but they c'udn't pin it on 'Lijah. So they schemed with a taxidermist. The feller wrote Elijah, saying that he understood of confidential parties that 'Lijah had a-quired a moose, an' that he, the taxi-dermist, wanted to buy a head an' was prepared to pay well for it.

"Elijah was lumberin' on the lower Enchanted. It happened that he had jist lost a roan hoss. It was out in back of the hovel, froze as stiff as an old maid at the North Pole. Elijah went out an' sawed off the roan's head, boxed it up, an' shipped it to the taxi-dermist—express collect. But . . . of course 'Lijah was a smart one."

It was obvious that Bill did not enjoy the implications. In fact, he scowled at Dud over ten days' growth of fertile whiskers.

"Dud," he said, "yer don't understand my case. 'Lijah Dole has been dead a good many years. Time has changed some things in a way that don't seem possible. When 'Lijah was cuttin' big punkin pine, they didn't put a man in jail fer followin' a bad-hit deer a lettle mite beyont sunset. In fact, thar warn't no fool sunset law in his day. Why, nowadays, they've got jurisdiction to put a man behind the bars fer jist spittin' on a sidewalk. I'm tellin' you that if 'Lijah was alive today, they'd have him down here permanently."

"Accordin' to the paper," drawled Dud, "you did your shootin' nearer to sunrise than sunset."

"Oh, so that's what they printed? Wa-al, let me tell yer, that this town is so full of prefabricators that thar's only room in this jail fer folks that tell the truth. Now see here, is a man supposed to keep lookin' at his watch every two er three min-its? How do they know a man owns a watch? Be they givin' them away with huntin' licenses?"

"The paper allowed that yer didn't have a huntin' license," remarked Dud.

"Why them cussed two-faced prefabricators! That editor had better leave this country before I git free."

"Did yer have a license, Bill?"

"Huh? Wa-al, I sorta spoke fer one; told the town clerk I'd be after one. Then it slipped my mind. But that hain't the p'int. The p'int is that I wounded a buck. He was bleedin' at every jump an' blattin' in awful pain."

"I never happened to hear a buck blat, exactly," said Dud.

"Is that so? Wa-al, yer sh'ud have been with me. An' if yer was, I know that yer w'ud have said that it w'ud be turrible cruelty to leave that critter to die in the dark. But what does the law say? The law says that I sh'ud have gone home an' let that buck die by inches of misery, becuz the sun had set offish'ly down in Augusty!"

Bill's voice had attained the edge of tears, but Dud was not moved.

"The paper didn't mention a buck," he said.

"Oh! It didn't, eh? Wa-al, that proves how far they was willin' to go to cover up them triflin' game wardens."

"The paper said they worked a trick on yer, Bill. Didn't say jist what it was, an' I wondered it if was sunthin' like they tried to pull on Elijah Dole, years ago."

The guise of noble tenderness fell from Bill's face, like a derby hat struck by a brick. His eyes grew black with indignation. And his teeth were grinding-angry when he spoke.

"So that's what they're telling—is it? They're backin' up them psychopathetic wardens—are they? By goshamighty, I'm a-goin' to sue that paper fer slanderous character. Can't I do it?"

"Wel-el, I guess yer c'ud sue," said Dud, cautiously, "but it might turn out expensive and embarrassing."

The suggestion of more expense sobered Bill. And he nodded solemnly at Dud. Then he said, "I guess it w'ud be cheaper to shoot the editor."

Dud chuckled. "Some public cemeteries," he said to me, "are a lot more crowded than Bill's private buryin' ground."

Bill sought refuge in a chew of tobacco. Then he said, "In a way, that's a fact, becuz I've always been too damned tender-hearted. Live an' let live has always been my principle, except when I got mad. But from now on, things is goin' to be differunt."

Dud shook his head in feigned seriousness. "It's no use, Bill. Ye'll have to take it. But if yer was as smart as 'Lijah was, or even some game wardens—"

"By tarnel," snarled Bill, kicking over a substantial bench, "I hain't goin' to let yer stay here an' call me a fool. I won't stand it from an illiterated feller like you, Dud Dean. I won't put up with it, not even in this place. All yer know erbout my case is what ye've read in the papers—"

"You been readin' the papers, Bill?"

"My glasses is broke. I can't see a thing, that is, near to."

Dud turned again to me. "Bill can't read a word er write his name down."

"Don't believe a word of that," cautioned Bill. "I don't lay claims to an eddication equal to some lawyers, but mine amounts to more than most guides has got."

"Seems to me," said Dud, "that it 'ud do yer good to tell us the truth erbout this case, after all the effort ye've made to tell everythin' but the truth."

"Bah. Wa-al, I don't mind tellin' you fellers, becuz yer can warn folks of the skulduggery that has been worked on honest men like me. Prima facie, I never wounded no buck—that is, not that I know of."

"Sounds pee-culiar to hear yer confess that," said Dud.

Bill continued. "Earnin' a living hain't like pickin' up quail the Lord has dropped in your lap. Times is hard. I can remember when a man c'ud git twenty-five dollars apiece fer all—take taxes. Nowadays, a man is like a poked sheep bein' led to the slaughter. Er look at it this way. If a man must work from sunup to sundown to git a livin' fer hisself an' his family, how is he goin' to git his deer legal? By geeprus, I had rather let the Almighty answer that 'un than them fellers that makes laws fer other folks to mind. Them fellers hain't got no more sense 'n a houn'-dorg with his head blowed off his neck. Gol durn it, I can remember when a common man had some rights, but not now. Why, them lawmakers hain't fit to 'sociate with mortality.

"I tell yer that's jist how it stands! So, one night, when the weather was on the edge of raining, thinks I, 'None of them tender-toed wardens will be outdoors tonight, an' therefore now is the time to exercise the natural-born rights of a man bred in a free country.' Yer see, I had been gittin' madder fer weeks at a time. An' when I git mad, sunthin' has got to give way."

"Wait a min-it," Dud said, "did you issue that warnin' to them game wardens, er how did they git wind of it?"

"Them fellers! Look here, I'd thank yer to understand that I don't 'sociate with no pinions of the law, not with sech game laws as we've got in this state, anyhow. Not me! Wa-al, I cleaned up old Bertha an' made sure I had plenty of ammunition. Then I oozes down to the old Ball place. As a matter of fact, I warn't too sure that I'd find anythin' down thar, becuz after ye've shot up a field three er four times, the deer git smartish. An' I had already killed— It was an awful black night. Somehow, the air felt wet, like bad luck, but I didn't pay much attention. Natcherly, I know better than to barge inter a place like that before

I've looked over the lay of the land. A man always has to make sure that none of them stinkers is sneakin' around. I thought that the coast was clear, near as I c'ud tell. But I listened some more.

"Ever notice how much a man can hear on a night like that? Maybe ye'll hear an owl away off in the woods, er somebudy shootin' a gun, but most of the sounds come a-whisperin' and a-rustlin'. The night feels like silk. Geeprus, when a man has been married as long as I have he can appreciate quiet, when it ain't too noisy. Then, by tarnel, here come them lawmakers, durn their shrunken hides. An' what do they cook up? They forbid a man to go huntin' when he wants to go hunting. What next? Next, they hire a gang of sneakin' wardens. Consider the dupliciousness of them creepin' wardens. They cal'late to deceive the very elected."

"Wait a min-it," interposed Dud, "be yer tryin' to say that a game warden 'ud try to outwit a politician?"

"No! Confound it. Don't the Book read erbout them that cal'-lates to deceive the very elected? Yer a purty one to incinderate that somebudy else is illiterated. Wa-al, listen to me. I say that them fellers in their reedick'lus fan-wing britches an' cow-boy hats hain't got no right to hinder freeborn citizens in the persuit of life, liberty, an' deer meat. So as soon as I felt reasonably sure that none of them sisters was thereabouts, I eased on my light. An' that light is a sweetheart. I can throw light clear across a hundred-acre lot. So I swung it around, slow an' methodistical. Jist when I was ready to give it up as a bad job, smack-o, a set of eyes burned back at me.

"Damn it, I warn't long erbout correspondin' to sech insolation. Bung! goes a flock of double-o buckshot. An' out goes them eyes. But that deer begun to let out the most unreasonable blats yer ever heard. Thinks I, 'Now ye've done it. They can hear that critter fer miles.' But I got my legs under me an' made a run fer it. When I got thar, she was kickin' like a hay tedder. I warn't long erbout slittin' her throat, let me tell yer."

"Her?" questioned Dud.

"Yeh. It was a big doe. After I fired at her, up jumps two of her lambs. Dang it, I had fergot to reload old Bertha. But fer that, I w'ud have had one of them."

"And that w'ud have made two," said Dud.

"Sure. An' I might have got the other one. But if yer want to hear this, don't keep buttin' in on me. Maybe yer don't know it, but night huntin' is sunthin' like murder in a book. Ye're in it head over heels. Thar hain't nothin' to be done that yer ain't already done, so yer might's well see it through. I dressed off the doe in the pitch dark—a trick them wardens c'udn't do to save their souls, if they had any, which they hain't. Then I loaded her inter the back seat of the old flivver. After that, I waited some. Then I eased her out to the main road without any headlights.

"So far, so good, as the preacher said after the wedding. An' if I had only gone home then an' thar, I w'udn't be here, durn their hides. But of course it felt to me as if the night was young an' auspacious. So I thought I'd like to go down the road to the old Owens place. With me, a thought like that is the same as done. Thank the good Lord, Parson, I had sense e-nough to take that doe out of the car an' to hide her back in the bushes."

Dud interrupted Bill. "Allowin' that we sh'ud fergit that yer was night huntin' ag'inst the law, didn't it come to your mind that the law only allows a man one deer in this state? Er did yer think that deer tags was hitched to a huntin' license like coupons on a gilt-edged bond?"

"Wa-al, I was goin' to mention the fact that my memory hain't so long as a miskeeter wiggler when I git to shootin' at deer. I can't help it, no more'n a person can go without food. However, if I had give the matter more thought that night, I w'ud have been a sorrier but happier man. But I didn't. I went down to the Owens place, backed the Ford inter the bushes out of sight, covered up the brass with a blanket, an' soft-footed up towards the old apple orchard. Jist beyond the bridge, over the brook from the beaver bog, it seemed to me I heard a noise. Of course I waited and listened careful. After maybe as much as ten minutes,

I snuck on the light. An' thar he was, maybe five er six rods away. Seems to me, now, that them eyes didn't look jist right. But the way a deer's eyes look under a light depends on the night air. I've seen them when they looked almost pink-red. Then ag'in, they'll look almost green, er white, like a star. But anyhow, I thought it was one of my nights. I must of been excited. Anyhow, I pulled."

"Can yer hold a light, an' shoot at the same time?" asked Dud. "I always heard it took two fellers to jack deer."

"Hah, some more of your ignorance. As I was saying, I let her go. Down goes them eyes. Sunthin' rattled in the bushes an' went thump on the ground. Natcherly, I run up to cut my deer's throat. Imagine how I felt! It was jist a moth-eaten buck's head that them sneakin' critters had tied up in the bushes. The plaster of Paris was tricklin' out of them buckshot holes an' runnin' away in leetle streams of dust. Crotchidy, I was took by surprise, an' it might have been as much as five seconds a-fore I jumped an' run— which didn't do me any good, becuz I landed in a game warden's arms.

"Jist try to imagine how I felt. I w'ud as soon be on the bosom of hell. He was a powerful cuss. I did all I c'ud to make him think that he had catched hold of a she-bobcat, but thar was two of them, an' only one of me. So it come to me that I w'ud have to do some stratifying. So I begun to laugh like it was all a joke. 'Ha, ha,' I says. 'You boys has had your fun an' I've had mine. Be yer foolish enough to think that yer c'ud fool me with that old trick? Why, I seen yer when yer put it up thar. An' thar sartinly hain't no law ag'inst shootin' a stuffed deer head.' "

" 'There's a law ag'inst huntin' in the dark with a jack light,' says the big feller, who was still huggin' me like a she-b'ar.

" 'Yess,' says the other feller, soft an' calm as sunthin' on ice. 'Yess,' he says. An' before I knew it, he had clicked a pair of hand-cuffs on me.

" 'He threw his flashlight over there in the alders,' says the big feller.

" 'Yess, I know,' says the second stinker, 'I found it.' "

"Crotch," exclaimed Dud, "so they worked that old stunt on yer? I knew that yer warn't so smart as some Presidents we've had, but I didn't realize that yer was as foolish as a porcupine. Crotch, an' they've been all these years at catchin' yer!"

"By tarnelnation," said Bill, scowling at Dud, "if that's all ye've to say when a neighbor is in affliction an' trouble, I w'ud thank yer to remove yerself outer my sight. Go hobnob with them deceivin' wardens."

"Wel-el, guess we might's well. But Bill, what became of that doe yer hid in the bushes before yer went down't the Owens place?"

"None of your damn business, Dud Dean, you duplicious turncoat."

"Too bad if it went to waste."

"Ask the old lady," said Bill, and he began to laugh as if that was the only pleasant angle. "She tells me that the meat is jist as prime an' tender as a defrosted rooster. Geeprus, how I'd like a fry of it. They feed a man down here like a hoss. But don't worry erbout that doe goin' to waste. My folks ain't starving, thanks to me an' no one else!"

When we walked away from the county jail, Dud said, "Now we can hunt up Malty, an' you can give her the ten dollars."

"It was only five," I said. "And thanks for the object lesson. Bill is an intriguing character, eh?"

Dud laughed. "Sech fellers are conundrums, but it beats me who thought them up in the fust place. It seems to me, sometimes, that life is a long parade. Them in the front gits tired of luggin' the banners, an' them in back hain't got the fainest notion what it's all erbout."

22. The Corduroy Pants

by

ERSKINE CALDWELL

TWO weeks after he had sold his farm on the back road for twelve hundred dollars and the Mitchells had moved in and taken possession, Bert Fellows discovered that he had left his other pair of corduroy pants up attic. When he had finished hauling his furniture and clothes to his other place on the Skowhegan road, he was sure he had left nothing behind, but the morning that he went to put on his best pair of pants he could not find them anywhere. Bert thought the matter over two or three days and decided to go around the back road and ask Abe Mitchell to let him go up attic and get the corduroys. He had known Abe all his life and he felt certain Abe would let him go into the house and look around for them.

Abe was putting a new board on the door step when Bert came up the road and turned into the yard. Abe glanced around but kept on working.

Bert waited until Abe had finished planing the board before he said anything.

"How be you, Abe?" he inquired cautiously.

"Hell, I'm always well," Abe said, without looking up from the step.

Reprinted from *Jackpot* by Erskine Caldwell by permission of the publishers, Duell, Sloan and Pearce, Inc. Copyright 1931, 1933, 1935, 1938 and 1940 by Erskine Caldwell.

Bert was getting ready to ask permission to go into the house. He waited until Abe hammered the twenty-penny into the board.

"I left a pair of corduroys in there, Abe," he stated preliminarily. "You wouldn't mind if I went up attic and got them, would you?"

Abe let the hammer drop out of his hands and fall on the step. He wiped his mouth with his hankerchief and turned around facing Bert.

"You go in my house and I'll have the law on you. I don't give a cuss if you've left fifty pair of corduroys up attic. I bought and paid for this place and the buildings on it and I don't want nobody tracking around here. When I want you to come on my land, I'll invite you."

Bert scratched his head and looked up at the attic window. He began to wish he had not been so forgetful when he was moving his belongings down to his other house on the Skowhegan road.

"They won't do you no good, Abe," he said. "They are about ten sizes too big for you to wear. And they belong to me, anyway."

"I've already told you what I'm going to do with them corduroys," Abe replied, going back to work. "I've made plans for them corduroys. I'm going to keep them, that's what I'm going to do."

Bert turned around and walked toward the road, glancing over his shoulder at the attic window where his pants were hanging on a rafter. He stopped and looked at Abe several minutes, but Abe was busy hammering twenty-penny nails into the new step he was making and he paid no attention to Bert's sour looks. Bert went back down the road, wondering how he was going to get along without his other pair of pants.

By the time Bert reached his house he was good and mad. In the first place, he did not like the way Abe Mitchell had ordered him away from his old farm, but most of all he missed his other pair of corduroys. And by bedtime he could not sit still. He walked around the kitchen mumbling to himself and trying to think of some way by which he could get his trousers away from Abe.

"Crusty-faced Democrats never were no good," he mumbled.

Half an hour later he was walking up the back road toward his old farm. He had waited until he knew Abe was asleep, and now he was going to get into the house and go up attic and bring out the corduroys.

Bert felt in the dark for the loose window in the barn and discovered it could be opened just as he had expected. He had had good intentions of nailing it down, for the past two or three years, and now he was glad he had left it as it was. He went through the barn and the woodshed and into the house.

Abe had gone to bed about nine o'clock, and he was asleep and snoring when Bert listened at the door. Abe's wife had been stone-deaf for the past twenty years or more.

Bert found the corduroy pants, with no trouble at all. He struck only one match up attic, and the pants were hanging on the first nail he went to. He had taken off his shoes when he climbed through the barn window and he knew his way through the house with his eyes shut. Getting into the house and out again was just as easy as he had thought it would be.

In another minute he was out in the barn again, putting on his shoes and holding his pants under his arm. He had put over a good joke on Abe Mitchell, all right. He went home and got into bed.

The next morning Abe Mitchell drove his car up to the front of Bert's house and got out. Bert saw him from his window and went to meet Abe at the door. He was wearing the other pair of corduroys, the pair that Abe had said he was going to keep for himself.

"I'll have you arrested for stealing my pants," Abe announced as soon as Bert opened the door, "but if you want to give them back to me now I might consider calling off the charges. It's up to you what you want to do about it."

"That's all right by me," Bert said. "When we get to court I'll show you that I'm just as big a man as you think you are. I'm not afraid of what you'll do. Go ahead and have me arrested, but if they lock you up in place of me, don't come begging me to go your bail for you."

"Well, if that's the way you think about it," Abe said, getting red in the face, I'll go ahead with the charges. I'll swear out a warrant right now and they'll put you in the county jail before bedtime tonight."

"They'll know where to find me," Bert said, closing the door. "I generally stay pretty close to home."

Abe went out to his automobile and got inside. He started the engine, and promptly shut it off again.

"Come out here a minute, Bert," he called.

Bert studied him for several minutes through the crack in the door and then went out into the yard.

"Why don't you go swear out the warrant? What you waiting for now?"

"Well, I thought I'd tell you something, Bert. It will save you and me both a lot of time and money if you'd go to court right now and save the cost of having a man come out here to serve the warrant on you. If you'll go to court right now and let me have you arrested there, the cost won't be as much."

"You must take me for a cussed fool, Abe Mitchell," Bert said. "Do I look like a fool to pay ten dollars for a hired car to take me to county jail?"

Abe thought to himself several minutes, glancing sideways at Bert. "I'll tell you what I'll do, Bert," he proposed. "You get in my car and I'll take you there and you won't have to pay ten dollars for a hired car."

Bert took out his pipe and tobacco. Abe waited while he thought the proposition over thoroughly. Bert could not find a match, so Abe handed him one.

"You'll do that, won't you Bert?" he asked.

"Don't hurry me—I need plenty of time to think this over in my mind."

Abe waited, bending nervously toward Bert. The match-head crumbled off and Abe promptly gave Bert another one.

"I guess I can accommodate you that little bit this time," he said, at length. "Wait until I lock up my house."

When Bert came back to the automobile Abe started the engine and turned around in the road toward Skowhegan. Bert sat beside him sucking his pipe. Neither of them had anything to say to each other all the time they were riding. Abe drove as fast as his old car would go, because he was in a hurry to get Bert arrested and the trial started.

When they reached the courthouse, they went inside and Abe swore out the warrant and had it served on Bert. The sheriff took them into the courtroom and told Bert to wait in a seat on the first row of benches. The sheriff said they could push the case ahead and get a hearing some time that same afternoon. Abe found a seat and sat down to wait.

It was an hour before Bert's case was called to trial. Somebody read out his name and told him to stand up. Abe sat still, waiting until he was called to give his testimony.

Bert stood up while the charge was read to him. When it was over, the judge asked him if he wanted to plead guilty or not guilty.

"Not guilty," Bert said.

Abe jumped off his seat and waved his arms.

"He's lying!" he shouted at the top of his voice. "He's lying—he did steal my pants!"

"Who is that man?" the judge asked somebody.

"That's the man who swore out the warrant," the clerk said. "He's the one who claims the pants were stolen from him."

"Well, if he yells out like that again," the judge said, "I'll swear out a warrant against him for giving me a headache. And I guess somebody had better tell him there's such a thing as comtempt of court. He looks like a Democrat, so I suppose he never heard of anything like that before." The judge rapped for order and bent over towards Bert.

"Did you steal a pair of corduroy pants from this man?" he asked.

"They were my pants," Bert explained. "I left them in my house when I sold it to Abe Mitchell and when I asked him for them he wouldn't turn them over to me. I didn't steal them. They belonged to me all the time."

"He's lying!" Abe shouted again, jumping up and down. "He stole my pants—he's lying!"

"Ten dollars for contempt of court, whatever your name is," the judge said, aiming his gavel at Abe, "and case dismissed for lack of evidence."

Abe's face sank into his head. He looked first at the judge and then around the courtroom at the strange people.

"You're not going to make me pay ten dollars, are you?" he demanded.

"No," the judge said, standing up again. "I made a mistake. I forgot that you are a Democrat. I meant to say twenty-five dollars."

Bert went outside and waited at the automobile until Abe paid his fine. In a quarter of an hour Abe came out of the courthouse.

"Well, I guess I'll have to give you a ride back home," he said, getting under the steering-wheel and starting the engine. "But what I ought to do is leave you here and let you ride home in a hired car."

Bert said nothing at all. He sat down beside Abe and they drove out of town toward home.

It was almost dark when Abe stopped the car in front of Bert's house. Bert got out and slammed shut the door.

"I'm mighty much obliged for the ride," he said. "I been wanting to take a trip over Skowhegan way for a year or more. I'm glad you asked me to go along with you Abe, but I don't see how the trip was worth twenty-five dollars to you."

Abe shoved his automobile into gear and jerked down the road toward his place. He left Bert standing beside the mailbox rubbing his hands over the legs of his corduroy pants.

"Abe Mitchell ought to have better sense than to be a Democrat," Bert said, going into his house.

BIOGRAPHICAL AND LITERARY NOTES
ON THE SELECTIONS

Dates of living authors are not given.

GORGES, 1565 or 66–1647. This first account of Maine as a place to live in forms part of a narrative published in London in 1622 and known to historians as *The Brief Relation*. It is the work of Sir Ferdinando Gorges, governor of the fort of Plymouth in Devon, and with Captain Robert Mason, proprietor of a grant he called "The Province of Maine." It is probably from Sir Ferdinando's employment of the term "Maine" that the word became established usage, and afterwards the name of the state.

BIARD, 1565–1622. Father Pierre Biard of Grenoble was one of the two Jesuit fathers brought to Acadia in 1611 by Charles de Biencourt, son of the Sieur de Poitrincourt, the associate of Champlain. The settlement at Mt. Desert represents an aspiration of the fathers to have a colonial station of their own, a hope frustrated by the destruction of the settlement by English from Virginia in its first year of existence.

GYLES, 1678–1740. John Gyles, taken prisoner at Pemaquid in 1689, as a boy of eleven, returned to Boston in 1698. He later became official Indian interpreter to the government of Massachusetts, and a captain in the colonial army. The extract is taken from his *Memoirs* written at the request of his second consort, 1736. It is the first of those narratives so particularly American, the *Indian Captivities*.

VINAL. Harold Vinal, poet and musician, was born on Vinalhaven Island in Penobscot Bay. It is to his poetry that State of Mainers turn for a native and distinguished awareness of the beauty and mystery of their islands and the cold Maine seas.

TOPHAM, 1742–1793. This "Informal Iliad" is printed even as it was written—in separate lines each beginning with a capital. It is the work of a young officer commanding a company under Arnold. Captain John Topham, born at Newport, R. I. was thirty years of age when he crossed the Maine wilderness. Taken prisoner at Quebec, he was later exchanged, and fought with distinction throughout the Revolution.

HENRY, 1758–1811. Judge John Joseph Henry dictated his famous account of his adventures as a member of the Arnold expedition to his daughter Anne Mary. He was born in Lancaster, Pa., and became a distinguished member of the Pennsylvania bar. Judge Henry's account is probably the most famous single account of the long struggle across the height of land.

BAILEY, 1731–1818. Parson Jacob Bailey, born in Rowley, Massachusetts, in early life relinquished the Congregational Ministry to become a devoted adherent of the Church of England. Sent as a missionary to what is now Dresden, Maine, he was exiled from his parish by the anti-British feeling of the Revolution and ended his days as Vicar of the Established Church at Annapolis Royal, Nova Scotia. A vigorous memory of his personality lingers in the Sheepscot region to this day.

VERRILL. A. Hyatt Verrill, author, naturalist, and explorer, here describes the arrival "downeast" of pioneers as such an event was recalled in the traditions of his own pioneer ancestors.

ROWE. William Hutchinson Rowe of Yarmouth, Maine, Secretary of the Maine Historical Society, is the leading authority on the ships and shipping of the state.

FIELD, 1894–1939. Rachel Field (Mrs. Arthur S. Pedersen) wrote several novels about the coast of Maine to which she had a life-long devotion. Born in New York City, she lived and worked during the summer at her home on Sutton's Island off Mount Desert.

INGRAHAM, 1809–1860. Rev. John H. Ingraham, Episcopal clergyman, was born in Portland, Maine, and spent his boyhood and youth at Hallowell. Moving to the southern states, he lived out the rest of his life as Vicar of a church in Mississippi. He was the author of more than a hundred novels, one of them, "The Prince of the House of David," a "best seller" of the mid-nineteenth century.

WELLS, 1788–1871. Captain Theodore Wells was born in Wells, Maine, and died in the same town. His book was published in Biddeford, Maine in 1874. The editor owes his knowledge of this volume to Mr. William Hutchinson Rowe.

PRINCE, 1817–1907. Captain George Prince was born in Thomaston, Maine. After an interesting and versatile career which included whaling, service in the Chilean army and navy, and a time spent as a cavalry officer in the Civil War, he settled down at home and devoted himself to business and the preservation of local history and its monuments. He is the author of *Old Times in Yarmouth, Maine,* published 1880.

LONGFELLOW, 1807–1882. Henry Wadsworth Longfellow, eldest son of an old and established Portland family, grew up in the heyday of the West India trade, and "The Spanish sailors with bearded lips" of the poem are probably seamen from the Spanish West Indies. "My Lost Youth" is incomparably the most distinguished poem ever written about an American city.

CARTER. Isabel Hopestill Carter, born at Woolwich across the Kennebec from Bath, spent her first ten years largely on shipboard, having come of four generations of seafaring ancestors on both sides of the family. Her fine novel "Shipmates" is a saga of the seafaring New England woman, based on her mother's life and her own experiences.

ROBINSON, 1869–1935. Edwin Arlington Robinson was born in Headtide, Maine, and spent his boyhood and youth in nearby Gardiner on the Kennebec, "The Town down the River." It is a Gardiner tradition that the poem reprinted refers to Captain Israel Jordan, a friend and neighbor of the Robinsons who was much loved by the children of the town. Together with his vessel, Captain Jordan disappeared in West Indian waters sometime in the 1880's, and nothing has ever been known of his fate.

STOWE, 1811–1896. Harriet Beecher Stowe lived in Brunswick for two and a half years while her husband, Calvin Stowe, held the professorship of "Natural and Revealed Religion" at Bowdoin College. Part of the house in which she wrote *Uncle Tom's Cabin* is now a restaurant, and the house (little changed) is open to the public.

BYNNER. Witter Bynner, poet and scholar, was born in Brooklyn, N. Y., and now lives in Santa Fe, N. M. "The old Second Maine," which left Bangor on May 14, 1861, was the first Maine regiment to arrive in Washington after the beginning of the Civil War.

LOWELL, 1819–1891. James Russell Lowell, poet and essayist; minister to England 1880–1885. The New England eminentissimi followed a fashion of the day in visiting the wilderness country of the Maine Woods.

CHAMBERLAIN, 1828–1914. General Joshua L. Chamberlain, graduate of Bowdoin College and the Bangor Theological Seminary, Colonel of the Twentieth Maine Regiment of Volunteers, and later President of Bowdoin is one of the memorable figures of nineteenth-century Maine. The holding of Little Round Top at Gettysburg with which his name is imperishably associated is probably the single most crucial episode of the entire Civil War, so great were the consequences. Had the Confederates carried the position, there is little doubt but that Gettysburg would have ended in a Union defeat.

For decades after the Civil War, the holding of Little Round Top was one of the state's proudest memories. Any number of local hillocks were renamed for the position, and even vessels were christened "Little Round Top." A tug of that name was to be seen at Ellsworth as late as the 1920's. Readers interested in the episode are advised to consult *Strong Vincent and his Brigade at Gettysburg* by Oliver W. Norton, Chicago, 1909.

RICHARDS. Rosalind Richards of Gardiner comes on her father's side of an old family settled on the Kennebec since early in the eighteenth century; her mother was Laura E. Richards, and her grandmother Julia Ward Howe, who wrote the "Battle Hymn of the Republic." In *A Northern Countryside* Miss Richards has gathered a lifetime of warm and delicate observation of the countryside and the people who live in it.

COATSWORTH. Elizabeth Coatsworth (Mrs. Henry Beston), poet and author of distinction in both the adult and juvenile fields, has in this selection taken as her scene the shores of Damariscotta Pond near the Beston farm. Local history says that the Indians abandoned this region to the whites with great reluctance.

RIDLON, 1841–1928. Rev. Gideon T. Ridlon, Sr., scholar, genealogist, and man of letters, was born in Yarmouth, Maine, and wrote with careful observation of the Maine he had known.

THOREAU, 1817–1862. Henry David Thoreau was in his thirtieth year when he climbed Katahdin. Rather characteristically, he did not follow any recognized route to the summit but starting from a point on the West Branch between outlets of Katahdin Stream and the Abol stream, took his compass and, going east of the Abol Slide, made his way up the south face of the mountain to South Peak. Vide *Thoreau's Route to Katahdin* by John W. Worthington, *Appalachia*, June, 1946.

VETROMILE, 1819–1883. Father Eugene Vetromile, missionary to the Indians of Maine and student of the Indian languages of the region, was born in Italy in the city of Gallipolis on the Gulf of Tarentum. Coming to America, he became a missionary priest, and spent various years of his life at Oldtown with the Penobscots. Father Vetromile's studies of Indian life and speech have high standing among scholars.

HALL. Leland Hall, close and realistic observer of Maine, is both a distinguished novelist and professor of music at Smith College.

BESTON. Henry Beston, naturalist and student of things American, lives in Nobleboro in Lincoln County. Among his books are *The Outermost House, The St. Lawrence River* and *Northern Farm,* a chronicle of Maine.

RICHARDS. John Richards of Gardiner (brother to Miss Rosalind Richards) was for many years head of the English department at St. Paul's School, Concord, N. H. Naturalist and scholar, he has an unusual knowledge of his native state together with a profound feeling for its quality and character.

SPRINGER, 1810–1870. John S. Springer, a native State-of-Mainer, wrote during the middle years of the nineteenth century.

HOLBROOK. Stewart H. Holbrook, born in Newport, Vermont, of a family with lumber interests, is the authority on lumbering in North America, covering with equal skill and sureness its economic and picturesque aspects.

WILLIAMS. Ben Ames Williams, born in Macon, Mississippi, had a middle-western boyhood, and went to college at Dartmouth in New England. He summers at Searsmont, Maine, and his skillful and authentic short stories of the region and its people are among the famous tales written about life in the state. He has also written several best seller novels dealing with nineteenth-century Maine.

RICH. Louise Dickinson Rich, who came from Massachusetts and married into Maine, has a profound and firsthand knowledge of what life is like in the Maine woods. She is the author of several books about the woods country.

ECKSTORM, 1865–1946. Mrs. Fannie Hardy Eckstorm, naturalist, historian, and student of the folklore and balladry of Maine, was born in Brewer. Her father dealt in furs, and having accompanied him on visits to the Maine Indians, she retained an unusual knowledge of the various Alonquin forms of speech. Mrs. Eckstorm was also a firsthand authority on the saga of the Maine rivers and the loggers.

CHASE. Mary Ellen Chase, the daughter of a judge in the little seaport of Blue Hill, Maine, has since 1926 been a professor of English Literature at Smith College. She is well known for her novels of seaboard life, of which "Mary Peters" is perhaps the most famous, but she has never written a more charming book than "A Goodly Heritage," an account of her own childhood in Blue Hill as one of a large family, and an evaluation of the old Yankee way of life.

COFFIN. Robert Peter Tristram Coffin, born at Brunswick, Maine, and now a professor at Bowdoin College, celebrates the good substantial life of a Maine seacoast farm as it was lived in the later nineties, together with everything that is beautiful and vital in the state. In his poetry and prose there is always something both of Nature and the human spirit.

JEWETT, 1849–1909. The "local color" tales of Sarah Orne Jewett picture the New England of the New England woman and the New England world which followed the Civil War. Told with simplicity, a native power of perception, and literary sureness, the stories have become a part of the regional tradition in American literature.

THAXTER, 1835–1904. Celia Laighton Thaxter born at Portsmouth, N. H., was taken when four years old to the lonely islet known as White Island in the Isles of Shoals where her father had been appointed keeper of the light. The group is divided between Maine and New Hampshire, and these vivid souvenirs of Appledore are memories of a Maine Island.

BISHOP, 1847–1923. William Henry Bishop, born at Hartford, Connecticut, and graduated at Yale in 1867, had a long career in the consular service of the Republic. His literary work, in the main, consists of novels and books of travel.

WASSON, 1855–1932. George Savary Wasson, born at Groveland, Massachusetts, was the son of a Maine family which had been established on Penobscot Bay since soon after the Revolution. Renewing his ties with Maine as a young yachtsman, he established himself at Kittery Point, and there began his life as a painter of the Maine coast. His intense interest and pleasure in his ancestral state soon led him to write about the country he knew so well by land and sea. Readers are advised to try the new edition of *Sailing Days on the Penobscot* with its fine introduction by Walter Muir Whitehill, and, if they can lay their hands on it, *Captain Simeon's Store*. In the editor's judgment, George

Wasson is the important Maine writer of his generation, no one surpassing him in vividness, authenticity, the power of narrative, and sense of character.

CRAWFORD, 1854–1909. Francis Marion Crawford was a popular American novelist at the end of the century, his romances oftenest concerning themselves with historical periods and life in European "society."

PARSONS. Elizabeth Parsons lives for much of the year with her children in a delightful house on the moors of Vinalhaven looking westward across Penobscot Bay to the rounded Camdens. A number of the stories printed in *An Afternoon* appeared in the New Yorker. Her feeling for atmosphere, and her power to convey the emotional climate rank her with the most distinguished short-story writers of our times.

COATSWORTH. See preceeding note.

DUNN, 1861–1937, Charles Dunn, Jr., was a distinguished member of the Maine bar. Born of pioneer stock in Aroostoock, it came to pass that because of his mother's death he was brought up by his grandparents on the great farm which they had hewed out of the wilderness. As his daughter, Professor Esther Cloudman Dunn of Smith College, writes in the introduction to *Cloudman Hill Heritage:* "The following papers were written by my father between the age of seventy-four and seventy-six as Christmas gifts for Marion Dodd who loved his boyhood recollections of life on this remote-self-contained Maine farm and asked him to write them down."

CARROLL. Gladys Hasty Carroll (Mrs. Herbert A. Carroll) has lived for the greater part of her life in South Berwick, Maine, where she was brought up on her grandfather's farm. The novel *As the Earth Turns* from which the selection was taken was written in 1933 at the beginning of five years spent in Minneapolis where her husband's work had taken them. It is a warm and rich story of country living, so well liked in the country of which it was written, that each summer the neighborhood gives a folk play based upon it, using its earnings to support the church, community center and library.

WHITE. Elwyn Brooks White was born in New York State and went to Cornell. From being a reporter he soon became a freelance writer, and is best known as a contributor to the New Yorker. For many years he lived at North Brooklin, Maine, in the shadow of Blue Hill. His best known book is probably the immensely popular "One Man's Meat," a series of essays whose intelligence and whose humor are alike in their distinction.

TIBBETTS. Pearl Ashby Tibbetts (Mrs. Raymond R. Tibbetts) lives in Bethel, Maine. Her mother was the daughter of Aroostook pioneers, and Mrs. Tibbetts here used the old family stories as a basis for her novel which is laid at her grandfather's farm.

GOULD. John Gould, State of Maine farmer, humorist, and chronicler of the way of life of the small town and the farmstead, lives at Lisbon Falls where he edits a newspaper, The Lisbon Enterprise ("subscription $2.00 a year").

STEPHENS, 1844–1931. Charles Asbury Stephens of Norway, Maine, a graduate of Bowdoin, was for some time an editor of the Youths Companion, and over many years wrote for that weekly "The Old Squire" stories of life in mid-nineteenth century rural Maine. So genuine are they and so well told that readers have been unwilling to let them perish as periodical literature, and they have recently been reissued in a series of very popular books.

EVANS. Abbie Huston Evans: On her father's side, Miss Evans is Welsh, and inherits the gift of poetry. On her mother's side her roots go deeply into the soil of seacoast Maine. She has published two books: *Outcrop,* with an introduction by Edna St. Vincent Millay who was once a student of hers, and *The Bright North.* Both are notable for an intense emotional force expressed in terms of closely observed nature.

COFFIN: See preceeding note.

BUTLER, 1890–1942. Katharine Butler (Mrs. Daniel Hathaway) was born in Salem, Massachusetts, and took a house at Castine, Maine, in the 1920's. She is the author of *The Little Locksmith.* Mrs. Hathaway's delight in Maine was one of the abiding joys of a life which was not always easy.

OGILVIE. Elisabeth Ogilvie, who writes most often of Criehaven Island in Penobscot Bay, has known the island intimately since childhood in both its summer and winter aspects. Her series of novels, *High Tide at Noon, Storm Tide* and *The Ebbing Tide* laid on the island, have all a strong factual quality, and she has a fine power to chronicle and describe nature. She now spends as much of the year as possible on an island off the coast near Thomaston, returning to Massachusetts for the winter.

MOORE. Ruth Moore was born on Gott's Island, where her father's people had long lived, and her mother came from Swan's Island. She went to school there, and later worked her way through High School at Ellsworth and went to the State Teachers College at Albany, N. Y. Since then she has done secretarial work and joined the staff of The Reader's Digest. Her first book, *The Weir,* is a powerful reconstruction of Gott's Island life: her second novel, *Spoonhandle,* deals with a larger island where the problems of the relationships between the native population and the summer people are more important.

RICH. See preceeding note.

Index

RIDEOUT, 1877–1927. Henry Milner Rideout was born at Calais, Maine, and went to Harvard College. After some years as an instructor in English he began writing, laying the scenes of his novels in the far East and in Maine. He had a fine sense of Maine people and the traditional values which sustained the way of life.

GRAHAM. Elinor Graham lives at Flying Point, below the little town of Freeport, with her husband David Graham. She was born in Hagerstown, Maryland, and after beginning her career on the stage, took up writing and has published two popular books, *Our Way Downeast* and *Maine Charm String*.

CASTNER. Harold W. Castner of Damariscotta is the careful historian of the Damariscotta region. Many of his sketches have appeared in the Lincoln County News. He is now publishing a series of pamphlets concerned with the picturesque side of local history.

FREEMAN. Jessie Wheeler Freeman, born in New Hampshire, came to Maine as the wife of a doctor in a seacoast village. She now lives in Gardiner. Her poems about men and women, often in their relationships to one another, are swift, dramatic, and memorable.

MACDOUGALL. Arthur R. MacDougall, Jr., poet, fisherman, and writer of wise and genial hunting and fishing stories, knows the upper Kennebec and the surrounding forest as well as any man in Maine. He has for many years been minister of the church at Bingham, Maine, where his annual sermon to fly-fishermen is attended from all over the country.

CALDWELL. Erskine Caldwell, born south of the Mason-Dixon line, spent five years in Maine. He has written a number of Maine stories, all of them marked by an ironic and vivid sense of regional character.